JUSTIN

EPITOME OF THE PHILIPPIC
HISTORY OF POMPEIUS TROGUS

AMERICAN PHILOLOGICAL ASSOCIATION

CLASSICAL RESOURCES SERIES

James J. Clauss, Series Editor

Number 3
JUSTIN
EPITOME OF THE PHILIPPIC
HISTORY OF POMPEIUS TROGUS

TRANSLATED BY
J. C. YARDLEY

WITH INTRODUCTION AND NOTES BY
R. DEVELIN

JUSTIN

EPITOME OF THE PHILIPPIC
HISTORY OF POMPEIUS TROGUS

TRANSLATED BY
J. C. YARDLEY

WITH INTRODUCTION AND EXPLANATORY NOTES BY
R. DEVELIN

SCHOLARS PRESS
ATLANTA, GA

JUSTIN
Epitome of the Philippic
History of Pompeius Trogus

Translated by
J. C. Yardley

With introduction and explanatory notes by
R. Develin

© 1994
The American Philological Association

On the covers:
Macedon
Phoenician Tetradrachm, 359-336 B.C.
Norman and Amelia Davis Classical Collection
SEATTLE ART MUSEUM
Photo credit: Paul Macapia

Library of Congress Cataloging in Publication Data
Justinus, Marcus Junianus.
 [Historiae Philippicae. English]
 Epitome of the Philippic history of Pompeius Trogus / Justin ;
translated by J. C. Yardley ; with introduction and explanatory notes
by R. Develin.
  p. cm. — (Classical resources series ; no. 3)
 "The translation is based on Seel's Teubner edition, (3rd ed.,
1971)"—Pref.
 Includes bibliographical references and index.
 ISBN 1-55540-950-4 (cloth). — ISBN 1-55540-951-2 (paper)
 1. History, Ancient. I. Trogus, Pompeius. Historia Macedonia.
II. Title. III. Series.
D58.J8 1994
930—dc20   93-46495
                                                               CIP

Printed in the United States of America
on acid-free paper

Table of Contents

Translator's Preface

THE TRANSLATION is based on Seel's Teubner edition (3rd ed., 1971); variations from that text are indicated in the notes and collected on page 339. I have tried as far as I could to steer a course between the Scylla and Charybdis of literal translation and paraphrase, and I hope that in my efforts to produce a readable version I have not sacrificed accuracy.

Thanks are due to the University of Ottawa for various grants which I have received for this project; to Oxford University Press for permission to reprint books 11–15, forthcoming in the Clarendon Ancient History series; to Waldemar Heckel of the University of Calgary for his work and comments on those and other books, as well as for the stemmata on pages 287 to 294, which he kindly prepared for me; and to the patient graduate students at Ottawa who proofread the translation in its numerous drafts. I must, however, single out for special thanks two people. My wife Norah read the penultimate version and removed many infelicities of English grammar and style; and Iolo Davies, my old friend and teacher, and one of the finest Latinists I know, read my initial draft in its entirety, saving me from many an error and suggesting alternative translations and interpretations. I suspect that the defects that remain occur at just those points where I failed to heed their advice.

J. C. Yardley

Acknowledgements

BEYOND the debts mentioned by the translator, we have to acknowledge the contribution of Catherine Côté and Sarah Parker for their diligence in compiling the index. Nor can we omit recognition of John Ramsey, William Race and James Clauss, who, as successive editors of the series, saw the book through the stages to publication with patience and attention. We owe much gratitude to Alexander MacGregor, the indefatigable reader who put more time and effort into his work than we could possibly have hoped. And finally, we thank Theodora MacKay for her painstaking work as compositor. We trust that all concerned enjoy the final product.

Bob Develin

Abbreviations

---

1. ANCIENT AUTHORS

Aesch.	Aeschines (orations cited by number)
Ath.Pol.	Aristotle(?), *Athenaion Politeia* (Constitution of the Athenians)
Dem.	Demosthenes (orations cited by number)
Diod.	Diodorus of Sicily
Her.	Herodotus
Plut.	Plutarch (lives cited by characters' names and *Moralia*)
Pol.	Polybius
Thuc.	Thucydides
Val.Max.	Valerius Maximus
Xen.	Xenophon

2. MODERN WORKS

AO	R. Develin, *Athenian Officials 684–321* B.C. (Cambridge 1989)
Bickerman	E. J. Bickerman, *Chronology of the Ancient World* (London 1968)
Burstein	S. M. Burstein, *Translated Documents of Greece and Rome* Volume 3: *The Hellenistic Age from the Battle of Ipsos to the Death of Kleopatra* (Cambridge 1985)
CAH	*The Cambridge Ancient History* Second edition
CHI 2	*The Cambridge History of Iran* Volume 2 (Cambridge 1985)
FGH	F. Jacoby, *Die Fragmente der griechischen Historiker* (by author and fragment numbers)
Gronovius	*Justini Historiae Philippicae ex editione Abrahami Gronovi cum notis et interpretatione in usum Delphini* (London 1822)

Harding   P. Harding, *Translated Documents of Greece and Rome* Volume 2: *From the End of the Peloponnesian War to the Battle of Ipsus* (Cambridge 1985)

MRR   T. R. S. Broughton, *The Magistrates of the Roman Republic* Volumes 1 and 2 (American Philological Association, 1951 and 1960)

Sherk   R. K. Sherk, *Translated Documents of Greece and Rome* Volume 4: *Rome and the Greek East to the Death of Augustus* (Cambridge 1984)

Introduction

In the twentieth century, translations of Justin's epitome of the universal history of Pompeius Trogus have appeared in French (E. Chambry and L. Thély-Chambry, Paris 1936), in German (O. Seel, Zürich-München 1972) and in Italian (L. Santi Amantini, Milano 1981). Yet, as generations have passed since the publication of J. Selby Watson's (not always available) English translation (London 1853, in the *Bohn's Classical Library* series), it is surely long overdue that a new—and, we hope, better—English translation be produced, and we are grateful for the American Philological Association's sponsorship of this volume, which aims to be of some value not only to Latinless students, but also to those who for other reasons may wish for convenient access to this work.

Why read Justin? His name is not on the lips of every student, and in areas where his account may be placed beside others, he has not always impressed. For example, his treatment of the growth of the Athenian empire at 3.6–7 has been called "a wildly erratic summary" (R. Meiggs, *The Athenian Empire* [Oxford 1972], 475). But such judgments should be made with caution. They are often reached with only partial knowledge of the work, and with Justin, as with any other historical writer, it is, I would urge, necessary to read the whole before employing or judging any part. To continue with the example, I have always felt that Meiggs's judgment on 3.6–7 was too harsh; after the work on this volume, I think I am better able to understand how that passage attained its form and thus to examine the credentials of its contents. To be sure, the text of Justin encompasses material of varying degrees of credibility, but an understanding of the whole will create perspective. This is of particular importance when it comes to those areas for which Justin is the major or even the only literary source. It must be emphasised that he is a fundamental source for Carthage and is the only surviving continuous narrative for the Hellenistic period, sketchy and confusing though his account may be.

But beyond Justin's importance for these particular areas, he has been a significant part of the historiographical heritage of the West. The work of Pompeius Trogus on which he drew was a considerable achievement, and thanks to Justin we enjoy the only pagan Latin universal history to survive, indeed the only universal history of any sort from before the Christian era to survive in its entirety. For this reason it has been preserved in some 200 manuscripts, being much read in the Middle Ages, known and used by writers such as Chaucer and Petrarch. Providing as it does a framework for a wide sweep of ancient history, the epitome extended its influence even into the nineteenth century.

It is necessary, therefore, to appreciate the nature and tone of the work overall; the complete history should be read reasonably quickly before any other use is made of it. But it is not for us to dictate every use or guide every opinion. We hope at least that we have made a useful text more accessible to all. What follows attempts to set out data and perspectives fundamental to an understanding of the work.

Pompeius Trogus

There can be few cases in the field of ancient historiography where the sum of knowledge concerning the persons of two writers is so scanty. Even authors represented by fragments are likely to have more personality, even if fictional, than Trogus, the historian living during the reign of Augustus, to say nothing of Justin, who produced the so-called "epitome" or abbreviated version of his work. Yet we must try as best we can to establish identities and milieus.

Outside the pages of Justin, we learn of Pompeius Trogus that he wrote a work *On Animals* ; some have detected this scientific interest within his history. Justin himself refers to Trogus' autobiographical notice at the end of Book 43. His family originated among the Vocontii, a Gallic tribe who came under Roman sway in 125/4 B.C. and were part of the new province of Gallia Narbonensis, created around 121 B.C. Roman citizenship had been granted to his grandfather by Pompey, under whom he served in Spain in the mid-70s. His uncle served under Pompey too, as a cavalry commander in the eastern war against Mithridates in the mid-60s. His father held a post under Julius Caesar, in charge of his correspondence and legations to him; the date is not specified, but the time of Caesar's dominance in the 40s seems to be indicated. Thus our Pompeius Trogus was a third generation Roman, bearing in his name the stamp of his Gallic origin (Trogus) alongside the customary acknowledgement of the Roman sponsor (Pompeius).

His father's occupation suggests a literary legacy, and there is no doubt of Trogus' immersion in the Roman rhetorical education. The very existence of his history testifies to that, but we also have the words of Justin in his preface. Many Romans of distinction had written their own history in Greek, says Justin, but Trogus, a man of old-fashioned eloquence, composed a history of Greek affairs and those of the whole world so that these could be read in Latin.

There is little more to say. The character might be fleshed out a little if our Pompeius were the addressee of a literary letter by Dionysius of Halicarnassus,[1] but that is only a speculation. It is clear enough that Trogus was born around the middle of the first century and lived and worked through the reign of Augustus. We cannot be precise as to a date of writing or publication; in all probability individual books became available to at least a select audience as they were initially completed. Evidence to be gleaned from the contents suggests that the final version dates to the early years of the Christian era, perhaps as late as A.D. 20. The work was available for use by Valerius Maximus and Velleius Paterculus under the emperor Tiberius (A.D. 14–37). At some unknown date the so-called "prologues" were compiled to indicate the contents of each of the 44 books of Trogus' history; these too are translated here.

We should conclude this section by noting that Trogus belonged to the canon of the four great Latin historians, along with Sallust, Livy and Tacitus.[2] We can only regret that we do not have at least as much of his text as we do of theirs.

JUSTIN

For us, then, Trogus is represented essentially through the epitome of Justin. We shall for convenience refer to this as an "epitome," though it will emerge that this is not quite appropriate. As to the compiler, he is a mystery. He tells us nothing of himself, though tantalizing clues appear in his preface. He constructed his work on a sojourn in Rome—evidently not his home—and he transmitted it to an unidentified singular "you," not, I think, to his readers in general, as has been asserted. His words can be taken to suggest that he was some sort of official: he felt it as necessary to account for his leisure as for his working hours. As has been frequently

---

1. See R. Develin, "Pompeius Trogus and Philippic History," *Storia della Storiografia* 8 (1985), 110ff.
2. Historia Augusta, *Aurelian* 2.1; *Probus* 2.7.

noted, we cannot even be sure of his name: it was either M. Iunianus Iustinus or, more likely, M. Iunianius Iustinus.

As to date, suggestions have ranged from the time of Antoninus Pius, even perhaps as specific as A.D. 144 or 145,[3] to as late as A.D. 395,[4] and everything in between. The arguments for the late date I find unconvincing, and I shall confine myself here to what seem to be positive indications. Certain statements in Justin would make no sense to his readers even if they were simply taken over from Trogus and published any time after about A.D. 230, when it was no longer possible to say that the Scythians had heard of, but not felt Roman arms (2.3.5), given the creation of a Roman province of Scythia; moreover, it would not be possible to write, as Justin does in books 41 and 42, in terms of a world divided between Rome and the Parthians, the latter having been replaced by the Sasanid monarchs. Attempts have been made to assess the date on the basis of Justin's language, but a full account must await an analysis using the Ibycus computer.[5] Preliminary results suggest a later second century date. No one could argue that such a date would be inappropriate for the sort of exercise which Justin undertook. The date is of some importance in locating the work as a cultural artefact; the scope of the present work, however, limits us to examining the nature of the text and its contents.

THE RELATIONSHIP OF JUSTIN TO TROGUS

English-speaking readers of this work, finding little modern discussion of Trogus or Justin in their own language, may be surprised to learn that there is a considerable literature in other languages, a sample of which is given below.[6] Suffice it to say that conclusions are often unscientific,

3. R. B. Steele, "Pompeius Trogus and Justinus," *American Journal of Philology* 38 (1917), 19ff.

4. R. Syme, "The Date of Justin and the Discovery of Trogus," *Historia* 37 (1988), 358ff.

5. See Syme (n. 4 above) and earlier Steele (n. 2 above) and F. R. D. Goodyear, "On the Character and Text of Justin's Compilation of Trogus," *Proceedings of the African Classical Associations* 16 (1982), 1–24. Goodyear was unable to conduct promised further studies, but Ibycus is being employed by the translator.

6. O. Seel, *Eine römische Weltgeschichte. Studien zum Text der Epitome des Iustinus und zur Historik des Pompeius Trogus* (Nürnberg 1972); in *Aufstieg und Niedergang der römischen Welt* II.30.2 (Berlin/New York 1982) the following: G. Forni and M.G. Angeli Bertinelli, "Pompeo Trogo come fonte di storia," 1298–1362; O. Seel, "Pompeius Trogus und das Problem der Universalgeschichte," 1363–1423; R. Urban, " 'Gallisches Bewußtsein' und 'Romkritik' bei Pompeius Trogus," 1424–

derived from easy assumptions and failing to recognize the fragility and subjectivity of the methods used. Some of the current orthodoxy and generally accepted facts will be found in J. M. Alonso-Núñez, "An Augustan world history: the *Historiae Philippicae* of Pompeius Trogus," *Greece and Rome* 34 (1987), 56–72.

For any assessment there is a compulsory first question: How far does Justin's work reflect that of Trogus? There is a widespread assumption— and it is usually taken for granted—that where Justin has long, continuous passages, these are lifted almost word for word from the text of Trogus. This, of course, is convenient for those who wish to study Trogus, but it is poorly grounded. What Justin says in his preface is that he "plucked out" ("excerpted") those items in Trogus which he found most worth knowing, omitting things which neither gave pleasure in the knowing nor were necessary as illustrations of behaviour, and made a sort of anthology—literally, "a little body of flowers"—to aid the memory of those who had studied Greek history and to instruct those who had not. There is nothing in this which asserts that his excerpts were taken *verbatim* from Trogus rather than reworked by himself. Indeed, we could gather from the last words of his preface that Justin had claims to his own style, unless we are to believe that the judgment of posterity which he mentions is to be based solely on the quality of his selection and the work from which he chose to select. Nor does the introduction to Mithridates' speech in Book 38 necessarily demonstrate, as many have thought,[7] that it is taken unchanged from Trogus.

Still, there seems to be much that comes from Justin himself, more indeed than merely in the more summary passages where this has been detected before. Prudence seems to require that when we find statements in the first person singular or words such as "now" or "to this day" we should take this as the voice of Justin. It remains true through all of this that Justin did not hesitate to reproduce choice phrases from his source; such a practice was normal even in what was considered a creative work. Small wonder, then, that in Justin we can detect reminiscences of Sallust and Livy ascribable to Trogus, though if Justin had (as he surely did) the rhetorical education advocated by Quintilian in the *Institutes*, he would

---

1443; H.-D. Richter, *Untersuchungen zur hellenistischen Historiographie. Die Vorlagen des Pompeius Trogus für die Darstellung der nachalexandrischen hellenistischen Geschichte (Iust. 13–40)* (Frankfurt/Bern/New York/Paris 1987).

7. Recently see F. R. D. Goodyear, "Pompeius Trogus and the Oxford Latin Dictionary," *Liverpool Classical Monthly* 7 (1982), 13f.

have absorbed his fair share of these authors, along with Cicero and Vergil. Further, it is enlightening to see how the fifth century Orosius has deviated from his source, Justin,[8] condensing, expanding and changing verbal expressions.

The term "epitome" is convenient, but difficult. Orosius (1.8) referred to Justin as an abbreviator and St Augustine (*City of God* 4.5) says he wrote a brief history following Trogus. Justin's own words show that he has not sought to give a résumé of Trogus, book by book, but has made a selection on the twin criteria of intrinsic interest and moral demonstration.[9] As a result, the books vary in length from one Teubner page to 22 (Books 40 and 2 respectively). The summaries of Livy's books which survive demonstrate that such things need not give a full and accurate representation of the actual contents. Still, the reader may gain an idea of what Justin has and has not chosen by comparing his text with the surviving prologues of Trogus. As for comparative size, estimates have varied. Alonso-Núñez and others have maintained that Justin amounts to about one-fifth the length of Trogus; at least Goodyear admitted that his one-seventh was a guess; if Trogus' books were about as long as Livy's, Syme's one-tenth is nearer the mark.

THE NATURE AND SOURCES OF THE HISTORY

I have allowed myself the luxury of referring to "*the* history," as if Trogus and Justin were one. To an extent this must be. In spite of what was said above, Justin must have found Trogus amenable, so that he could readily draw upon the original for moral examples. Everything points to that conclusion. In the historiographical tradition, to characterise Trogus as possessing "old-fashioned eloquence" suggested the moralism which was part and parcel of such writing. Moreover, I have argued that the title "Philippic History" had no special reference to Philip II or a succession of Philips, but was reminiscent of the caustic moralizing typified by Theopompus.[10] With due caution, therefore, we can use Justin to shed light on Trogus.

---

8. See Steele (above n. 2) 27.

9. Interestingly, this recalls the grounds on which Arrian, a second-century A.D. historian, says he chose between different versions in the preface to his *Anabasis of Alexander*. Very sensible on this question is P. Jal, "A propos des *Histoires Philippiques*: quelques remarques," *Revue des Etudes Latines* 65 (1987), 194ff. at 196ff. Evidently the word "epitome" is used in the heading of only one manuscript, a late one at that.

10. Above n. 1. On Theopompus' *Philippica*, see below.

Some things about Trogus' history are reasonably clear and uncontroversial. His work fell into the genre of universal history. Somewhat earlier, Diodorus of Sicily had produced 40 books in an attempt to encompass the history of the known world from mythical times to 59 B.C. Trogus' contemporary Nicolaus of Damascus produced a massive 144 books, stretching from Ninus of Assyria to 4 B.C. The difference in Trogus' work was that it was in Latin and that it concentrated on Near Eastern and Greek affairs, relying essentially on Greek sources. He also picked up on the theme of succeeding empires: Assyria, Medes, Persia, Macedonian kingdoms, Rome (but nothing substantial), Carthage, and then the Parthians in Books 41 and 42. It follows that the work concentrates on the deeds and behaviour of kings and tyrants.

The idea of a succession stretches all the way back to Herodotus. Indeed, Herodotus had a substantial influence upon succeeding historiography, as is clear from the letter of Dionysius of Halicarnassus (who favoured Herodotus over Thucydides) mentioned above.[11] Dionysius also places in the Herodotean stream Theopompus, the fourth-century B.C. writer who produced an epitome of Herodotus, as well as his 59 books centring on the history of Philip II of Macedon. If Trogus was not the addressee of Dionysius' letter, he was surely part of a similar milieu. In any case, his history was in the manner of these predecessors. He would provide ethnographic discourses (some would say digressions) on the peoples who came into his narrative, show an interest in the origins of customs and the like. Indeed, the subtitle of the work, if you will, was "the origins of the whole world, and its terrain," which underscores his interest in ethnography and geography. Above all, he would satisfy the demand established by literary criticism for treatment of character and emotion. Rhetoric lent its force to the delineation of virtues and (better still) vices, and created vivid scenes of high emotion.

All these elements may be found in Justin and are evident straight from the first book, where the central figures are monarchs and not only is imperialism seen to begin, but empire itself goes through its first passage. Such elements would be appropriate in Trogus' time, when the Roman world was becoming used to autocracy, and at Justin's, whenever that was in the developed empire. Justin, indeed, demonstrates an interest in hereditary succession and primogeniture;[12] this is one of those elements which shows us Justin, even if he found it in Trogus.

11. See n. 1.
12. See 2.10.2; 3.2.5f.; 16.2.7; 21.1.1.

Another element is a continuing appeal to the workings of fortune, something which scholars who want to see the words of Trogus in Justin have sought to exploit. Briefly, the ascription of Roman successes to good luck (30.4.16; 39.5.3) contrasts with the rise of Macedon, owing to the virtues of the latter's kings combined with the diligence of the people (7.1.1 and thereafter); this is part of an anti-Roman bias in Trogus, taken over from a source of such tendency. This goes hand in hand with the supposition that Trogus meant to flatter his fellow Gauls. Neither of these conclusions should be allowed to stand—if Trogus had good words for his ancestors, it is hardly surprising. It should not, however, be used to argue that Justin too was from Gaul, since many other peoples receive extended treatment as they catch his interest; none would suppose him a Scythian, though that race crops up constantly. More importantly, no one who has read the beginning of Book 43 ought to see Trogus as anti-Roman, and anyone familiar with his contemporaries Livy and Vergil, not to mention the public and official media of coin legends and buildings, ought to realize the *pride* the Romans felt in the fact that their efforts had been promoted by fortune, which is more than mere "good luck." Moreover, if 36.4.12 records the influx of vices after Asia became subject to Rome, it again accords with what may be found in mainstream Roman historiography.[13] It is also a basic tenet, though too often ignored, that sentiments found in speeches attributed to characters in a history are not simply to be taken as those of the author.

We are much safer in seeing any non-Roman point of view in Trogus as owing to his use of Greek sources.[14] We have been brought into the area of what Syme in his article called the "torture and tedium of 'Quellenforschung'." The scientific-sounding German word merely means the search for the sources drawn upon by surviving writers. It is especially applied to writers who are perceived as transcribing or translating in some degree one particular source at a time, with the result that blocks of narrative in, for example, Livy and Diodorus are derived closely from particular predecessors. Despite continuing expressions of hope that this line of research is moribund, its funeral has not yet been held. The subject cannot be avoided, though we may avoid taking it to the brink of tedium.

Trogus has come under this sort of scrutiny, though it is particularly dangerous, of course, to draw conclusions on the basis of an intermediary such as Justin. Now sometimes it *is* clear enough to which author an

13. See, e.g., Sallust *Catiline* 11f.
14. See Jal (above n. 9), 203.

account goes back, when, that is, there is a closeness to a surviving text or another definite clue. But when the supposed sources are works which survive only in fragments or not at all, conclusions reached by this method cannot, to say the least, be automatically relied upon. Such conclusions may, nonetheless, be found stated with undue confidence, and some become orthodoxy. With Trogus, the figure of his contemporary Timagenes, who also focussed on monarchs, is often featured as a mediating source, but this is a supposition based on very little beyond convenience.[15] Much else is pure guesswork and playing with names. And what is gained? If an author takes over the perspectives of his source, it is not mere slavish copying. Nor need any conclusion ultimately affect the historicity of the basic data: a good source can transmit wrong information and *vice versa*, so one still has to weigh the credentials of what is in the text at hand. So in most cases the historical soundness of what we actually find in Justin is not a question decided by speculative reference to the sources of Trogus. The notes to this translation will often mention possible sources, but it should be remembered that in few instances is there any certainty.

Greek though the sources were, some terms are quite naturally Romanised: a prominent example is the use of "senate" for varieties of deliberative councils. The reader should have little trouble with these. There are other areas of the account where events have been depicted in colours familiar to Roman readers. This is hardly surprising, any more than are the ubiquitous workings of portents and divine forces. Nor will it be necessary to search long for Trogus/Justin's view of women— they should be like Theoxena at 23.2.6ff., but many are not. General tendencies are easily identified.

One area where Trogus differed from other ancient historians was in the matter of speeches. The placing of speeches composed by the author in the mouths of characters was standard practice, but we learn from 38.3.11 that Trogus went out of his way to criticize Livy and Sallust on the ground that their practice exceeded the permissible limits of history. So while there are in Justin short snatches of direct speech, longer orations (the longest being that of Mithridates in Book 38) are reported as indirect speech. The contents are nonetheless rhetorical, to the extent of frequent overstatement.

Trogus attempted both to construct his work chronologically and to follow a given series of events from start to finish, as Justin indicates in the

15. This goes back especially to A. von Gutschmid, "Trogus und Timagenes," *Rheinisches Museum für Philologie* 37 (1882), 548ff.

preface. Yet these two principles were not always compatible. Not only did Trogus go back over the history of a nation when it emerged as a major player in the narrative, but he also found it expedient to follow through a connected set of events in one theatre and then go back in time when he turned to another. Because of this practice the notes to the translation must provide dates and connections between interrupted narrative. Comparison with Diodorus in particular shows that this was an almost inevitable consequence of any attempt to write a universal history.

This also may account for some of the reader's difficulties in following Justin, as the sequence of events can be confused even further through selection and compression. For it must be stressed again that Justin has fashioned his own history out of his predecessor's. It is all but certain that Justin's own methods in picking from Trogus' account have created further distortions and misunderstandings. While the major scenes which he has selected maintain internal coherence, the more summary passages seem to have been constructed with less attention and can muddle events as well as skip over a long interval in a few words. One particular aspect of this which will be encountered often is Justin's use of terms such as "meanwhile" as a link word in his narrative, when in fact the events concerned are not contemporaneous at all. Such a translation is accurate, yet highly misleading. To add one more example, if Justin seems to be contradictory in reporting the story that Aristaeus first revealed to men the use of bees and honey (13.7.10), while saying much the same about Gargoris in Spain (44.4.1), we need not lay this at the door of Trogus, who quite possibly recorded both stories as part of the lore attached to the different areas with which he was dealing. With Justin, any such context has been removed.

Perhaps on occasion Justin causes difficulties because he worked from notes. Perhaps he was affected by a desire to pass on as quickly as possible to the next good story. More to the point, however, is Justin's own intent and interest, his principles of selection. This may be summed up in Jal's statement that he was "more orator than historian,"[16] and consequently saw no need for identifying tags to distinguish between Hellenistic monarchs of the same name. Such imprecision had no relevance to the rhetorical and moral significance of what was recounted. We return finally to the point that the work here translated is that of Justin, not Trogus.

16. Jal (above n. 9), 199.

The Notes

In the notes to this translation I have, as already remarked, tried to aid the reader with indications of chronology and possible sources. Where relevant, reference has been made to *AO* and *MRR* (see the list of abbreviations), since they provide convenient repositories of ancient sources. I have also tried to indicate major parallel accounts of events, where possible (which is by no means always) those earlier than Trogus, but I have not thought it necessary to point up all the discrepancies between versions (such as conflicting numbers, a constant problem for ancient historians who believe that one set might be correct), which interested readers can pursue for themselves. Remarks on the text have been kept to a minimum. Other notes refer to problems and attempt clarification. It is not appropriate here to provide substantial bibliography, but sometimes modern works have been noted where they seem particularly helpful or place emphasis on the sources, Justin included. When events fall in the realm of the mythological (or legendary), I have provided no note unless the text would be hard to understand without one—handbooks are available. Internal references to Justin use the term "section" to refer to the larger subdivisions marked in boldface, while the sign § applies to the subdivisions of each section. As with any work of this sort, it is not possible to please everyone. Yet a full commentary was not the intention, and any comments must to a degree reflect the interests and idiosyncrasies of the commentator.

Bob Develin

Justin's Epitome of
the Philippic History of Trogus

PREFACE

[1] MANY Romans, even men of consular rank, had already composed Roman history in a foreign language—Greek—but Pompeius Trogus chose Latin as the medium for his history of Greece and the whole world. Possessed of an eloquence characteristic of the ancients, he was motivated either by a desire to rival the fame of these authors or by the originality of his project, his intention being that Greek history should be as accessible in our language as ours is in Greek. Thus he embarked on an enterprise which called for great enthusiasm and stamina. [2] For since most authors engaged in the history of single rulers or peoples find that even their work demands intense effort, then we must recognize that Pompeius demonstrated an enterprise worthy of Hercules in undertaking a universal history, his books encompassing the annals of every period, king, nation and people. [3] And whereas Greek historians approached their work as specialists, each following his own interests and omitting what did not serve his purpose, Pompeius summarized all their material within a chronological framework while also pursuing a topic from start to finish. [4] During a period of free time which we had in the City, I excerpted from his forty-four published volumes all the most noteworthy material. I omitted what did not make pleasurable reading or serve to provide a moral, and I produced a brief anthology to refresh the memory of those who had studied history in Greek, and to provide instruction for those who had not. [5] This I have sent on to you, not so much for your information as for your criticism, and so that you may also have some justification of my period of free time, which Cato thinks should be accounted for, too.[1] [6] For the time being, your judgment will have to suffice; among later generations, once malicious criticism has ceased, my industry will be duly acknowledged.

---

1. See in particular Cicero *Pro Plancio* 66.

BOOK 1

1 [1] IN the beginning, authority over the peoples and nations of the world lay with monarchs, who rose to supreme power not because they courted popular support but because their restraint won the approval of honest men. [2] There were no laws to regulate the masses; the decisions of the leaders were the law. [3] It was customary to guard the boundaries of one's empire rather than to advance them: each ruler's kingdom was confined to the land of his fathers.

[4] It was the Assyrian king Ninus[1] who first exchanged this ancient and virtually hereditary custom for an unprecedented lust for dominion. [5] He was the first to make war on his neighbours and, as far as the boundaries of Libya, he brought under his domination nations as yet unskilled at self-defence. [6] He was, it is true, preceded by the Egyptian Vezosis and King Tanaus of Scythia, of whom the former advanced to the Pontus and the latter, as far as Egypt; [7] but these were engaged in distant, not local, wars and their goal was not empire for themselves but glory for their people.[2] Satisfied with victory, they shunned dominion. Ninus, however, secured by continuous occupation of territory the wide empire he had won. [8] He subjugated his immediate neighbours; then, strengthened by this acquisition of power, he passed on to others, each successive victory being the means for gaining the next, and thus he conquered the peoples of the entire East. [9] His final campaign was against Zoroaster, king of Bactria, who, they say, was the inventor of magic and a diligent student of cosmology and the movements of the stars.[3] [10] After killing Zoroaster,

1. See Diod. 2.1ff., whose source is the same as that of Trogus, Ctesias of Cnidus. See R. Drews, "Assyria in Classical Universal Histories," *Historia* 14 (1965), 129–142. Ninus is probably Tukulti-Ninurta I (1244–1208).

2. The Egyptian king is Sesostris in Her. 2.102ff., Sesoöstris in Diod. 1.53ff., and is likely to be Ramses II (1290–1224), though not all the actions attributed to Sesostris may belong to Ramses. Tanaus, who does not appear in Justin Book 2, is evidently the eponym of the Tanais river (the modern Don).

3. The name "Zoroaster" naturally suggests the prophet of Ahura-Mazda, whose worship was adopted by the Achaemenids of Persia, but Diod. 2.6.3 calls this man Oxyartes, a name otherwise borne by the Bactrian-Sogdian chieftain whose daughter Roxane married Alexander the Great.

Ninus himself died, leaving behind a young son, Ninias, and a widow, Semiramis.[4]

2 [1] Semiramis did not dare entrust the throne to an immature boy, but no more would she openly occupy it herself. The many great nations of their empire had barely submitted to Ninus, a man; much less would they submit to a woman. She pretended, therefore, to be the son of Ninus rather than his wife, a boy rather than a woman. [2] For mother and son were of average height, had high-pitched voices and bore a facial resemblance to each other. [3] Semiramis kept her arms and legs covered and wore a turban on her head; and, to avoid the impression that this new mode of dress was concealing something, she gave orders that her people be similarly clothed—a fashion universally maintained by the race since that time.[5] [4] By so disguising her sex from the start, she passed for a boy. [5] Her subsequent achievements were impressive and, when she felt them great enough to have overcome any possible resentment, she revealed her identity and the imposture. [6] Nor did the admission detract from the prestige of her rule; indeed it served to increase admiration for her—a woman surpassing not only women but men, too, in manly achievement! [7] She founded Babylon and encircled it with a wall of baked brick, which she mortared with bitumen instead of sand since this substance is found seeping from the ground throughout the region. [8] This queen had many other illustrious achievements to her credit; for, not content with maintaining the frontiers of the empire won by her husband, she also added Ethiopia to her rule. [9] She even attacked India, a country penetrated by none save herself and Alexander the Great. [10] In the end, she tried to have sexual relations with her son and was murdered by him, thirty-two years after succeeding Ninus on the throne. [11] Her son, Ninias, was content with the empire built up by his parents and completely abandoned military activity. Further, almost as if he had exchanged sex with his mother, he was rarely seen by men and he grew old surrounded by women. [12] Following this example, his successors also gave official responses to their subject peoples through

4. For the contents of the following section see Diod. 2.4ff., again based on Ctesias and containing details at variance with the account here. On Semiramis' sexual behaviour see Orosius 4.4ff.

5. Hardly true, and Diod. 2.6.6 indicates that Semiramis dressed thus only for her journey to Bactria.

intermediaries. [13] The Assyrians, who were later called the Syrians, ruled this empire for 1300 years.[6]

3 [1] The last Syrian ruler was Sardanapallus, a man, but more degenerate than a woman.[7] [2] His own governor of the Medes, who was called Arbactus, sought an audience with him, a privilege hitherto granted to no one. When, after a great deal of soliciting, Arbactus finally succeeded in gaining admission, he found Sardanapallus surrounded by troops of whores. He was spinning purple wool with a distaff and, dressed like a woman (though he was more effeminate in his appearance and more wanton in his glances than any woman), apportioning tasks of wool to the young girls of the household. [3] On seeing this, Arbactus was incensed that so many warriors were subject to such a "woman" and that men who bore swords and armour served someone who worked with wool. He went to his comrades and told them what he had seen, adding that he could not take orders from someone who preferred to be a woman rather than a man. [4] Thus a conspiracy was formed and hostilities commenced against Sardanapallus. On hearing of this, Sardanapallus reacted not like a man about to defend his kingdom, but as women do when fearful for their lives. First he looked for a place to hide, but soon proceeded to battle with a small and disorderly force. [5] Defeated, he fell back on his palace, where he built and lit a funeral pyre and then flung himself and his riches into the flames—in this action alone behaving like a man. [6] The man responsible for his death, Arbactus, the former governor of Media, was made king after him. Arbactus transferred the empire from the Assyrians to the Medes.[8]

4 [1] After many kings, the throne came down in due succession to Astyages.[9] [2] He dreamed that a vine sprouted from the womb of his only daughter to cast a shadow with its branches over all Asia. [3] When the soothsayers were consulted, they responded that Astyages would have a grandson from this daughter, that the grandson's greatness was foretold, but Astyages' loss of the throne was likewise predicted. [4] This response terrified the king, who refused to have his daughter married

6. Diod. 2.28.2 agrees on this figure, but see Drews (above n. 1), 138ff.

7. Her. 2.150; Diod. 2.23ff., where Arbactus appears as Arbaces. Sardanapallus may well be Ashurbanipal (668–629). From this point, and especially from section 4, the reader should consult the relevant sections of *CHI* 2.

8. Whatever is meant by this, Her. 1.106 says the Assyrians were conquered by Cyaxares the Mede.

9. For the contents of sections 4 to 6 see Her. 1.107ff., where there are slight differences.

either to a prominent man or to a fellow-citizen, for he feared that noble parentage on both the father's and the mother's side would strengthen the grandson's spirit. Instead he married her off to Cambyses, a man of humble birth who belonged to the as yet undistinguished Persian race. [5] Even that did not remove the fear inspired by his dream, and when his daughter became pregnant he summoned her to him so that the child could be killed at birth right before its grandfather's eyes. [6] The baby was born and Harpagus, a confidant of the king, was assigned the murderous task. [7] Harpagus was afraid that if the throne should pass to the king's daughter when Astyages died (for he had produced no male heir), then she, unable to avenge the infant's death by taking action against her father, would do so by punishing his henchman. Accordingly, he handed the boy over to the herdsman of the king's cattle to be exposed. [8] It so happened that at the same time a son had been born to the herdsman also, [9] and when his wife heard of the order for exposure of the royal child she earnestly begged that the boy be brought and shown to her. [10] Worn down by her entreaties, the herdsman returned to the wood to find a bitch at the infant's side offering the child her teats and keeping away wild animals and birds. [11] Struck with the same compassion which he had seen in the dog, the herdsman took the boy to his cottage, the dog following anxiously behind. [12] When the woman took the baby in her arms, he snuggled into her as if he knew her, and there seemed to be such vitality in him and so winsome was the affectionate child's smile that the wife actually asked the herdsman to expose her own baby in place of the royal infant and allow her to bring up the boy, thus bringing to realization either his fortune or her own hopes. [13] And so the youngsters' fates were interchanged, the one being raised as a herdsman's son and the other exposed as the king's grandchild. [14] The child's nurse was later named Spargos, that being the Persian word for "dog."[10]

5 [1] Later on, because he had an air of authority with the herdsmen, the boy was given the name Cyrus.[11] [2] Soon afterwards, he was chosen king by lot while playing with his friends and he mischievously gave a whipping to those who disobeyed him. Hence a complaint was brought to the king by the boys' parents, angry that free children had been flogged

10. The word appears as "Spako" in Herodotus, with the Greek equivalent "Cyno." Herodotus also notes that it was the woman's name that gave rise to the story above about the nursing dog.

11. The Greek "kyrios" means "lord," which is, of course, an irrelevant coincidence.

like slaves by a slave of the king. [3] Astyages sent for the boy and questioned him. When Cyrus declared with a completely straight face that he had acted like a king, Astyages, struck by his self-confidence, was put in mind of his dream and its interpretation. [4] And since the boy's facial resemblance, the date of exposure and the herdsman's confession all fitted together, he acknowledged him as his grandson. [5] Furthermore, since the boy's reign among the herdsmen appeared to have fulfilled the dream-prophecy, he dropped his threatening demeanour, at least as far as the boy was concerned. [6] But he was furious with his friend Harpagus. To repay him for saving the grandchild, he killed Harpagus' own son and served the flesh to him as a meal. [7] Harpagus concealed his anguish for the moment and postponed venting his hatred for the king until an opportunity for revenge should present itself.

[8] Time passed, Cyrus grew up and Harpagus, spurred on by the pain of his bereavement, informed him by letter of how he, Cyrus, had been banished to Persia by his grandfather;[12] how the latter had ordered his murder when he was a baby and how he had been rescued by Harpagus' own kindness; how he, Harpagus, had displeased the king and thus had lost his own son. [9] He urged Cyrus to raise an army and embark on the easy road to the throne, promising that the Medes would defect to him. [10] Since the letter could not be carried openly because the king's guards were blocking all the roads, it was put inside an eviscerated hare, which was then handed to a trusty slave to be carried to Cyrus in Persia. The slave was also given nets to make him look like a hunter and so provide cover for the plot.

6 [1] After reading the letter, Cyrus was told in a dream to embark on this very enterprise, but he was further advised in the dream to accept as partner in the undertaking the first person he happened to meet the next day. [2] Setting out on the open road before dawn, he met a slave named Sybares who belonged to the work-house of a certain Mede. [3] Cyrus questioned the man about his birth and, when he heard that he had been born in Persia, he removed his fetters and, taking him as his companion, returned to Persepolis. [4] There he called a meeting of the people and told them all to come with axes and fell the wood that bordered the road. [5] This they did energetically, and on the following day Cyrus invited them to a banquet he had prepared. [6] When he saw that the banquet had warmed their spirits, he asked them which

12. Banishment to Persia has not figured in the story, but Herodotus shows Cyrus residing in Persia.

manner of life they would choose if given the option, yesterday's labour
or today's banquet. "Today's banquet", they all cried out, whereupon
Cyrus declared that, as long as they obeyed the Medes, their whole life
would be like yesterday's labour whereas, if they followed him, it would
be like today's banquet. [7] They were all delighted with this and Cyrus
marched against the Medes.

[8] Astyages entrusted the direction of the war to Harpagus, forgetting
his own "services" to the latter. [9] Once Harpagus took command of the
troops, he promptly surrendered them to Cyrus and by this treacherous
desertion took his revenge for the king's cruelty. [10] When Astyages
heard this, he gathered fresh forces from all quarters, marched into
Persia in person and recommenced the struggle with some vigour. He
positioned a portion of his army behind those who were already in combat
and ordered them to drive back into the enemy at sword point any who
hesitated. [11] He told his soldiers that, if they did not win, they would
find at their rear troops just as formidable as those in front; they should
decide, therefore, whether to break the one line by fleeing or the other by
fighting. [12] Forced to do battle, his army experienced a great surge
of morale. [13] The Persian line was hit hard and was gradually giving
ground when the mothers and wives of the men came running to meet
them, begged them to return to battle [14] and, as the men hesitated, lifted
up their dresses and revealed their private parts, asking if they wanted
to seek refuge in the wombs of their mothers or wives. [15] Checked
by this rebuke, the Persians returned to the field, made an assault and
forced into flight the enemy from whom they had themselves been fleeing.
[16] Astyages was captured in this battle, but Cyrus merely deprived him
of his kingdom, and then behaved towards him more like a grandson
than a victor, setting him over the mighty nation of the Hyrcanians (since
Astyages himself did not want to return to the Medes). [17] Thus it was
that the empire of the Medes came to an end after a rule of 350 years.

7 [1] At the beginning of his reign, Cyrus made Sybares governor of
Persia and gave him his sister in marriage. (It was Sybares who had
been a partner in Cyrus' enterprise from the beginning, the man whom,
in accordance with the dream, he had freed from the workhouse and
had taken as his companion in everything.) [2] But the states which
had formerly paid tribute to the Medes believed that the change in
government also meant a change in their status, and so they revolted from
Cyrus, an event which proved the ultimate cause of many wars for the
king. [3] After reducing most of the rebels, he was on campaign against
the Babylonians when King Croesus of Lydia (whose power and wealth

were famous at the time) came to their aid.[13] Croesus was defeated and, fearful now for his own safety, he retreated into his kingdom. [4] After his victory and after settling matters in Babylonia, Cyrus pushed the war into Lydia. [5] There he had no difficulty in scattering the army of Croesus, which was already demoralized by the fortunes of the previous battle, and Croesus himself was taken prisoner. [6] But Cyrus' victory was as humane as his campaign had been free of danger. [7] Croesus was granted his life, a portion of his fortune and the city of Beroe in which to lead a life that at least approached a royal dignity, even if it was not that of a king. [8] Such mercy benefited the conqueror as much as the conquered [9] for, when it became known that Croesus was under attack, help began to flow to him from all over Greece, as if to extinguish a fire that was perceived as threatening everyone. [10] Such was the affection felt for Croesus throughout the city-states, and Cyrus would have faced a serious war with Greece if his treatment of Croesus had been at all harsh.

[11] Some time later, when Cyrus was busy with other wars, the Lydians revolted.[14] [12] Defeated once more, they were now deprived of weapons and horses and ordered to restrict their activities to inn-keeping, theatrical performances and the maintaining of brothels. [13] So it was that a people, once powerful through its energy and brave in battle, became corrupted by easy living and profligacy, and lost its former virtue. Men invincible in their campaigns down to the time of Cyrus now succumbed to luxury and were overcome by peace and lethargy.

[14] Before Croesus the Lydians had many kings who were remarkable for the vicissitudes of their lives, but none had a fate to compare with that of Candaules.[15] [15] He had a wife with whom he was desperately in love because of her beauty, and he would sing her praises to everybody. Not satisfied with the private enjoyment of his marital bliss, he would even divulge the secrets of the marriage bed, [16] just as if silence on that subject detracted from her beauty. [17] Finally, to gain credence for his claims, he showed her naked to his companion Gyges, [18] by which he made an enemy of his friend, who was now tempted to seduce the wife, while he also alienated his wife by virtually giving her love to another man. [19] For shortly afterwards the murder of Candaules became the price of her marriage to Gyges, and the wife, with her husband's blood

13. See Her. 1.71ff., which is not the immediate source here; neither perhaps is Ctesias, who calls Beroe "Barene" (§ 4 [Photius]). Cyrus' campaign against Croesus dates to 547. The capture of Babylon actually occurred in October 539.
14. Her. 1.154ff.
15. Her. 1.8ff.

as her dowry, handed over to her lover both herself and her husband's throne.

8 [1] After reducing Asia and all the East, Cyrus invaded Scythia.[16] [2] The queen of the Scythians at that time was Tamyris, who, in a most unwomanly fashion, was not intimidated by the approach of her enemies. She could have prevented them from crossing the river Araxes, but instead she allowed them to pass because she believed that a battle fought within the boundaries of her empire would be to her advantage, and also that the river would form an obstacle to impede the enemy's flight. [3] Accordingly, Cyrus took his troops across and, after advancing some way into Scythia, pitched camp. [4] Then, the next day, he pretended to panic, and abandoned his camp as if in flight, leaving behind large quantities of wine and all the makings of a feast. [5] When news of this was brought to the queen, she sent her young son with a third of her forces in pursuit of the king. [6] The young man, however, had little military experience and, when he reached the camp of Cyrus, it was as if he had arrived for a banquet, not a battle: forgetting the enemy, he allowed his barbarians, who were not used to wine, to drink too heavily, [7] with the result that the Scythians were overcome by drunkenness before they were overcome in battle. [8] On learning this Cyrus returned by night, fell upon them when they were still the worse for drink and killed them all, including the queen's son.

[9] After losing this large army—and, a more grievous bereavement, her only son—Tamyris, far from dissolving in tears at the pain of her loss, instead contemplated revenge to ease her grief. She actually caught her enemies, as they gloated over their recent victory, with a ruse similar to the one which they had used themselves. [10] Feigning loss of confidence after the blow she had received, she retreated and lured Cyrus into a narrow pass [11] where, laying an ambush in the hills, she slaughtered 200,000 Persians along with their king. [12] What was also remarkable about this victory was that there was not a single Persian survivor to bring back news of the catastrophe. [13] The queen ordered Cyrus' head to be cut off and thrust into a wineskin filled with human blood, adding these words of rebuke for his ruthlessness: "Glut yourself with blood—you always had a thirst for it and could never get enough." [14] Cyrus reigned thirty

---

16. Her. 1.201ff., where the objects of Cyrus' ambition are the Massagetae (Derbekes in Ctesias § 8), whom some said were Scythians, and the queen is Tomyris. There are other differences of detail.

years and had a remarkably distinguished record of successes throughout his reign, not just at its beginning.

9 [1] Cyrus was succeeded by his son Cambyses,[17] who added Egypt to his father's empire; [2] but, taking offence at the superstitions of the Egyptians, Cambyses ordered the destruction of the temples of Apis and the other gods. [3] He also sent an army to capture the famous temple of Hammon, but the force was destroyed when it was overtaken by storms and buried in massive drifts of sand. [4] Subsequently, Cambyses had a dream that his brother Mergis would be king, [5] and this so terrified him that he did not hesitate to add fratricide to his acts of sacrilege. [6] For it was truly difficult for someone who showed no respect for religion, and who had attacked even the gods, to spare his own family!

[7] For this ruthless service he selected from among his friends a certain Magus named Cometes. [8] In the meantime, Cambyses himself died from a serious wound in his thigh inflicted when his sword unsheathed itself, and thus he paid the penalty, whether for the fratricide he had commissioned or for the sacrilege he had committed. [9] When this was reported to him, the Magus hurriedly perpetrated his crime before word of the king's death could get out, and substituted his own brother Oropastes for Mergis, the rightful heir to the throne, whom he had murdered. [10] In fact, Oropastes closely resembled Mergis both facially and in physique and, since none suspected that imposture was involved, he was declared king in Mergis' place. [11] The affair was all the more easily concealed because among the Persians the king is kept from sight, ostensibly to protect his royal dignity. [12] So now the two Magi attempted to win over popular support by granting remission of taxes and exemption from military service over a three-year period, [13] thus trying to consolidate by extravagant largesse a throne which they had procured by duplicity. [14] The first to entertain suspicions was Hostanes, a nobleman with very sharp powers of deduction. [15] He used messengers to ask his daughter, who was one of the royal concubines, whether the king really was Cyrus' son. [16] She replied that she did not know and

---

17. In the sources relevant to section 9 there are discrepancies as to names, sequence, and more, and it is likely that Cambyses' name has been unduly blackened. See Her. 3.1ff., 61ff.; Ctesias §§ 9ff.; Darius' Behistun inscription (J. M. Balcer, *Herodotus and Bisitun* [Historia Einzelschriften 49, 1987]); the inscription of Udjahorresnet (A. B. Lloyd, "The Inscription of Udjahorresnet: a Collaborator's Testament," *Journal of Egyptian Archaeology* 68 (1982), 166ff.); T. C. Young in *CAH* vol. 4, 1–52; M. A. Dandamaev, *A Political History of the Achaemenid Empire* (trans. W. J. Vogelsang, Leiden 1989). Trogus, it seems, followed Herodotus' version.

could find out from no one else because the concubines were confined and segregated. [17] Hostanes then told her to feel the king's head while he was sleeping, since Cambyses had cut off both ears of the Magus. [18] When he was later informed by his daughter that the king had no ears, he divulged the matter to some Persian noblemen whom he then incited and bound by a solemn oath to murder the imposter. [19] Only seven were party to the conspiracy. These hid swords under their clothes and proceeded immediately to the palace so that the plot might not be revealed by any of them should they be given time for a change of heart. [20] Killing all who stood in their way at the palace, they made their way to the Magi. The latter showed no lack of spirit in defending themselves, [21] for they both drew their swords and killed two of the conspirators. [22] But they were overwhelmed by superior numbers. One of them was seized around the waist by Gobryas, whose companions hesitated, afraid they might run him through instead of the Magus since the action was taking place in the dark; but he told them to stab the Magus even through his own body. [23] As luck would have it, however, the Magus was killed and Gobryas was unharmed.

10 [1] On the death of the Magi, the noblemen enjoyed great prestige for having recovered the throne; but they gained even more from being able to agree in their discussion of the future of the kingdom.[18] [2] They were so evenly matched in personal integrity and noble birth that this very equality made the choice from among them difficult for the people. [3] The nobles themselves therefore devised a means of assigning the decision to their religion and to chance. [4] They agreed among themselves that early in the morning of a predetermined day they should all lead their horses before the palace, and the one whose horse neighed first as the sun rose should be king ([5] for the Persians believe the sun to be the one and only god and they claim that horses are sacred to that god). [6] Now among the former conspirators was one Darius, son of Hystaspes, who was anxious about the impending kingship. His groom told him that if the neighing of the horse was all that stood in the way of success, there really was nothing to worry about. [7] During the night before the prescribed day, he took Darius' horse to the appointed place and coupled it with a mare, believing that the horse's sensual pleasure would yield a certain result—as, in fact, it did. [8] When the noblemen all met the next day at the hour specified, Darius' horse, recognizing the spot and feeling desire for the mare, immediately neighed and, while the

18. Her. 3.8off.

other animals did nothing, was the first to emit the happy omen for its master. [9] Such was the integrity of the other nobles that as soon as they heard the omen they jumped from their horses and hailed Darius as king. [10] The people, too, unanimously accepted the decision of the nobles and confirmed him as king. [11] Thus it was that the throne of Persia, won by the courage of seven men of the highest rank, was conferred for such an insignificant reason on one of their number. [12] Such acquiescence in regard to the throne is truly amazing on the part of these men when they had been prepared to face death to wrest it from the Magi.

[13] And yet Darius' handsome appearance and personal qualities fitted him for the throne; besides which, he had family ties with the former kings. [14] Right at the start of his reign he married Cyrus' daughter, using this royal wedding to strengthen his rule by making it appear that the throne had now been returned to the family of Cyrus rather than handed over to a stranger.[19]

[15] After an interval the Assyrians revolted and seized Babylon.[20] Reducing the city proved difficult and Darius was incensed. Then Zopyrus, one of the killers of the Magi, ordered himself lashed all over his body in his own home, and his nose, ears and lips cut off. In this state he presented himself to the unsuspecting king. [16] Darius was thunderstruck. He asked the reasons for the hideous disfigurement and the name of the culprit. Zopyrus then explained in secret the motive for his actions, and after establishing his plan for the future set off for Babylon, posing as a deserter. [17] There he displayed his mutilated body to the people and complained about the cruelty of the king, whose superiority in the contest for the throne lay in an omen, not merit—in the neighing of a horse, not the rational appraisal of men. [18] He told them to use this example of Darius' treatment of his friends to gauge what his enemies should prepare for, [19] and urged them to put their trust in their arms rather than their walls and permit him to direct a combined operation against Darius, since his resentment towards the king was the fresher. [20] All were aware of the man's breeding as well as his courage, and there was no concern about his trustworthiness, for which they had his wounds and disfigurement as guarantee. [21] So Zopyrus was unanimously elected general, and at the head of a small company of

19. Darius was, as he himself says in the Behistun inscription, one of the Achaemenids. He in fact married two daughters of Cyrus, Atossa and Artystone (Her. 3.88).

20. Her. 3.150ff. Zopyrus was in fact the son of Megabyzus, the one who had been among the killers (Her. 3.70).

men he fought one or two successful engagements, the Persians making a pre-arranged retreat before him. [22] Finally, the entire rebel army was put in his charge; this he betrayed to Darius and brought the city itself into the king's power. [23] Following this Darius invaded Scythia, the history of which campaign will be recounted in the next volume.

BOOK 2

1 [1] To give an account of the impressive and magnificent history of the Scythians, one must go back to their beginnings; [2] for their early years were as distinguished as the period of their empire, nor did the men outshine the women in heroic exploits. [3] The men established the Parthian and Bactrian empires, but the women were the founders of the Amazonian kingdom. [4] In fact, when one considers the achievements of the males and those of the females, it is difficult to decide which of the two sexes had the more distinguished history.[1]

[5] The Scythian race is always regarded as the oldest in the world, though there was a longstanding dispute between the Scythians and the Egyptians over the age of their peoples. [6] The Egyptians claimed that at the beginning of creation certain countries were scorched by excessive heat from the sun while others froze in a brutally cold climate. These latter, said the Egyptians, could not be the first lands to produce mankind; indeed, they were not even able to welcome and provide shelter for immigrants until the invention of clothing to protect the body against heat and the cold, and until their inhospitable environment could be tempered by technological advances. [7] The climate of Egypt, on the other hand, had always been so temperate that its inhabitants were bothered neither by cold in winter nor by heat in summer, [8] while its soil was so fertile as to be surpassed by no other land in the production of food for human consumption. [9] So, the Egyptians claimed, it was reasonable to accept the place where men could most easily be nurtured as the place of their origin.

[10] For their part, the Scythians thought that a temperate climate was no proof of antiquity. [11] In giving different regions varying degrees

1. Her. 4 begins with a long treatment of the Scythians, but this was certainly not the direct source of Trogus. At Her. 4.5.1 we find the Scythian claim to be the *youngest* of peoples, and at 2.2 the Egyptians concede the issue of antiquity to the Phrygians. The Scythians are dealt with by T. Sulimirski in chapter 4 of *CHI* 2.

of heat and cold, they said, Nature had also immediately produced animals capable of adapting to their environment, [12] and she had also diversified species of trees and crops according to local climatic conditions. [13] The Scythian climate was, indeed, harsher than the Egyptian; that only meant that the Scythians were physically and mentally all the more robust than the Egyptians. [14] Besides, the world, which is now made up of regions, was once an undivided whole, and at the beginning of creation the earth was either submerged in floodwater or else engulfed in the fire out of which the universe was born. Either cosmic theory favoured the priority of the Scythians. [15] If the earth was originally covered by fire, which gradually died down and gave place to land, then no region can have been detached from the fire by the severity of its winter earlier than the north, where it is so harsh that even now there is no area more icebound. [16] Egypt, however, and all the rest of the East, must have been the latest to cool, for even today it still bakes in the torrid heat of the sun. [17] If, alternatively, the entire world was once submerged in deep water, then certainly it was all the higher ground which was first uncovered by the retreating flood, whereas the water would have remained longest on the lowest soil, [18] and the sooner a part of the world dried out the sooner it would have begun to generate living creatures. [19] Now Scythia, they argued, was so much higher than other countries that all rivers rising within it flow into Lake Maeotis,[2] and then into the Pontus and Egyptian sea.[3] [20] Egypt was another matter. So many kings over so many centuries had directed their attention and money to protecting it against flooding, constructing huge barrages to combat the violence of the inundations and digging many canals, the former to keep back the waters, the latter to siphon them off; and even so the land could not be cultivated unless the Nile were driven back.[4] So Egypt could not be thought to have the most ancient population; indeed, its barrages, whether constructed by its kings or formed by the accumulation of the silt of the Nile, would suggest it to be the most

2. The Sea of Azov.

3. So the text, but unless Trogus made some comparison with the low, inundated areas of Egypt, "Egyptian sea" is perhaps an error (on the part of Justin or a scribe) for "Aegean sea," given the proximity of "Egypt." The Pontus is the Black Sea.

4. An emendation suggested by Shackleton Bailey in *Phoenix* 34 (1980), 3 would render the translation "unless the Nile receded," referring to the annual retreat of the floodwaters.

recent of countries. [21] The Egyptians were defeated by such arguments and ever since then the Scythians have always been thought the older.

2 [1] Scythia stretches eastward and is bordered on one flank by the Pontus, on the other by the Riphaean Mountains, and to the rear by Asia and the river Phasis. [2] It is an extensive country both in length and breadth. [3] Its various peoples have no fixed boundaries; they do not engage in agriculture, and they have no home nor hut nor even fixed abode. Instead they pasture their cattle and sheep throughout the year, and live a nomadic life in the desolate wilds. [4] They transport their wives and children with them in wagons which they cover with hides as protection against rain and winter cold, and use as houses. [5] Their justice derives from the natural bent of their race rather than from codified law. [6] No crime is more serious than theft—naturally, for since they have no buildings to safeguard their sheep and cattle, what would they have left amid the forests if robbery were condoned? [7] They do not lust after silver and gold like other human beings, [8] and their diet consists of milk and honey.

[9] They know nothing of the use of wool, much less clothing, and, despite the blistering cold to which they are continually subjected, their dress consists only of hides and the skins of small animals. [10] This simple life-style has also bestowed upon them an equitable character, for they do not covet another's property—the lust for riches is to be found only where they are in use. [11] One would wish that the rest of mankind exhibited similar moderation and self-restraint with regard to the property of others. [12] Then for sure there would not be so many wars following one after the other in every age and every land; [13] nor would sword and shield eliminate more people than natural causes determined by Fate. [14] In fact, it seems amazing that nature should bestow on the Scythians what the Greeks have been unable to achieve with all the protracted teachings of their sages and the precepts of their philosophers, and that a refined morality should suffer by comparison with that of uncultured barbarians. [15] So much more has ignorance of vice benefited the Scythians than knowledge of virtue has the Greeks.

3 [1] The Scythians three times aspired to domination in Asia, while they themselves remained continuously free from either challenge or defeat by a foreign power. [2] They drove the Persian king Darius in ignominious flight from Scythia, [3] and massacred Cyrus and his entire army.[5] [4] They likewise annihilated Alexander the Great's general Zopyrion and all his forces.[6] [5] They have heard of the military might of Rome but not experienced it. [6] They were themselves the founders of the Parthian and Bactrian empires.[7] [7] A people hardened by the rigours of war and possessing enormous physical strength, they have no wish to acquire anything they would be afraid to lose, and they want nothing from victory but glory. [8] The first person to declare war on the Scythians was the Egyptian king, Vezosis,[8] who sent ahead embassies to dictate terms of submission to his enemy. [9] The Scythians, however, forewarned of the king's coming by their neighbours, replied to the ambassadors [10] that the leader of such a rich people had made a foolish mistake in commencing hostilities against a poor one: [11] he was thus making more precarious his domestic situation because the outcome of the war was uncertain, the rewards of victory non-existent and the losses from defeat obvious. [12] Accordingly, the Scythians were not going to wait for Vezosis to come to them, since there was so much more to whet the appetite on the enemy side; instead, they would come themselves to advance toward their spoils. [13] Action immediately followed words, and when the king learned that the Scythians were advancing at top speed he turned to flight, abandoned his army with all its military equipment and retreated in panic into his kingdom. [14] It was the marshlands which prevented the Scythians from entering Egypt.

[15] Returning from there they conquered Asia and imposed taxes upon it, but at a modest rate which was more a token of their authority than a real prize of victory. [16] They delayed fifteen years in pacifying Asia before they were finally recalled by the importunate pleas of their wives, who informed them by an embassy that, if their men failed to return, they themselves would have children by their neighbouring peoples and would not as women be responsible for the extinction of the Scythian race. [17] Asia continued to pay taxes to the Scythians for fifteen hundred years [18] until Ninus, king of the Assyrians, put an end to the tribute.

4 [1] In the meantime, in Scythia, two young princes, Plynos and Scolopitus, were driven from home by the aristocratic faction. They took with them a large number of the younger Scythians [2] and settled on the

---

5. These events are chronologically reversed: see above 1.8 and below 2.6.9–11.

6. See 12.1.4–5, 16–17.

7. See 41.1.1–2, 2.3–4.

8. See 1.1.6 and note.

coast of Cappadocia near the river Thermodon, where they conquered and occupied the plains of Themiscyra. [3] There, over a period of many years, they regularly plundered the neighbouring peoples, until the latter eventually banded together to ambush and massacre them. [4] Their wives now perceived that they were widows as well as exiles. They therefore took up arms and undertook the defence of their territory, at first by driving back aggressors and presently by offensive action. [5] They also dismissed all thought of intermarriage with their neighbours, calling it slavery rather than marriage. [6] They embarked instead upon an enterprise unparalleled in the whole of history, that of building up a state without men and then actually defending it themselves, out of contempt for the male sex. [7] They even put to death the men who had remained at home, so that some of them would not appear more fortunate than others. [8] They also gained their revenge for the killing of their husbands by destroying the neighbouring tribes. [9] Then, with peace assured by their military success, they entered into sexual relationships with surrounding peoples so that their line would not die out. [10] Males born of such unions they put to death, but girls they brought up in a way that adapted them to their own way of life, [11] training them in armed combat, horse-riding and hunting instead of keeping them in idleness or working with wool. And so that their archery would not be handicapped, they cauterized their right breasts during infancy—hence their name "Amazons."[9]

[12] They once had two queens, Martesia and Lampeto. Already famous for the power which they held, these divided their forces in two and waged war in turns, each alternating offensive action with defence of the country's boundaries. [13] To add authority to their successes, they claimed to be daughters of Mars.

[14] After conquering most of Europe, they also seized a number of city-states in Asia. [15] Here they founded Ephesus and several other cities, after which they sent home part of the army with a huge quantity of plunder. [16] The rest of the Amazons who had stayed behind to guard their empire in Asia were all killed, along with their queen, Martesia, when the barbarians made a concerted attack on them.

[17] Martesia was succeeded on the throne by her daughter Orithyia, who won great admiration not only for her superlative military skills but also because she kept her virginity throughout her life. [18] The splendid reputation of the Amazons was so enhanced by her valour

9. Literally meaning "breastless," though the left was retained for the nursing of children.

that Hercules was ordered by the king to whom he owed the twelve labours to bring back for him the arms of the Amazonian queen, as though this were an impossible order. [19] Hercules therefore set sail for those regions with nine warships, accompanied by the leading young heroes of Greece, and took the Amazons by surprise. [20] At that time two sisters ruled them, Antiope and Orithyia, but Orithyia was abroad on campaign, [21] and when Hercules landed on their shore Antiope, who had no fear of an enemy attack, had with her only a small retinue. [22] Thus it transpired that few of the Amazons could take up arms in response to the surprise attack and so they presented their enemy with an easy victory. [23] Many were killed or taken prisoner, including the two sisters of Antiope, Menalippe and Hippolyte, the former captured by Hercules and the latter by Theseus. [24] Theseus, who was awarded Hippolyte as a prize of war, married her and by her had his son Hippolytus. [25] Hercules after his victory restored the captive Menalippe to her sister and, as the price of her ransom, was given the arms of the queen. His mission thus accomplished, he returned to the king.

[26] When Orithyia learned that her sisters had been attacked and that their abductor was the king of Athens, she urged her companions to seek revenge, and declared that they had wasted their time in conquering the Gulf of Pontus and Asia if they were still exposed not so much to a war as to piracy from the Greeks. [27] She then asked for assistance from Sagylus, king of Scythia. She told him that the Amazons were of Scythian origin, that their husbands had been massacred and that they themselves had been obliged to take up arms, and she presented her reasons for going to war. She added that, by their valour, they had proved that the Scythians had women as spirited as their men. [28] Stirred by national pride, Sagylus sent his son Panasagorus and a large contingent of cavalry to assist them. [29] A disagreement arose before the battle, however, and the Amazons, abandoned by their allies, were defeated in the field by the Athenians. [30] Nevertheless, they found shelter in the encampment of their allies, with whose help they returned to their kingdom without being attacked by other tribes.

[31] Penthesilea came to the throne after Orithyia. There survive great tributes to her valour during the Trojan War when, bringing assistance to the Trojans against the Greeks, she fought amidst the most intrepid heroes. [32] After Penthesilea was killed and her army wiped out, the few Amazons who had remained in the kingdom found it difficult to defend themselves against the neighbouring tribes, but they managed to survive down to the time of Alexander the

Great. [33] One of these, the queen Minithyia (or Thalestris), was granted leave to sleep with Alexander for thirteen days in order that she could have a child by him.[10] She then returned to her kingdom and died soon afterwards, and with her died all trace of the Amazonian name.

5 [1] The Scythians had been away from their wives and children for eight years on their third expedition into Asia, and they now faced a war with their slaves at home.[11] [2] The wives had tired of the long wait for their husbands and, thinking that they had been wiped out in battle rather than merely detained by the war, married the slaves who had been left in charge of the cattle. [3] When their masters returned victorious, the slaves armed themselves and drove them back from the borders as though they were foreigners. [4] The outcome was still in doubt when the Scythians were prompted to change their method of fighting. They realized that the adversaries they had to fight were not a freeborn enemy but their own slaves, whom they should bring to heel by their authority as masters rather than by arms; that they should carry whips instead of weapons into battle and, laying aside their swords, acquire canes and lashes and all the other equipment used to strike terror into slaves. [5] The plan won general approval, and they all fitted themselves out with the recommended equipment. When they engaged their enemy, they brandished the whips before the unsuspecting slaves, and struck such terror into them that they were able to conquer by the fear of the lash men whom they could not conquer by the sword, men who now took to their heels not like a defeated enemy but like runaway slaves. [6] Any who could be captured were punished by crucifixion; [7] moreover, the wives, beset by a guilty conscience, resorted to suicide, some by the sword, others by hanging themselves. [8] Following this, the Scythians had peace right down to the time of King Ianthyrus. [9] The Persian king, Darius, was refused the hand of Ianthyrus' daughter and made war on him, as was mentioned above.[12] [10] He invaded Scythia with an armed force of 700,000, but his enemy afforded him no opportunity for pitched battle; and so, frightened that his retreat might be cut off if the bridge over the Ister were cut down, he pulled back in panic, losing 80,000 men. [11] However, when such vast Persian numbers were involved, the loss

10. See 12.3.5–7 with note.
11. The following story is told in Her. 4.2ff., though without the details in §§ 6–7 here.
12. See 1.10.23. For the following cf. Her. 4.87ff.; Ianthyrus appears at 4.126 and 127 as Idanthyrsus.

was not considered a serious setback. [12] Darius then subdued Asia and Macedonia, and he also defeated the Ionians in a naval battle[13] [13] Next, when he learned that the Athenians had helped the Ionians against him, he turned the whole offensive against them.

6 [1] We have now arrived at the wars of the Athenians. These they brought to a conclusion in a manner that not only exceeded all hopes at the time, but strained belief after the event; and the achievements of the Athenians were greater in the outcome than they could have prayed for. A short excursus on the city's origins is therefore called for, [2] especially since the Athenians differ from other peoples in not having risen to greatness from mean beginnings.[14] [3] For they are unique in priding themselves on their origins as well as their development. [4] It was not immigrants or a motley rabble of people brought together at random that founded the city; rather, the Athenians were born from the land which they inhabit, and their home is also their place of origin. [5] They were the first to teach how to work with wool, and the use of olive oil and wine; and when men were still eating acorns the Athenians showed them how to plough and also to sow grain. [6] As for literature, the art of speaking and the whole civilization which we possess today—Athens is their shrine.

[7] Before the time of Deucalion, their king was Cecrops, who, they claimed (for all early history is based on myth), had the attributes of both sexes, this because he was the first to join male and female in marriage.[15] [8] Cecrops was succeeded by Cranaus, whose daughter Atthis gave the

13. The text refers to Asia, but we might rather expect mention of Thrace, subdued with Macedonia by Darius in 513. The naval battle would seem to be that at Lade, which preceded the fall of Miletus in 493, signalling the end of the Ionian revolt in the early chapters of Her. 6. The Athenians had withdrawn their aid earlier.

14. The notion of Athenian autochthony is commonplace (see, e.g., Thuc. 1.2). Early Athenian history, with all its variants, was the subject of reconstruction, especially by the series of Atthidographers, which really began in the mid-fourth century with Cleidemus (though earlier Hellanicus of Lesbos had produced a short treatment) and led to the most compendious and later most consulted of them, Philochorus, in the third century. The fragments are collected in *FGH*, beginning at no. 323. See also C. Hignett, *A History of the Athenian Constitution* (Oxford 1952), chapter 2.

15. Elsewhere Cecrops is described as part man, part snake and is credited with the introduction of monogamy, the division of Attica into twelve communities (Athens was previously called Cecropia), and much else. He himself is said to have married a daughter of Actaeus, Attica's first king. Perhaps Justin has misunderstood what he found in Trogus.

region its name, [9] and after Cranaus the king was Amphictyonides, who was the first to dedicate the city to Minerva and give the city-state the name of Athens. [10] It was during Amphictyonides' time that a flood destroyed most of the peoples of Greece. [11] The only survivors were those who found refuge in the mountains or those who escaped by boat to the Thessalian king, Deucalion, to whom, as a result, was attributed the founding of the human race. [12] The throne then came down, by due order of succession, to Erechtheus, during whose reign the planting of grain was discovered by Triptolemus at Eleusis [13] (and it is in honour of Triptolemus' benefaction that the nocturnal rites were instituted there). [14] Another Athenian king was Theseus' father, Aegeus, whom Medea divorced when she saw she had a stepson who was an adult. After that she returned to Colchis with Medus, the son whom she had had by Aegeus. [15] Theseus was king after Aegeus, and after Theseus came his son, Demophoön, who gave aid to the Greeks against the Trojans.

[16] Between the Athenians and the Dorians there were longstanding grievances.[16] Determined to settle these by military means, the Dorians consulted the oracle about the outcome of the war they contemplated, [17] and received the answer that they would prevail provided that they did not kill the Athenian king. [18] When the conflict began, the Dorian soldiers were instructed that, above all, they were to leave the Athenian king unscathed. [19] At that time the king of the Athenians was Codrus, who, when he learned of the oracle of the god and the instructions issued by the enemy, changed from his royal robes into rags, and went into the enemy encampment carrying a bundle of sticks on his back. [20] Here, amid a crowd of Dorians who stood in his way, he was killed by a soldier whom he had deliberately wounded with a sickle. When the Dorians recognized the king's corpse they quit the field without a fight. [21] Thus the Athenians were spared a war through the valour of a king who sacrificed himself to save his country.

7 [1] After Codrus there were no more kings of Athens, and this is explained by the deference granted to his memory.[17] [2] The government

16. The three major divisions of the Greek peoples were the Ionians (including the Athenians), the Dorians (including the Spartans and the Megarians, mentioned below), and the Aeolians. The oracle at Delphi figures prominently in Greek history.

17. Athenian tradition held that between the end of the kingship and the beginning of the annual archonship there were 7 ten-year archons. Developments are summarily treated in *Ath. Pol.* 3. The first annual archon dates to the end of the 680s (*AO* 27f.). There was in fact a codification of sorts by Draco in (probably)

of the state was left to annually elected officers, [3] but the city in that epoch had no written laws because the will of the kings had been the law. [4] So it was that Solon, a man of renowned impartiality, was selected virtually to refound the state on the basis of codified law, [5] and he exercised such moderation in dealing with the commons and the senate that, although any measure adopted on behalf of one order seemed likely to antagonize the other, he won equal support from both sides. [6] Amongst his many remarkable achievements is his memorable intervention [7] in the armed conflict between the Athenians and the people of Megara for possession of the island of Salamis, a struggle which had almost destroyed both states. [8] After numerous bitter defeats it became a capital offence at Athens to propose legislation designed to reclaim the island, [9] and this put Solon in a quandary, for he feared that silence on his part would hurt the interests of the state, while stating his opinion would hurt his own. He therefore feigned a sudden attack of insanity, [10] which gave him the excuse not only to make public pronouncements which were against the law, but also to put them into effect. [11] Dressed in slovenly clothes he rushed out in public like a lunatic. A crowd gathered around him and, the better to disguise his intentions, he proceeded to give his illegal exhortation to the people in poetry, a medium which he was unaccustomed to using.[18] [12] He so thoroughly won over the minds of all that war was immediately declared on the Megarians, the enemy was defeated and the island became Athenian territory.

8 [1] The Megarians meanwhile had not forgotten the war against the Athenians which they had started and then broken off, and they wished to avoid the impression that their campaigns had achieved nothing.[19]

621/0 (*AO* 31f.), but the full code came with Solon, who was archon in 594/3 (*AO* 37f.). Solon's moderation is a commonplace derived from his own poetry. For a developed treatment see Plutarch's biography, and for the affair with Megara *AO* 33.

18. Strange as this last phrase reads, it translates the "insolitis sibi versibus" of the manuscripts. Better sense is given if we accept the reading "ibi" preferred by some editors: "something quite unheard of in Athens" (i.e. giving political advice in elegiac couplets).

19. Pisistratus became tyrant for the first time in 561/0; the events described here should be only a short time before that date: see *AO* 41f. The story here is very close to that in the fourth-century Aeneas Tacticus 4.8ff.: see D. Whitehead, *Aineias the Tactician* (Oxford 1990), 107f. The earliest and basic account of the events in the rest of section 8 is Her. 1.59ff., although the epitome omits the two expulsions and returns of Pisistratus (see *AO* xi). Pisistratus died in 528/7.

They therefore boarded their ships in order to make a surprise attack by night on the Athenian matrons at the Eleusinian Mysteries. [2] On learning this, the Athenian general, Pisistratus, set some young men in an ambush and instructed the matrons to practice their rites with the usual cries and hubbub, even when the enemy were approaching, so that the latter would not realize that their plan had been discovered. [3] When the Megarians disembarked, Pisistratus fell on them unawares and wiped them out. Then he promptly hurried to Megara with the fleet which he had seized, setting among his soldiers a number of women to play the part of the captured matrons. [4] Recognizing the shape of their vessels as well as the plunder which had been their goal, the Megarians came to meet them at the harbour. Pisistratus cut them down and came close to capturing the city. [5] Thus the Dorians, falling into their own trap, gave the victory to their enemy.

[6] Pisistratus, however, apparently regarded this as a victory for himself rather than for his native land and now resorted to subterfuge to make himself tyrant. [7] In his home he deliberately had himself beaten, and then he appeared in public with his injuries. [8] He called an assembly, showed his bruises to the people and complained about the brutality of the aristocrats, by whom he falsely claimed he had been assaulted. [9] Tears were added to his allegations; with an inflammatory oration he roused the passions of the gullible crowd, pretending that the senate hated him because of his love for the common people. [10] He was awarded a train of attendants as a bodyguard, and with these he seized the tyranny for himself and reigned for thirty-three years.

9 [1] After Pisistratus' death, one of his sons, Diocles, was assassinated by the brother of a young woman whom he had raped.[20] [2] The other son, whose name was Hippias, now occupied the throne of his father, and he ordered the arrest of his brother's killer. [3] When the latter was forced under torture to name his accomplices in the murder, he named all of the tyrant's friends. [4] Hippias executed these and then asked the assassin if any accomplices still remained. No, he replied, there was now nobody left whom he still wanted to see die, apart from the tyrant himself. [5] With this declaration he revealed that he had got the

20. There is no consistency in the versions of the immediately following events; Justin's has affinities with *Ath.Pol.* 18 (see also Her. 5.55ff.; Thuc. 6.54ff.). Hippias' brother was Hipparchus, who was killed in 514 by Harmodius and Aristogeiton; Hippias was ousted in 511/10. He did indeed go to Persia, and for the rest of section 9 see Her. 6.102ff.; for the Athenian protagonists *AO* 56f. (the year 490/89).

better of Hippias, after taking revenge for his sister's honour. [6] The man's courage prompted the community to reflect on its lost liberty, and eventually Hippias was deposed and driven into exile. [7] He went to Persia, where Darius, as noted above, was commencing an offensive against the Athenians, and he offered himself as his guide, against his own fatherland.

[8] When the Athenians heard that Darius was coming, they sought assistance from the Spartans, with whom, at that time, they had an alliance; [9] but they could see that the latter would be delayed for four days by religious observances, and so they did not wait for Spartan aid. Instead, they drew up 10,000 citizens and a thousand Plataean auxiliaries and marched into battle against 600,000 of the enemy on the plains of Marathon. [10] Miltiades was the Athenian commander in chief and also the man who had advised against waiting for support; he was so full of confidence that he set more store by speed of action than he did by his allies. [11] As the Athenians went into battle, such was the fervour in their hearts that, even though a mile separated the two armies, they broke into a run and reached the enemy before the latter had time to release their arrows. And their daring met with success. [12] They fought with such heroism as to make one think that there were warriors on one side and cattle on the other. [13] The defeated Persians fled back to their ships, many of which were sunk and many captured.

[14] So great was the valour of individual Athenians in the battle that it appeared difficult to determine who should have the highest praise. [15] However, one of those who gave a dazzling performance was the young Themistocles; even then his qualities were obvious and betokened his future greatness in military leadership. [16] The superb achievements of the Athenian soldier Cynegirus have also drawn accolades from historians. [17] After dispatching countless Persians in the battle, Cynegirus took part in the pursuit of the enemy back to the ships and there he held on with his right hand to a ship loaded with men, refusing to let go until he lost his hand. [18] Then, although his right hand had been severed, he gripped the vessel with his left hand and finally, when he had lost that one as well, held on to the ship with his teeth. [19] Such was his courage that, showing no fatigue after killing so many and, undaunted by the loss of both his hands, he fought on to the end, despite his mutilation, using his teeth like a wild animal. [20] The Persians lost 200,000 in the engagement or from shipwreck. [21] Hippias, tyrant of Athens, who was the instigator and fomenter of that war, also fell, the avenging deities of his native land exacting their penalty for his treason.

10 [1] Meanwhile Darius also died, in the midst of preparations for
the war he was renewing against Athens. He left numerous sons who
were born to him both during his reign and before it;[21] [2] the eldest
of these was Ariamenes, who asserted his claim to the throne by virtue of
his age, for the right of succession for all peoples has been established
by priority of birth and nature herself. [3] Xerxes, however, wanted
the question decided not on the ground of primogeniture, but on the
circumstances prevailing at the time of birth, [4] arguing that while
Ariamenes was indeed Darius' first-born, he was born while Darius was
still a private citizen, whereas Xerxes was his first son after he became
king. [5] The brothers born before him, he argued, could lay claim to
whatever personal estate Darius had possessed at that time, but not to the
throne, for he himself was the first child recognized by their father after
his accession. [6] There was the further point that, at the time of his birth,
not just Ariamenes' father but his mother too were ordinary citizens, as
was his maternal grandfather. [7] Xerxes, on the other hand, was born
when his mother was queen, had never seen his father as anything other
than king and had also had, as grandfather on his mother's side, King
Cyrus, the founder of their great empire, not merely the heir to it. [8] So
even if their father had left the two brothers on equal terms, Xerxes still
had the superior claim because of his mother and grandfather. [9] This
dispute they agreed to refer to their uncle Artaphernes as a kind of family
judge; [10] and he, examining the case within the home, decided in
favour of Xerxes. But so fraternal was the disagreement that there was
no superciliousness on the part of the winner or resentment on the part of
the loser. Indeed, while the matter was actually in dispute they sent each
other gifts and invited each other to banquets where the atmosphere was
not simply one of trust but of conviviality as well; and the decision itself
was reached without the need for witnesses and without recrimination.
[11] So much more reasonable were brothers then in apportioning huge
empires between themselves than they are now when they split up a paltry
estate.

[12] Xerxes spent five years preparing for the war against Greece
which his father had initiated.[22] [13] News of this came to Demaratus,

21. Darius died in November 486. The following story is also told in Her. 7.2f.,
though with differences of detail and personnel and with Darius still alive.
22. The essential account of Xerxes' invasion, beginning 481/0, is, of course,
Her. 7–9, which, however, could hardly have been Trogus' direct source. The
story of Demaratus is not in Her.; the numbers given at §§ 18–20 are at best
confused when compared with Her. 7.60, 89, 97; similarly, 11.2 compared with

the Spartan king. Demaratus was then in exile at Xerxes' court, but he remained more loyal to his native city, despite his banishment, than to the king, despite Xerxes' benefactions. Accordingly, lest the Spartans be crushed by a war which they did not expect, he gave a complete account of the preparations to their magistrates in a message written on wooden tablets, and rendered the message illegible by pouring wax over it, [14] taking care that no uncovered piece of writing betray him, and also that the freshness of the wax not give away his scheme. He then handed the tablets to a trusty slave for transportation, ordering him to pass them on to the Spartan magistrates. [15] On their arrival, the matter gave rise to long speculation in Sparta: the magistrates could see no writing, and yet they surmised that the tablets had not been sent without a purpose; and the puzzling nature of the question made them think it all the more important. [16] While the men were still engaged in guesswork, the sister of King Leonidas hit upon the intent of the writer. [17] The wax was scraped away, and the plans for the campaign were brought to light.

[18] Xerxes had already put under arms 700,000 men from his own kingdom plus 300,000 auxiliaries, [19] so that there is justification for the tradition of rivers being drained by his army and of the whole of Greece being scarcely capable of containing the force. [20] It is also said that he had 1,200 men-of-war and 3,000 transport vessels. [21] What this huge armament lacked was a general. Looking at the king, one might compliment him on his riches, but not on his ability as a leader. [22] Such were the resources within his kingdom that, even when rivers were being depleted because of the size of his army, he was still left with wealth on a truly royal scale at home. [23] But Xerxes himself was always observed to be the first to flee and the last to fight, cowardly in the face of danger and arrogant once the danger was past. [24] Before he had experience of war, he was confident in his strength and behaved as though he were lord of Nature herself: he levelled mountains, filled in valleys, spanned some seas with bridges and rendered others more accessible by canals that shortened distances.

11 [1] But the terror inspired by Xerxes' entry into Greece was matched by the shameful humiliation of his retreat. [2] When Leonidas, king of Sparta, took possession of the pass of Thermopylae with 4,000 men, Xerxes, contemptuous of his numbers, ordered into battle the men whose kinsmen had been killed in the battle of Marathon; [3] and in attempting

---

Her. 7.202. The story of Leonidas' attack on the Persian camp is not in Her.; but see Diod. 11.9f., which may point to Ephorus as the source.

to avenge their relatives these became the first victims of the debacle. As they were replaced by an ineffectual rabble, the slaughter only increased. [4] For three days the battle went on, to the distress and indignation of the Persians; [5] but on the fourth news was brought to Leonidas that the top of the hill was in the hands of an enemy force of 20,000. The king then urged the allies to retreat and keep themselves in reserve for a better opportunity to serve their fatherland, [6] adding that he and his Spartans were obliged to put Fortune to the test; he was more indebted to his country than he was to life, he said, whereas the others should be preserved for the defence of Greece. [7] On hearing the king's command, the other allies left, and only the Spartans remained.

[8] At the start of the war the oracle at Delphi had been consulted and had foretold that the Spartans were destined to lose either a king or their city; [9] and for this reason King Leonidas had, when he was setting off to war, steeled his men's resolve and made them aware that he was going into battle ready to face death.[23] [10] This was why he had taken possession of the pass, so that victory with his handful of men would be more glorious, while defeat would be less detrimental to the state. [11] Now, after discharging the allies, he encouraged the Spartans to keep in mind that die they must, no matter how they fought, and that they must avoid seeming to have been braver in their decision to stay than in the fight itself. [12] Rather than wait to be surrounded by the enemy, he said, they should take advantage of the night to fall on them while they were off their guard and enjoying themselves, [13] for nowhere could victors die with greater honour than in the camp of the enemy. [14] Persuading men who had already persuaded themselves to die was not difficult. [15] They immediately took up their weapons and 600 men burst into a camp of 500,000. They headed straight for the tent of the king, intending either to die along with him or else, if they were overpowered, to die right where he himself was. [16] The entire camp was in an uproar. Not finding the king, the Spartans ranged triumphant the length of the camp, creating wholesale slaughter and destruction in the knowledge that they were fighting not in the hope of victory but to avenge their own deaths. [17] The battle lasted from nightfall through the best part of the day [18] and when the Spartans finally went down, amid huge contingents of enemy dead, they were not so much defeated as exhausted from defeating the enemy. [19] After

23. The Latin is unclear. Some translators (e.g. Seel) would prefer "*they* were going into battle...."

two setbacks in battle on land, Xerxes now decided to try his luck at sea.

12 [1] However, the Athenian leader, Themistocles, had observed that the Ionians, on whose account they undertook the war against the Persians in the first place, had come with their fleet to support the king, and he determined to entice them over to his side.[24] [2] Since he had no opportunity to confer with them, he had signs erected at points where they were to land and the following words written on the rocks: [3] "Ionians, are you mad? What crime are you planning? Do you intend making war on people who were once your founders and recently your defenders, too? [4] Is that why we established your city walls—so that we should have people to destroy *ours*? [5] The cause of our conflict with Darius in the past, as with Xerxes now, was obviously our refusal to abandon you when you rebelled. [6] Why not cross over from that prison of yours to this camp to which you really belong? [7] Or, if this is too risky, at least back off when the fighting begins; row astern and leave the battle."

[8] Before this battle at sea Xerxes had sent 4,000 armed men to Delphi to plunder the temple of Apollo. [9] It was just as if he were taking on in war not only the Greeks but the immortal gods as well. [10] The contingent was entirely wiped out by thunderstorms, to make Xerxes aware of how utterly powerless humans are before the gods. [11] After this he burned Thespiae, Plataea and Athens, all abandoned by their peoples, and, unable to wreak havoc on human foes with the sword, he did so on their buildings with fire. [12] Now after the battle of Marathon Themistocles had forewarned the Athenians that their victory over the Persians would not mean the end of the war but would rather be a reason for its escalation, and they therefore constructed 200 ships.[25] [13] As Xerxes approached they had consulted the oracle at Delphi, receiving the response that they should protect themselves with wooden walls; [14] and Themistocles, who believed that this referred to protection afforded by their ships, persuaded everybody that the fatherland consisted of its citizens, not its walls, that a state existed in its inhabitants, not its buildings, [15] so that it would be a better idea to entrust their safety to their ships rather than to their city, which was the advice, he claimed,

24. Her. 8, though again Trogus shows other influences. This section begins after Artemisium, omitted by Justin. For the basis of Themistocles' appeal cf. above n. 16 on 2.6.16. There is also a reference to the aid Athens sent to the Ionians when they attempted to revolt from Persian control between 499 and 494, something which has been also passed over by Justin.

25. See Her. 7.140ff. and *AO* 58 (the year 483/2).

also given by the god. [16] His recommendation won approval and the Athenians, abandoning their city, deposited their wives and children together with their most precious possessions on some remote islands. They themselves took up arms and boarded their ships. [17] Other cities also followed the example of the Athenians.

[18] The entire allied fleet was now united and ready for the sea battle, and the allies had occupied the strait of Salamis to prevent an encircling movement by the superior Persian numbers. Then a quarrel arose with the leaders of the allied states. [19] Since they wanted to abandon the campaign and disperse to protect their own territories, Themistocles was afraid that the strength of the Greeks would be impaired by the departure of the allies. He therefore used a trusty slave to send the message to Xerxes that Greece was his for the taking since it was then drawn together in one spot. [20] If, however, the various states which now wanted to retreat actually dispersed, he would face the harder task of taking them on individually. [21] By this ploy Themistocles induced the king to give the signal for battle, and the Greeks, surprised by the approach of the enemy, entered the fray with their forces combined. [22] The king, meanwhile, remained on the beach with some of his ships as a spectator of the battle.

[23] Artemisia, queen of Halicarnassus, who had come to support Xerxes, fought with great spirit amongst the foremost generals; [24] indeed, one could see in a man a woman's timidity, and in a woman a man's courage. [25] When the battle was still undecided, the Ionians followed Themistocles' instructions and began to withdraw little by little from the fight, and their desertion broke the spirit of the others. [26] As they cast around for a means of escape the Persians were pushed back and, soon afterwards, vanquished and put to flight. In the chaos many ships were captured and many sunk, but the majority, fearing the cruelty of the king as much as the enemy, slipped away home.

13 [1] Shattered by this defeat, Xerxes was wondering what to do when Mardonius came to him. [2] He encouraged him to return to his kingdom so that reports of his unsuccessful campaign, exaggerating everything as usual, should not foment rebellion, [3] and he requested that Xerxes leave him 300,000 soldiers selected from amongst all his troops. With this force he would either subjugate Greece entirely, which would redound to the king's credit, or else, if matters turned out otherwise, his submission to the enemy would not discredit Xerxes. [4] Since Mardonius' advice met with Xerxes' approval, he was assigned an army and the king himself prepared to lead the rest of his forces back into his kingdom. [5] But on hearing of the king's flight, the Greeks formulated the plan of breaking down the bridge which Xerxes, as "lord of the sea," had constructed at Abydus; thus, his retreat cut off, he would either be destroyed along with his army, or be compelled to sue for peace, overwhelmed by his desperate situation.[26] [6] Themistocles, however, was afraid that cutting off the enemy might transform their desperation into courage, and that they would resort to the sword to hew a path that could not be opened up by other means (and he kept repeating that enough of the enemy were left in Greece as it was, and their numbers should not be increased by holding Xerxes back). [7] Seeing that he could not convince the others of his point of view, he sent the same slave to Xerxes, informing him of the plan and telling him to hasten his retreat and secure his crossing before the Greeks arrived. [8] Shocked by the news, Xerxes assigned the task of leading his troops to his commanders while he himself hurried to Abydus with a few men. [9] Here he found his bridge broken by the winter storms, and he crossed in a panic in a fishing boat. [10] That was a turn of events worth contemplating for the light it sheds on the human condition: by an amazing reversal of fortune, to see the man whom recently the entire ocean could barely contain, and whose armies had burdened the earth by their numbers, now hiding in a tiny boat and completely deprived of the assistance of even his slaves! [11] Nor was the return journey easier for the infantry whom he had assigned to his commanders, since in addition to their daily hardships—for men in fear enjoy no rest—they had also faced starvation. [12] Then a large number of days without food had brought disease, and such was the horrible and deadly effect that the roads were filled with corpses, and birds of prey and wild animals followed the army, attracted by the carrion.

14 [1] In Greece, meanwhile, Mardonius captured Olynthus.[27] [2] He also made overtures to the Athenians with the promise of a peace treaty and alliance with the king, pledging to rebuild on an even grander scale their city, burned by the Persians. [3] But when he saw them unwilling to barter their freedom at any price, he burned the buildings which he had actually started to rebuild and moved his troops into Boeotia. [4] The Greek army, numbering 100,000, followed him and it was here that battle was joined. [5] But the king's fortunes did not change along with

26. This is quite garbled compared with Her. 8.107ff.
27. Her. 8.127 has Artabazus, not Mardonius. After this we move into Her. 9 and the end of the war. The distinctions at the end of section 14 could represent a confused version of what is found in Diod. 11.27.

the general: Mardonius was defeated and he fled from the shipwreck, as it were, with a handful of men. [6] His camp, filled with royal treasure, was captured, and it was then, after they divided amongst themselves the Persian gold, that a taste for extravagance first overtook the Greeks.

[7] It so happened that, on the very day that Mardonius' forces were destroyed, a naval battle against the Persians was fought in Asia off the promontory of Mycale. [8] Before the engagement, as the fleets were facing each other, the rumour reached both armies that the Greeks had prevailed and Mardonius' troops had been cut to pieces. [9] The report had spread with such speed, it is said, that although the battle had only been fought that morning in Boeotia, news of the victory reached Asia about noon, crossing all those seas and so much land in such a short time. [10] When, on the termination of the war, the award of prizes to the various states was discussed, the valour of the Athenians was unanimously voted supreme above all the rest; [11] and amongst the generals, too, Themistocles was adjudged the greatest, in the declared opinion of the city-states, and thus raised further the prestige of his fatherland.

15 [1] The Athenians, their power increased by the spoils of war and their enhanced reputation, now set about rebuilding their city.[28] [2] Since they had marked out walls of a greater compass than before, they roused the anxiety of the Spartans, who considered what the fortification of the city would confer upon a people whose power had been increased even by its destruction. [3] They therefore dispatched an embassy to advise the Athenians against building what could serve as fortresses for their enemies and places of refuge in a future war. [4] Themistocles could see the envy generated by his city's aspirations but he did not think an impulsive response advisable, and he replied to the embassy that delegates would come to Sparta to discuss the issue with them. [5] Dismissing the Spartans with this response, he urged his countrymen to accelerate the work. [6] Then, after a lapse of time, he set out in person with the delegation and, by feigning illness en route or, at another time, criticizing the tardiness of colleagues without whom discussions could not legitimately be held, he kept procrastinating and playing for time for the completion of the work. [7] Meanwhile, word was brought to the Spartans that the work at Athens was being accelerated, and they immediately sent ambassadors to look into the matter anew. [8] At this point Themistocles sent a slave with a letter to the Athenian magistrates telling them to put the ambassadors in irons and hold them as security

---

28. For Themistocles' embassy see *AO* 65f. (the year 479/8).

against reprisals being taken against him. [9] He then went to the assembly of the Spartans and declared that Athens was entirely fortified and could withstand an attack with its walls as well as its arms. [10] He added that in the event of their deciding on reprisals for this against himself their ambassadors had been detained as a surety in Athens. [11] He then took them to task severely for seeking to establish their superiority not by their valour but through weakness on the part of their allies. [12] He was allowed to leave and was welcomed by his fellow-citizens as if he had triumphed over Sparta.

[13] To avoid impairing their strength by inactivity and to gain revenge for the two Persian invasions of Greece, the Spartans next took the initiative and began to raid Persian territory.[29] [14] As commander in chief of their army and that of their allies they chose Pausanias but he, with the aim of exchanging his command for monarchic power over the whole of Greece, struck a bargain with Xerxes, who was to give him the hand of his daughter as the price of Pausanias' treason. To keep the king to his word in the matter by a favour, Pausanias returned all the Persian prisoners-of-war. [15] He also wrote a letter to Xerxes telling him to put to death any messengers he might send, so that their compact should not be betrayed by loose talk. [16] But the Athenian general, Aristides, who shared with Pausanias the conduct of the war, blocked his colleague's manoeuvres and took some appropriately astute measures, so that he thwarted his plans for betrayal. Not long afterwards Pausanias was brought to trial and found guilty.

[17] When he saw that the treasonable plot had been brought to light, Xerxes recommenced hostilities.[30] [18] The Greeks, for their part, now appointed as their general the Athenian Cimon, son of Miltiades (under whose command the battle of Marathon had been fought), a young man whom a number of instances of filial piety had already marked out for future greatness. [19] His father had been thrown into prison on a charge of embezzlement and had died there; Cimon took on his fetters himself and redeemed the body for burial. [20] Nor on the field of battle did he disappoint the judgment of those who chose him: his merits were not inferior to those of his father, and after defeating Xerxes on land and sea he forced him to withdraw in fear into his kingdom.

29. Again, the following is closer to Diod. 11.44f. than anything else (cf. Thuc. 1.128ff.). For Aristides see *AO* 66f. (the year 478/7).

30. Cf. Diod. 11.6off. The references to Cimon are very general, but see *AO* 67 (the year 478/7) and under subsequent years; also Plutarch's biography. For Miltiades see *AO* 56 (the year 490/89).

BOOK 3

1 [1] Xerxes, king of Persia, who had formerly struck terror into the whole world, began to be regarded with contempt even by his subjects after the unsuccessful campaign in Greece.[1] [2] As the king's prestige weakened day by day, Artabanus, one of his officers, began to entertain hopes of gaining the throne and, one evening, accompanied by his seven robust sons, he entered the palace (which was always open to him because of his friendship with Xerxes), murdered the king, and then began to use duplicity to remove Xerxes' sons, who now stood in the path of his ambition. [3] He was less concerned about Artaxerxes, who was just a boy, and so he invented the story that the king had been killed by Darius, who was a young man, the sooner to gain the throne, and he induced Artaxerxes to punish one parricide with another. [4] When they arrived at Darius' home, the young man was found sleeping, but they put him to death anyway, alleging that he was just pretending to be asleep. [5] Artabanus saw that after his crimes there remained only one son of the king, but he feared competition for the throne amongst the nobility, and he therefore enlisted Baccabasus as an associate in his intrigue. [6] Baccabasus, however, was content with the current regime, and disclosed the matter to Artaxerxes, telling him how his father had been killed and his brother eliminated through a baseless suspicion of parricide, and how, finally, a plot was being hatched against Artaxerxes himself. [7] After hearing this, Artaxerxes, apprehensive about the number of Artabanus' sons, gave orders that the army be at the ready under arms the following day for him to carry out an inspection of their numbers and of their individual proficiency in combat. [8] Artabanus himself took up his position under arms along with the rest. The king pretended that his cuirass was too short and told Artabanus to exchange his with him. While the officer was removing his cuirass and was thus unprotected, Artaxerxes ran him through with his sword; then he ordered the arrest of the sons. [9] So it was that at one stroke this fine young man avenged his father's assassination and his brother's death, and also rescued himself from the machinations of Artabanus.

2 [1] While this was taking place in Persia, all Greece split into two alliances, under the leadership of the Spartans and the Athenians

---

1. For the following cf. Ctesias §§ 33f.; Diod. 11.69. The Baccabasus mentioned below is Megabyzus.

respectively, and turned its arms from wars abroad against its own vitals. [2] A single people thus became two distinct bodies, and men who had shared a camp were divided into two opposing armies. [3] On the one side the Spartans augmented their strength by winning over the forces of the city-states which had formerly been part of the cooperative effort; on the other the Athenians, renowned for the antiquity of their nation as well as for their achievements, relied on their own strength.[2] [4] Thus the two most powerful peoples of Greece, equally great because of Solon's ordinances and Lycurgus' legislation, proceeded to rush headlong into war through jealousy of each other's strength.[3]

[5] Lycurgus, since he was next in line after his brother, Polydectes, king of Sparta, could well have claimed the throne for himself, but instead he demonstrated consummate loyalty in relinquishing it in favour of Charillus, Polydectes' posthumous son, when he came of age. [6] He wanted everybody to realize how much more important the claims of family loyalty were to men of integrity than any kind of power. [7] In the meantime, while the child was growing up and Lycurgus was acting as his guardian, he established a legal system for the Spartans, who did not have one, and he earned as much distinction from his own exemplary conduct as he did from drafting the laws, [8] since he refused to legislate for others any behaviour which he did not first put into practice himself by way of example. [9] He strengthened the obedience of the people to the authorities, and the impartiality of the authorities in their exercise of power. [10] He encouraged thrift in the whole population, believing that the hardships of military life would be made easier by their constantly practising frugality. [11] He issued orders that all commerce be based on barter rather than money, [12] and abolished the use of gold and silver on the premise that they were the source of all criminal behaviour.

3 [1] Government of the state he divided amongst the classes. [2] To the kings he granted the authority to conduct war; to the magistrates

---

2. This is very schematic and inaccurate. The Greeks had formed an alliance against Xerxes, but after the war the Athenians became leaders of its naval arm, conventionally described by the modern term "Delian League," an organization which became in effect an Athenian empire; see R. Meiggs, *The Athenian Empire* (Oxford 1972). The Spartans remained associated with other states in mainland Greece and in particular dominated the Peloponnese.

3. On Lycurgus and the Spartan system, to which we are taken back, there are a number of sources, including Plut. *Lycurgus*. See in general P. Cartledge, *Sparta and Laconia. A Regional History 1300–362 B.C.* (London 1979), with a discussion of the king lists in Appendix 3 (see also Bickerman 156). As sources for Trogus on Sparta, Phylarchus, Ephorus, Antiochus and Timaeus have all been proposed.

he assigned the administration of justice, providing replacements for them every year; to the senate he gave custody of the laws; and to the populace he granted the right to choose the senate and whatever magistrates they wanted.[4]   [3] He divided the communal farmland equally amongst all the citizens, so that equality of possessions would prevent one person having more power than another. [4] He ordained that all meals be public affairs to prevent anyone hiding his wealth or a luxurious standard of living. [5] Young men were allowed to wear no more than a single garment a year, and no one could appear in public better dressed than anyone else or eat more expensive meals. He did not want imitation to lead to extravagance. [6] He directed that, at the age of puberty, boys be taken not to the forum, but to the country, to spend their early years at work and manual labour rather than in easy living. [7] He gave instructions that they should not sleep on bedding of any kind, that they live on a diet of plain food and not return to town before reaching manhood. [8] Young girls he ordered to marry without a dowry so that it was the wife, not money, that was being selected, and so that husbands would be stricter in controlling their spouses when free from the restrictions of a dowry. [9] He decreed that the greatest deference be shown not to the rich and powerful, but to the old according to their seniority; and old age certainly enjoys more respect in Sparta than anywhere else in the world.

[10] Lycurgus could see that these laws were stringent at their inception, following as they did a period of permissive morality, and so he made up the story that it was Apollo at Delphi who had drafted them and that he, Lycurgus, had brought them back from there on the god's instructions. He hoped that religious awe would prevail over the people's reluctance to accommodate themselves to the new system. [11] Then, to give his laws an eternal validity, he had the whole community take an oath not to make any changes to them until he returned, and he pretended that he was going to Delphi to consult the oracle on appropriate additions and modifications to them. [12] In fact, he set off for Crete where he lived in permanent exile, giving instructions on his deathbed for his bones to be thrown into the sea so that the Spartans could not carry them back to Lacedaemon and thus consider themselves freed from the obligations of their oath not to repeal his legislation.

4. Sparta had two kings; the magistrates are the ephors; the senate is the gerousia.

4 [1] Thanks to this system of values the state quickly became strong,[5] so much so that when the Spartans went to war with the Messenians over the latters' violation of some young Spartan women during a religious festival in Messenia, they bound themselves with the most solemn oath not to return before taking Messenia, a vow which they made to themselves from confidence either in their strength or in their fortune. [2] It was this that started the dissension in Greece and proved to be the ultimate cause of internal warfare. [3] Contrary to their expectations, the Spartans were forced into a ten-year siege of the city, while their wives complained of the long period without their husbands and kept calling them home. [4] The Spartans came to fear that if they persevered with the war, they would do themselves more harm than they would the Messenians. The latters' casualties among their younger citizens were made good by the fertility of their females, while the Spartans faced continuous attrition in battle and the fertility of their spouses meant nothing in the absence of their husbands. [5] They therefore selected young men from that group of soldiers who had arrived as reinforcements in the period after the oath was taken, and sent them back to Sparta with permission to have promiscuous sexual relations with all the women there, [6] in the belief that conception would occur earlier if each of the women tried to achieve it with a number of men. [7] Children born of these parents were called Partheniae in memory of their mothers' shame.[6]

[8] When the children reached the age of thirty, they were afraid of being left penniless, for none of them had a father whose estate he could hope to inherit. Accordingly, they took as their leader Phalantus, who was the son of Aratus, the man who had given the Spartans the idea of sending the young men home to procreate; [9] thus, as his father had once been responsible for their birth, the son would now be responsible for their prospects and their social standing. [10] Without saying goodbye to their mothers, to whose adultery they thought they owed their disgrace, the Partheniae set out in search of a home. [11] After a long time and many adventures, they finally landed in Italy where they seized the citadel of

---

5. The fullest source for the Messenian Wars is Pausanias Book 4, where the named sources are Rhianus of Bene and Myron of Priene. Trogus may have followed Ephorus (cf. *FGH* 70 F 216) and there is a summary treatment at Diod. 15.66, but the only contemporary source was the seventh century poet Tyrtaeus (see below). The first war with Messenia took place about 735–715; the second, which Pausanias dates 685–668, was in fact slightly later.

6. "Partheniae" means something like "virgin births" or "births produced by women who should have been virgins."

Tarentum, defeated the former inhabitants and established their home.[7]
[12] After a number of years, however, their leader, Phalantus, was driven
into exile during a political upheaval, and he came to Brundisium, the
town to which the former citizens of Tarentum had retired after being
driven from their homes. [13] On his deathbed he persuaded the former
Tarentines to crush his bones and other mortal remains and have them
secretly scattered in the forum of Tarentum, [14] claiming that Apollo at
Delphi had foretold that in this way they could recover their homeland.
[15] They believed that Phalantus had revealed the destiny of his citizens
in order to avenge himself, and carried out his instructions. In fact, the
meaning of the oracle was the contrary of what he said, [16] for it had
promised continued possession rather than the loss of the city if this were
done. [17] Thus did the scheme of a leader in exile and the services
rendered by his enemy secure perpetual occupation of Tarentum for the
Partheniae. [18] As a memorial of his benefaction they decreed divine
honours for Phalantus.

5 [1] In the meantime the Messenians, although they could not be
vanquished by the valour of the Spartans, fell prey to their treachery.
[2] For the eighty years which followed they were subjected to the brutal beatings given to slaves, and frequently also to imprisonment and
other forms of maltreatment meted out to a captured city. Finally, after enduring these punitive measures for a long time, they renewed the
war. [3] The Lacedaemonians were also all the more united in their
resolve in taking up arms because they thought that it was going to be
a war against their serfs. [4] Hence, spirits were inflamed by a feeling of injustice on one side and indignity on the other. The Spartans
consulted the Delphic oracle about the outcome of the war and were
told to request a commander in chief from the Athenians. [5] When
they learned of the oracle's response, the Athenians sent, as an insult
to the Spartans, a lame poet, Tyrtaeus.[8] [6] He, after three defeats in
the field, reduced the Spartans to such desperation that they freed[9] their

---

7. The traditional date is 706, which is roughly consistent with the archaeological remains.

8. Tyrtaeus' Athenian origin (also found at Pausanias 4.15.6) is a later invention
as lame as the poet was supposed to be. See M. R. Lefkowitz, *The Lives of the
Greek Poets* (London 1981), 35, 38f.

9. The translation of the sentence to this point reflects Seel's text, where
"fusus" refers to Tyrtaeus. Perhaps "fusos" should be read. The translation
would then be: "Three defeats had driven the Spartans to such despair that
Tyrtaeus could convince them to free . . . ."

slaves to supplement their forces, and promised them the wives of those who were killed in action, [7] so that they would not only make good the numbers of the citizens who had fallen but also inherit their social position. [8] The Spartan kings, however, wanted to withdraw the army from fear of bringing further damage on their state by fighting against destiny, [9] and were stopped only by the intervention of Tyrtaeus, who, at a public gathering, recited to the army poetry of his own composition in which he had included exhortations to valour, consolation for losses suffered and military advice. [10] Such was the enthusiasm that he inspired in the men that they were no longer concerned for their own self-preservation, only that they achieve proper burial; and they accordingly fastened to their right arms tokens bearing their own names and the names of their fathers, [11] so that, should they all lose their lives in an unsuccessful engagement and the passage of time disfigure their physical appearance, they could still be given burial from information provided on the tokens. [12] When the kings saw such enthusiasm in their army, they took steps to have the matter reported to the enemy. [13] This, however, far from striking panic into the Messenians, instead encouraged them to rise to the challenge. [14] The battle was joined with such fervour that rarely was there ever a bloodier fight. [15] Finally, victory went to the Spartans.

6 [1] Time passed and the Messenians renewed the war for the third time; [2] and the Spartans called all their allies, including the Athenians, to assist them.[10] [3] The Spartans, however, doubted the reliability of the Athenians, and dismissed them from the war on the pretext that they were not needed. [4] This so offended the Athenians that they transferred from Delos to Athens the money contributed by all Greece to finance the war against Persia, so that the Spartans could not pillage and loot it if they seceded from the alliance. [5] But the Spartans did not sit idly by; since they were embroiled in the war with Messenia, they sent other Peloponnesian states to fight the Athenians. [6] At that point the

---

10. The epitome rushes through the period covered by Thuc. 1–5 and Diod. 11–12; Ephorus may have been the source. On the date of Athenian assistance to Sparta see *AO* under 463/2 and 462/1. The transfer of the treasury to Athens is traditionally dated to 454, but a date in the 460s is supported by what little literary evidence we have (N. D. Robertson, "The True Nature of the 'Delian League' 478–461 B.C.," *American Journal of Ancient History* 5 [1982], 112ff.). The so-called First Peloponnesian War began in 459. Athens' involvement in Egypt is usually dated 460–454, but the six-year commitment could have begun a year or two earlier.

Athenians were under strength because they had sent a fleet into Egypt, and thus they were easily defeated in a sea battle. [7] Then, some time later, when the return of their men had increased both their naval and infantry strength, they took up the fight again. [8] By now the Spartans had abandoned the Messenian campaign and also taken up the fight against the Athenians. [9] Victory hung in the balance a long while, and finally the two sides parted on equal terms.

[10] The attention of the Spartans was now brought back to the Messenian war and, since they were reluctant to leave the Athenians at peace in the meantime, they struck a bargain with the Thebans to restore to them their hegemony in Boeotia (which they had lost during the time of the war with Persia), on the condition that they take up the war with the Athenians. [11] Such was the fury of the Spartans that, despite their involvement in two wars, they did not refuse to take on a third, provided that they could set adversaries on their enemy. [12] Confronted with this storm of a war, the Athenians appointed two generals: Pericles, a man of proven courage, and Sophocles, the writer of tragedies.[11] [13] These split the army in two, laid waste Spartan territory and also added many of the city-states of Asia to the Athenian empire.

7 [1] Daunted by these reverses, the Spartans concluded a thirty-year peace, but their enmity towards Athens would not permit such protracted inactivity.[12] [2] Thus they broke the treaty after a period of fifteen years and, with contempt for gods and men, ravaged the territory of Attica. [3] To avoid the impression that they had come in order to plunder rather than do battle, they tried to provoke the enemy to combat [4] but the Athenians, on the advice of their leader, Pericles, postponed their revenge for the unjust pillaging of their land to a more appropriate time, considering pitched battle unnecessary when they could avenge themselves on the enemy without risk. [5] Then, after a few days, they boarded their ships and, with the Spartans suspecting nothing, pillaged all the territory of Sparta, carrying off much more than they had lost before. [6] In fact, if one compared the losses suffered, the retaliatory raid far surpassed the original injury.

11. This is the height of confusion. Pericles and Sophocles were generals together, but in 441/0 in another theatre (*AO* 89f.); what seems to be meant here is the activity of Tolmides and Pericles in 456/5 and 455/4 (*AO* 76f.) and developments of subsequent years.

12. The peace was made in 446/5 and war broke out in 432/1.

[7] The expedition brought fame to Pericles, but he gained much more from his indifference towards his personal property.[13] [8] The fields of everyone else were ravaged, but the enemy had left his intact, hoping to expose him to danger through jealousy or to disgrace from suspicion of treason. [9] This, however, Pericles had anticipated, and he had forewarned the people that it would happen; and so, to avoid being the object of jealousy, he had made a gift of his land to the state. [10] Thus he gained the greatest renown from what had been intended to bring him into danger.

[11] Some days passed and the adversaries met in a sea battle, in which the Spartans were defeated and put to flight. [12] After this, the two sides butchered each other incessantly on land and sea, in battles fought with varying success. [13] Eventually, tired of their many reverses, they concluded a fifty-year peace, which they respected for only six years.[14] [14] For they would break the truce, which they had made in their own names, by using their allies as a front, [15] as if they were perjuring themselves the less by assisting their allies than by engaging in open warfare. [16] From here the theatre of war was transferred to Sicily, but before I give an account of that I must say a little about Sicilian geography.

BOOK 4

1 [1] They say that Sicily was once attached to Italy by a narrow isthmus and that it was torn from the main body of the land by the buffeting of the Upper Sea, which pounds that area with the full force of its waves.[1] [2] The land there is fine and friable, and so perforated with caverns and grottos that it is exposed to the wind almost all the way through. [3] Furthermore, the composition of the soil is naturally suited to generating and supporting combustion, containing, it is said, an inner layer of sulphur and bitumen. [4] Thus it is that, when the

13. The following story seems to be an embellishment on Pericles' promise to give his lands to the state; they remained untouched (Thuc. 2.13.1).

14. The Peace of Nicias in 421.

1. The Upper Sea should be the Adriatic, but the Tyrrhenian is meant here. Thuc. 6–7 deals with the Sicilian expedition, including remarks on the nature of Sicily, but this is not the direct source of the present account. Again one thinks of Ephorus, especially with the expedition of 427/6 (below), and Philistus has been detected behind details of the later expedition.

wind and the subterranean fire come to grips with each other, the earth frequently belches forth flames, or vapour, or smoke in several places, [5] and this is why the fire of Mount Aetna has lasted for so many centuries. [6] Furthermore, when an unusually fierce gust has blown down the air vents formed by the caverns, piles of sand are expelled.

[7] The Italian promontory closest to Sicily is called Rhegium because that is the name given in Greek to things "broken off."[2] [8] And it should cause no surprise if the early history of this area is full of myth when it is a combination of so many wonders. [9] In the first place, there exist nowhere else on earth straits so stormy,[3] with a current that is not only fast but violent, so that it is frightening not just to those who are on it but even to those looking at it from a distance. [10] Indeed, the waves crash against each other in such conflict that one can see some of them sink to the depths as if in flight, while others rise into the air like victors; and at one moment can be heard the roar of the boiling surf, at the next the groan of it sinking into a whirlpool.

[11] Then there are also, close by, the perennial fires of Mount Aetna and the Aeolian islands, their combustion seemingly fuelled by the waters themselves; [12] and, in fact, a fire of such magnitude could not have lasted so many centuries within such a narrow compass without being fed by a fuel derived from the moisture. [13] This is the source of the myths of Scylla and Charybdis, of the barking sounds and the monster which people think they have seen; sailors were terrified by the great whirlpools formed by the sinking of the sea, and they thought that the barking was coming from the waves as they collided in the maelstrom when the current sucked them down. [14] The same natural causes lie behind the permanent fires of Mount Aetna. [15] The waters as they clash entrap air and drag it along with them to the seabed, where they keep it compressed until it seeps through the vents in the soil to ignite the combustible materials within it.

[16] Furthermore, the fact that Italy and Sicily are so close, and their promontories so similar in height, means that the wonder we experience now is as intense as was the terror felt by the ancients, who believed that whole ships were caught and swallowed as the promontories clashed and again separated. [17] And the ancients did not just make this up as a tale for entertainment; its inspiration was the terror and awe experienced by travellers in those parts. [18] For the natural features of the area are such that, viewing them from a distance, one would think one saw a gulf

2. From the Greek verb "rhegnumi," to break.
3. The Straits of Messina.

in the coastline rather than a strait and, at closer quarters, one would believe that what had formerly been promontories joined together were parting and pulling away from each other.

2 [1] At first Sicily was called Trinacria[4] and later it was given the name Sicania. [2] Originally it was the home of the Cyclopes, and when these died out Cocalus seized control of the island. [3] After Cocalus each of its city-states fell under the power of tyrants, produced more abundantly here than in any land. [4] One of these was Anaxilaus, who was as just in his conduct as the others were cruel, and who gained no small return from his restraint.[5] [5] For, when he died, he left behind infant sons, whom he entrusted to the guardianship of Micalus, a slave of proven loyalty; and Anaxilaus was remembered by all the people with such affection that they preferred to be ruled by a slave than to abandon the king's children—even the most prominent citizens, with no thought for their personal dignity, left the sovereignty of the state in the hands of a slave. [6] The Carthaginians, too, tried to gain control of Sicily, and fought its tyrants with mixed success. [7] Eventually they lost their general, Hamilcar, along with his army, and the defeat rendered them inactive for some time.

3 [1] Meanwhile, the people of Rhegium were beset by internal conflicts, and the dissension split the state into two factions.[6] Some veterans from Himera were invited by one side to assist them, and these, expelling the people against whom they had been called to fight, and soon afterwards killing those whom they had assisted, took possession of the city along with the wives and children of their erstwhile allies. [2] This was a crime that no tyrant could match; defeat would have been better than victory for the people of Rhegium. [3] For even if the terms of captivity had made them slaves to their conquerors or if they had been obliged to go into exile after losing their country, at least they would not have been slaughtered amid their altars and domestic gods, to leave behind them their fatherland, their wives and their children as plunder for utterly ruthless despots.

[4] Further, the people of Catana were suffering under the oppressive domination of the Syracusans; with no confidence in their own strength,

4. Meaning "three-cornered."

5. Anaxilaus of Rhegium died in 476/5; Diod. 11.48.2, where the regent is Micythus. For the Carthaginians see below Book 19.

6. This story seems to have escaped Diodorus, unless it is alluded to at 11.76.5 (the year 461/0).

they sought help from the Athenians.[7] [5] possibly the Athenians wished
to expand their empire, having already driven deep into Asia and Greece,
or else they were alarmed by the fleet which the Syracusans had constructed, fearing that this would augment the might of the Spartans; at all
events, they sent the general Lamponius with a fleet to Sicily, ostensibly
to aid the people of Catana, but really to make a bid for mastery of the
island. [6] Since the initial stages of the campaign had proved successful,
with heavy enemy losses, the Athenians mounted a second expedition to
Sicily, this time with a larger fleet and stronger army, under the leadership
of Laches and Chariades. [7] But because they feared the Athenians or
because they were tired of the war, the people of Catana had sent back
the Athenian reinforcements and made peace with the Syracusans.

4 [1] Then, later, since the terms of the peace were not respected
by the Syracusans, the citizens of Catana again sent a deputation to
the Athenians.[8] The ambassadors appeared before the assembly in
mourning: filthy clothes, unkempt hair and beards, and a generally
miserable appearance designed to excite pity. [2] Tears accompanied
their entreaties, and such was the compassion aroused in the people by
their appeals that a motion was passed condemning the generals who
had withdrawn the reinforcements from them. [3] An enormous fleet
was voted to the Syracusans, and Nicias, Alcibiades and Lamachos were
made its commanders.[9] So large was the force with which the Athenians
once more headed for Sicily that they struck terror even into those whom
they were being sent to help. [4] Shortly afterwards, Alcibiades was
recalled to stand trial, and Nicias and Lamachos fought two successful
battles on land. [5] Then they surrounded Syracuse with siege walls,
pinned down the enemy within the city and cut them off even from
supplies arriving by sea. [6] Crushed by these reverses, the Syracusans

7. This version is nearer to that at Diod. 12.53f. than to that in Thucydides,
even to the spelling of Charoiades' name as Chariades. The latter and Laches
were generals in 427/6 (*AO* 124f.); Charoiades died, and Laches was succeeded in
the next year by Pythodorus. Justin's Lamponius is a mystery, unless he represents
a Lampon and an otherwise unattested generalship for (perhaps) *AO* no. 1772.
A further mystery is why the people of Catana, who in the later expedition had to
be forced to side with Athens, have replaced the Leontini here and the Egestans
in section 4.

8. See last note. The Diodoran account is 12.82ff. The reference in § 2 seems
to be to 425/4, for which see *AO* 129f. For the Athenian commanders see *AO*
under the years 416/5 to 413/2.

9. While "Lamachos" is a deviation from Latinate versions of names, it reflects
the manuscripts.

sought assistance from the Spartans, [7] who sent them only one man, Gylippus, but in him the Syracusans had the equivalent of a whole army of reinforcements. [8] On his way to Sicily, Gylippus had heard that the war was going badly for the Syracusans, and so he raised auxiliary troops both in Greece and in Sicily and then seized some ground which would be tactically useful for the conduct of the war. [9] He was then defeated in two battles, but he engaged in a third in which, killing Lamachos, he at one stroke put to flight the enemy and delivered his allies from the siege. [10] The Athenians now switched from land to naval warfare, and Gylippus accordingly sent for a fleet along with reinforcements from Lacedaemon. [11] On learning this, the Athenians for their part sent out Demosthenes and Eurymedon to replace their fallen general, and reinforcements with them. [12] The Peloponnesians, too, through a joint decree of their states, sent assistance on a massive scale to the Syracusans. It was as if the war in Greece had been transferred to Sicily, and both sides were pursuing it with all their might.

5 [1] In the first naval engagement the Athenians were defeated, and they also lost their camp together with all the wealth belonging to the state and even to private citizens. [2] To these reverses was also added defeat in battle on land, and then Demosthenes began to express the opinion that they should quit Sicily while their situation, poor though it was, was not completely hopeless. [3] They should not, he said, persist with a war which had started so inauspiciously while they had more important and possibly more damaging[10] wars to fight at home, for which they should be preserving their city's military resources. [4] Nicias was adamant that they stay; he was either ashamed of their poor performance, or afraid of frustrating the hopes of his countrymen, or simply driven on by destiny. [5] So war was resumed at sea and their spirits were revived, after the last storm of misfortune, to optimism for the next encounter; [6] but because of the incompetence of the commanders, who made an attack on the Syracusans while the latter could defend themselves in a narrow strait, the Athenians were easily defeated. [7] First to fall was the commander Eurymedon, putting up a valiant fight in the front line, and the 30 ships under his command were burned. [8] Demosthenes and Nicias also suffered defeat, and they disembarked their armies in the belief that flight overland would be safer. [9] Gylippus took possession of the 130 ships which they abandoned and then set off in pursuit of the

---

10. Translating "infeliciora." Perhaps we should read "feliciora," giving the sense "more promising."

crews, capturing some of the fugitives and killing others. [10] His army lost, Demosthenes spared himself surrender by taking his own life with his sword, [11] [11] but Nicias did not even learn the lesson of self-respect from Demosthenes' example and made his countrymen's defeat the more bitter by the ignominy of capture.

BOOK 5

1 [1] For two years the Athenians waged war in Sicily, with more ardour than success.[1] During this period, the expedition's prime mover and leader, Alcibiades, was charged at Athens in his absence with divulging the holy mysteries of the rites of Ceres, whose sanctity lay primarily in their secrecy. [2] He was recalled from the war to face trial but, whether from guilt or injured innocence, he instead slipped off quietly into exile in Elis. [3] He then discovered that he had not only been found guilty, but also solemnly consigned to the nether powers by the sacred oaths of the entire priesthood, whereupon he left Elis for Sparta, [4] and there urged the Spartan king to attack the Athenians, who were now in disarray after the defeat in Sicily. [5] The Spartans agreed and all the Greek states[2] flocked to their assistance to extinguish what they perceived as a fire that threatened them all—[6] so intense was the hatred the Athenians had incurred by the ruthless oppressiveness of their empire. [7] Furthermore, the Persian king, Darius, remembering the enmity of his father and grandfather towards that city, made a pact with the Spartans through his satrap of Lydia, Tissaphernes, promising to cover all the expenses of the war.[3] [8] Such, at least, was his alleged reason for joining the

---

11. This detail is unique to this account; in both Thucydides and Diodorus Demosthenes is also captured and put to death.

1. This is a carryover from the last book in terms of sources. From 1.11 on, cf. Thuc. 8 and Diod. 13.36ff. See also Plut. *Alcibiades* and for the profanation of the mysteries Andocides *On the Mysteries*. A recent treatment of Alcibiades is W. M. Ellis, *Alcibiades* (London and New York 1989). We know that Alcibiades went from Argos to Sparta, but since Nepos *Alc.* 4.4 says he went from Elis to Thebes, we may be dealing with the variant account of Ephorus. The defeat in Sicily dates to 413.

2. Strangely, Justin wrote "regna," literally "kingdoms."

3. This king is Darius II, who ruled from 426 to 403. Darius' father, Artaxerxes II, had in fact concluded at least one peace with Athens, so perhaps Trogus had meant Darius' grandfather Xerxes and great-grandfather Darius I.

Greeks; in reality, he was afraid that after defeating the Athenians the Spartans would turn their weapons on him. [9] Little wonder, then, that the flourishing power of Athens should have collapsed when all the East came together to crush a single city. [10] But the Athenians did not go down without a fight or without drawing blood. They fought to the last, sometimes winning, and rather than being defeated conclusively they were worn out by the fickleness of Fortune. [11] At the start of the conflict all their allies had, predictably, deserted them; whichever way Fortune inclines, the favour of human beings follows.[4]

2 [1] Alcibiades also assisted with the war which he had fomented against his homeland, not as a common soldier but by his qualities of leadership. [2] Given command of five ships, he moved swiftly to Asia where he used the prestige of his own name to incite to rebellion the states paying tribute to Athens. [3] These states knew of his fame at home and, in their eyes, exile had not diminished his stature; for them it was less a case of his being deprived of an Athenian command than his being granted a Spartan one, and his new powers compensated for those which he had lost. [4] Amongst the Spartans, however, Alcibiades' qualities aroused more jealousy than gratitude. [5] The leading citizens had even ordered his assassination, seeing him as a rival to their reputations, but Alcibiades found out about it through his adulterous affair with the wife of King Agis.[5] He sought refuge with Tissaphernes, satrap of King Darius, into whose graces he quickly insinuated himself with his courteous behaviour and obsequious charm. [6] For he was in the prime of his life, strikingly handsome and equally renowned for his oratory, even amongst the Athenians. [7] He was, however, better at making friends than he was at keeping them, because the flaws in his character were initially hidden behind the screen of his eloquence. [8] He persuaded Tissaphernes not to give so much financial support to the Spartan fleet, [9] arguing that the Ionians should be called upon to share the cost, since it was for their liberation from paying tribute to Athens that the war had been undertaken in the first place.[6] [10] Tissaphernes, he went on, should

4. "The start of the conflict" presumably relates to the new circumstances of 412/11.

5. A notorious affair which, whether genuine or not, had the consequence that Agis' son Leotychidas was regarded as illegitimate, giving Agis' brother Agesilaus the succession.

6. See above 5.1.7. The aid channeled through the satrap Tissaphernes went mainly for a fleet to challenge Athenian naval superiority. The freeing of the Ionians and other Aegean states under Athenian domination had been Spartan

not be too energetic in assisting the Spartans; he should bear in mind that he was laying the foundations for someone else's victory, not his own; the war should be subsidized only to the point that it not be abandoned for want of funds. [11] For while the Greeks quarrelled, he continued, the Persian king would be the arbiter of peace and war, and he would defeat with their own weapons enemies he could not defeat with his, whereas if the war were terminated he would immediately be obliged to fight the winners. [12] Greece should be ground down by internal wars so she would not be free to take on wars abroad; the strength of the two sides should be kept equal and the weaker one given help. For, he said, the Spartans would not sit back after a victory in this war, because they had declared themselves the champions of the liberty of Greece. [14] Tissaphernes approved of what he said. He became sparing in the supplies which he provided, and he did not send the Spartans the whole of the king's fleet for fear of giving them a clear victory or obliging the combatants to cease hostilities.

3 [1] Meanwhile Alcibiades was making his countrymen well aware of the service he was doing them. [2] When ambassadors from the Athenians came to him, he promised them an alliance with the king if the government were transferred from the popular assembly to a senate.[7] [3] His hope was that the factions of the state would reach an understanding and that he would be the unanimous choice to direct the war, or else that in the event of a conflict between the classes he would be called to the aid of one or other of the parties. [4] In fact, the threat of war hanging over them made the Athenians more concerned with their self-preservation than their self-esteem; [5] and, with the agreement of the common people, power was therefore transferred to a senate. [6] The senators, however, with the arrogance natural to their class, proceeded to treat the commons with cruelty, as individuals appropriated to themselves the unbridled power of tyrants; whereupon Alcibiades

---

propaganda from the beginning of the Peloponnesian War, though part of the understanding with Sparta was that these states should again come into Persian possession, freedom from which had brought them into Athens' sphere after 479.

7. In Athenian terms, a (or the) "senate" can only mean the *boule*, which was to be of 400, with citizen rights confined to the 5000, who eventually became the essential body after the demise of the closer oligarchy; though they are still in control at the end of Thucydides, they soon gave way to the resurgent democracy. On these complicated events see A. W. Gomme, A. Andrewes and K. J. Dover, *A Historical Commentary on Thucydides* vol. 5 (Oxford 1981), 184ff.; P. J. Rhodes, *A Commentary on the Aristotelian Athenaion Politeia* (Oxford 1981), 362ff.

was recalled from exile by the army and put at the head of the fleet.
[7] Alcibiades immediately sent a letter to Athens saying that he would
instantly come with the army and wrest the rights of the people back from
the Four Hundred, if the latter did not restore them of their own accord.
[8] The threat terrified the aristocrats. At first they tried to betray the
city to the Spartans but then, when they failed to do so, they went into
exile. [9] His homeland delivered from its internal difficulties, Alcibiades
now focussed all his attention on equipping the fleet and proceeded to
war against the Spartans.

4 [1] The Spartan generals, Mindarus and Pharnabazus, were already
waiting for Alcibiades at Sestus with their vessels drawn up for combat,
[2] but when battle was joined victory went to the Athenians.[8] In that
engagement most of the enemy force and almost all their senior officers
were killed, and 80 ships were captured. [3] Furthermore, a few days later,
when the Spartans had switched from sea to land operations, they were
defeated once again. [4] Dejected by these reverses they sued for peace;
they failed to achieve this because of the efforts of those who would profit
from a continuation of the war. [5] Meanwhile, an attack launched on
Sicily by the Carthaginians forced the recall of the auxiliary forces sent by
the Syracusans. [6] These factors left the Spartans helpless. Alcibiades
now proceeded to lay waste Asia with his victorious fleet, engaging in
battles in a number of places. Emerging the victor in all of these, he
retook the cities that had defected and captured several others which
he annexed to the empire of the Athenians. [7] Having re-established
Athens' former prestige at sea and added to it the further distinction of
his operations on land, he returned to Athens the darling of his people.
[8] In all these battles 200 enemy vessels and an enormous amount of
booty were taken.

[9] On the triumphal return of the army, the people streamed out
in a welcoming body, expressing admiration for all the soldiers, but for
Alcibiades in particular. [10] It was on him that the whole community
fixed its eyes, on him it gazed in suspense, on him people looked as if
he were sent from heaven and as if he were the personification of victory.

---

8. Evidently the battle of Cyzicus. Pharnabazus was not a Spartan general,
but the Persian satrap of Hellespontine Phrygia. Though Xenophon's *Hellenica*
takes up where Thucydides leaves off, the account in Justin does not come close to
that in Xenophon until section 6, leaving Ephorus as the likely source at least until
that point; see Diod. 13.42ff. There is a biography of Lysander by Plutarch. The
Carthaginian attack on Sicily dates to 410/09 and Alcibiades' return to Athens to
407/6.

[11] They applauded what he had done for his country, but they had no less admiration for what he had done against it during his exile, defending this on the grounds that he had acted in anger and under provocation. [12] This one man wielded such authority, they said, that he had been responsible for bringing down the mightiest empire, and then setting it up again; wherever he stood, victory took his side, and amazing reversals of fortune attended him. [13] They loaded him with honours of all kinds, divine as well as human, and were at odds with each other as to which was the greater, the disgrace of their expelling him or the honour of his recall. [14] Carrying the very gods before whom they had cursed him earlier, they came to congratulate him, [15] and the man to whom they had refused any kind of human assistance they now wanted to set in heaven, if that were possible. [16] They outweighed their earlier insults with honours, the losses imposed on him with gifts, the curses with prayers. [17] What they talked about was not the defeat in Sicily but the victory in Greece; not the fleets lost because of him, but those which he had taken; it was not Syracuse that they remembered, but Ionia and the Hellespont. [18] Whether the feelings which Alcibiades inspired in his countrymen were of hatred or of approval, they were never lukewarm.

5 [1] In the meantime, Lysander was given charge of the fleet and of the conduct of the war by the Spartans, while Darius, king of Persia, made his own son, Cyrus, governor of Ionia and Lydia in place of Tissaphernes. Cyrus provided the Spartans with reinforcements and financial assistance, and rallied them to hopes of regaining the fortunes they had formerly enjoyed. [2] Alcibiades now set off for Asia with a hundred ships and, heedless of all danger, was plundering territory that a long period of peace had left rich, with his men scattered about enjoying the looting and not fearing an ambush. The Spartans, their strength augmented by Cyrus, appeared suddenly and overwhelmed them. [3] The straggling troops incurred such slaughter that the losses in that engagement exceeded those which they had inflicted in the earlier ones, [4] and such was the despair of the Athenians that they immediately replaced Alcibiades as commander in chief with Conon,[9] [5] thinking that their defeat had come not from the fortunes of war but from treachery on the part of their general, with whom their former rejection counted for more than their recent benefactions. [6] For they concluded that his sole purpose in winning in the previous campaign was to show the enemy what kind of commander they had spurned and to make them buy victory more dearly. [7] In fact, his quick

9. This is the defeat at Notium in 407/6; see *AO* 174f.

intelligence and moral depravity made anything believable in Alcibiades' case. [8] Accordingly, fearing the violent reaction of the mob, he went into voluntary exile a second time.

6 [1] Conon, who replaced Alcibiades, was well aware of the qualities of the man he had succeeded as commander and he took great pains over equipping the fleet. [2] But the ships were short of fighting men since the best had been lost on the marauding expedition in Asia. [3] However, old men and young boys were armed for battle, and the number of the soldiers was made to pass muster without any increase in the army's real strength. [4] They were of an age ill suited for combat, and they could do little to prolong the war; they were massacred on all sides, or captured as they fled, and so disastrous were their losses, either in casualties or men taken prisoner, that it seemed as if the very name of Athens, not just its empire, had been eradicated. [5] The battle left the Athenians in ruin and despair. They were now at such an impasse that, having exhausted the age-group for military service, they granted citizenship to foreigners, emancipation to slaves, and pardon to condemned criminals. [6] Such were the dregs of society from which the erstwhile masters of Greece raised an army and with which they were now with difficulty seeking to safeguard their freedom. [7] Even so they decided to try their luck once more at sea. [8] So resolute were they that, though lately despairing of their lives, they did not now despair of victory. [9] But these were not soldiers of the calibre needed to defend the name of Athens, nor did they have the strength with which they had grown accustomed to achieving victory; and men who had served time not in camp but in irons lacked the necessary military expertise. They were all either taken prisoner or killed in action.[10] [10] Conon, the sole senior officer to survive the battle, feared savage reprisals from his fellow-citizens and withdrew to Evagoras, king of Cyprus, with eight ships.

7 [1] After his successes, the Spartan general, Lysander, proceeded to taunt his enemies in their misfortune. [2] He sent to Sparta, along with the spoils of war, the captured ships decorated as if for a triumph, [3] and he also accepted the voluntary surrender of the tributary states which fear of the vacillating fortunes of the war had kept loyal to Athens. Of the Athenian empire he left nothing but the city itself.

[4] When a full report of this was brought to Athens, the inhabitants all left their homes and went rushing in blind panic through the streets,

---

10. This is the battle of Aegospotami in 405/4; see *AO* 180f.

asking each other for information and trying to find the source of the news. [5] Boys were not kept at home by their immaturity, nor old men by their feebleness, nor women by the weakness of their sex; to such an extent had the realization of the enormous calamity permeated all ages. [6] Then they assembled in the forum and there repeatedly lamented their common calamity the whole night through. [7] Some wept for brothers, sons or parents; others for kinsmen; others for friends who were dearer than kinsmen; and they mourned at once the public lot and their private misfortunes. [8] At one moment they thought the end was near for themselves, at the next for the fatherland, and they judged the fate of the survivors more piteous than that of the fallen. [9] They all pictured to themselves siege, starvation and an enemy arrogant in victory; [10] they pondered now the destruction and burning of the city, now the captivity which they all faced and the abject misery of enslavement; [11] and they thought of the earlier destruction of the city as being far less disastrous in that it had cost them the ruin of buildings alone while sparing sons and fathers. [12] Now, however, they had no fleet left to which they could resort for safety, as they had done in the past, and no army whose courage could rescue them and enable them to construct finer walls.

8 [1] The enemy then fell upon the city which had been so bitterly lamented and was as good as lost. They laid siege to it and proceeded to starve out the beleaguered population. [2] They knew that few imported supplies remained; and they had taken measures to prevent fresh ones being brought in. [3] The will of the Athenians was broken by these blows and, after prolonged starvation and constant deaths from it, they sued for peace; but there was a protracted debate among the Spartans and their allies as to whether it should be granted. [4] Many were in favour of wiping the name of Athens off the map and destroying the city by fire; but the Spartans declared that they would not dash out one of the two eyes of Greece; [5] and they promised peace if the Athenians demolished the twin walls which extended down to Piraeus, surrendered the ships that still remained to them, and accepted from Sparta thirty governors to manage their affairs of state. [6] The city surrendered on these terms and the Spartans assigned its reorganization to Lysander. [7] This year was notable for the death of Darius, king of Persia, and the exile of the Sicilian tyrant Dionysius, as well as for the capture of Athens.[11]

---

11. The year is 405/4. Diod. 14.8f. details the problems and virtual exile of Dionysius, on whom see below Book 20.

[8] The change in the Athenian constitution brought with it a change in the condition of its citizens.[12] [9] Thirty governors were duly appointed for the state, and these turned into thirty tyrants. [10] From the start they assigned themselves 3,000 bodyguards (almost the entire citizen population of Athens to have survived all its calamities)[13] [11] and, as if this were too small a number to keep the city under control, they were given a further 700 soldiers by the victors.[14] [12] There followed a purge of the citizenry, which the Thirty inaugurated with Alcibiades so that he could not again seize control of the government under the guise of liberating the city. [13] When they learned that he had left for the court of Artaxerxes, the Persian king, they sent assassins at a rapid pace to head him off. [14] Alcibiades was overtaken by them, and, since he could not be killed openly, he was burned alive in the room in which he was sleeping.[15]

9 [1] Thus freed from fear of an avenger, the tyrants now sought to destroy the pitiful remnants of the city with further murders and looting. [2] When they learned that one of their number, Theramenes, disapproved of their conduct, they killed him, too, in order to intimidate everyone else. [3] There was, as a result, a general exodus from the city in all directions, and Greece was filled with Athenian refugees. [4] When these unfortunates were deprived even of this assistance by a Spartan edict forbidding the Greek city-states from accepting fugitives, they all converged on Argos and Thebes, [5] where they not only passed their exile in security but even regained hopes of recovering their fatherland.[16]

[6] Amongst the exiles was a nobleman of forceful character, Thrasybulus. He felt that a bold gesture should be made for their homeland and their common safety, even at the risk of his life. He therefore brought the exiles together and seized the stronghold of Phyle in Attic territory. [7] And he was not without support from a number of states which sympathized with the Athenians in their cruel misfortunes. [8] Ismenias,

12. To the continuing sources add, for Athenian affairs, primary and secondary references found in *AO* under the years 404/3 to 401/0.

13. The parenthesis translates what the Latin (albeit strange) seems to say, but in fact elsewhere we hear of 300 armed attendants; the Thirty conceived the idea of limiting citizenship to a body of 3000, later gaining discretionary authority to put to death anyone not on this list. These facts seem to have been confused.

14. The Spartan garrison under Callibius.

15. There are various versions of Alcibiades' death, of which Val. Max. 1.7 ext. 9 perhaps follows Trogus; also Nepos *Alc.* 10; Diod. 14.11; Plut. *Alc.* 38f. The ultimate source of Trogus' account could well have been Theopompus.

16. Xen. *Hell.* 2.4.1 has Megara and Thebes.

for example, a leading citizen of Thebes, unable to help them with public assistance, helped them from his private means, [9] and Lysias, the
Syracusan orator, who was then himself in exile, equipped 500 soldiers at
his own expense and sent them to succour the country which was the
common homeland of the art of rhetoric. [10] There was a fierce engagement. But since those on one side were battling with all their strength
for their own country while those on the other were fighting cautiously to
keep control of another's, the tyrants were vanquished. [11] Defeated,
they fled back into the city which they had already exhausted by bloodshed and which they were despoiling even of its arms. [12] Then, since
they suspected all the Athenian citizens of treachery, the tyrants ordered
them to move out of the city and make their homes within the lines of
the demolished double walls, and used non-Athenian soldiers to bolster
their regime. [13] After this, they attempted to bribe Thrasybulus by
promising him a share in the government; [14] failing to gain his assent,
they asked for assistance from the Spartans. When this arrived, they
fought another battle [15] in which the most ruthless of all the tyrants,
Critias and Hippolochus,[17] met their end.

10 [1] After the other tyrants were defeated and their army, which was
composed mainly of Athenians,[18] began to flee, Thrasybulus asked in
a loud voice why they were running from him as from a conqueror rather
than helping him as a champion of their common liberty. [2] He told
them to remember that the battleline which they saw was composed of
their fellow-citizens not foreign enemies; that he had taken up arms not
to seize anything from them after their defeat, but rather to restore what
had been taken from them, and that he was not making war on the state
but on their thirty masters. [3] He then reminded them of their common
ancestry, of the laws and religious observances which they shared, of
their long comradeship in many a campaign, and he begged them, even
if they could passively submit to slavery, at least to show compassion
towards their exiled compatriots, to give him back his fatherland and
accept their own liberty in turn. [4] He made such an impression with
these words that the army returned to the city and ordered the thirty
tyrants to move to Eleusis, putting ten men in their place to govern the
state. [5] These men, however, totally unperturbed by the example of

17. Xen. *Hell.* 2.4.19 has Hippomachus.
18. These were, of course, those Athenian citizens who by choice or duress
were on the side of the tyrants, a point made here mainly to create the context
for Thrasybulus' remarks, but also perhaps to emphasize the fact that foreign
troops were in a minority and this was essentially a civil war.

the previous administration, set out on the same ruthless path as their predecessors.

[6] Meanwhile, it was announced in Sparta that war had flared up among the Athenians, and King Pausanias was sent to suppress it. [7] Pausanias was moved to compassion for a whole people in exile; he restored their homeland to the unfortunate citizens and ordered the ten tyrants to leave the city and join the others at Eleusis. [8] Peace was restored by these measures, but some days later the tyrants were suddenly overcome with resentment, as much at the recall of the exiles as at their own banishment—as if the liberty of others constituted slavery for themselves—and they launched an attack on Athens. [9] But as they came forward to parley, on the understanding that their power was to be returned to them, they were ambushed and slaughtered, sacrificial victims to peace, as it were. The people whom the tyrants had ordered out of the city were recalled; [10] and at last a state which had been broken down into its many individual members was reconstituted as a whole body. [11] To forestall any dissension which might arise from what had happened before, they all swore to observe an amnesty for the events of the civil strife.

[12] Meanwhile, the Thebans[19] and the Corinthians sent ambassadors to the Spartans to ask for their share of the proceeds from the sale of plunder taken in a war in which they had all faced the dangers together. [13] The request was refused. While these two states did not openly declare war on the Spartans, in their hearts they secretly felt such anger that it could be inferred that war was on the horizon.

11 [1] It so happened that at about this time the Persian king Darius died, leaving two sons, Artaxerxes and Cyrus.[20] [2] In his will he bequeathed to Artaxerxes his kingdom, and to Cyrus the provinces of which he was the governor. [3] Cyrus, however, thought his father's decision unfair; and he secretly began to prepare for war with his brother. [4] When this was reported to Artaxerxes, the king summoned his brother and imprisoned him in chains of gold—Cyrus all the time feigning innocence

19. While the Thebans had been on the Spartan side in the war, their disagreements had begun immediately after. Thwarted in their motion for Athens' destruction, they had even harboured Athenian fugitives; see above 5.8.4 (without naming the Thebans) and 5.9.4f.

20. See above 5.8.7 for Darius' death. For the Greek involvement in the following events and especially the return of the 10,000, see Xen. *Anabasis*; also Xen. *Hell.* 3.1; Ctesias §§ 19–20; Diod. 14.19ff., with which the present text shows some affinity.

and disclaiming any hostile intent—and he would have put him to death if their mother had not stopped him. [5] Released by Artaxerxes, Cyrus now began to prepare for war overtly and without concealment, making no secret of his intentions but openly declaring them, and assembling reinforcements from all quarters. [6] The Spartans remembered the strong support he had given them in their war against Athens, and they decreed that assistance be given to him when his enterprise required it, pretending ignorance of the identity of the intended foe. [7] In this way they sought to win Cyrus' good will and also at least the chance of a pardon from Artaxerxes, should the latter prove victorious, since they would have made no public declaration against him. [8] In battle, however, the fortunes of war brought the two brothers face to face. Artaxerxes was wounded first, [9] but he managed to ride out of harm's way. Then Cyrus was overwhelmed and killed by the royal bodyguard. Thus Artaxerxes prevailed and at a stroke took possession of the plunder from the war with his brother, and his brother's army along with it.

[10] In that battle, there were 10,000 Greeks on Cyrus' side. These were victorious on the wing on which they had been stationed, and after Cyrus' death they could not be conquered by the Persian army, for all its size, nor could they be caught in a trap. [11] They returned by a route that took them through a large number of savage tribes and barbarous peoples, covering huge distances, and they defended themselves by their courage all the way to the boundaries of their country.

BOOK 6

1 [1] The more the Spartans had the more they coveted—for such is human nature. Not content with doubling their strength by acquiring the resources of Athens, they began to strive for empire over the whole of Asia. Most of it, however, was under Persian rule. [2] The man chosen as leader for this campaign, Hercylides,[1] saw that he had to confront two of King Artaxerxes' satraps, Pharnabazus and Tissaphernes, who had at their disposal the strength of powerful nations. He therefore decided that he should first make peace with one or the other of them. [3] Tissaphernes seemed the better choice since he was both more energetic and better

---

1. Dercylidas, correctly given in the prologue of Trogus. We are in 399/8 and the following events are covered by Xen. *Hell*. 3.1.8ff. and into Book 4; Diod. 14.38ff.

equipped, having under his command the troops of the late prince Cyrus, and it was he who was therefore invited to a meeting by Hercylides. Terms were negotiated and the satrap was taken out of the war. [4] Pharnabazus lodged a complaint about this with their king, alleging that when the Spartans had entered Asia Tissaphernes had not driven them back by armed force but had maintained them at the king's expense, [5] that he was now buying from them a postponement of hostilities instead of fighting them, as if every loss incurred did not affect the totality of the empire. [6] It was a disgrace, Pharnabazus said, for warfare to be a matter of bribery rather than action, for an enemy to be bought off rather than driven back by force of arms. [7] With such arguments he alienated the king from Tissaphernes, and urged him to replace the latter, as commander of the war at sea, with Conon the Athenian, who was at that time in exile in Cyprus after losing his fatherland in the war.[2] [8] The Athenians still had their naval expertise, said Pharnabazus, even if their power was broken, and a better man could not be found even if they had unlimited choice. [9] Pharnabazus was therefore given 500 talents and instructed to put Conon in charge of the fleet.

2 [1] On learning this, the Spartans for their part sent an embassy to request assistance in the war at sea from King Hercynio of Egypt, [2] by whom they were sent 100 triremes and 600,000 bushels of wheat.[3] They also amassed powerful auxiliary forces from their other allies. [3] But what this huge army, facing a great leader, really lacked was a competent general. [4] The allies demanded Agesilaus, who was then king of Sparta, but the Spartans long debated his appointment to supreme command because of a prophecy of the Delphic Oracle [5] which foretold an end to their empire "when the royal power became lame"—and Agesilaus was club-footed. [6] Eventually they decided that it was better to have a king who was lame in his walk than a kingdom that was lame in its exercise of power. [7] Accordingly, they sent Agesilaus into Asia with a large force, and I would find it hard to cite another opposing pair of generals as evenly matched as these. [8] In age, courage, strategic acumen and intelligence they were almost identical; and their military records were equally illustrious. [9] To each fortune gave qualities comparable in all

2. Tissaphernes met his end in 395/4, but it cannot be said that he was replaced by Conon.

3. See Diod. 14.79ff., where the Egyptian king is called Nephereus. Xenophon and Plutarch both wrote biographies of Agesilaus, who ruled in Sparta from 399 to 360. He had been in Asia for some time and was recalled because of the Corinthian War in 394.

respects, but yet kept either from being defeated by the other. [10] The preparations for the campaign were on a large scale and great exploits were performed by both generals. [11] Conon, however, was forestalled by a mutiny of the soldiers, whom the king's officers had systematically defrauded of their pay. The troops grew all the more insistent in their demands for their due, assuming that the campaign would be the harder for being directed by a great leader. [12] Conon long importuned the king in his dispatches to no effect and finally came to him in person, [13] but was refused an audience because he would not do obeisance before him in the Persian manner. [14] Nevertheless, he communicated with him through intermediaries and complained that campaigns being fought by the wealthiest of kings were flagging for want of funds; that although he had an army to match the enemy's, the king was being beaten through failure to spend money, an area in which he had the advantage, and that he was found wanting in precisely that sphere in which he was by far superior. [15] Conon demanded that he be assigned a finance officer on the grounds that entrusting that job to several people was ruinous. [16] He was given his money and sent back to the fleet, whereupon he immediately went into action, performing many exploits as successful as they were valiant: he ravaged the countryside of the enemy, took cities by storm, wrought wholesale destruction like a very whirlwind. [17] Alarmed by Conon's accomplishments, the Spartans recalled Agesilaus from Asia to defend the fatherland.

3 [1] In the meantime Pisander, left in charge of the country by Agesilaus when he set out, devoted all his energies to equipping a huge fleet, intending to try the fortunes of war.[4] [2] On the verge of his first encounter with the enemy, Conon also took great care in deploying his forces. [3] As a result, in that battle there was intense competition, not just between the generals, but among the rank and file as well. [4] For even the commander Conon was less committed to the Persians than he was to his country, [5] and just as he had been the man responsible for the loss of their empire when Athens fell, so now he also wanted to be regarded as its restorer, as well as to recover for himself by victory the fatherland he had lost through defeat. [6] His achievement would be all the more spectacular because he would be taking into the fight not the

4. Xen. *Hell.* 4.3.10ff.; Diod. 14.83. Pisander was Agesilaus' brother-in-law. The battle is that of Cnidus in 394. If Justin is placing the restoration of democracy in this year, he is obviously mistaken, but perhaps the impression comes from condensation of a longer summary in Trogus.

military resources of Athens but those of a foreign nation, and when he fought it would be the king who risked defeat, whilst victory would benefit Conon's native land. He would aspire to glory by means different from those of past leaders of his city: [7] they had defended their country by defeating the Persians; Conon would re-establish it by giving the Persians victory.

[8] Then there was Pisander. Kinship led him to emulate Agesilaus' virtues, and he made every effort not to fall short of his relative's achievements and illustrious reputation, or to overthrow by a moment's failure an empire built up through so many wars and over so many centuries. [9] His soldiers and all his oarsmen felt the same anxiety; they were tortured not so much by fear of losing their recent gains as by concern that the Athenians might recover what they once enjoyed. [10] But the brilliance of Conon's victory was as great as the violence of the battle. [11] The defeated Spartans fled and the enemy garrison was withdrawn from Athens. [12] The people had their former standing restored and their subject status removed, while many cities of their empire were retaken.

4 [1] This was the beginning of the recovery of the power of Athens, and the end of that of Sparta, [2] for the Spartans now began to lose the respect of their neighbours, as if along with their empire they had also lost their valour.[5] [3] The first to take the offensive against them, with Athenian support, was Thebes, [4] a city-state which, after growing in power at the expense of its neighbours, now rose through the courage of Epaminondas to hopes of domination over Greece. [5] There was a battle on land, in which Spartan fortunes were just as they had been in the naval battle against Conon. [6] In that engagement Lysander, under whom Sparta had defeated Athens, lost his life. [7] In addition, the other Spartan leader, Pausanias, went into exile after being accused of treason. [8] On winning their victory, the Thebans marched their entire army to the city of Sparta, thinking they could easily storm it since the Spartans had been totally deserted by their allies. [9] It was fear of this that prompted the Spartans to recall to the defence of the fatherland their king, Agesilaus, who was then campaigning very successfully in Asia, [10] for after Lysander fell they trusted no leader but Agesilaus. [11] Since he was late in coming, however, they raised an army and went

5. We have for the following period the continuing accounts of Xenophon and Diodorus. Justin is condensed and confused. Lysander died at Haliartus in 395/4, which battle Justin has evidently confused with the battle of Leuctra in 371.

out to meet the enemy. [12] But, defeated once already, their spirits and their strength were inadequate to face their recent conquerors, and they were vanquished at the first charge. [13] It was when these forces of his countrymen had already been destroyed that Agesilaus appeared on the scene, but he renewed the fight and, with troops that were fresh and hardened by many campaigns, had little difficulty in snatching victory from the enemy, though he was seriously wounded himself.

5 [1] When they learned of these events, the Athenians were afraid of being reduced to their former state of serfdom if the Spartans were once more victorious. [2] They therefore put an army together and ordered it to be taken by Iphicrates to assist the Boeotians. Iphicrates was only twenty years old but a young man of great talent. [3] The youth was possessed of astonishing valour beyond his years, [4] and never before, despite all their great leaders, had the Athenians enjoyed a general of greater potential or more precocious genius. [5] His abilities transcended the military sphere to embrace rhetoric as well.[6]

[6] When Conon heard of Agesilaus' return, he too came back from Asia in order to lay waste Spartan territory, [7] and the Spartans, encircled and with the menace of war echoing all round them, were reduced to the depths of despair. [8] Conon, however, after laying waste the enemy's land, made for Athens. Here he was welcomed with great joy by his fellow-citizens, but he nevertheless felt more dejection at the burning and destruction of his country by the Spartans than happiness at having returned to it after so long a time. [9] He restored what had been burned from the proceeds of his booty and by using the Persian army; and he rebuilt what had been demolished. [10] Such was the fate of Athens: burned earlier by the Persians, it had been rebuilt by their hands; now, sacked by the Spartans, it was being restored by spoils taken from the Spartans. [11] And, the tables turned, the city now had as allies its former enemies, and regarded as its enemies the people with whom at an earlier time it had once had the closest ties.

6 [1] While this was going on King Artaxerxes of Persia sent a deputation to Greece bearing his order for a general cessation of hostilities.[7] He threatened to treat as an enemy any who failed to comply, and he restored to the city-states their independence and all their property. [2] This gesture was prompted not by concern for the hardships of the Greeks and

6. The date is 393/2; see *AO* 211.
7. A Persian embassy did come to Greece in 392/1, but peace was made later, in 387/6 (the Varronian date for the Gallic sack of Rome).

for the wars which arose from their interminable and deadly animosities; [3] rather, Artaxerxes was now involved in a campaign in Egypt (he had undertaken this because reinforcements against his satraps had been sent to the Spartans from Egypt) and he wished to ensure that his armies were not detained in Greece. [4] Exhausted by all their wars, the Greeks were eager to comply. [5] This year was noteworthy not only because peace suddenly fell over the whole of Greece, but also because it was at this time that the city of Rome was captured by the Gauls.

[6] The Spartans now waited for a time when the Arcadians were away from their city; then, feeling safe, they made a surprise attack, stormed and occupied an Arcadian stronghold and stationed a garrison within it.[8] [7] The Arcadians in turn equipped and mobilized an army and, enlisting the help of the Thebans, attempted to win back by war what they had lost. [8] In that battle the Spartan leader, Archidamus, was wounded, [9] and when he saw his men being cut to pieces, clearly defeated, he employed a herald to claim the bodies of his men for burial [10]—the sign of conceding victory amongst the Greeks. Satisfied with this acknowledgment, the Thebans gave the sign to show mercy.

7 [1] Neither side resumed the offensive, and there was a truce as if by tacit agreement. A few days later, the Lacedaemonians proceeded to mount other attacks on their neighbours; and the Thebans, led by Epaminondas, conceived the hope of capturing the city of Sparta. [2] They set off for Lacedaemon in silence at nightfall, but they failed to make a surprise attack [3] because the old men of the city and the others who were not of fighting age had a premonition of the enemy's approach and went to meet them, in arms, right in the narrows of the city gates. [4] Here, facing a force of 15,000 soldiers, as few as one hundred men of advanced age committed themselves to the fight. [5] Such courage and strength does the sight of one's country and one's home inspire, and so much the fiercer is the spirit induced by their presence than by the mere recollection of them. [6] For when these men saw where they were fighting and what was at stake, they resolved on victory or death. [7] Thus a few old men held at bay an army to which a whole force of men in their prime had proved unequal days before. [8] In that battle two enemy generals were killed. [9] Meanwhile, with the news of Agesilaus' coming, the Thebans withdrew. [10] But the conflict was not postponed

8. We have now leapt to 365/4 and events covered (but with no mention of the Thebans) by Xen. *Hell.* 7.4.19ff. The confusion continues through section 7, where we are into 363/2 and the battle of Mantinea; Xen. *Hell.* 7.5; Diod. 15.82ff.

for long; the young men of Sparta, fired by the valour and glory of the old, could not be restrained from immediately deciding the issue in the field. [11] Victory was going to the Thebans when Epaminondas, fulfilling the role of a brave soldier as well as general, was seriously wounded. [12] News of this brought grief and terror to the one side and stupefied the other with joy, and they left the battle as if by common consent.

8 [1] A few days later Epaminondas died, and with him perished the power of his state. [2] Break off the sharp tip of a javelin and you have deprived the rest of the weapon of its capacity for damage; just so the removal of the Theban general, who represented the javelin point, blunted the strength of the state, so that Thebes appeared not so much to have lost him as to have died with him in entirety. [3] For before the time of his leadership the Thebans waged no war of note, and afterwards they were distinguished not for their military prowess but their defeats. It is evident, therefore, that his country's period of glory was born and died with him.

[4] It was unclear whether it was as a man or as a general that he had the better qualities. [5] He never sought power for his own advantage, only for that of his country, [6] and to money he was so indifferent that not enough was left by him to pay for his funeral. [7] He craved reputation no more than he did money, for all his appointments were heaped on him against his will, [8] and he functioned in these positions in such a way that he seemed to be adding prestige to the office rather than gaining it himself. [9] Further, his literary interests, as well as his erudition in philosophy, were so great that it seemed amazing that a man with a natural bent for literature should have acquired such a remarkable knowledge of military science. [10] Nor was the way in which he died at odds with the style of life which he had adopted. [11] He was carried half-dead back to the camp. He recovered consciousness and the power of speech, and put just one question to the men standing around him: whether the enemy had taken his shield from him when he fell. [12] When he was told that the shield had been recovered, he had it brought to him and kissed it as being his companion in his toil and his glory; then he asked one more question—which side had won? [13] On hearing that it was the Thebans, he said that all was well, and expired giving congratulations to his native land.[9]

---

9. Epaminondas' death here is apparently much swifter than at 6.8.1—"a few days later"!

9 [1] With the death of Epaminondas the valour of the Athenians likewise perished, [2] for on the loss of their traditional rival they slipped into lethargy and torpor [3] and, instead of spending their state revenues on their fleet and land forces as in the past, they now squandered them on festivals and putting on public games.[10] [4] They flocked to the theatres, along with their famous actors and poets, making more frequent visits to the stage than to the camp and praising versifiers as greater men than generals. [5] It was at this time that state income, formerly used for the maintenance of soldiers and oarsmen, began to be distributed to the urban populace.

[6] These factors brought about the emergence of the hitherto undistinguished, little-known name of Macedon, while the Greeks were amusing themselves; [7] and Philip, kept as a hostage for three years in Thebes where he was trained in those qualities possessed by Epaminondas and Pelopidas, began to impose the hegemony of Macedonia, like the yoke of slavery, on the shoulders of Greece and Asia.[11]

BOOK 7

1 [1] Macedonia was formerly called Emathia, after King Emathion, whose primitive heroism lives on to this day in those regions.[1] [2] In keeping with its modest beginnings its territory was very restricted; [3] the inhabitants were called Pelasgians and the country Bottia. [4] Later, thanks to the valour of the kings and the enterprise of its people, it subjugated first its neighbours and then other peoples and tribes, extending its empire to the furthest limits of the East. [5] Pelegonus, father of Asteropaeus (one of the most distinguished champions in the Trojan War, we are told), is

---

10. We may detect here the moralizing tone of Theopompus. In the wake of a debilitating war with some of their allies, the Athenians instituted economies through a budget system wherein the theoric fund, technically meant to provide the cost of theatre attendance to citizens, became the repository of excess revenues. See *AO* 7.

11. Philip's sojourn in Thebes is noted also by Diod. 15.67.4 (under the year 369/8) and Plut. *Pelopidas* 26.4f.

1. It is as likely as can be that Trogus' source for Macedonian affairs was Theopompus. The history of Macedon to the death of Philip may conveniently be followed in *A History of Macedonia* (Oxford), vol. I to 550 by N. G. L. Hammond (1972), vol. II 550–336 by Hammond and G. T. Griffith (1979).

said to have reigned in Paeonia, which is now part of Macedonia. [6] In another quarter, in Europa, a man called Europus occupied the throne.

[7] Caranus also came to Emathia with a large band of Greeks, being instructed by an oracle to seek a home in Macedonia. Here, following a herd of goats running from a downpour, he seized the city of Edessa, the inhabitants being taken unawares because of heavy rain and dense fog. [8] Remembering the oracle's command to follow the lead of goats in his quest for an empire, he established the city as his capital, [9] and thereafter he made it a solemn observance, wheresoever he took his army, to keep those same goats before his standards[2] in order to have as leaders in his exploits the animals which he had had with him to found the kingdom. [10] He gave the city of Edessa the name Aegaeae and its people the name Aegeads in memory of this service.[3]   [11] Then, after driving out Midas—he, too, ruled part of Macedonia—and other kings, he supplanted them all as sole ruler, [12] and was the first to unify the tribes of different nations and make a single body of Macedonia, establishing a firm basis on which his expanding kingdom could grow.

2 [1] The king after Caranus was Perdiccas,[4] who was known both for his illustrious life and for his memorable final instructions, which resembled an oracular utterance. [2] When on his deathbed, the aged Perdiccas indicated to his son, Argeus, the place where he wished to be buried, and gave orders that not merely his own bones but also those of his successors to the throne be laid in that spot, [3] declaring that the throne would stay in their family as long as the remains of their descendants were buried there. [4] It is on account of this piece of superstition that people believe that the line died out with Alexander, because he changed the place of burial.[5] [5] Argeus ruled with restraint and won the affection of the people. He left as his successor his son, Philip, who succumbed to an early death, appointing as his heir Aëropus, who was but an infant. [6] Now, the Macedonians were continually at war with the Thracians and Illyrians, and with these campaigns for their routine training they became so hardened that they began to alarm their neighbours with their illustrious military reputation. [7] Accordingly the Illyrians, with

2. So indeed the Latin, but surely the truth was that the goats were represented *on* the standards.

3. The Greek for goat was "aigos," which would be Latinized as "aegus."

4. Cf. Her. 8.137ff., where the succession is as here, except that Alcetas is between Aëropus and Amyntas.

5. Alexander the Great, that is, who supposedly asked to be buried at the oracle of Ammon in Libya, but was finally entombed at Alexandria in Egypt.

disdain for the tender years of the child monarch, launched an attack on the Macedonians. [8] The latter, defeated in battle, carried forward their king in his cradle, placed him to the rear of their battle-line and renewed the fight with greater spirit, [9] imagining that the reason for their earlier defeat was that they had fought without the auspices of their king. [10] Now, however, they were going to win because from that superstition they had drawn the determination to do so. [11] At the same time they were gripped by pity for the child, since defeat would evidently make their monarch a prisoner. [12] So, once battle was joined, they routed the Illyrians with great slaughter and showed their enemies that what the Macedonians had lacked in the previous encounter was their king, not courage. [13] Aëropus was succeeded by Amyntas, who enjoyed particular renown both for his own merits and because of the outstanding character of his son, Alexander, [14] who was naturally endowed with all manner of superb abilities, to the extent that he even competed in the Olympic games in a variety of events.[6]

3 [1] In the meantime Darius, king of Persia, after being driven from Scythia in ignominious flight, was concerned that he might be discredited everywhere because of his military losses.[7] He therefore sent Magabasus with some of his troops to conquer Thrace and the other kingdoms of that area, to which Macedonia would be added as a place of little importance. [2] Magabasus quickly executed the order of his king and sent an embassy to Amyntas, king of Macedonia, demanding to be given hostages as a guarantee of peace in the future. [3] The ambassadors were given a cordial reception but, becoming the worse for wine during the course of the dinner, they asked Amyntas to add to the magnificence of the feast the privileges of intimate friendship by inviting his daughters and wives to his banquet; for this, they said, was regarded amongst the Persians as a binding pledge of hospitality. [4] When the women arrived, the Persians began to fondle them in too familiar a manner, whereupon Amyntas' son, Alexander, asked his father to have regard for his dignity as an older man and leave the banquet, promising that he would moderate the exuberance of the guests. [5] When Amyntas left, Alexander also called the women away from the banquet for a short while, ostensibly to have them made up more attractively and bring them back more desirable. [6] He put in their place some young men dressed as women and told

---

6. This is Alexander I Philhellene (Her. 5.22), who ruled c.495–452.
7. See Her. 5.14ff. "Magabasus" is Megabazus. For Darius and the Scyths see above 2.5.10f.

them to use their swords, which they carried beneath their dress, to curb the forwardness of the ambassadors. [7] And so all the Persians were killed. When his embassy failed to return, Magabasus, not knowing what had happened, dispatched Bubares with part of his army to the area on what he thought would be an easy campaign of little significance; [8] he did not deign to go in person, for fear of demeaning himself by taking on such a contemptible people in battle. [9] Bubares, however, fell in love with Amyntas' daughter before war could commence and abandoned the campaign. He married her and, renouncing hostile intentions, entered into a regular family relationship with Amyntas.

4 [1] After Bubares left Macedonia King Amyntas died. The family ties which his son and successor, Alexander, enjoyed with Bubares not only ensured him peace in the time of Darius but also put him on such good terms with Xerxes that when the latter swept through Greece like a whirlwind he granted Alexander authority over all the territory between Mt Olympus and Mt Haemus. [2] But Alexander extended his kingdom as much through his own valour as through Persian generosity.

[3] The throne of Macedonia then came by order of succession to Amyntas, son of Alexander's brother Menelaus.[8] [4] He, too, was remarkable for his energy and was possessed of all the qualities befitting a general. [5] He had three sons by Eurydice: Alexander, Perdiccas, and Philip, the father of Alexander the Great of Macedon, as well as a daughter, Euryone. By Gygaea he had Archelaus, Arridaeus and Menelaus. [6] Amyntas undertook difficult campaigns against the Illyrians and the Olynthians. [7] Moreover, Amyntas would have fallen victim to the treachery of his wife Eurydice (she had made a pact to marry her son-in-law, undertaking to kill her husband and hand the crown to her lover) had their daughter not divulged her mother's liaison and criminal intentions. [8] After surviving all these dangers Amyntas died an old man, passing on the throne to his eldest son, Alexander.

5 [1] Right at the start of his reign, Alexander averted further war with the Illyrians by agreeing to pay them tribute and giving them his brother,

8. Alexander was succeeded by his son Perdiccas II (c.452–413) and he by Archelaus (413–399). Four brief and turbulent reigns preceded that of Amyntas III, father of Philip, 392–370. Alexander II then lasted until his murder in 368, Ptolemy until 365, when he was killed by Perdiccas III, who ruled until 359, when in fact he fell in battle against the Illyrians. Events through this period surface occasionally in Diodorus. There was enough intrigue among Macedonian royalty, but Justin's account has gone even beyond what we learn elsewhere.

Philip, as a hostage. [2] Some time later he again used Philip as a hostage to re-establish peace with the Thebans, and it was this that most served to develop Philip's exceptional genius.[9] [3] Kept as a hostage at Thebes for three years, Philip spent the earliest stages of his boyhood in a city characterized by old-fashioned austerity and in the home of Epaminondas, the great philosopher and general. [4] Shortly afterwards, Alexander succumbed to the treachery of his mother Eurydice. [5] Although Eurydice had been caught red-handed, Amyntas had nevertheless spared her life for the sake of the children they had in common, unaware that she would one day prove their undoing. [6] Alexander's brother, Perdiccas, likewise became the victim of a treacherous plot on her part. [7] It was indeed a cruel blow that these children should have been murdered by their mother and sacrificed to her lust when it was consideration of these same children which had once rescued her from punishment for her crimes. [8] The murder of Perdiccas seemed all the more scandalous in that the mother's pity was not stirred even by the fact that he had an infant son.[10] [9] So it was that for a long period Philip was guardian for the minor rather than king himself [10] but, facing the threat of more serious wars, and at a time when any assistance to be expected from the infant was too far in the future, he was constrained by the people to take the throne.

6 [1] When he assumed power, everybody had great expectations of him both because of his natural ability, which held out promise of a great man, and because of the old prophecies concerning Macedonia [2] which had predicted that "Macedonia would enjoy great prosperity in the reign of one of Amyntas' sons."[11] The wickedness of Philip's mother had left only Philip to realize that hope. [3] At the start of his reign the green youth of the novice was plagued by trouble: the murder of his brothers, so cruelly done away with; the large number of his enemies; the fear of treason; the poverty his kingdom suffered, exhausted by interminable warfare. [4] Then, too, there were wars brewing simultaneously in different quarters, as if many nations were conspiring to crush Macedonia. Philip could not take on these wars

9. See above 6.9.7.

10. He would have been Amyntas IV; it is debatable whether or not Philip II (359–336) began as regent for the latter.

11. The narrative account of the period of Philip's reign is Diod. 16 (with interspersed attention to Sicily in particular). Two recent treatments of the Macedonian are J. R. Ellis, *Philip II and Macedonian Imperialism* (London 1976) and G. Cawkwell, *Philip of Macedon* (London 1978).

all at once, [5] and he decided they should be dealt with separately. Some he settled by negotiation and others by paying out money, while he attacked all the enemies who were easiest to conquer, so that by victory over these he might both strengthen his men's wavering resolve and also remove his enemies' disdain for him. [6] His first fight was with a contingent of Athenians; he defeated them in an ambush and, although he could have annihilated them, fear of a more serious conflict prompted him to let them go unharmed and without ransom. [7] After the Athenians, Philip shifted his attack to the Illyrians, killing many thousands of the enemy. [8] He next took Thessaly, where war was the last thing anyone expected, by a surprise attack, not because he wanted plunder but because he was eager to add the strength of the Thessalian cavalry to his own army. [9] He then amalgamated the cavalry and infantry to create an invincible army. He also captured the famous city of Larissa. [10] While these matters were proceeding successfully, he married Olympias,[12] daughter of Neoptolemus, king of the Molossians; [11] the match was arranged by Arrybas, king of the Molossians, who was the girl's cousin and guardian and was married to her sister, Troas. This was the cause of Arrybas' downfall and of all his troubles. [12] For, while he was hoping to increase his kingdom through his family ties with Philip, he was stripped of his own kingdom by the latter and grew old in exile.[13]

[13] After these achievements Philip was no longer satisfied with defensive campaigns but even went on the offensive against peaceful nations. [14] He was engaged in an attack on the the city of Mothone[14] and was passing before its walls when an arrow fired from the defences struck out the king's right eye, [15] but the injury did not make him any the less effective in combat or more savage in his treatment of his enemies. [16] On the contrary, when, a few days later, the enemy sued for peace, he granted it, and showed not merely restraint but leniency in dealing with the defeated enemy.

12. In 357. Arrybas was the brother of Neoptolemus, who was king before him, and so Olympias' uncle.

13. This came in 342; below 8.6.7.

14. Methone, in 353. If Diod. 16.34.4f. is to be believed, Philip was hardly so lenient.

BOOK 8

1 [1] As for the Greek states, for all their attempts to impose their rule on each other, they only succeeded in losing their ability to rule themselves.[1] [2] With no restraint they rushed into mutual destruction, and realized only in subjection that what they forfeited individually constituted a loss for them all. [3] For Philip of Macedon, as though reconnoitring from a watch tower, was scheming against the liberty of them all. Sustaining their disputes by helping the weaker side, he forced winners and losers alike to become slaves to his royal power.

[4] The prime responsibility for this disaster lay with the Thebans who, at the time of their hegemony, had insufficient strength of character to deal with their success. After defeating the Spartans and the Phocians in the field, they high-handedly impeached them before the combined council of Greece, as though slaughter and pillage had been too small a punishment for them.[2] [5] The Spartans were charged with seizure of the citadel of Thebes during a time of truce, the Phocians with having laid waste Boeotia—[6] as if, after armed conflict, the two sides had left room for legal solutions. [7] Since the victors had the last word in determining the verdict, the defendants were fined more than they were able to pay. [8] The Phocians stood to be deprived of their lands, children and wives. Led by a certain Philomelus, they in desperation seized the temple of Apollo at Delphi, as though venting their anger on the god. [9] Enriched with gold and money from there, they hired mercenaries and launched an attack on the Thebans. [10] The action of the Phocians, generally abhorred because of the sacrilege involved, generated still greater resentment against the Thebans, by whom they had been driven to such desperate measures, than it did against the Phocians themselves. [11] Help was therefore sent to the Phocians both by the Athenians and by the Spartans. [12] In the first encounter Philomelus pillaged the Theban camp, [13] but in the ensuing battle he was the first

---

1. For other accounts and Trogus' probable source see above at 7.6.
2. The council is that of the Amphictyons of Delphi, the year 355/4. Diod. 16.14.3 names Demophilus and other sources. The charge against Sparta relates to the seizure of the Cadmeia in 382 (Xen. *Hell.* 5.2.25ff.), but the charge had been laid after Leuctra in 371 (Diod. 16.23.2). The major sin of the Phocians was to have cultivated the sacred plain of Cirrha (Diod. 16.23.3). Philomelus' death came in 354/3.

to fall, fighting in the thick of the fray, and with his impious blood paid the price for his sacrilege. [14] Onomarchus replaced him as general.

2 [1] Against Onomarchus the Thebans and the Thessalians chose as general not one of their own citizens—they were afraid that the power victory gave such a man would be more than they could put up with—but Philip, king of Macedonia, [2] and they freely submitted to a foreigner's exercise of such power as they feared to see in the hands of their own people. [3] Philip, posing as the avenger of sacrilege rather than the champion of the Theban cause, ordered all his men to put on laurel crowns, with which they marched into battle, as though the god were going before. [4] Catching sight of the emblems of the deity, the Phocians were terror-stricken as they thought of their misdeeds. They flung down their arms, took to their heels and paid for their desecration with the bloodbath that followed.[3] [5] It is difficult to believe how greatly this redounded to Philip's credit amongst all nations; [6] he was held up as the avenger of sacrilege, the champion of religion. Here was a crime which the world's forces should have united to avenge, and Philip had stood alone to demand atonement. [7] The man who had championed the majesty of the gods deserved to be regarded as second only to the gods. [8] When the Athenians heard the result of the battle, they seized the pass at Thermopylae in order to block Philip's advance into Greece, just as they had done in earlier days when the Persians were coming, but though their tactics were the same as then neither their courage nor their cause was at all comparable. [9] On the earlier occasion they fought for the freedom of Greece, now for a public sacrilege; then to defend their temples from pillaging by an enemy, now to defend the pillagers of temples against an avenging army. [10] They were acting as the defenders of a crime, the vindication of which would have disgraced others, let alone the Athenians. [11] They had clearly forgotten that in the hazardous times of their own past it was Apollo whose advice they had followed; that it was under his leadership that they had marched successfully into so many wars, founded so many cities with favourable auspices and won such a great empire by land and sea; and that they had never embarked on any enterprise, either as individuals or as a city, without his divine sanction. [12] To think that intellects steeped in all branches of learning and shaped by the most enlightened legal and political institutions should have committed so foul a crime that they lost the right to censure barbarians in the future!

---

3. This is the battle of the Crocus Field in 352.

3 [1] Philip, however, showed no more integrity in his dealings with his allies. [2] Apparently frightened of being outdone by his enemies in sacrilegious crime, he overran and pillaged the states whose leader he had been a short while before, states which had fought under his supreme command and which had congratulated him and themselves on their victory. [3] He auctioned off the women and children from each, [4] and spared neither the temples of the immortal gods, nor holy shrines, nor even the guardian deities, public and private, into whose presence he had recently come as a guest. [5] The result was that he appeared less the avenger of sacrilege than one who had sought a licence to commit it. [6] Next, as though he had achieved great success, he crossed to Thrace,[4] where he fought in the same treacherous fashion, capturing by subterfuge and putting to death neighbouring kings until he annexed the entire province to the Macedonian empire. [7] Then, to remove the bad name which he had acquired—he was the most infamous man of his epoch—he sent men through the kingdoms and richest city-states [8] to spread the word that King Philip was spending large sums of money on the construction of walls, shrines and temples throughout the states, and to issue invitations to contractors for the works. [9] When these contractors arrived in Macedonia, however, they were put off by various excuses and so they left without complaint out of fear of the violent character of his rule.

[10] After this Philip attacked the people of Olynthus for having shown compassion and given shelter to two of his half-brothers after he had murdered the third.[5] These were the sons of his stepmother,[6] and Philip desperately wished to do away with them since he saw them as potential claimants to the throne. [11] For this reason he annihilated a famous old city, subjected his brothers to the fate for which he had long before marked them out and indulged himself with a huge amount of plunder as well as the fratricide which he had prayed for. [12] Next, as though he had the right to realize any scheme whatsoever that occurred to him, he seized the gold mines in Thessaly and the silver mines in Thrace [13] and, to leave no law or convention unbroken, he turned his hand to piracy as well.

4. Thus the text of Seel, as against "Cappadocia," which makes no sense. The Thracian Chersonese may be presumed.
5. The serious campaign against the Olynthians began in 349/8. Demosthenes, particularly in his Olynthiac orations, is a major, if hardly dispassionate, source. Philip's immediate aim in Thrace was the kingdom of Cersebleptes.
6. Gygaea: above 7.4.5.

[14] After this, it so happened that two brothers, who were kings in Thrace, chose him as an arbiter of some differences which they had, not out of any regard for his fairmindedness but from fear on the part of each that Philip might add his strength to the other's. [15] Philip, in keeping with his character, appeared for the case as if for a war, with his army drawn up for battle, taking the brothers by surprise. He behaved not like an arbiter, but with the criminal duplicity of a thief, despoiling both of them of their kingdoms.

4 [1] In the meantime an Athenian embassy came to him suing for peace.[7] [2] Philip heard them out, then in his turn sent ambassadors to Athens bearing his conditions for peace; and there a peace treaty was concluded to their mutual benefit. [3] Embassies also arrived from the other Greek city-states, motivated by fear of war rather than love of peace. [4] The Thessalians and the Boeotians, as their rancour increased, begged him to show himself the leader of the Greeks against the Phocians, as he had claimed to be. [5] Such was the burning hatred that they felt for the Phocians that, oblivious to their own catastrophes, they would rather perish themselves than fail to destroy them, and they preferred to endure the cruelty of Philip, which they had already experienced, than show mercy towards their enemies. [6] The ambassadors of the Phocians, on the other hand, with the support of the Spartans and the Athenians, kept begging him to renounce hostilities (they had already bought a postponement from him on three occasions). [7] This truly was a disgraceful and pathetic sight: Greece, still the world leader in military strength and reputation, the country which had always been the conqueror of kings and nations, and which was still mistress of many cities—Greece waiting patiently at the court of a foreigner to beg for peace or war. [8] It was shameful to see these liberators of the world place all their hopes in outside assistance, reduced by internal strife and civil war to fawning upon what had but lately been a minor client-state, [9] and especially to see this done by the Thebans and Spartans, who previously had competed for hegemony and now strove only to win the favour of a despot.

[10] Meanwhile, flaunting his supremacy, Philip affected contempt towards these great cities as he pondered to which of the adversaries he should show favour. [11] He granted private audiences to embassies

---

7. For their various accounts of the embassies of 347 and 346 see Dem. 19 and Aesch. 2, and from shortly after the Peace of Philocrates Dem. 5. See also *AO* 318ff.

from both sides, promising the one not to open hostilities and binding the ambassadors with an oath not to divulge his response to anyone, and assuring the other that he would join them and bring them assistance. He told both sides not to make preparations for war or have any fear of it. [12] He put everybody at ease with these conflicting responses and then seized the pass at Thermopylae.

5 [1] It was now that the Phocians realized for the first time that they had been caught in Philip's trap, and they rushed to arms in panic. [2] But they had no opportunity to prepare for war and no time to amass support, and Philip was all the while threatening them with annihilation if they failed to surrender. [3] Victims of necessity, they struck a bargain for their lives and capitulated. [4] But Philip's commitment was as trustworthy as his earlier promise to avert hostilities. [5] The Phocians were slaughtered indiscriminately and taken captive; parents were not left their children, nor husbands their wives, nor temples their statues of the gods. [6] The wretched survivors had but one consolation: since Philip had cheated his allies of their share of the plunder, the Phocians saw none of their property in the hands of their enemies.

[7] Philip returned to his kingdom and, just as shepherds drive their flocks at different times into winter or summer pastures, so he now capriciously transplanted whole peoples and cities as he felt regions needed to be populated or depopulated. [8] Everywhere it was a dismal picture, almost one of desolation. [9] True, it was not a scene of panic inspired by an enemy; there was no movement of troops through a city, no armed melée, nor the plundering of property and abduction of people; but there was silent, forlorn dejection, [10] as men feared that even their tears might be taken to signify opposition. [11] Grief is actually intensified when repressed, becoming the more deeply rooted the more its expression is denied. [12] The evacuees looked wistfully now at the tombs of their forefathers, now at their ancient family deities, now at the houses in which they had been born and had themselves produced children, [13] sorrowing at one moment for their own fate, for having lived to see that day, and at the next for that of their children, for not having been born after it.

6 [1] Some of these peoples Philip settled right on his borders as a bulwark against his enemies, others he set on the remote frontiers of the empire, and some, who were prisoners-of-war, he distributed to supplement the populations of his cities. [2] Doing this he made one kingdom and one people from large numbers of different clans and tribes.

[3] After organizing and settling affairs in Macedonia, Philip next outwitted and defeated the Dardanians and his other neighbours.[8] [4] He did not keep his hands from kindred blood either; for he decided to drive from his throne Arrybas, king of Epirus, who was a very close blood-relation of his wife, Olympias, [5] and then he summoned to Macedonia Arrybas' stepson, Alexander, a good-looking but virtuous young boy and the brother of his own wife, Olympias. Philip summoned him in his sister's name [6] and then made every effort to seduce him, holding out the promise of his stepfather's throne and pretending to be in love with him, until he drove the boy into a homosexual liaison with him. His motive was to gain greater submissiveness from the boy, either through a guilty conscience or the prospect of the throne. [7] So when Alexander reached the age of twenty, Philip gave him, though he was hardly more than a boy, the throne which he had taken from Arrybas, and thus was villainous in his dealings with both. [8] For in the case of the man from whom he took the throne he failed to respect the rights of kinship; as for the other to whom he gave it, he made him a catamite first, and then a king.

BOOK 9

1 [1] What had incited Philip to come to Greece was the prospect of looting a few cities; but when, on his arrival, he calculated the collective wealth of all of the cities from the plunder taken from some smaller ones, he decided to make war on Greece as a whole.[1] [2] He thought that it would be highly beneficial to his prospects of success if he brought under his control the famous maritime city of Byzantium, which would serve as a safe base for his land and sea forces; but the town shut its gates against him and he laid siege to it. [3] The city had been originally founded by Pausanias, king of Sparta, and had remained in his power for seven years, after which, as victory changed hands, it was regarded at one time as being under the sway of the Spartans, at another of the Athenians. [4] The result of this disputed sovereignty over the town

8. We are in 344/3. On Arrybas cf. above 7.6.10ff.; he was expelled in 342 (Dem. 7.32; Diod. 16.72.1).
1. The year is 340 (Diod. 16.74); Philip's assault began with Perinthus, near Byzantium. For Pausanias see above 2.15.14ff. and *AO* 67f.

was that, since nobody gave it support as being his own possession, it preserved its independence all the more resolutely.

[5] Exhausted by the protracted siege, Philip now resorted to piracy in order to generate funds. [6] He captured 170 merchant ships, sold them and thus brought some slight relief to his acute financial needs. [7] Then, rather than have such a huge force preoccupied with the siege of a single city, he set off with his finest troops and stormed a large number of cities in the Chersonese. [8] He also summoned his son Alexander, who was 18 years old, to receive his initial training under his father in the field.[2] [9] In addition, he made a predatory expedition into Scythia in the spirit of a merchant, trying to make good the expenses of one war with the profits from another.

2 [1] The king of the Scythians at that time was Atheas, who, hard pressed in a war with the Histriani, used the people of Apollonia as intermediaries to request support from Philip, whom he would then adopt as his heir to the throne of Scythia.[3] [2] In the meantime, however, the king of the Histriani died, thereby freeing the Scythians from the threat of war and the need to seek assistance. [3] Atheas, therefore, sent back the Macedonians and had a message sent to Philip that he had neither asked for his help nor authorized his adoption, [4] for, he said, the Scythians had no need of the protection of the Macedonians, to whom they were superior, while he himself did not lack an heir since he had a son still alive. [5] On hearing this Philip sent envoys to Atheas requesting a contribution towards expenses of the siege of Byzantium so that he should not be obliged to abandon the campaign for lack of funds. [6] Atheas, he said, ought to be all the more willing to comply because, when the troops had been sent to his aid by Philip, Atheas had not given them even travelling expenses, much less paid for their service. [7] Atheas now used as an excuse his kingdom's harsh climate and barren soil which, so far from enriching the Scythians, barely kept them fed; he replied that he had no resources with which to satisfy such a great king [8] and he felt it was more insulting to discharge a small part of his debt than to default completely. [9] After all, the Scythians were renowned for their courage and physical toughness, not for their wealth.

2. Alexander was in fact some 16 years old and according to Plut. *Alex.* 9 was left in charge in Macedonia.

3. Diodorus (16.1.5) obviously knew of the following episode, but Justin is the only extant source. See in general T. S. Brown, "Herodotus and Justin 9.2," *The Ancient History Bulletin* 2 (1988), 1ff.

[10] Slighted by this, Philip raised the siege of Byzantium and opened hostilities against the Scythians, first sending envoys to allay the enemy's fears. They were to report to Atheas that during the siege of Byzantium Philip had vowed a statue to Hercules, [11] that he was now coming to set it up at the mouth of the Ister,[4] and that he requested a safe passage to discharge his religious obligations to the god since he would be coming as a friend of the Scythians. [12] Atheas replied that, if Philip wished to fulfil his vow, the statue should be sent to him, and he promised not only to have it set up but also that it would remain inviolate; but he would not permit an army to enter his territory. [13] If Philip erected the statue against the wishes of the Scythians, he continued, Atheas would demolish it when he left and turn the bronze of the statue into arrowheads. [14] With feelings bruised on both sides, they now engaged in a battle, in which the Scythians, though superior in valour and determination, were defeated by the cunning of Philip. [15] Twenty thousand children and women were captured along with a large number of cattle, but no gold or silver. That was the first time that reports of the the poverty of the Scythians were corroborated. [16] Twenty thousand thoroughbred mares were sent to Macedonia for breeding purposes.

3 [1] During his return march from Scythia, Philip was met by the Triballians, who said that they would not allow him to pass unless they were given part of his plunder. [2] A quarrel broke out, which soon led to a battle, in which Philip received such a serious wound to the thigh that the weapon passed right through and killed his horse.[5] [3] Everyone thought he was dead, and so the plunder was lost. Thus it was that the spoils of Scythia, as though under a curse, very nearly brought the Macedonians to grief.

[4] As soon as he had recovered from his wound, Philip proceeded against Athens in a war on which he had long been secretly resolved.[6] [5] The Thebans embraced the cause of the Athenians from fear that, if the latter were defeated, the war, like fire on a neighbour's property, might spread to them. [6] An alliance was therefore struck between two city-states which a short time before had been mortal enemies. These went on to ply Greece with deputations, expressing the opinion that their common enemy should be repelled by their common forces, [7] and that if Philip met with success at the start he would not stop short of

4. The Danube.
5. Cf. Marsyas of Pella *FGH* 135/6 F 17, without comment on the horse's fate.
6. For events leading up to the battle of Chaeronea in 338 see also Dem. 18.

bringing all Greece under his yoke. [8] Some states were persuaded by these arguments and joined the Athenians, but fear of going to war against Philip actually drove others to his side. [9] Battle was joined, and although the Athenians were far superior numerically they were defeated by a Macedonian valour that had been tempered by incessant warfare. [10] Yet they fell remembering their former glory, for they all had their wounds in front, and covered with their dying bodies the posts they had been given to defend by their generals. [11] For the whole of Greece this day marked the end of its glorious supremacy and of its ancient independence.

4 [1] Philip shrewdly concealed his joy at this victory.[7] He did not offer the customary sacrifices that day, nor did he laugh at dinner; he permitted no games during the feasting, used no garlands or perfume. As far as he could, he conquered without making anyone feel that he was a conqueror. [2] He issued orders that he be addressed not as "king of Greece" but as "general". [3] He showed such restraint, concealing his joy and respecting his enemies' distress, that he avoided the impression of either gloating amongst his own countrymen or of being insulting towards the vanquished. [4] It was the Athenians whom he had found to be his bitterest foes, but he released their prisoners-of-war without ransom and also surrendered to them the bodies of their dead for burial, actually encouraging them to carry the remains to the tombs of their forefathers. [5] Furthermore, he sent to Athens his son Alexander with his friend, Antipater, to conclude a peace treaty and an alliance with its people. [6] In the case of the Thebans, however, he set a price not only on the prisoners but even on the burial of their dead; [7] and the leading citizens of the community he either beheaded or sent into exile, confiscating the property of every one of them. [8] Next he repatriated those who had been unlawfully exiled, appointing 300 of their number as judges and governors over the city. [9] Before the latter all the most powerful citizens were arraigned on the very charge of having unlawfully driven them into exile, and these continued to be so unrelenting that they all declared themselves guilty, arguing that the interests of the state had been better served by the exile of these men than by their restoration. [10] This was truly amazing fortitude on their part: as far as they could, they were delivering a verdict on their judges who had the power of life and death over them; they had no concern for the acquittal which their

7. Philip's reaction as here portrayed contrasts markedly with Diod. 16.87 (though there Demades changes the king's demeanour) and Plut. *Dem.* 20.3.

enemies could award them; and since they could not gain revenge by action they preserved their freedom in their speech.

5 [1] After settling matters in Greece, Philip had delegates of all the cities summoned to Corinth to ratify the current state of affairs.[8] [2] There he laid down the conditions for peace for all Greece according to the merits of the individual states, and he selected from the entire gathering a common council, a single senate, as it were. [3] The Spartans alone snubbed the king and his terms, thinking that what was not agreed on by the cities but imposed by a conqueror was not peace but servitude. [4] Then a list was made of the auxiliary forces to be supplied by each state to assist the king in the event of his being attacked, or to conduct offensive war under his leadership. [5] Clearly, the objective of these preparations was the Persian empire. [6] The total of these auxiliary troops was 200,000 infantry and 15,000 cavalry, [7] in addition to which there were also the armies of Macedonia and the subject barbarian tribes on the borders. [8] At the onset of spring Philip sent ahead three generals into Persian territory in Asia: Parmenion, Amyntas and Attalus, [9] whose sister he had recently married after repudiating Olympias, the mother of Alexander, because he suspected her of adultery.[9]

6 [1] In the meantime, as the auxiliary troops from Greece were assembling, Philip celebrated the marriage of his daughter Cleopatra to the Alexander whom he had made king of Epirus.[10] [2] The day was remarkable for its sumptuous preparations which befitted the greatness of the two kings, the one giving away a daughter and the other taking a wife. [3] There were also splendid games. Philip was hurrying to see these, flanked by the two Alexanders, his son and his son-in-law, without bodyguards, [4] when Pausanias, a young Macedonian nobleman whom nobody suspected, took up a position in a narrow alleyway and cut Philip

8. On the agreement made at Corinth see also Dem. 17 and the inscription translated as Harding no. 99.

9. Diod. 16.91 does not include Amyntas. Philip had no need to divorce Olympias to marry another wife, who was Cleopatra, Attalus' *niece* (whom Arrian 3.6.5 calls Eurydice).

10. Alexander I of Epirus, Olympias' brother; cf. 8.6.4ff. On the problem of Philip's murder in 336 see the diametrically opposed views of R. Develin, "The Murder of Philip II," *Antichthon* 15 (1981), 86ff.; J. R. Ellis, "The Assassination of Philip II," in *Ancient Macedonian Studies in Honor of Charles F. Edson* (Thessaloniki 1981), 99ff.; also W. Heckel, "Philip and Olympias (337/6 B.C.)," in *Classical Contributions. Studies in Honour of M. F. McGregor* (Locust Valley, New York 1981), 51ff.

down as he went by, thus spoiling with the sorrow of a funeral a day intended for merriment. [5] In the early years of puberty Pausanias had been sexually abused by Attalus, and to that indignity had been added a further outrage: [6] Attalus had taken him to a banquet, made him drunk and subjected him not only to his own carnal desires but, like a prostitute, to those of his fellow-diners as well, so making the boy an object of universal ridicule amongst his peers. [7] Outraged by this treatment, Pausanias had frequently complained to Philip, only to be put off by various excuses, not without ridicule as well, while he could at the same time see his enemy honoured with the rank of general. He then directed his rage against Philip himself, and exacted from the unfair judge the vengeance he could not exact from his enemy.

7 [1] It was also believed that Pausanias had been suborned by Olympias, mother of Alexander, and that Alexander himself was not unaware of the plot to murder his father. [2] For Olympias was thought to have felt no less resentment over her repudiation and the fact that Cleopatra had been preferred to her than Pausanias felt over his sexual abuse. [3] As for Alexander, it was believed that he feared that a brother born to his stepmother would be a rival for the throne, and that this had occasioned his quarrelling at a banquet, first with Attalus and then with Philip himself, [4] so acrimoniously that Philip lunged at him with sword drawn and was only just prevailed upon not to kill his son by the entreaties of his friends. [5] That was why Alexander had gone with his mother to his uncle in Epirus, and after that to the kings of Illyria, [6] and he was with difficulty reconciled to his father, when Philip recalled him, and barely persuaded to return by the entreaties of his relatives. [7] Olympias was also trying to induce her brother Alexander, the king of Epirus, to go to war, and she would have succeeded if Philip had not forestalled him by giving him his daughter in marriage. [8] It is thought that Olympias and her son, goaded to wrath by these exasperations, incited Pausanias to proceed to so heinous a crime while he was making his complaints about the abuse going unpunished. [9] At all events, Olympias had horses ready for the assassin's getaway. [10] Afterwards, when she heard of the king's assassination, she came quickly to the funeral, ostensibly doing her duty; and on the night of her arrival she set a golden wreath on Pausanias' head while he still hung on the cross,[11] something which no

---

11. The crucifixion of Pausanias was either execution itself or his corpse was crucified, which would be in line with Diodorus' report that he was killed immediately after the murder.

one else but she could have done while Philip's son was still alive. [11] A few days later, she had the assassin's body taken down and cremated it over the remains of her husband; she then erected a tomb for him in the same place and, by inspiring superstition in the people, saw to it that funerary offerings were made to him every year. [12] After this she forced Cleopatra, for whom Philip had divorced her, to hang herself, having first murdered her daughter in the mother's arms; and it was with the sight of her rival hanging there that Olympias achieved the revenge to which she had hastened by murder. [13] Finally she consecrated to Apollo the sword with which the king was stabbed, doing so under the name Myrtale, which was the name that Olympias bore as a little girl.[12] [14] All this was done so openly that she appears to have been afraid that the crime might not be clearly demonstrated as her work.

8 [1] Philip died at the age of 47 after a reign of 25 years. [2] By a dancer from Larissa he had a son, Arridaeus, who was king after Alexander; [3] he also fathered many other children from the different wives which he had, as kings do. Some of these died of natural causes, others violently. [4] He was a king with more enthusiasm for the military than the convivial sphere; [5] in his view his greatest treasures were the tools of warfare. [6] He had a greater talent for acquiring wealth than keeping it, and thus despite his daily pillaging he was always short of funds. [7] His compassion and his duplicity were qualities which he prized equally, and no means of gaining a victory would he consider dishonourable. [8] He was charming and treacherous at the same time, the type to promise more in conversation than he would deliver, and whether the discussion was serious or lighthearted he was an artful performer. [9] He cultivated friendships with a view to expediency rather than from genuine feelings. His usual practice was to feign warm feelings when he hated someone, to sow discord between parties that were in agreement and then try to win the favour of both. [10] Besides this he was possessed of eloquence and a remarkable oratorical talent, full of subtlety and ingenuity, so that his elegant style was not lacking fluency, nor his fluency lacking stylistic elegance. [11] Philip was succeeded by his son Alexander, who surpassed his father both in good qualities and bad. [12] Each had his own method of gaining victory, Alexander making war openly and Philip using trickery; the latter took pleasure in duping the enemy, the

---

12. She was also known under two other names, Polyxena and Stratonice (Plut. *Mor.* 401a–b). The dedication of the sword also appears at Val. Max. 1.8. ext. 9, possibly derived from Trogus.

former in putting them to flight in the open. [13] Philip was the more prudent strategist, Alexander had the greater vision. [14] The father could hide, and sometimes even suppress, his anger; when Alexander's had flared up, his retaliation could be neither delayed nor kept in check. [15] Both were excessively fond of drink, but intoxication brought out different shortcomings. It was the father's habit to rush from the dinner-party straight at the enemy, engage him in combat and recklessly expose himself to danger; Alexander's violence was directed not against the enemy but against his own comrades. [16] As a result Philip was often brought back from his battles wounded while the other often left a dinner with his friends' blood on his hands.[13] [17] Philip was unwilling to share the royal power with his friends; Alexander wielded it over his. The father preferred to be loved, the son to be feared. [18] They had a comparable interest in literature. The father had greater shrewdness, the son was truer to his word. [19] Philip was more restrained in his language and discourse, Alexander in his actions. [20] When it came to showing mercy to the defeated, the son was temperamentally more amenable and more magnanimous. The father was more disposed to thrift, the son to extravagance. [21] With such qualities did the father lay the basis for a world-wide empire and the son bring to completion the glorious enterprise.

BOOK 10

1 [1] The Persian king Artaxerxes[1] had 115 sons by his concubines, but only three fathered within a legitimate marriage: Darius, Ariaratus and Ochus. [2] In the case of Darius, Artaxerxes broke with Persian custom, amongst whom there is a change of king only through death. Because of his tender feelings for Darius the father made him king during his own lifetime, [3] believing that nothing he bestowed on his son was lost to himself and anticipating a truer pleasure from being a father if he lived to see his son wearing the royal insignia. [4] Darius, however, after this extraordinary proof of paternal devotion, harboured the design of killing his father; [5] crime enough if he had plotted the parricide alone, but

13. Probably a rhetorical plural referring to the killing of Cleitus in 328 (below 12.6).
    1. Artaxerxes II Mnemon (405–359), whose biography was composed by Plutarch. Cf. Diod. 15.93.1 (the year 362/1).

greater yet because he enlisted fifty of his brothers as accomplices in the act, making parricides of them as well. [6] It is truly miraculous that, when so many were involved, a murder could not merely be undertaken as a cooperative effort, but also kept secret, that amongst fifty children not one should be found who could be kept from such a heinous crime by the father's dignity, or by respect for an old man or considerations of their father's fondness for them. [7] Can the word "father" have been held so cheap by such a multitude of sons? With such a retinue, Artaxerxes should have been well protected even from his foes; instead, surrounded by the treachery of his sons, he was in less danger from his enemies than from his own children.

2 [1] The motive for the prospective murder was more wicked than the plot itself. [2] After Cyrus was killed in the war between the two brothers, which was mentioned above,[2] King Artaxerxes had married Cyrus' mistress, Aspasia. [3] Darius had later demanded that his father cede her to him as he had ceded the crown, and with his characteristic indulgence towards his children Artaxerxes had initially agreed to do so. [4] Subsequently he had a change of heart and, so that he could with honour refuse what he had too hastily promised, he appointed Aspasia priestess of the sun, by which office she was perpetually forbidden sexual relations with all men. [5] This infuriated the young man, driving him into an outburst of quarrels with his father and then into the plot which he formed with his brothers. But he was caught, along with his accomplices, while he was preparing the coup against his father, and he paid the price of the intended murder to the gods who avenge disrespect for a father's dignity. [6] The wives and children of all the conspirators were also put to death, to eliminate every last trace of such a wicked crime. [7] After this Artaxerxes died of a sickness brought on by grief, a more successful king than he had been a father.

3 [1] The kingdom now passed to Ochus, who, fearing a similar conspiracy, filled the palace with his kinsmen's blood and with the slaughter of his most prominent citizens.[3] Nothing moved him to compassion: not family ties, not sex, not age—he clearly did not want

---

2. 5.11.1ff. On Aspasia see Xen. *Anab.* 1.10.2; Plut. *Artax.* 26.3ff.—at 27.3 she is priestess of Artemis [Anaitis] at Ecbatana.

3. Artaxerxes III Ochus (359–338). See Diod. 17.5.3ff. Ochus was poisoned and his youngest son Arses placed on the throne; he too was murdered, just before the death of Philip in 336. Darius III then eliminated the dual murderer Bagoas. Darius ruled until 330; see Books 11 and 12.

to be considered more ineffectual than his parricidal brothers. [2] After thus purifying his kingdom, as it were, he made war on the Cadusians. [3] In this campaign, one of the enemy issued a challenge to single combat and a certain Codomannus went forward to face him, cheered on by the whole army. The Persian dispatched his adversary and restored to his countrymen both the victory and their glorious reputation which they had almost lost. [4] For this noble feat Codomannus was made satrap of Armenia. [5] Then, some time later, King Ochus died, and because the memory of Codomannus' exploit of old still lived on he was appointed king by the people and given the name Darius so that his royal status would be complete. [6] He fought a protracted war against Alexander the Great with varying success and great courage but eventually he was defeated by Alexander and murdered by his own kinsmen, and with him died the empire of the Persians.

BOOK 11

1 [1] In Philip's army, reactions to his death varied with the different nationalities of which it was composed.[1] [2] Some renewed their hopes of liberty believing they were held in unjust servitude; [3] others, tired of service far from home, were happy to have been spared the expedition; [4] a number grieved that a torch lit for a daughter's marriage had been put to her father's funeral pyre. [5] The sudden turn of events had also caused the late king's friends[2] no little trepidation as their thoughts turned to Asia, which had been challenged to fight; then to Europe, which was still not totally subdued; [6] then to the Illyrians, the Thracians, the Dardanians and the other barbarian tribes of dubious loyalty and unstable character—a simultaneous uprising by all these peoples would be impossible to check.[3] [7] Alexander's arrival remedied the situation: [8] he addressed the entire host in an assembly, offering them such timely

---

The translation of Books 11 to 15 is published separately in the Clarendon Ancient History Series with a full commentary by Waldemar Heckel, which, with the author's permission, I have plundered for these more modest notes, and to which I direct the interested reader's attention. For the period to 301 see *A History of Macedonia* vol. III (Oxford 1988), Part One (by N. G. L. Hammond).

1. For Philip's death see 9.6f.

2. This probably has a technical reference. The prominent nobles of the king's entourage were known as "hetairoi," "companions."

3. There are many modern works on Alexander, and the major parallel narratives are Diod. 17, Curtius Rufus and Arrian, to which we can add Plutarch's biography. The question of Trogus' immediate source is a vexed one.

consolation and encouragement as to eliminate the anxiety of the fearful and inspire hope in them all. [9] He was twenty years old, at which age he demonstrated great promise, but he did so with such restraint that he seemed to have still more in reserve than was then apparent. [10] He exempted the Macedonians from all obligations except military service, and this won him the unanimous support of the people, so much so that they said they had exchanged their king's identity, not his merits.

2 [1] His primary concern was for his father's funeral, at which his first instruction was that all involved in the assassination be put to death at tomb of his father.[4] [2] The only person he spared was Alexander of Lyncestis, the brother of the assassins,[5] for he wished to preserve in that man's person the good omen for his reign, since it was the Lyncestian who had first saluted him as king. [3] He also arranged the murder of his half-brother, Caranus, son of his stepmother, who was his rival for the throne. [4] Alexander's early achievements included the suppression of many insurgent nations and the snuffing out of a number of incipient rebellions. [5] Encouraged by these successes he swiftly marched into Greece, where, following his father's example, he summoned the city-states to Corinth and was appointed successor to Philip as their commander in chief. [6] Then he applied himself to the Persian war which his father had begun. [7] While he was busy with preparations for this, he was brought word that the Athenians and Spartans[6] had defected from him and gone over to the Persians, and that the man responsible for their defection was the orator Demosthenes, whom the Persians had bribed with a large quantity of gold. [8] Demosthenes, he was told, claimed that all the Macedonian forces, together with their king, had been wiped out by the Triballians, and had brought into the meeting a witness to testify that he had personally received a wound in the battle in which the king was killed. [9] Believing this, nearly all the city-states had undergone a change of heart, and now the Macedonian garrisons were under siege. [10] To

4. For what this might mean and individuals involved see the works cited in the note to 9.6. Alexander of Lyncestis was Antipater's son-in-law and was executed for treason in 329 after being kept in chains for 3 years (see 11.7.1 and 12.14.1). Caranus is widely held to be a fiction.

5. Justin here reflects claims other than that Pausanias had been a lone assassin; see the works referred to in the note to 9.6 above. The text, however, is difficult and the presence of "assassins" is due to conjecture.

6. The Spartans in fact had not joined the alliance nor did they take action until later. Perhaps the Thebans belong here. For Demosthenes and Athens see *AO* 364f., 373ff. (the years 336/5 and 335/4).

meet these uprisings head-on, Alexander raised and equipped an army and overran Greece with such speed that the Greeks, unaware of his approach, could scarcely believe their eyes.

3 [1] On his way he had offered encouragement to the Thessalians and reminded them of the services rendered to them by his father Philip and of his kinship with them on his mother's side because of her descent from the Aeacids.[7] [2] The Thessalians had listened eagerly to all this and, like his father before him, Alexander had been appointed supreme commander of their entire people, all their taxes and revenues being made over to him. [3] As for the Athenians, just as they had been first to defect, so they were also the first to regret their action. [4] Their disdain for their adversary turned to admiration, and the youth of Alexander, which had previously earned their contempt, they now extolled as superior to the heroism of the leaders of old. [5] Accordingly they sent ambassadors with an appeal for peace, and after giving them an audience and a stern reprimand Alexander ceased hostilities with Athens.

[6] Next he directed the army towards Thebes, intending to show the same mercy if he met with similar contrition. [7] But the Thebans resorted to arms rather than entreaties or appeals, and so after their defeat they were subjected to all the terrible punishments associated with a humiliating capitulation. [8] When the destruction of the city was being discussed in council, the Phocians, the Plataeans, the Thespians and the Orchomenians, Alexander's allies who now shared his victory, recalled the devastation of their own cities and the ruthlessness of the Thebans, [9] reproaching them also with their past as well as their present support of Persia against the independence of Greece.[8] [10] This, they said, had made Thebes an abomination to all the Greek peoples, which was obvious from the fact that the Greeks had one and all taken a solemn oath to destroy the city once the Persians were defeated. [11] They also added the myths of earlier Theban wickedness—the material with which they had filled all their plays—in order to foment hatred against them not only for their treachery in the present but also for their infamies in the past.

---

7. The Molossian royal house, of which Olympias was a member, claimed descent from Neoptolemus, son of Achilles, and Achilles came from Phthia, probably Pharsalus in Thessaly.

8. Most recently Plataea, Thespiae and Orchomenus had been destroyed by Thebes in the 370s and 360s. Thebes had gone over to the Persians in 481 and in the aftermath the city was threatened (Her. 9.86ff.).

4 [1] Then one of the captives, Cleadas, was given permission to speak.[9] The Thebans had not defected from the king, he said—for they had been told he was dead—but from the king's heirs. [2] Whatever wrong they had done must be blamed on their gullibility, not disloyalty, and for this they had already paid a heavy price with the loss of their young warriors. [3] All that was left to them now was an enfeebled and harmless population of old men and women, who had themselves been subjected to violence and outrage more bitter than anything they had ever experienced. [4] Their entreaties, he continued, were no longer for their fellow-citizens, of whom so few remained, but for the harmless soil of their fatherland and for a city which had given birth not only to men but to gods as well. [5] Cleadas even appealed to the king's personal devotion to Hercules, who was born in their city and from whom the clan of the Aeacidae traced its descent, and to the fact that his father Philip had spent his boyhood in Thebes.[10] [6] He asked Alexander to spare a city which worshipped his ancestors born within it as gods and which had also witnessed the upbringing of the most eminent of kings. [7] But anger prevailed over entreaties. The city was destroyed, its lands divided among the victors, [8] and the prisoners were auctioned off, their price being pushed up not by the bidders' desire to make a bargain, but by the intensity of the hatred for an enemy. [9] The Athenians found the whole affair heart-rending and, in contravention of an edict issued by the king, threw open their gates to the refugees. [10] This so incensed Alexander that, when the Athenians sent a second embassy to beg him to refrain from military action, he let the envoys depart only on the condition that the Athenians surrender to him their orators and generals, confidence in whom so often induced them to rebel.[11] [11] Since the Athenians were ready to go to war rather than be forced into this, the matter was resolved by their keeping their orators, but sending their generals into exile. [12] The latter immediately went over to Darius and provided a considerable addition to Persian strength.

5 [1] As he was setting off for the war in Persia, Alexander put to death all those of his stepmother's relatives whom Philip had promoted to high office and awarded military commands; [2] nor did he spare any of his own family who appeared likely candidates for the throne—he did not

9. This character appears in no other source and may have been invented for the purpose of the speech (by Cleitarchus?).

10. Hercules (Heracles) was the mythical ancestor of the Macedonian royal house, which was in fact the Argeadae. Alexander's emulation of Hercules is constantly attested. For Philip in Thebes see above 7.5.1ff.

11. Cf. *AO* 373ff. (the year 335/4).

want any basis for unrest left behind in Macedonia while he was involved in operations far away.[12] [3] He also took along with him to fight at his side any of the tribute-paying kings of more than ordinary ability, leaving the less energetic ones to safeguard the kingdom. [4] He then brought his troops together and embarked them on ships. The sight of Asia prompted him to unimaginable elation, and he erected twelve altars to the gods as votive offerings for a successful campaign. [5] All his ancestral domains in Macedonia and Europe he distributed amongst his friends, declaring that Asia was enough for him; [6] and before any of the ships left shore he sacrificed animals, asking the gods for victory in a war in which he had been chosen to avenge the numerous Persian assaults on Greece. [7] The empire of the Persians, he said, had lasted long enough and was ready for the taking—it was time they were replaced by others who would do better. [8] Nor were the army's expectations any different from the king's: [9] forgetting wives and children and the realities of a campaign far from home, they were all already thinking of Persian gold and the riches of the entire East virtually as their personal plunder, and it was not war and its dangers that they had in mind but treasure. [10] On reaching the mainland Alexander first hurled his spear into the soil which was his enemy, and leapt fully armed from the ship like a man performing a dance. [11] He then offered up sacrificial victims, praying that those lands be not unwilling to accept him as their king. [12] He also conducted sacrifices at Troy, before the tombs of the heroes who had died in the Trojan war.

6 [1] From there Alexander proceeded against the enemy. He barred his men from pillaging Asia, telling them they should spare their own property and not destroy the things which they had come to possess. [2] In his force were 32,000 infantry, 4,500 cavalry and 182 ships. [3] With so small an armament it is debatable which is more amazing: that he conquered the whole world or that he dared make the attack in the first place. [4] When he was levying troops for this hazardous campaign, rather than take sturdy young men or those in the first flower of youth he selected instead veterans, some already past military age, men who had fought alongside his father and his uncles. [5] One might have thought he had chosen not soldiers but men to teach soldiering! [6] Moreover, no

---

12. "His stepmother's relatives" in fact refers only to Cleopatra's uncle Attalus. Other than Amyntas son of Perdiccas, it is hard to imagine any potential rivals for the throne. The kings mentioned are the Thracian prince Sitalces and Ariston of Paeonia.

company commander was less than sixty years old;[13] hence a glance at the headquarters of the camp would have suggested that here was the senate of some republic of bygone times. [7] And so, in battle, no one thought of flight, only victory, and no one placed his hopes in fleetness of foot rather than the strength of his arm.

[8] For his part, the Persian king, Darius, had such confidence in his strength that he refused to employ subterfuge—a strategy based on deception, he told his men, would mean a victory gained by cheating— [9] and so far from repelling the enemy from his borders he allowed Alexander to advance into the heart of his empire, thinking there was more honour in throwing back an invader than in blocking his entry. [10] The first encounter took place in the plains of Adrasteia.[14] [11] In the Persian line there were 600,000 men, but they turned and fled, defeated as much by Alexander's tactics as by the valour of the Macedonians. There were heavy casualties on the Persian side, [12] while in Alexander's army nine infantrymen fell and 120 cavalry. [13] These the king buried at great expense to console the others, awarding them equestrian statues and granting their relatives immunity from taxation. [14] After the victory most of Asia went over to him. [15] Alexander also fought a number of battles with subordinates of Darius,[15] who were defeated more by the panic inspired by his name than actual force of arms.

7 [1] In the meantime Alexander was brought news, based on information from a prisoner, that a plot was being engineered against him by Alexander the Lyncestian, son-in-law of Antipater (who had been left in charge of Macedonia), [2] and so he had him imprisoned, fearing rebellion in Macedonia if he had him put to death.[16] [3] He then made for the city of Gordium, situated between Greater and Lesser Phrygia. [4] He was seized by an urge to take this city, not so much for its spoils as because he had heard that the yoke of Gordius was lodged there in the temple of Jupiter, and that ancient oracles had foretold dominion over all of Asia for any man who succeeded in untying its knot.

[5] Why and how this came about is as follows. Gordius was ploughing in these regions with hired oxen when birds of all kinds began to flutter around him. [6] He went to consult the soothsayers in a neighbouring

13. A clear exaggeration. Of the generals only Parmenion (born around 400) is demonstrably over 60.

14. This is the battle at the Granicus river in 334. Numbers are, as often, variable, but in Latin 600,000 can mean "countless thousands."

15. Notably at Miletus and Halicarnassus.

16. See above II.2.I.

city and at the city gate he met a young woman of extraordinary beauty of whom he enquired which soothsayer he would be best advised to consult. [7] The woman knew the art of prophecy, which she had been taught by her parents; on hearing the reason for his consultation she replied that he was destined to hold royal power, and she offered to marry him and share his prospects. [8] Such a fine match struck him as being the start of the good fortune that should attend his rule. [9] After the wedding civil discord arose among the Phrygians, [10] and when they consulted the oracles about terminating the conflict, the reply they received was that to do this they needed a king. [11] When they questioned the oracle a second time on the identity of the king, they were instructed to return and accept as their king the first person they found coming in a wagon to the temple of Jupiter. [12] The person they met was Gordius, and they immediately hailed him as king. [13] Gordius lodged in the temple of Jupiter the wagon in which he had been riding when the throne was conferred on him, consecrating it to the majesty of kings. [14] He was succeeded by his son Midas, who, after receiving religious initiation from Orpheus, filled Phrygia with religious cults, and this, throughout his life, protected him more effectively than could an armed guard.

[15] Alexander took the city and, entering the temple of Jupiter, asked where the wagon yoke was to be found. [16] It was pointed out to him but he was unable to find the ends of the thongs, since they were hidden within the knots and so, interpreting the oracle in a somewhat forceful manner, he slashed through the thongs with his sword, thus undoing the knots and finding the ends hidden within them.

8 [1] While he was thus occupied, Alexander was told that Darius was approaching with a huge army [2] and so, apprehensive of the restricted terrain, he swiftly crossed the Taurus mountains, covering, in his haste, five hundred stades in a single day's march.[17] [3] Arriving in Tarsus he was so taken by the beauty of the River Cydnus, which flows through the centre of the town, that he threw down his arms and, covered as he was with dust and sweat, hurled himself into its icy waters. [4] Suddenly his muscles stiffened, to such an extent that he could not speak, and no way of arresting the malady could be found, much less the hope of a cure.[18] [5] One doctor alone, by the name of Philip, promised a cure, but he was

17. Roughly 50–60 miles, 80–100 kilometres.
18. The disease may have been malaria, or possibly pneumonia. Only Justin has Parmenion in Cappadocia at this time.

under suspicion because of a letter of Parmenion sent from Cappadocia on the previous day. [6] Unaware of Alexander's illness, Parmenion had written to tell him to be on his guard against Philip, who, he claimed, had been suborned by Darius with a large bribe. [7] Nevertheless, Alexander decided that trusting a doctor of questionable loyalty was safer than facing certain death from the illness, [8] so he took the cup, handed the letter to the doctor and, as he drank, gazed intently at the man's face while he read. [9] When he saw Philip unperturbed, his spirits rose and he recovered three days later.

9 [1] Darius meanwhile advanced to offer battle with 400,000 infantry and 100,000 cavalry.[19] [2] The enemy numbers disturbed Alexander when he considered the smallness of his own; but he also reflected on what brilliant victories he had won with that same small force and what powerful nations he had defeated. [3] Hope began to overcome his anxiety and, thinking it riskier to postpone the fight and thereby allow despondency to grow amongst his men, he rode round his troops addressing remarks tailored to each nationality among them. [4] The Illyrians and Thracians he inspired by bidding them consider the wealth and opulence of the enemy; the Greeks, by reminding them of past wars and of their deadly hatred for the Persians. [5] To the Macedonians he mentioned Europe, which they had already conquered, and Asia, their present objective; and he boasted that no soldiers had been found to rival them throughout the world. [6] This fight, he added, would mark both the end of their hardships and the crowning of their glory. [7] While he was doing this he would frequently tell the line to halt, intending by such pauses to accustom the men to bear the sight of the enemy hordes. [8] Darius, for his part, did not remain idle, but set his battleline in order; as though to usurp his generals' responsibilities, he went the rounds in person, encouraging individual soldiers, and reminding them all of the ancient glories of the Persians and of the divine providence that had bestowed perpetual dominion upon them.

[9] After this the battle began, a furious one in which both kings were wounded, and the outcome remained in doubt until the moment when Darius took flight. [10] What followed was a slaughter of the Persians: 61,000 Persian infantry and 10,000 cavalry fell, and 40,000 prisoners were taken. Of the Macedonians 130 infantrymen were lost and 150 cavalrymen. [11] In the Persian camp large quantities of gold and other treasures were found, [12] and among the prisoners taken in the camp

19. The battle of Issus in November 333.

were the mother of Darius, his wife (who was also his sister) and his two daughters. [13] Alexander came to pay them a visit and give them some encouragement, but at the sight of his armed escort the women embraced each other, believing their death imminent, and let out sorrowful cries. [14] Then, throwing themselves before Alexander's feet, they begged not for their lives but only for a stay of execution until they could bury Darius' body. [15] Moved by such loyalty on the women's part, Alexander informed them that Darius was still alive, dispelled their fear of execution and gave orders that they be treated and addressed as queens. [16] He also told the daughters to expect marriages not unbefitting their father's rank.

10 [1] When, after this, Alexander looked upon the treasures and extravagant riches of Darius, he was overcome with awe at such splendour.[20] [2] It was now that he first started to hold sumptuous banquets and splendid dinners; now, too, that he began to fall in love with the prisoner Barsine because of her beauty [3] (by her he later had a son whom he named Hercules). [4] He was well aware, however, that Darius was still alive, and so he dispatched Parmenion to surprise the Persian fleet and others of his friends to take the cities of Asia. [5] These cities immediately fell into the hands of the conquerors when word of the victory was received, Darius' governors actually surrendering themselves along with a large quantity of gold. [6] Alexander then set out for Syria, where he met many of the eastern kings, who came to him wearing the fillets of suppliants.[21] [7] He accepted a number of them as allies, according to the deserts of each, while others he deprived of their thrones, replacing them with new rulers. [8] Particularly notable was Abdalonymus, who was made king of Sidon by Alexander.[22] [9] Alexander had made him a king although previously he had eked out a miserable existence as a hired labourer drawing water and irrigating gardens; candidates from the nobility were passed over so that men would not think the appointment due to birth rather than the benefaction of the giver.

[10] The city of Tyre had sent Alexander a deputation with a heavy crown of gold in a show of congratulation. He accepted it with gratitude, then said he wished to go to Tyre to discharge his vows to Hercules. [11] The ambassadors, trying to deny him entry, replied that it would

20. These treasures were in fact taken later at Damascus, along with Barsine.
21. In antiquity, the wearing of a fillet around the head was a common symbol for people thus craving favour.
22. Around the turn of 333/332.

be more appropriate for him to do this in Old Tyre, which furthermore had a temple of greater antiquity. Alexander was so infuriated that he threatened to destroy the city.[23] [12] He immediately brought his troops up to the island, but faced armed resistance from the Tyrians, their spirits raised by their confidence in Carthaginian support. [13] Tyrian resolve was strengthened by the example of Dido, who had founded Carthage and gone on to conquer a third of the world.[24] They thought it humiliating if their womenfolk had shown more courage in acquiring an empire than they themselves did in safeguarding their independence. [14] They therefore evacuated all who were not of age for fighting to Carthage, whence they called for assistance; but not long afterwards they were captured through treachery.

11 [1] After that Alexander took Rhodes, Egypt and Cilicia without a fight, [2] and then proceeded to the temple of Jupiter Hammon to consult the god about future events and about his own birth. [3] For his mother, Olympias, had confessed to her husband, Philip, that it was not by him that she had conceived Alexander but by a huge serpent. [4] Moreover, shortly before his death, Philip had publicly declared that Alexander was not his son, [5] and had for that reason repudiated Olympias as guilty of adultery.[25] [6] So it was that, wishing both to claim divine birth and also to clear his mother of infamy, Alexander sent men ahead to bribe the priests to give the responses he wanted.[26] [7] When he entered the temple, the priests immediately hailed him as the son of Hammon [8] and he, delighted at his divine adoption, ordered that he be henceforth regarded as the god's son. [9] Alexander then asked whether he had punished all his father's assassins. The reply was that his father could not be assassinated and could not die, but that King Philip had been fully avenged. [10] In answer to his third question he was informed that he was being granted victory in all his wars and possession of the whole world. [11] His companions were also told by the oracle to venerate Alexander as a god rather than a king. [12] This all served to increase the king's vanity and swell his pride to a startling degree, eliminating the geniality which he had acquired from Greek literature and Macedonian upbringing. [13] On his return from the temple of Hammon, he founded

23. The siege of Tyre lasted seven months into July or August 332.
24. See 18.4f., where the lady is called Elissa.
25. See above 9.5.9. For the serpent see Plut. *Alex.* 2.6, 3.1f.
26. Justin is the only extant source to contain the imputation of bribery.

Alexandria and gave orders that the Macedonian colony be the capital of Egypt.[27]

12 [1] After fleeing to Babylonia, Darius entreated Alexander by letter to grant him leave to ransom his female prisoners, offering him a large amount of money. [2] As the price of these prisoners, however, Alexander demanded not money but all Darius' kingdom. [3] Some time later, further letters from Darius reached Alexander, offering him marriage to Darius' daughter and a portion of the kingdom. [4] Alexander, however, wrote back that he was being offered what was already his, and he told Darius to come to him as a suppliant and leave to the victor all decisions about the empire. [5] At this, with all hope of a peace treaty lost, Darius prepared for a renewal of hostilities, and marched to meet Alexander with 400,000 infantry and 100,000 cavalry. [6] While on the march, he was brought news that his wife had died after a miscarriage, that Alexander had shed tears over her death and given her a generous funeral, and that he had done this not from physical attraction for her but out of human compassion. [7] For, the report continued, Alexander had set eyes on her only once, whereas he frequently went to console Darius' mother and young daughters. [8] At this point Darius realized he was truly beaten: first the battles, and now to be outdone by his enemy even in acts of benevolence! But it was comforting, he thought, to lose to such a man if winning proved impossible. [9] He therefore wrote a third letter thanking Alexander for not behaving as an enemy towards his family, [10] and he went on to offer him the greater part of his empire short of the Euphrates river, as well as the hand of one of his two daughters, and 30,000 talents in addition, for the rest of the prisoners. [11] To this Alexander replied that thanks from an enemy were worthless; [12] he had done nothing with the object of flattering his enemy or of seeking lenient terms of peace when the outcome of the war was uncertain, [13] but rather he was acting out of magnanimity, which had taught him to fight against his enemy's strengths, not his misfortunes. [14] He promised to grant what Darius wished, if he was willing to be considered second to Alexander and not his equal. [15] The universe could not be guided by two suns, he said, nor could the countries of the world safely have two supreme rulers. [16] Therefore, Darius must prepare to surrender on

27. The foundation of Alexandria probably equates with April 7, 331 (R. Bagnall, "The Date of the Foundation of Alexandria," *American Journal of Ancient History* 4 [1979], 46ff.), but it did not become capital of Egypt until 320 or 312 at the instigation of Ptolemy.

this day or to do battle on the next; and he should promise himself no more victory beyond what he had already enjoyed.

13 [1] The following day they led out their armies for combat.[28] Then, just before the engagement, Alexander, exhausted from worry, fell asleep. [2] Since the battle lacked only the king, he was awakened, with difficulty, by Parmenion. When everyone asked him how he could sleep when beset by danger, especially when he always went with little sleep when not on active service, Alexander replied that he had been freed from a deep uneasiness, [3] and that his sudden release from anxiety had permitted him to sleep; he could now come to grips with all Darius' troops together—he would have feared a protracted campaign if the Persians had divided their forces. [4] Before the battle began, the two armies afforded each other a diverting spectacle. [5] The Macedonians marvelled at the Persian numbers, their stature and the beauty of their weapons; the Persians were astonished that so many thousands of their soldiers had been vanquished by so few. [6] Their commanders meanwhile were constantly making the rounds of the men, [7] Darius claiming that a reckoning would reveal barely one enemy for every ten Armenians,[29] [8] and Alexander warning his Macedonians not to be overawed by the enemy's numbers, size or strange colour. [9] He told them to bear in mind only that this was their third battle with the same enemy; they were not to suppose that flight had made the Persians into better soldiers since they bore with them into battle the depressing memory of the crushing defeats they had suffered and all the blood spilled in the two previous engagements; [10] and while Darius had the greater numbers, Alexander had more real men. [11] He urged them to show contempt for this army agleam with gold and silver, which represented for them booty rather than a threat—for victory was to be won not by ostentatious equipment but by prowess with the sword.

14 [1] Then the battle got under way. With disdain for an enemy they had defeated so often, the Macedonians threw themselves into the fray; on the other side the Persians preferred death to defeat. [2] Rarely in any battle has so much blood been shed. [3] When Darius witnessed his men going down in defeat he himself wished to die, but he was constrained by his entourage to make his escape. [4] Then several of

---

28. The battle of Gaugamela in October 331.
29. "Armenians" translates the text, but their presence here is inexplicable except by error. Professor A. MacGregor suggests the reading "Achaemenians."

them urged him to have the bridge over the river Cydnus severed to block the enemy advance, but Darius declared that he was opposed to having such provision made for his own security as would throw so many thousands of his comrades on the enemy's mercy—others should also have access to the same means of escape as he.

[5] Alexander meanwhile was engaging himself wherever danger was greatest, and ever plunging himself into those areas where he saw the enemy densest and the fighting keenest—he wanted himself rather than his men to take the risks. [6] It was with this engagement that he seized control of Asia in the fifth year after his accession to the throne, [7] and his triumph was so complete that none dared rebel thereafter, while the Persians, after so many years of dominion, submissively accepted the yoke of enslavement. [8] The men were rewarded and granted thirty-four days' rest, after which Alexander made an inventory of the spoils and [9] discovered a further 40,000 talents in the city of Susa. [10] He also captured the Persian capital, Persepolis, a city which had enjoyed many years of renown and which was filled with spoils from all over the world, though these only came to light after its fall. [11] It was at this time that Alexander encountered some 800 Greeks who had been mutilated and kept in captivity. They asked him to avenge them—as he had avenged Greece—for the barbarous treatment they had received from the enemy. [12] Given the opportunity of returning home, they chose rather to accept a land grant, for they feared that instead of bringing joy to their relatives they might cause revulsion by their appearance.

15 [1] Meanwhile, in the Parthian village of Thara,[30] Darius was bound in fetters and chains of gold by his own kinsmen, who wished to conciliate the victor. [2] It was, I suppose, the decision of the immortal gods that the Persian Empire should come to an end in the land of those destined to succeed to it![31] [3] Moving at a rapid pace, Alexander arrived there the following day, only to discover that Darius had been removed at night in a covered carriage. [4] Accordingly, he told the main body to follow behind and pressed on after the fugitive with 6,000 cavalry, fighting many hazardous battles on the way. [5] After covering many miles and finding no trace of Darius, he gave the horses a breathing space, and it was then that one of his men, making for a nearby spring, came upon Darius in his carriage. The king had been stabbed several times but was still breathing.

30. The name is another detail found only in Justin.
31. Namely the Parthians; see Book 41.

[6] A captive was brought and from his speech Darius recognized him to be a fellow-countryman. Darius said that this at least brought him some consolation in his present misfortune since he would now be talking to someone who would understand him, and not uttering his final words in vain. [7] He then ordered that the following message be taken to Alexander: that though he had done the Macedonian no favours, he now died indebted to him for the greatest services, since in the case of his mother and children he had found Alexander's character to be that of a king rather than an enemy, and that he had been luckier in the enemy whom fate had allotted him than he had been in his relatives and kinsmen. [8] For, Darius explained, his wife and children had been granted their lives by that enemy, whereas he himself had now been deprived of his by his relatives, men to whom he had granted both their lives and their provinces. [9] And for this act they would now receive the recompense which Alexander as victor decided to give them. [10] To Alexander he said he was showing his gratitude in the only manner a dying man could, by his prayers to the gods above and below, and to the patron deities of royalty, that he achieve the conquest and dominion of the whole world. [11] For himself he was asking a favour that was just and easily granted—burial. [12] As for revenge, the reason for exacting it was no longer just Darius; now it was a question of precedent and the common cause of all kings—and for Alexander to ignore this would be dishonourable as well as dangerous, since it was a matter both of his sense of justice, on the one hand, and expediency, on the other. [13] To which end he was giving the soldier his right hand, as the supreme guarantee of the kingly trust that he was to take to Alexander. He then stretched out his hand and died.[32] [14] This was reported to Alexander and when he saw the body he wept at the thought of Darius' succumbing to a death so unworthy of his exalted position. [15] He ordered that the body be given a royal burial and his remains laid in the tombs of his ancestors.

32. July 330.

BOOK 12

1 [1] Alexander went to great expense to bury the men whom he had lost in the pursuit of Darius, and he distributed 13,000 talents amongst those who remained from the campaign. [2] Most of the horses were lost because of the heat, and even those which survived were disabled. [3] Alexander's entire treasure, which amounted to 190,000 talents, was deposited at Ecbatana in the charge of Parmenion. [1]

[4] In the meantime, the king received dispatches from Antipater in Macedonia containing news of the war against the Spartan king Agis in Greece, of the war fought by Alexander, king of Epirus, in Italy, and also of the campaign of his governor Zopyrion in Scythia.[2] [5] The tidings inspired mixed emotions in him, but his elation on learning of the deaths of his two royal rivals outweighed his distress at the loss of the army with Zopyrion. [6] For after Alexander's departure virtually the whole of Greece had rushed to arms to seize the opportunity to recover its independence, [7] following the lead of the Spartans, who had been alone in repudiating the peace of Philip and Alexander and in rejecting their conditions. The leader of this campaign was Agis, king of Sparta. [8] Antipater concentrated his forces and put down the insurrection right at its outbreak, [9] though there were heavy casualties on both sides. [10] When King Agis saw his forces take to their heels, he discharged his bodyguard—to show himself second to Alexander only in luck, not in courage—and wrought such havoc amongst his enemies that, at times, he drove back whole companies of men. [11] He was finally overcome by their superior numbers, but in glory he defeated them all.

2 [1] Alexander, king of Epirus, had been invited into Italy when the people of Tarentum petitioned his aid against the Bruttii.[3] He had embarked on the expedition enthusiastically, as though a partition of the world had been made, the East being allotted to Alexander, son of his sister Olympias, and the West to himself, [2] and believing he would have

---

1. Parmenion remained at Ecbatana as Alexander journeyed east.

2. For Alexander of Epirus, uncle of Alexander the Great, see below 2.1, for Zopyrion, 2.16f. On Agis' movement there is an additional contemporary source in Aesch. 3.165. The Spartans had not joined the Greek alliance (cf. 11.2.7n.). Agis was in fact supported by most of the Peloponnesians, but Thebes had been destroyed and the Athenians held back.

3. See Livy 8.24, where Alexander is said to have died in the same year as the foundation of Alexandria, which is 331/0, not Livy's 326.

no less scope to prove himself in Italy, Africa and Sicily than Alexander was going to have in Asia and Persia. [3] There was a further consideration. Just as the Delphic Oracle had forewarned Alexander the Great of a plot against him in Macedonia,[4] so an oracular response from Jupiter at Dodona had warned this Alexander against the city of Pandosia and the Acherusian River; and since both were in Epirus [4]—and he was unaware that identically named places existed in Italy—he had been all the more eager to opt for a campaign abroad, in order to avoid the perils of destiny. [5] On his arrival in Italy, he first went to war with the Apulians, [6] but when he discovered what was prophesied for their city, he lost no time in concluding a peace-treaty and an alliance with their king. [7] In that period, Brundisium was a city belonging to the Apulians, though it had been founded by the Aetolians, followers of Diomedes, the leader who had won great fame and renown for his exploits at Troy. [8] The Aetolians, however, had been driven out by the Apulians. Subsequently, consulting the oracles, the Aetolians had received a response that the people who reclaimed the territory would possess it forever, [9] and for that reason they had sent ambassadors to demand, with threats of military force, that the city be restored to them by the Apulians. [10] The oracle, however, was made known to the Apulians, who then murdered the ambassadors and buried them in the city so that these would for ever have a place there. Thus fulfilling the oracle, the Apulians had now enjoyed a long occupation of the city, [11] and when Alexander became aware of this, he renounced his war with them out of respect for the prophecies of old. [12] He commenced hostilities with both the Bruttii and the Lucanians, capturing many of their cities, and he concluded treaties and alliances with the Metapontines, the Poediculi and the Romans. [13] The Bruttii and the Lucanians, however, gathered auxiliary forces from their neighbours and resumed their war with increased fervour. [14] During this campaign the king was killed in the vicinity of Pandosia and the River Acheron. He did not discover the name of the fateful region until he fell, and only when he was dying did he realize that the death which had led him to flee his native land had not threatened him there after all. [15] The people of Thurii ransomed and buried his body at public expense.

[16] It was while this was going on in Italy that Zopyrion, who had been left as governor of Pontus by Alexander the Great, also gathered an army of 30,000 and launched a campaign against the Scythians, for he thought himself indolent if he took no action on his own initiative. [17] He

---

4. Neither the oracle nor the plot is known from elsewhere.

was wiped out with all his forces and paid the price for an impulsive attack on an unoffending people.[5]

3 [1] News of all this was brought to Alexander in Parthia. He affected sorrow because of his kinship with Alexander of Epirus and prescribed for the army a three-day period of mourning. [2] After this all his soldiers were expecting to return home, for they believed that the war was over,[6] and they were already embracing in their imagination their wives and children. At this point Alexander summoned the army to an assembly. [3] He told them that their illustrious battles meant nothing while the barbarians of the East remained secure, that it was not Darius' life but his kingdom that had been his objective and that they should hunt down the men who had rebelled against Darius' rule. [4] Inspiring anew the hearts of his men with this speech, he went on to subjugate Hyrcania and the Mardians. [5] It was here that he encountered Thalestris, or Minythyia, the queen of the Amazons.[7] Accompanied by three hundred women, she had travelled thirty-five days through thickly populated[8] terrain in order to have a child by the king. [6] Her appearance and the purpose of her coming aroused general surprise: she was strangely dressed for a woman and she came seeking sexual intercourse. [7] The king paused for thirteen days for this purpose and Thalestris left when she thought she had conceived.

[8] After this Alexander assumed the dress of the kings of Persia and a diadem, something former Macedonian kings had never worn— submitting as it were to the rules of those whom he had defeated. [9] In order to avoid excessive animosity, if he were seen to be alone in adopting such garb, he also instructed his friends to wear long gold and purple robes. [10] To copy the Persians in their excesses as well as their dress, he divided his nights among the troops of royal concubines, women of superlative beauty and noble birth. [11] To all this he added enormous, sumptuous banquets—so as to remove any trace of parsimony or meagreness from his extravagance—and he embellished his dinner-parties

5. Cf. 2.3.4; 37.3.2. Zopyrion was general in Thrace.
6. On the ground that the aims of the crusade against Persia seemed to have been achieved.
7. See 2.4.33; 42.3.7.
8. This translates the received text "inter confertissimas gentes." Supposing a better sense could be gained, Goodyear, *Proceedings of the African Classical Associations* 16 [1982], 10 strongly advocated the old emendation "infestissimas," thus having the journey proceed "through most hostile peoples."

with games in keeping with royal splendour. [12] He had forgotten that great power is lost, not won, by such conduct.

4 [1] Meanwhile there was general resentment throughout the camp that Alexander had so far fallen away from his father Philip's example as to disown the glory of his fatherland and adopt the habits of the Persians—on whom those very habits had brought defeat at his hands! [2] But lest he appear alone in succumbing to the vices of the people he had conquered in battle, he also allowed his soldiers to marry any of the captive women with whom they were cohabiting, [3] for he thought they would be less eager to return home if they had in the camp some semblance of a home and domestic setting. [4] He also believed that the rigours of the campaign would make the pleasures of wedlock all the more agreeable. [5] Moreover, to keep the troops up to strength, he thought there would be less of a drain on Macedon if his veterans could be replaced by their sons, who as young recruits would serve on the ramparts on which they had been born, [6] and these would be all the more steadfast for having spent not just their training but even their infancy right in the camp.[9] [7] This practice in fact persisted even in the time of the successors of Alexander. [8] Accordingly, as boys they received a statutory allowance of food and as young men they were equipped with arms and horses, while their fathers were recompensed according to the number of children they had. [9] Orphans still continued to draw the pay of fathers who died in battle, and their boyhood years were spent in the field on various campaigns. [10] Thus, toughened by hardship and danger from a tender age, they constituted an unbeatable army: for them the camp was home and every battle victory. [11] These children bore the title "The Descendants."[10] [12] Alexander then conquered the Parthians, and a Persian nobleman, Andragoras, was appointed their governor; it was from him that the Parthian kings of later times were descended.[11]

---

9. Reinforcements had from time to time come from Macedon; see A. B. Bosworth, "Alexander the Great and the Decline of Macedon," *Journal of Hellenic Studies* 106 (1986), 1ff.

10. This term, "Epigoni," is properly applied to the 30,000 young men of native extraction whom Alexander ordered to be recruited before he left Bactria for India (Curtius 8.5.1), but who did not join him until he returned to Susa in 324. These "Descendants" could only have been at most five or six years old at Alexander's death!

11. There is evident confusion here. Arrian 3.25.7 suggests the name was Arsaces. There was a Seleucid satrap named Andragoras, who was defeated by the Arsaces who was founder of the Parthian kingdom (see 41.4.6ff.).

5 [1] Alexander began in the meantime to terrorize his men with an animosity characteristic of an enemy, not of one's own king. [2] He was particularly incensed at being criticized in their gossip for having repudiated the ways of his father, Philip, and of his country. [3] It was such charges that led to the execution of the elderly Parmenion, whose authority was second only to that of the king, along with his son, Philotas, after both had been subjected to torture.[12] [4] This aroused general rancour throughout the camp, the men being moved to pity for the fate of the innocent old man and his son, and sometimes saying that they should expect no better themselves. [5] When this was reported to Alexander, he was afraid that such talk might permeate even to Macedonia and his glorious victory be sullied by the stigma of ruthlessness. He therefore pretended that he was going to send home a number of his friends to report their victory, [6] and urged the men to write to their families, since the opportunities to do so would diminish as the campaign became more remote. [7] He then secretly confiscated the packets of letters that were handed in, [8] from which he was able to ascertain what each man thought of him. He concentrated in a single company those who had been somewhat critical of the king, intending either to wipe them out or to plant them among the colonies he founded in far-off lands.

[9] Next Alexander conquered the Drancae, the Euergetae or †Arimaspi†,[13] the Parapamesadae and the other tribes living in the foothills of the Caucasus, [10] and during this time one of Darius' friends, Bessus, was brought to him in chains. Bessus had not only betrayed his king but had actually murdered him; [11] and so, to make him pay for his treason, Alexander surrendered him to Darius' brother for torture. He felt that Darius had been less his enemy than the "friend" by whom the king had been assassinated. [12] To leave his name in these lands he founded the city of Alexandria on the river Tanais,[14] completing its wall, which measured six miles, in 17 days, and transferring to it the populations of three towns which Cyrus had founded.[15] [13] He also founded twelve

12. Philotas had not passed on information brought to him of a plot in late 330; now in 329 he was condemned and executed and his father murdered (though not tortured, as his son had been).
13. This is an addition to the text in a form commonly found (see Her. 4.13.1), though it belongs better to a Scythian tribe and the correct form is probably "Ariaspi" (so Arrian 3.27.4).
14. The Jaxartes.
15. That is, Cyrus the Great in the sixth century.

cities in Bactria and Sogdiana, dispersing amongst them those members of his army whom he regarded as malcontents.

6 [1] This done, he invited his friends to a banquet on a feast day.[16] [2] Here, the topic of Philip's achievements arose in their drunken conversation, and Alexander began to set himself above his father and to praise his own magnificent exploits to the skies, with the acquiescence of most of the guests. [3] One of the senior men, Clitus, confident of his position in the first rank of the king's friends, began to defend Philip's memory and to praise his achievements, which so annoyed the king that he grabbed a spear from a guard and murdered Clitus at the table. [4] Revelling in the bloodshed he proceeded to taunt the dead Clitus with his vindication of Philip and his eulogy of the latter's military ability. [5] Then, sated with blood, his temper abated and anger gave way to reflection. He considered who it was he had killed and his motive for the killing, and now he began to repent his action, [6] sorry that praise of his father had roused him to a pitch of anger that insults would not have merited and that he had killed an elderly and innocent friend in a setting of feasting and drinking. [7] As violently shaken by remorse as he was earlier by anger, he decided to die. [8] First, bursting into tears, he put his arms around the dead man, touched his wounds and, as if Clitus could hear, admitted to him that he had been out of his mind. Then he seized a weapon, turned it on himself and would have carried out the deed but for the intervention of his friends. [9] His longing for death persisted even throughout the days that followed. [10] For his regret was intensified as he remembered his own nurse, who was Clitus' sister;[17] even in her absence it was she who aroused in him the deepest shame [11] as he reflected on how despicably she had been recompensed for nursing him—after spending his infancy in her arms Alexander was now, a man and victorious, repaying her with death instead of kindness. [12] Then he considered how much idle rumour and animosity he had created in his own army as well as among the conquered nations, how much fear and resentment of himself amongst his other friends, [13] and into what a bitter tragedy he had turned his own banquet—making himself as terrifying a figure at banquet as when he stood armed in battle. [14] His thoughts

16. Versions of this incident differ in detail. Clitus had been an important commander, but at this time, autumn 328, was chosen to succeed to the satrapy of Bactria (Curtius 8.1.19).

17. Arrian (4.9.3) calls her Lanice, Curtius (8.1.21) Hellanice. A great deal is made of such details by E. D. Carney, "The Death of Clitus," *Greek, Roman, and Byzantine Studies* 22 (1981), 149ff.

then turned to Parmenion and Philotas, to his cousin Amyntas, to his murdered stepmother and brothers, to Attalus, Eurylochus, Pausanias and the other Macedonian chieftains he had eliminated.[18] [15] Because of this, he went without food for four days, until he was won over by the entreaties of the troops, who as one begged him not to let his grief for a single man's death destroy them all; [16] for, they said, after leading them to the furthest frontier of barbarian territory he would be abandoning them amongst hostile tribes now stirred to war. [17] The entreaties of the philosopher Callisthenes proved especially effective; he was on intimate terms with Alexander because they had both been pupils of Aristotle, and he had also been invited by the king to be the author of the latter's chronicles.[19] [18] So he turned his attention back to the campaign, and accepted the surrender of the Chorasmi and the Dahae.

7 [1] Next came a piece of vanity characteristic of Persian royalty, the adoption of which Alexander had postponed for fear of provoking undue animosity by changing everything at once: he ordered people to do obeisance before him instead of saluting him.[20] [2] The most outspoken of the objectors was Callisthenes, and this spelled death for him and many prominent Macedonians, who were all executed, ostensibly for treason. [3] Even so the Macedonians retained the conventional method of saluting their king and obeisance was rejected.

[4] Alexander now made for India, intending to establish the Ocean and the furthest limits of the Orient as the boundaries of his empire. [5] To match his army's equipment to the glory of its enterprise, he had the horses' trappings and the men's arms overlaid with silver, and he called the army "the Argyraspids," after their silver shields.[21] [6] On his arrival at the city of Nysa, the townspeople offered no resistance,

---

18. The figures from Parmenion to Attalus have been mentioned earlier. Eurylochus was the one who revealed to Alexander the conspiracy of the pages, which came later, so there is confusion of some sort here. Pausanias seems to be the assassin of Philip and the others could be the Lyncestians, including Alexander of Lyncestis (cf. 11.2.1, 7.1).

19. Callisthenes of Olynthus is also said to have been a nephew of Aristotle,

20. This normal Persian practice, called "proskynesis" in Greek, did not imply the divinity of the Persian king to his subjects; but for Greeks and Macedonians it was an honour reserved for immortals. The consequences for Callisthenes and others, including the royal pages who conspired, are told in greater (and not wholly consistent) detail in other accounts.

21. The Argyraspids, "Silvershields," were not the entire army, but a special unit of some sort, their exact nature being a matter of debate.

trusting in the local cult of Father Liber,[22] by whom the city had been founded; Alexander ordered them spared, pleased not only that he had emulated the god's campaign but had even followed in his footsteps. [7] Then he took the army to see the holy mountain, which was as luxuriantly covered with a natural growth of vine and ivy as if it had been cultivated and attentively tended by gardeners. [8] But his troops, on reaching the mountain, in a sudden frenzy proceeded to rush off crying the holy cry of the god to the consternation of the king—but without sustaining any harm. So it was that the king came to understand that sparing the townspeople had been more in his own army's interest than theirs. [9] From there he headed for the Daedalian mountains and the realm of Queen Cleophis. She surrendered to Alexander but subsequently regained her throne, which she ransomed by sleeping with him, attaining by sexual favours what she could not by force of arms. [10] The child fathered by the king she named Alexander,[23] and he later rose to sovereignty over the Indians. [11] Because she had thus degraded herself Queen Cleophis was from that time called the "royal whore" by the Indians. [12] After traversing India Alexander now reached a rocky eminence which was extremely high and precipitous, on which many tribes had sought refuge; and he was told that Hercules had been prevented from capturing this by an earthquake. [13] So it was that, overcome by an urge to better Hercules' exploits, he braved extreme hardship and peril to take the height, finally accepting the surrender of all the local tribes.[24]

8 [1] One of the Indian kings, who was called Porus, was a man equally remarkable for his physical strength and for greatness of spirit. [2] He had heard of Alexander's reputation and had long been preparing for war in anticipation of his arrival.[25] [3] When battle was joined, Porus ordered his troops to attack the Macedonians but insisted on having the king for himself as his own personal enemy. [4] Alexander did not hang

22. Dionysus, hence the identification of the city as Dionysopolis. The holy mountain was called Meros or Meron. Dionysus is another figure whom Alexander consciously imitated.

23. Curtius 8.10.36 attests to the son, but neither he nor any other author asserts Alexander's paternity. Trogus' readers may have been reminded of Cleopatra, who bore a son to Caesar and is called "whore queen" by Propertius 3.11.39 and Pliny *NH* 9.119.

24. The height was called Aornus ("Birdless"). For emulation of Hercules see 11.4.5.

25. This is the battle at the Hydaspes river in 326.

back from the fight; but at the first clash his horse was wounded and the king was thrown to the ground, to be saved only when attendants rushed to his aid. [5] Porus, overwhelmed by many wounds, was captured; [6] but he was so distressed at his defeat that, when spared by his enemy, he refused to take food or have his wounds looked after, and was only with difficulty prevailed upon to remain alive. [7] As a mark of respect for his courage, Alexander restored him safe and sound to his kingdom. [8] In this area he founded two cities, calling one Nicaea and the other Bucephala, after his horse. [9] He then defeated the Adrestae, the Catheani, the Praesidae, and the Gangaridae, annihilating their armies.[26] [10] Arriving in the kingdom of Sophites, he found 200,000 enemy infantry and 20,000 cavalry waiting for him. At this point, the whole army, exhausted as much from the number of its victories as the hardships endured, tearfully pleaded with him [11] to bring the wars to an end and at long last give some thought to returning home, taking into account the age of his men, [12] who barely had enough years of life left to get back.[27] They showed him their grey hair, or their wounds, or their bodies decrepit with age or covered with old scars, [13] declaring that they were unique in having borne uninterrupted service under two kings, Philip and Alexander. [14] All they asked for, they said, was that he finally take back their remains to the tombs of their fathers; it was not fighting spirit they lacked but youth, [15] and if he would not spare his men he should at least spare himself, to avoid overtaxing his good fortune. [16] Moved by their reasonable entreaties, and as though to crown his victorious campaign, he had the camp made on a grander scale than usual, hoping the proportions of its construction would intimidate his enemies and make him an object of wonder for posterity. [17] There was no task that the men attacked with more enthusiasm. And so, after annihilating the enemy, they returned joyfully to the camp.

9 [1] From there Alexander proceeded to the river Acesines and sailed down it to the Ocean, [2] where he accepted the surrender of the Agensonae and the Sibi, whose founder was Hercules.[28] [3] From here he sailed to the Mandri and Sudracae, tribes which faced him with an armament of 80,000 infantry and 60,000 cavalry. [4] He defeated them

26. There are problems of identification and chronology. The readings "Catheani" here and "Sophites" in the next sentence appear by emendation.
27. This is the mutiny at the Hyphasis river.
28. In fact, the army came first to the Acesines and thence to the Hydaspes to meet a fleet, late in 326. The readings "Agensonae" and "Sudracae" are emendations. The "Mandri" are the Mallians.

in the field and then led his army to their city. [5] The first to scale its wall, he observed that the city was without defenders and so, without a single bodyguard, he leapt down to the ground within. [6] When the enemy saw him thus isolated, they raised a shout and rushed at him from all sides in the hope of terminating with the life of a single man a world-wide war, and of avenging so many nations. [7] Nevertheless, Alexander resolutely defended himself and single-handedly engaged several thousand men. [8] Incredibly, he was not terrified by the enemy numbers, by their dense shower of missiles or the loud cries of his attackers; on his own he cut down or drove back many thousands. [9] When, however, he saw that he was being overwhelmed by their numbers, he pressed himself against the trunk of a tree which at that time stood close to the wall [10] and, using this to protect himself, long kept the horde at bay until, learning of his perilous situation, his friends leapt down to join him, many of them being killed by the enemy. [11] The battle long remained undecided until the wall was breached and the entire army could come to their comrades' aid. [12] In that engagement, Alexander was struck by an arrow beneath the breast. Weakened from loss of blood, he dropped to one knee and continued fighting until he killed the man who had wounded him. [13] The treatment was riskier than the wound.

10 [1] When, after great fear for his life, Alexander was finally restored to health, he dispatched Polyperchon to Babylonia with the army while he himself and a select body of men boarded some ships and followed the coastline of the Ocean.[29] [2] He then came to the city of King Ambus, whose inhabitants, hearing that he could not be vanquished by the sword, dipped their arrows in poison and, thus inflicting wounds that were doubly lethal, repulsed the enemy from their walls, killing large numbers of them. [3] Among the many casualties was Ptolemy, who time and again seemed on the point of death. Then the king was shown in a dream a herb that would serve as an antidote to the poison, and when Ptolemy took this in a drink, he was immediately delivered from danger. Most of the troops were saved by this antidote. [4] Alexander then took the city by storm, returned to his ship and offered sacrifices to the Ocean, praying for a safe return home. [5] And now his chariot had, as it were, passed the turning-point: he had established boundaries for his empire as

29. Craterus was the major figure sent, though Polyperchon (the correct Greek spelling) may well have gone with him. Carmania would be the precise destination, but Justin is vague. At this point Alexander had not reached the coast, but was following the Indus. The king next mentioned is otherwise called Sambus. The story about Ptolemy is held to be fiction.

far as the deserts would permit one to advance on land and as far as the sea could be navigated—and so he came sailing on a favorable tide into the estuary of the river Indus. [6] There, to commemorate his exploits, he founded the city of Barce,[30] set up altars and left one of his friends as governor of the coastline of India. [7] Then, on the point of starting the land journey, he was told of the deserts along his way, and he ordered wells to be dug at convenient points; copious quantities of sweet water were found which enabled him to return to Babylonia.[31] [8] There many of the subject nations brought before him charges against their governors, and Alexander had the latter put to death in the presence of the ambassadors, disregarding any ties of friendship he had with them. [9] After this he married Darius' daughter, Statira; [10] at the same time he presented to the Macedonian noblemen unmarried girls selected from the best families amongst all the conquered peoples, so that any recrimination against the king might be lessened through their complicity in his action.

11 [1] Alexander then summoned the troops to an assembly and promised to discharge all their debts at his own expense, so that they could take home intact their booty and prizes.[32] [2] This generosity was remarkable not only because of the large sum involved but also because it was given as a gift; and the creditors were as grateful as those in debt, since collecting was as difficult for the former as payment for the latter. [3] Twenty thousand talents were expended to this end. [4] Alexander then discharged his veterans and made up their numbers with younger men; [5] but those who were retained resented the fact that the veterans were leaving and demanded demobilization for themselves too, insisting that their years of service be counted rather than their ages and observing that it was only fair that those recruited together be released together. [6] Matters had by this time gone beyond entreaties to actual insults; the men bade him go to war on his own, along with his "father" Hammon, since he had no respect for his soldiers. [7] For his part Alexander now rebuked the men, now proffered gentle advice against tarnishing a glorious campaign with mutiny; [8] finally, since words were of no avail, he leapt down from the dais, unarmed, into the armed assembly to arrest the ringleaders of the mutiny and, meeting no opposition, seized thirteen of them with his own hands and led them off for execution. [9] So far

---

30. Otherwise unknown. The governor was Peithon son of Agenor.
31. Gross misrepresentation of the hellish trek through the Gedrosian desert. Again, Carmania is the actual arrival point (see above n. 29). The marriages took place at Susa, which Alexander reached in spring 324.
32. These events took place at Opis in the summer of 324.

did dread of their king make them willing to accept their death; so far did military discipline strengthen Alexander's resolve to carry out the execution.

12 [1] Then, in a separate meeting, he addressed the Persian auxiliaries. [2] He praised them for their unfailing loyalty both to himself and their former kings, and reminded them of his acts of kindness towards them: how he had never regarded them as a defeated enemy but as partners in his victory; how he had adopted their modes of conduct and not imposed his own on them; how by the bonds of marriage he had brought conquered and conqueror together. [3] Furthermore, he said, from now on he would entrust his personal protection to them as well as to the Macedonians. [4] And so he selected a thousand young men from their number to join his bodyguard and incorporated in his army a group of auxiliaries who had received Macedonian training. [5] This was resented by the Macedonians, who complained that the king had transferred their duties to their enemies, [6] and they all came in tears to the king and begged him to vent his displeasure by punishing rather than humiliating them. [7] By this moderate request they prevailed upon him to discharge 11,000 veterans. [8] A number of his friends who were at an advanced age were also released: Polyperchon, Clitus, Gorgias, Polydamas and Antigenes. [9] Craterus was put at the head of those who were discharged, with instructions to succeed Antipater as governor of Macedon, and Alexander summoned Antipater, with a force of new recruits, to take Craterus' place. [10] Those now discharged received their pay as if they were still on active service.

[11] At this time one of his personal friends died—Hephaestion, a favourite of Alexander's because of his good looks and boyish charms as well as his absolute devotion to the king. [12] Disregarding kingly decorum, Alexander spent a long time mourning him, built him a tomb at a cost of 12,000 talents and ordered that he be worshipped posthumously as a god.[33]

13 [1] While he was on his way back to Babylonia from the remote shores of the Ocean, Alexander was brought word that his arrival in Babylonia was awaited by embassies from Carthage and the other African states, and also by embassies from Spain, Sicily, Gaul and Sardinia, as well as a few from Italy. [2] So far had the terror of his name pervaded the whole world that all nations were ready to fawn upon him as though he were destined

---

33. Hephaestion, Alexander's closest friend, died at Ecbatana in October 324. Strictly speaking he was worshipped as a hero, not a god, with his shrine in Egypt.

to be their king. [3] For this reason he was making all haste to Babylonia to preside over what seemed to be a world-wide assembly. Then one of his Magi forewarned him against entering the city of Babylon, declaring the place was destined to be fatal for him.[34] [4] Alexander therefore passed by Babylon and withdrew across the Euphrates to the long-deserted city of Borsipa. [5] There he was prevailed upon by the philosopher Anaxarchus to disregard the predictions of the Magi as false and unreliable: what was subject to fate was beyond the knowledge of mortals, and what was due to nature could not be changed. [6] He therefore turned back towards Babylon, where he gave the army several days' rest; and during this time he resumed his old practice, now long discontinued, of the ceremonial banquet. [7] Abandoning himself completely to revelry, he spent a day and a night without sleep. As he was leaving the dinner, the Thessalian Medius decided to renew the festivities and invited Alexander and his companions to join him. [8] Alexander took a cup, but had not yet drunk more than half of it when he suddenly uttered a groan as if he had been pierced by a spear [9] and was carried half conscious from the banquet. He was racked with such agony that he asked for a sword to put an end to it, and the pain on being touched was like that of a wound. [10] His friends put it about that the cause of his illness was excessive drinking, but in fact it was a conspiracy, though the scandal was suppressed by the power of the successors.[35]

14 [1] The instigator of the conspiracy was Antipater. He could see that his closest friends had been put to death by Alexander; that his son-in-law, Alexander the Lyncestian, had been killed by him;[36] [2] that his own great achievements in Greece had earned him the king's envy rather than appreciation; [3] and that he had also been the object of various accusations made by Alexander's mother, Olympias. [4] Then there were the cruel executions, a few days before, of the governors of the conquered nations. [5] On the basis of all this Antipater thought he had been summoned from Macedonia not to join the campaign but to face punishment. [6] So, to anticipate the king's move, he suborned his own son Cassander, who, along with his brothers Philip and Iollas, used to wait upon the king. He gave Cassander a poison, [7] the virulence of which was such that it could not be contained by bronze, iron or earthenware; it

34. The Magi were the Median priestly class; in other accounts they are Chaldaean astrologers. Borsipa was not deserted until much later.
35. A very confident assertion of something which is (and was) at least debatable.
36. See 11.7.1.

could be transported only in a horse's hoof. He forewarned his son to trust no one but his brothers and the Thessalian. [8] This was why the drinking-party was arranged and restarted in the Thessalian's quarters. [9] Philip and Iollas, who used to taste and add the water to the king's drinks, put the poison in cold water and added this to his cup after they had performed the tasting.

15 [1] After three days Alexander felt that his death was certain and he declared that he could recognize the fate that had overtaken the house of his forefathers, for most of the Aeacids were dead by their thirtieth year.[37] [2] Then the soldiers became restless, suspecting that their king was dying because of treachery; but Alexander himself placated them. He had himself carried to the highest spot in the city, where he let them all come to see him and, as they wept, held out his hand for them to kiss. [3] They were all in tears, but Alexander, so far from weeping, gave not the slightest indication of being in low spirits—he actually comforted some who could not control their grief and gave others messages for their parents. [4] He was as undaunted in the face of death as he had been in the face of the enemy.

[5] When the men were dismissed, he asked his friends at his bedside if they thought they would find a king like him again. [6] All were silent; then Alexander himself added that, while he did not know the answer to that question, he did know something else, which he could predict and almost see with his own eyes, namely how much blood Macedonia would shed in this struggle, how much slaughter and gore she would sacrifice to his ghost. [7] Finally he gave instructions that his body be buried in the temple of Hammon. [8] When his friends saw that he was sinking, they asked him whom he appointed as heir to his throne, to which he replied "the most deserving man." [9] Such was his greatness of spirit that although he was leaving a son, Hercules, a brother, Arridaeus, and a wife, Roxane, who was pregnant, he gave no thought to family ties and named as his heir the most deserving man.[38] [10] He implied it was wrong for a brave man to be replaced by anyone but a brave man, or for the power of a great kingdom to be left to any but those of proven worth. [11] It was as if by these words he had given the signal for war amongst his

37. Alexander was in fact almost 33 when he died in June 323; see below 16.1.
38. For Hercules see 13.2.7. Roxane, daughter of the Sogdian Oxyartes, had married Alexander in 327. Her child would be Alexander IV, a pawn not a ruler, even though his mother did away with her rival Statira soon after Alexander's death.

friends, or thrown amongst them the apple of Discord.[39] They all rose to compete with each other, and canvassing the mob sought in secret the favour of the troops. [12] On the sixth day Alexander's voice failed. He removed his ring and handed it to Perdiccas, a gesture which quelled the growing dissension amongst his friends. [13] For even though Perdiccas had not been verbally designated heir by Alexander, it seemed that he was the chosen one in the king's judgment.

16 [1] Alexander died in the month of June at the age of thirty-three. He was a man endowed with superhuman greatness of spirit. [2] On the night of his conception, his mother Olympias dreamed that she was entwined with a huge serpent, and the dream did not mislead her, for what she bore in her womb was certainly more than mortal.[40]

[3] Her renown derived from her descent from the Aeacids, a family dating back to earliest times, and from the fact that her father, her brother, her husband and all her ancestors had been kings; but not one of their names conferred greater distinction on her than her son's. [4] A number of prodigies foretelling his greatness appeared at the moment of his birth. [5] On the day on which he was born two eagles perched all day long on the roof of his father's house, predicting the double empire of Europe and Asia. [6] On the same day his father received word of two victories, one in the Illyrian war, the other in a race at Olympia for which he had entered four-horse chariots, and this was an omen that foretold victory over the whole world for the infant. [7] As a boy Alexander was a very enthusiastic student of literature, [8] and when his boyhood was over he had five years of instruction under Aristotle, the most renowned philosopher in the world. [9] Then, succeeding to the throne, he gave orders that he be called the king of all lands and of the world, [10] and he inspired such confidence in his men that, if he were present, they would fear the army of no enemy, even if they themselves were unarmed. [11] So it was that he did battle with no adversary without defeating him, besieged no city without taking it, and attacked no tribe without crushing it entirely. [12] In the end he was brought down not by the valour of an enemy, but by a plot hatched by his own men and the treachery of his fellow countrymen.

---

39. The golden apple thrown into the banquet celebrating the marriage of Peleus and Thetis that ultimately brought about the Trojan War.
40. See 11.11.3.

BOOK 13

1 [1] When Alexander died, in the prime of his life and in the full flush of victory, there was a dismal silence throughout Babylon.[1] [2] The conquered nations, however, did not credit the report because they believed him immortal as well as invincible. [3] For they remembered how often he had been snatched from the jaws of death, how often when he was thought lost he had suddenly appeared before his men, not only safe and sound but victorious. [4] When confirmation of his death arrived, all the barbarian tribes which had recently been conquered by him grieved for him not as an enemy but as a father. [5] Furthermore, although the loss of her son had brought the disgrace of captivity after a station of such grandeur, the mother of Darius had not until that day felt tired of life, but on hearing of Alexander's death she committed suicide, [6] not because she preferred an enemy to her son but because she had felt the affection of a son in a man she had once feared as an enemy. [7] The Macedonians, on the other hand, were for their part delighted: it was not a fellow-countryman they had lost or a glorious sovereign, but an enemy, and they cursed his excessive severity and the endless risks they had run in battle. [8] Furthermore, the officers had their eyes on the empire and positions of authority, the rank and file on Alexander's war chest and its great hoards of gold, an unexpected prize. The former dreamed of accession to the throne, the latter of a legacy of wealth and riches; [9] for there were 50,000 talents in the treasury, and tribute generated 30,000 a year. [10] But Alexander's friends were justified in having their eyes set on the throne since their qualities and the respect they enjoyed were such that one might have taken each one of them for a king, [11] all of them possessing handsome features, a fine physique and great powers of body and mind alike—so much so that a stranger would have supposed that they had been selected not from one people only but from all the world. [12] For never before that time did Macedonia, or indeed any other nation, produce so rich a crop of brilliant men, [13] men who had been picked out with such care, first by Philip and then by Alexander, that

---

1. The major narrative source for the successors of Alexander is Diodorus, from Book 18 onwards, generally thought to depend upon Hieronymus of Cardia (as probably did Trogus) along with Duris of Samos. Arrian also wrote of the successors, and there are Plutarch's biographies of Eumenes and Demetrius (which parallel Justin to the end of Book 14). See in general N. G. L. Hammond in *A History of Macedonia* vol. III (Oxford 1988), 95ff.

they seemed chosen less as comrades in arms than as successors to the throne. [14] Little wonder then that the world was conquered by officers of this mettle, when the Macedonian army was under the direction of so many men who were kings rather than generals. [15] Such men would never have met their match had they not clashed amongst themselves, and the province of Macedonia would have produced many Alexanders if Fortune had not armed them to destroy each other by making them equals in merit.

2 [1] But Alexander's death, while bringing them joy, did not also bring them security: they were all contenders for a single position, [2] and they were no less afraid of the common soldiers than they were of each other, since the indiscipline of the troops was greater and their sympathies unpredictable. [3] The equality among the officers actually served to increase their discord since none was so preeminent that anyone else would submit to him.

[4] Thus they assembled under arms at the royal tent to resolve the present difficulties. [5] Perdiccas proposed that they await the birth of the child of Roxane, who was then eight months pregnant by Alexander; if her child were a boy, he should be made his father's heir.[2] [6] Meleager declared that they should not delay their decision through doubt as to what would be born; they should not await the birth of kings when they could have recourse to some already born. [7] If they wanted a boy, there was at Pergamum a son of Alexander by Barsine, Hercules by name; [8] if they preferred a young man, they had in the camp Alexander's brother, Arridaeus, an affable fellow and a very acceptable choice for all, not only in his own right but also on account of his father Philip. [9] Roxane, he added, was of Persian descent, and it was not right to appoint kings for the Macedonians from the bloodline of those whose kingdoms they had crushed. [10] Not even Alexander himself had wanted that, he said, and in fact he had on his deathbed made no mention of the child. [11] Ptolemy rejected Arridaeus' claim to the throne, not only because of his low birth on his mother's side—he was purportedly the son of a prostitute from Larissa—but also because of the serious disability from which he suffered, which might mean a regent holding the real power while Arridaeus was king in name only. [12] Better, he said, to choose from those who stood close to their late king in personal qualities, who were the governors

2. On Roxane and her child (Alexander IV) and Hercules see 12.15.9. Arridaeus (below), considered to be feebleminded, was about 34 years old; his mother was no whore (see below), but Philina of the Aleuadae of Larissa in Thessaly.

of provinces, who were entrusted with military campaigns—rather that than be subjected to the domination of unworthy men while the king had but nominal power. [13] It was Perdiccas' proposal that won the day, with unanimous approval, [14] and it was decided that they should await the birth of Roxane's child. In the event of male issue, they appointed as guardians of the child Leonatus, Perdiccas, Craterus and Antipater, and immediately took an oath of allegiance to them.

3 [1] The cavalry followed the same course but the infantry were furious at being left no say in the matter, so they declared Alexander's brother Arridaeus king, appointed guards for him from amongst their own number and issued orders that he be addressed by his father's name, Philip. [2] When this was reported to the cavalry, they sent two of their officers, Attalus and Meleager, as envoys to soothe the infantry's feelings; but, seeking to gain power by courting the mob, these abandoned their mission and threw in their lot with the soldiers. [3] The mutiny immediately gained momentum, since it now had leadership and a plan of action. [4] They all took up arms and burst into the royal tent with the purpose of wiping out the cavalry, [5] the news of which sent the latter in panic from the city. They pitched camp and proceeded in their turn to intimidate the infantry.

[6] Meanwhile the mutual animosities of the generals did not abate. [7] Attalus sent men to murder Perdiccas, the leader of the other party, [8] but since he was armed and even challenged the assassins to fight, they did not dare confront him. So fearless was Perdiccas that he even went to the infantry, summoned them to a meeting and informed them what manner of crime they were about to commit. [9] He told them to bear in mind against whom they had taken up arms; to remember it was not against Persians but Macedonians, not their enemies but their countrymen, most of them even their blood relatives and certainly their comrades in arms, men who had shared with them the same camp, the same dangers. [10] A fine sight they would provide for their foes, he said, their internecine slaughter giving joy to those who were smarting from military defeat at their hands, and their own blood making atonement to the spirits of the enemies they had killed.

4 [1] After presenting these arguments with his unique eloquence, Perdiccas so impressed the infantry that his advice was accepted and he was unanimously elected their leader. [2] Then a reconciliation was effected with the cavalry, who agreed on the choice of Arridaeus as king, [3] with a part of the empire held in reserve for a son of Alexander, should one be born. [4] These arrangements they made with the body of Alexander set in their midst so that its majesty would witness their decisions.

[5] With the matter of the succession settled, next Antipater was made governor of Macedonia and Greece, Craterus was given charge of the royal treasury, and Meleager and Perdiccas were to look after the camp, the army and its affairs.[3] [6] King Arridaeus was instructed to escort Alexander's body to the temple of Hammon.[4] [7] After this Perdiccas, furious at those responsible for the mutiny, announced suddenly, and without consulting his colleague, that because of the king's death there would be a ceremonial purification of the camp the following day. [8] He drew up the troops under arms upon an open plain and, to the general approval of the men, called out from individual companies, as he passed along the lines, those involved in the mutiny, secretly relaying orders for their execution. [9] On his return, he distributed provinces among the officers with the twofold aim of disposing of rivals and also making such awards of power seem like personal favours on his part.[5] [10] First of all, Egypt and part of Africa and Arabia were allotted to Ptolemy, whom Alexander had promoted from the ranks for his personal qualities; [11] to administer the province Ptolemy was also assigned Cleomenes, the man who had built Alexandria, as his adjutant. [12] The province adjacent to this, Syria, was given to Laomedon of Mitylene, and Cilicia to Philotas. [13] Pithon the Illyrian was made governor of Greater Media and Perdiccas' father-in-law, Atropatos, of Lesser Media. [14] The people of Susiana were assigned to Coenus, Greater Phrygia to Antigonus, son of Philip. [15] Nearchus was allotted Lycia and Pamphylia, Cassander Caria and Menander Lydia. [16] Lesser Phrygia fell to Leonatus, Lysimachus was given Thrace and the coastline of Pontus, and Eumenes Cappadocia and Paphlagonia. [17] To Seleucus, son of Antiochus, fell supreme command of the camp, [18] and Cassander, son of Antipater, was put in charge of the royal entourage and guards. [19] In Further Bactria and the various parts of India the former governors were retained, [20] and

3. This was hardly an effective arrangement. Craterus was in fact made guardian of Arridaeus' kingdom, Perdiccas remained chiliarch, a vague "first man after the king," Meleager being his right-hand man. The King Arridaeus next mentioned is a different man, later satrap of Hellespontine Phrygia. The words "its affairs" here translates the Latin "rerum" of the manuscripts. Seel, however, prints Madvig's "regum," "kings"; the post of supervisor is attested elsewhere, but at this point there was only one king to be concerned with.

4. Perdiccas intended Alexander's body to go for traditional burial at Aegae in Macedon, but it ended up in Alexandria after the machinations of Ptolemy.

5. Justin does not provide the best guide through this maze; cf. Diod. 18.3.

Taxiles took control of the Seres[6] between the Hydaspes and Indus rivers. [21] Pithon, son of Agenor, was sent out to the colonies established in India; Oxyartes was granted the Parapameni in the furthest part of the Caucasus; [22] Sibyrtius was given the Arachosians and Cedrosians; Stasanor the Drancae and Arei. [23] Amyntas was allotted the Bactrians, †Soleus Staganor† the Sogdians, Philip the Parthians, Phrataphernes the Hyrcanians, Tleptolemus the Carmanians, Peucestes the Persians, Archon of Pella the Babylonians, and Arcesilaus Mesopotamia. [24] For each general the allocation was virtually a gift from heaven, but for a large number of them it also provided an excellent opportunity to expand their domains; [25] for shortly afterwards, as though they had been apportioning kingdoms rather than provinces, they became kings instead of governors, not simply acquiring great power for themselves but even bequeathing it to their descendants.[7]

5 [1] While these things were going on in the East, in Greece the Athenians and the Aetolians were devoting all their energies to the war which they had started when Alexander was still alive.[8] [2] What had prompted the hostilities was a letter written by Alexander on his return from India which restored those exiled from all the cities with the exception of condemned murderers. [3] The letter was read out at the Olympic festival, at which all of Greece was gathered, and caused a great uproar [4] because large numbers of the exiles had been expelled not by due process of law but by political factions made up of prominent citizens who now feared that the exiles, if recalled, would gain greater political power than the authorities themselves. [5] As a result, many cities angrily and openly proclaimed at the time that they would assert their independence by military means, [6] but foremost among them were the Athenians and Aetolians. [7] When news of this was brought to Alexander, he had given instructions for 1,000 warships to be levied from the allies to conduct the war in the West and he had intended making an expedition with a powerful force to destroy Athens. [8] The Athenians accordingly raised a force of 30,000 men and 200 ships and now opened hostilities against Antipater, who had received Greece in the allocation. Antipater, however, refused to meet them in battle, and instead took

6. This term usually indicates the Chinese, but that is clearly not so here.

7. Of course, a great deal of shifting and rearrangement occurred first and the power which became kingship devolved on only a few.

8. The Lamian War, put down in 322. Alexander's letter had been read at the Olympic games of 324. Additional sources are Plut. *Phocion* 23ff.; Plut. *Demosthenes* 27ff.; *AO* 406ff. (the years 323/2 and 321/0).

shelter behind the walls of the city of Heraclea, to which the Athenians laid siege. [9] Now, at this time, the Athenian orator Demosthenes happened to be in exile in Megara, banished from his homeland on a charge of accepting a bribe from Harpagus[9]—who had fled from Alexander's brutal reprisals—to urge his city to make war on Alexander. [10] Learning that Hyperides had been sent by the Athenians on a mission to induce the Peloponnese to join their uprising, Demosthenes went with him and used his oratory to win over Sicyon, Argos, Corinth and other cities to the Athenian cause. [11] In return for this, a ship was sent by the Athenians to meet him and he was recalled from exile. [12] However, while Antipater was still besieged, the Athenian leader Leosthenes was killed by a weapon hurled at him from the city walls as he was passing by, [13] and this so raised Antipater's spirits that he even ventured to break down the Athenian siege rampart. [14] He then sent envoys to request assistance from Leonatus; but when the Athenians received word that Leonatus was coming with an army they moved to confront him in battle formation and in the ensuing cavalry engagement Leonatus received a serious wound from which he died. [15] Although Antipater saw that his reinforcements had been defeated, he was nevertheless glad at Leonatus' death, congratulating himself on the simultaneous removal of his rival and acquisition of the latter's forces. [16] So he immediately took over Leonatus' army and, since he now considered himself a match for his enemy even in the field, broke out of the siege and withdrew to Macedonia. [17] The Greek forces also dispersed to their various cities now that the enemy had been driven from Greek soil.

6 [1] Perdiccas meanwhile had launched a campaign against Ariarathes, King of Cappadocia.[10] He defeated him in battle but left the field with his wounds and the dangers he had faced as his only prize; [2] for when the enemy returned to the city from the battle, they all killed their wives and children, set fire to their homes and all their possessions and, [3] after throwing in even their slaves, hurled themselves into the flames—so that the victorious enemy might enjoy nothing of their property other than the sight of its burning. [4] Then, to bolster his strength with royal dignity, Perdiccas turned his thoughts to marriage with Cleopatra, sister of Alexander the Great and former wife of the other Alexander,[11] a

---

9. I.e. Harpalus.

10. Justin conflates campaigns in Cappadocia (322) and Pisidia (321); see Diod. 18.16.1ff. and 18.22.

11. Alexander of Epirus, who had died in 331 (12.2.1ff.). Cleopatra's daughter was named Nicaea.

match to which Olympias, her mother, voiced no objection. [5] First, however, he wished to use the pretext of family alliance to ensnare Antipater. [6] He therefore pretended that he wished to marry the latter's daughter, his object being to facilitate the acquisition of fresh levies of recruits from Macedonia. [7] But Antipater saw through the ruse, and Perdiccas' simultaneous courtship of two women eventually left him with neither. [8] War between Antigonus and Perdiccas followed. [9] Craterus and Antipater supported Antigonus, making peace with the Athenians and appointing Polyperchon governor of Greece and Macedonia.[12] [10] Perdiccas removed to Cappadocia Arridaeus and the son of Alexander the Great, the kings who had been placed in his charge, and he consulted his friends on the conduct of the war. [11] Some were in favour of transferring the theatre of operations to Macedonia, the very source and heart of the empire: [12] there they would have Olympias, mother of Alexander, to add significant support to their cause, as well as the favour of the citizens because of the names of Alexander and Philip. [13] Nevertheless, it seemed an expedient measure to start with Egypt in case Asia were seized by Ptolemy after their departure for Macedonia. [14] Paphlagonia,[13] Caria, Lycia and Phrygia were added to the provinces which Eumenes had already received, [15] and he was instructed to await Craterus and Antipater in his territory. To assist him he was assigned Perdiccas' brother, Alcetas, and Neoptolemus, along with their armies; [16] Clitus was put in charge of the fleet; Cilicia was taken from Philotas and given to Philoxenus; and Perdiccas himself made for Egypt with a mighty army. [17] So it was that Macedonia, her leaders split between warring factions, armed herself to stab her own vitals, turning her sword from war against a foe to shed the blood of countrymen, and ready, like the insane, to lacerate her own hands and limbs.

[18] Meanwhile, in Egypt, Ptolemy had been shrewdly accumulating considerable resources. [19] He had won the support of the Egyptians by his exceptional restraint, and he had also put the neighbouring monarchs in his debt by his benefactions and indulgent behaviour towards them. [20] He had, in addition, extended the bounds of his empire by the acquisition of the city of Cyrene,[14] and so powerful had he become that, rather than fearing his enemies, he was now to be feared by them.

12. Arrangements with Athens had been made in 322, the previous year. At this time, they were concerned with the Aetolians (Diod. 18.25).

13. As Eumenes had been given Paphlagonia in 323, perhaps Pamphylia is meant here.

14. For the details of which see Diod. 18.19ff.

7 [1] Cyrene had been founded by Aristaeus, who had the name Battos because he was tongue-tied.[15] [2] His father Grinus, king of the island of Thera, was ashamed that this son, though an adolescent, was still unable to speak, and he came to the oracle at Delphi to beg for the god's help. The response which he received was that his son Battos should make for Africa and found the city of Cyrene, where he would be granted the use of his tongue. [3] The oracle seemed absurd: the island of Thera was sparsely populated and yet the instructions were that colonists should go from there to found a city in the vast territory of Africa. The matter was accordingly dropped. [4] Some time later, the Therans' defiance of the god was punished by a plague, which finally forced them to obey him, but their numbers were so remarkably small that they barely filled a single ship.

[5] Arriving in Africa, they took possession of Mt Cyra, driving off the indigenous population, because it was an attractive region and also because it had a copious supply of water. [6] Here their leader, Battos, found his tongue loosened and began to speak for the first time, a phenomenon which, since they saw the god's prophecy partially fulfilled, encouraged the people to hope that the city could also be founded. [7] For this reason they encamped there. They then got wind of an old tale according to which Cyrene, a virgin of striking beauty, had been abducted by Apollo on Mt Pelion in Thessaly and brought to the very mountain range that included the hill they had occupied. Pregnant by the god, she had given birth to four boys, Nomius, Aristaeus, Autuchus and Agraeus. [8] Meanwhile, men had been sent by Cyrene's father, Hypseus, king of Thessaly, in search of the girl but, captivated by the beauty of the spot, they had settled in the same place as she. [9] On reaching manhood, three of Cyrene's sons returned to Thessaly, where they inherited their grandfather's kingdom, [10] while Aristaeus ruled an extensive kingdom in Arcadia, where he was the first to teach mankind how to keep bees, produce honey and make cheese, and the first to discover the rising of the constellation at the solstice.[16] [11] On hearing this story, Battos, who recognized the girl's name from the oracle, founded the city of Cyrene.

---

15. For versions of the founding of Cyrene, which took place around 630, see Her. 4.150ff., where Battos' father is Polymnestos and Grinnus is the son of Aesanius; compare Pindar *Pythian* 4. The Battiad kings ruled until about 440.

16. The constellation will be that of Sirius, the Dog Star.

8 [1] So, his strength augmented by the acquisition of this city, Ptolemy prepared for war as he awaited Perdiccas,[17] [2] but what harmed Perdiccas more than the strength of his enemy was the loathing he incurred by his arrogance; this won the hatred even of his allies, who deserted in droves to Antipater. [3] Neoptolemus, too, who had been left behind to assist Eumenes, was inclined not only to desert but even to betray his party's troops. [4] Realising this in time, Eumenes felt it essential to decide the issue with the traitor in battle. [5] Neoptolemus was defeated. He fled to Antipater and Polyperchon[18] and persuaded them to overtake Eumenes by forced marches while the latter was still jubilant from his victory and unconcerned because of Neoptolemus' flight. [6] Eumenes, however, was not deceived, and the ambush was turned back on its perpetrators: believing they were going to attack Eumenes while he was off guard, they were marching along off guard themselves, and exhausted from no sleep the previous night, when Eumenes fell on them. [7] Polyperchon died in the engagement. [8] Neoptolemus engaged Eumenes in single combat and, after a long struggle in which each man wounded the other, was finally overcome and killed. [9] Thus, by two consecutive victories in the field, Eumenes went some way towards reviving the fortunes of his party, which the defection of his allies had left badly flagging. [10] Finally, however, Perdiccas was murdered; Eumenes, Pithon the Illyrian and Perdiccas' brother, Alcetas, were declared outlaws by the army; and the war against them was put under the direction of Antigonus.[19]

BOOK 14

1 [1] Once Eumenes had learned that Perdiccas had been killed and that he himself had been declared a public enemy by the Macedonians and command in the war against him entrusted to Antigonus, he volunteered the information to his soldiers. [2] He was afraid rumour would

17. The narrative goes back to the year 321. From § 3 the scene switches to the Hellespont.

18. Here and at 8.7 the name should be Craterus, as in the prologue to the book.

19. Perdiccas was killed in Egypt and Antigonus' appointment as "General of Asia" came only when the army had reached Triparadeisus in northern Syria, where a new distribution of satrapies took place.

exaggerate matters or that the unexpected turn of events would generate panic in his men, [3] and he also wished to find out what their feelings were towards him so that he could base his strategy on their general mood. [4] Even so, he insisted that anyone alarmed by the situation was free to leave. [5] By this announcement he won them all over to his cause, so much so that to a man they urged him to open hostilities and declared that they would rescind the decrees of the Macedonians by the sword. [6] Eumenes then moved his army forward into Aeolia,[1] where he levied monies from the cities and plundered those which refused to pay, treating them as enemies. [7] He next moved on to Sardis and Alexander the Great's sister, Cleopatra, with the intention of using her influence to secure the loyalty of his centurions and senior officers, who would think that royal authority rested on the side favoured by Alexander's sister. [8] Such was the respect that Alexander's greatness commanded that even women were used as a path to the prestige conferred by his hallowed name.

[9] On his return letters were found scattered throughout the camp specifying rich rewards for any who brought Eumenes' head to Antigonus. [10] When he learned of this, Eumenes summoned his men to an assembly. He began by offering them his thanks that no one had been found who would set the prospect of blood money above loyalty to his oath of allegiance, [11] but then he craftily added that the letters had actually been concocted by himself to test the feelings of his men. [12] His security depended on them all, he said; moreover, neither Antigonus nor any other of the generals wanted victory on terms that would establish a terrible precedent that could recoil on himself. [13] In this way, he was able, for the moment, to curb the spirit of those who were wavering and also make provision for the future so that, in the event of a similar occurrence, the men would not think that they were being offered bribes by the enemy but rather being put to the test by their commander. [14] And so they all now vied with each other in offering their services as members of his bodyguard.

2 [1] Meanwhile Antigonus arrived with his army. He pitched camp and the next day proceeded to offer battle.[2] [2] Eumenes did not hesitate to take up the fight, but he was defeated and sought refuge in a fortress.

---

1. In northwestern Asia Minor; the year is 320. Cleopatra had moved to Sardis in 321.

2. This is the battle of Orcynii in early 319, after which Eumenes was besieged at Nora (the fortress).

[3] Since he saw that he would be facing the hazards of a siege in this place, he dismissed most of his troops to prevent his being surrendered to the enemy by a majority vote, and also so that the hardships of the siege would not be aggravated by sheer numbers. [4] He then sent legates to Antipater to beg for assistance, since he alone seemed to be a match for Antigonus in military strength; and when Antigonus learned that reinforcements had in fact been sent to Eumenes by Antipater he raised the siege.[3] [5] Eumenes was for the moment relieved of the fears he had for his life, but with his army demobilized his prospects of survival were small.

[6] When he examined all his possible courses of action, it seemed best to turn to the Argyraspids of Alexander the Great, an invincible force which by its many victories had won a brilliant reputation.[4] [7] But after Alexander the Argyraspids had little respect for any leader, for after all the memories of their great king, they thought it an indignity to serve under others. [8] Eumenes, therefore, proceeded with flattering entreaties addressed to them individually, now hailing them as "comrades" and "protectors," now styling them variously his "partners in the dangers of the East" and "the last hope for his survival and his sole protection." [9] He reminded them that they alone had conquered the East by their valour, they alone had eclipsed the campaigns of Father Liber and the immortal deeds of Hercules. [10] It was because of them, he said, that Alexander had become great, because of them that he had gained divine honours and deathless glory. [11] He begged them to accept him not so much as a leader but as a comrade and to enlist him as a member of their order. [12] Accepted by them on these terms, he little by little arrogated supreme command to himself, first by advising the men individually and then by leniency in correcting misconduct, until in the camp nothing could be done without him, no action taken without recourse to his expertise.

3 [1] Finally, when the news arrived that Antigonus was coming with his army, Eumenes managed to force his men to take the field, [2] but since they ignored the orders of their general they were defeated by a

3. Antipater died in autumn 319. Antigonus came to terms with Eumenes after the siege had lasted a year.
4. For the Argyraspids see 12.7.5. They were now guarding the royal treasure in Cilicia and in fact were ordered to obey Eumenes through a letter from Polyperchon.

valiant enemy.[5] [3] In that battle they lost not only the glory that was theirs from so many campaigns, along with their wives and children, but also the rewards which they had gained in the course of their long service. [4] But Eumenes, who was responsible for the defeat and who had no other hope of saving himself, kept urging on his defeated men. [5] He claimed that they had proved superior to their enemy in valour, having cut down five thousand of them, and that if they persevered in the fight it would, in fact, be the enemy who would sue for peace. [6] The losses which they thought meant defeat, he said, amounted to two thousand women, a few children and some slaves; these they would be better able to recover by winning rather than by abandoning a victory almost won. [7] The Argyraspids, however, said that they would not attempt a retreat after losing their property and their wives, nor yet would they do battle against their own children; [8] and they actually berated Eumenes for bringing them back, on the very point of demobilization, to a new campaign and further warfare without end, after so many years of service and at a time when they were going home laden with the spoils of numerous wars. [9] He had deceived them with empty promises, they said, and practically taken them away from their homes and the very threshold of their fatherland, [10] and not even now, when they had lost all the profits won in successful campaigns and suffered defeat, would he leave them in peace to a wretched old age of penury. [11] Then, without the knowledge of their officers, they hurriedly sent a deputation to Antigonus with the request that he order the restitution of their property, and Antigonus undertook to return it if they surrendered Eumenes to him. [12] As soon as he found this out, Eumenes tried to escape with a few men, but he was brought back and, in desperation, when a crowd of soldiers converged on him, he requested permission to deliver one last address to the army.

4 [1] He was called upon by all to speak, silence fell and his fetters were loosened. He stretched out his hand and let the crowd see it, manacled as he was.[6] [2] "Men," he said, "you see the clothing and decorations worn by your leader. No enemy put them on me—even that would have brought me some consolation. [3] It is you who have transformed me from victor to vanquished, from commander to captive, you who three

---

5. The battle of Gabiene in 316/5, though three years of fighting have been conflated.

6. It is indicative of the rhetorical freedom of ancient historiography that the speech at Plut. *Eum.* 17.6ff. is different in content.

times in the course of this year have sworn an oath of loyalty to me.
[4] But I say nothing of that; recriminations ill suit those in wretched
circumstances. [5] This is all I ask: if what Antigonus intends above
all else is my death, permit me to die amongst you. [6] It is nothing to
Antigonus how or where I die, and I shall be spared a shameful death.
[7] If I am granted this, I release you from the oaths by which you have
time and time again bound yourselves to me. [8] If, despite my request,
shame prevents you from doing violence to me, give me a sword and
let your general do on your behalf, without the obligation of an oath,
what you have sworn to do for your general."

[9] When he failed to gain his request, he turned from entreaty to
anger. [10] "You accursed scoundrels," he said, "may the gods who
punish perjury take note of your conduct and bring you to the end you
yourselves have given your leaders. [11] Yes, it was you who a short time
ago bespattered yourselves with the blood of Perdiccas and also devised
the same fate for Antipater.[7] [12] You would have killed Alexander himself, had Heaven willed that he could die at a mortal's hand; you did your
worst and bedevilled him with mutinies. [13] Now I am the last victim of
your treachery and I call down on you this infernal curse: [14] may you
spend all eternity exiled to this camp, poverty-stricken and homeless, and
may you be destroyed by your own weapons with which you have more
often destroyed generals of your own side than those of your enemies."

[15] After this, seething with rage, he set off at the head of his bodyguards for the camp of Antigonus, [16] followed by an army which,
through the betrayal of its leader, was itself captive and was now conduct-
ing towards the victor's encampment a triumphal procession in victory
over itself, [17] and surrendering to the victor, too, all the honours of King
Alexander and the palms and laurels of so many campaigns. [18] And, to
complete the procession, elephants and the auxiliary troops from the East
brought up the rear. [19] For Antigonus this was a victory finer than all
those which Alexander had won: the latter had conquered the East, but
Antigonus had triumphed even over those by whom the East had been
won. [20] So Antigonus distributed these world conquerors amongst his
troops, restoring to them the possessions which he taken from them in
victory. [21] Out of respect for their former friendship, he would not
allow Eumenes to come into his presence but had him assigned to the
custody of his guards.

7. A reference to the sedition which met Antipater at Triparadeisus (Arrian
Succ. 1.30ff.).

5 [1] Meanwhile Eurydice, wife of King Arridaeus, had learned that Polyperchon was returning to Macedonia from Greece and that he had sent for Olympias.[8] [2] Prompted by womanly jealousy and taking advantage of the illness of her husband, whose functions she was beginning to usurp, [3] Eurydice wrote to Polyperchon in the king's name and told him to hand over the army to Cassander since the king had transferred the administration of the kingdom to him. She sent the same message by letter to Antigonus, in Asia. [4] Indebted to her for the favour, Cassander did everything in accordance with the whims of this headstrong woman. [5] Then he left for Greece, where he made war on numerous cities, [6] and their destruction alarmed the Spartans, like a fire next door. So, disregarding the prophecies and the glorious reputation of their forefathers, they lost faith in their prowess in battle and encircled with protective walls the city which they had always defended with arms rather than fortifications. [7] So inferior to their ancestors had they become! For centuries their wall had been the valour of the citizens, but now the citizens felt they would be safe only when hiding behind actual walls.

[8] Meanwhile, the unsettled condition of Macedonia brought Cassander home from Greece. [9] For when Olympias, mother of King Alexander, was coming from Epirus to Macedonia in the company of Aeacides, king of the Molossians, Eurydice and King Arridaeus attempted to keep her from entering the land. [10] The Macedonians, who were roused either by the memory of her husband or the greatness of her son, and by the humiliation caused by the act, transferred their allegiance to Olympias, on whose orders both Eurydice and the king were executed. Arridaeus had held the throne for six years after the death of Alexander.

6 [1] Olympias did not rule for long either. Acting more like a woman than a monarch, she resorted to wholesale slaughter of the nobility and turned the support she had gained into hatred. [2] And so, once she learned of Cassander's arrival, out of mistrust of the Macedonians she withdrew to the city of Pydna with her daughter-in-law, Roxane, and

---

8. Polyperchon had succeeded Antipater as general of Macedonia and guardian of the kings in 319, whereupon he had summoned Olympias. On his return from Greece see Diod. 18.71f. (the year 317). For the current events see Diod. 19.11ff. (the year 317/6). Cassander was the son of Antipater, who had been irked when Polyperchon was preferred to him.

her grandson, Hercules.[9] [3] She was accompanied on the journey by Deidamia, daughter of King Aeacides, by her stepdaughter Thessalonice, who herself enjoyed some distinction because of the name of her father Philip, and by numerous other ladies from the nobility, a group that was more distinguished than capable. [4] When this news was brought to Cassander, he arrived at Pydna by forced marches and laid siege to the city. [5] Feeling the pressure of starvation and military force, and weary of the long siege, Olympias struck a bargain for her life and surrendered to the victor. [6] Cassander, however, summoned the people to a meeting to ascertain what they wanted done with Olympias, and he bribed relatives of men who had been put to death by her to put on mourning garb and denounce the woman's atrocities. [7] Roused to anger by these people and with no thought for her former royal dignity, the Macedonians decreed that she be executed, [8] ignoring the fact that it had been her son and her husband who not only guaranteed their security amongst their neighbours, but also enabled them to acquire great wealth and worldwide domination. [9] When Olympias saw men with weapons approaching her, intent on carrying out the sentence, she went to meet them of her own accord, dressed in her royal attire and leaning on two maidservants. [10] The sight of this astonished the assassins, who reflected on her erstwhile majesty and on the names of all the kings that she brought to mind; they stopped short, [11] and finally soldiers were sent by Cassander to run her through. She did not run from the sword, nor from their blows, nor did she scream like a woman. She faced death the way courageous men do, upholding the glorious reputation of her ancient family; you could recognize Alexander even in his mother's death. [12] It is said that as she lay dying she arranged her hair and covered her legs with her dress so that there would be nothing undignified in her bodily appearance. [13] Subsequently Cassander married Thessalonice, daughter of King Arridaeus,[10] and he sent Alexander's son along with the mother to be held in the citadel of Amphipolis.

---

9. Confusion, as Hercules was the son of Barsine. Roxane and her son, Alexander IV, took refuge with Olympias in the winter of 317/6 (Diod. 19.35.5). During this winter Olympias was besieged in Pydna. She died in the spring.
10. Actually daughter of Philip II, not Arridaeus (Philip III).

BOOK 15

1 [1] Now that Perdiccas was dead, along with his brother, and also Eumenes, Polypercon[1] and the other generals who had been on the opposing side, the war amongst the successors of Alexander seemed to be at an end. Then, suddenly, a rift appeared among the victors themselves. [2] Ptolemy, Cassander and Lysimachus demanded a distribution of the money which had been captured as booty as well as a division of the provinces, but Antigonus refused to consider sharing profits from a war in which he alone had faced the dangers; [3] and, to give the impression that the war he was undertaking against his allies was an honourable one, he made it known that he meant to avenge the death of Olympias, who had been killed by Cassander, and to free from their imprisonment at Amphipolis the son of Alexander, his king, along with the boy's mother. [4] On learning this, Ptolemy and Cassander allied themselves with Lysimachus and Seleucus and energetically prepared for war on land and sea.

[5] Ptolemy held Egypt and most of Africa, as well as Cyprus and Phoenicia; Macedonia and Greece were under Cassander's control; [6] Antigonus had seized Asia and parts of the East. In the first encounter of the war Antigonus' son, Demetrius, was defeated by Ptolemy at Galama,[2] [7] a battle in which Ptolemy's clemency won him more renown than the actual victory; [8] for he released Demetrius' friends and not only let them keep their own property, but made them further gifts as well. He also restored all Demetrius' personal belongings and slaves, [9] adding the magnanimous comment that his aim in going to war was not plunder but honour—he was angry that, after the defeat of the generals who had opposed them, Antigonus had seized for himself alone the profits of the victory which they had won together.

2 [1] Meanwhile, on his way back from Apollonia,[3] Cassander came upon the Audariatae, who had left their native soil because of an infestation of frogs and mice and were then searching for a new home. [2] Since he was afraid that they might seize Macedonia, he came to an agreement with them, accepted them as allies and assigned to them the

---

1. As at 13.8.5, 7, Justin should mean Craterus. Polyperchon lived at least until the end of the century. We have reached the winter of 316/5 and Diod. 19.57.

2. So Justin, but the battle is that of Gaza in 312, as in Trogus' epitome.

3. Cassander acquired this city in southern Illyria in 314; cf, 17.3.16ff.

most remote territory of Macedonia. [3] He was now afraid that Alexander's son, Hercules, who had passed his fourteenth birthday, might be invited to occupy the throne of Macedonia because of the prestige of his late father's name. Cassander therefore ordered that he and his mother Barsine be secretly killed and their bodies buried without ceremony lest their violent deaths come to light if a funeral were held.[4] [4] It was as if his crime in killing first the king, then that king's mother, Olympias, and his son was somehow insufficient, [5] for he also went on to murder in the same treacherous manner Alexander's other son along with the mother, Roxane, evidently thinking that he could attain his goal, the throne of Macedonia, only by crime.

[6] Meanwhile, Ptolemy again clashed with Demetrius, this time at sea. Losing his fleet in this battle,[5] he conceded victory to his enemy and sought refuge in Egypt. [7] Demetrius, prompted by the kindness he had been shown on the previous occasion, sent back to Egypt Ptolemy's son, Leontiscus; his brother, Menelaus; and his friends, along with their personal entourage and belongings. [8] To make it appear that they were driven by hope of glory and honour, not animosity, they were actually competing with each other, in the throes of war, to confer gifts and kindnesses. [9] In those days wars were conducted with so much more honour than friendships are today. [10] Elated by the victory, Antigonus gave orders that both he and his son, Demetrius, be addressed as "kings" by the people. [11] So that he would enjoy no less dignity among his own people, Ptolemy was also given the title "king" by the army.[6] [12] When they heard this news, Cassander and Lysimachus, in their turn, claimed royal status for themselves. [13] They had all refrained from adopting the trappings of royalty as long as sons of the king had been able to survive, and [14] such was the respect they felt for Alexander that, even when they enjoyed the royal power, they were content to forego the title "king" as long as Alexander had a legitimate heir. [15] Ptolemy, Cassander and the rest of the generals could see that they were being picked off one by one by Antigonus, but they had all regarded the war as belonging to each of them individually rather than as something to be

4. Though the fourteenth birthday is symbolic of reaching manhood, Hercules was at the time of his death in 309 seventeen or eighteen years old. Justin alone notes his mother's death, but it is likely enough, given the fate of Roxane and Alexander IV.

5. The battle of Salamis in the spring of 306; Diod. 20.47.7ff.

6. Not an immediate reaction: Ptolemy did not employ the title until early 304.

fought together, and so had refused to give each other assistance, thinking that victory would belong to one of them rather than to the whole group. [16] But now they bolstered each other's resolve by letter, agreed on a time and place to assemble, and prepared to fight with their forces united. [17] Cassander could not join the struggle because of a war he was fighting with his neighbours, and so he sent Lysimachus to assist his allies with a large force.

3 [1] Lysimachus had been born into a distinguished Macedonian family, but all his pedigree paled before the demonstrable instances of his moral worth; [2] for this was so exceptional in him that in greatness of spirit he went beyond even the teachings of philosophy, and he also surpassed all the conquerors of the East in his reputation for physical strength.[7] [3] The following episode illustrates his character. Alexander the Great was furious with the philosopher Callisthenes' opposition to the use of the Persian method of salutation and had falsely alleged that Callisthenes was party to a conspiracy that was afoot against him.   [4] Brutally mutilating all his limbs and cutting off his ears, nose and lips, Alexander reduced him to a hideous and pitiful spectacle, [5] and he even had him carried around shut up in a cage with a dog to intimidate the others. [6] Lysimachus, who had been a student of Callisthenes and used to ask his advice on moral issues, felt pity for this great man who was being punished not for a crime but for speaking his mind, and gave him poison to relieve his sufferings.   [7] So incensed was Alexander that he had Lysimachus thrown to a ferocious lion.   [8] However, when the lion, enraged at the sight of his victim, leapt at him, Lysimachus wrapped his hand in his cloak, plunged it into the lion's mouth and killed the beast by ripping out its tongue.   [9] When this was reported to the king, his admiration led him to forget the offence, and his affection for Lysimachus increased on account of the latter's unshakable courage. [10] Furthermore, Lysimachus accepted with magnanimity the king's humiliation of him, as though it came from a father.   [11] Eventually, the memory of the incident passed completely from his mind and, later on, in India, when the king was in pursuit of some enemy stragglers and became separated from his troop of attendants because his horse was so fast, it was Lysimachus alone who accompanied him across huge sand

---

7. There is some confusion as to Lysimachus' origins. For Callisthenes, who was more historian than philosopher, see 12.6.17; the manner of his death is variously reported. For a parallel treatment of Lysimachus see Pausanias 1.9.5ff. The story of the lion was legendary, but for an alternative see Curtius 8.1.14ff.

dunes. [12] Before this Lysimachus' brother Philip had volunteered to perform the same service, but he had died in the king's arms.[8] [13] Now, however, as Alexander dismounted, he accidentally wounded Lysimachus on the forehead with the tip of his spear, so seriously that the only way of staunching the flow of blood was by the king taking his diadem from his own head and putting it on Lysimachus' in order to close up the wound. [14] This was the first omen that royal authority was to come to Lysimachus. [15] Further, after the death of Alexander, when the provinces were being divided amongst his successors, it was Lysimachus who was assigned the fiercest tribes on the assumption that he was the bravest of them all. [16] So far, by universal agreement, did he excel the others in courage.

4 [1] Before the commencement of the war which pitted Ptolemy and his allies against Antigonus, Seleucus, who had returned suddenly from Greater Asia, appeared on the scene as a new foe for Antigonus. [2] Seleucus was renowned for his valour, and the circumstances of his birth were astounding.[9] [3] His mother was Laodice, wife of Antiochus, who had been a distinguished general under Philip. She dreamed that she had conceived after sleeping with Apollo, [4] that when she was pregnant she had received from the god, as a present for having slept with him, a ring with a stone on which an anchor was carved, with instructions to give this to the son she was to bear. [5] Two things made this dream astounding. The first was a ring that was found in the bed the following day bearing that very motif, and the second a birthmark in the shape of an anchor on the infant Seleucus' thigh. [6] Laodice gave this ring to Seleucus when he went off with Alexander the Great on the Persian campaign, explaining to him how he had been born. [7] After Alexander's death Seleucus gained control of the East, and he founded a city in which he immortalized the memory of his double conception [8] by naming the city Antioch after his human father and consecrating the adjacent fields to Apollo. [9] The emblem of his birth persisted in the succeeding generations, since his sons and grandsons had an anchor on the thigh as a congenital mark of their ancestry.

[10] After the partitioning of the Macedonian empire amongst the allies,[10] Seleucus fought many wars in the East. [11] First of all he took

8. In 328/7; see Curtius 8.2.33ff.

9. Nothing more is known of his parents. The ring story is found in Appian *Syr.* 56.

10. Seleucus, Lysimachus, Cassander and Ptolemy. Seleucus took Babylon in 312. See Appian *Syr.* 54f.

Babylon, after which, his strength augmented by the victory, he conquered the Bactrians. [12] Then he crossed into India which, following Alexander's death, had shaken from its shoulders the yoke of servitude and put to death his governors. [13] The man responsible for this liberation was Sandrocottus.[11] After his victory, however, he had turned the so-called liberty they had gained back into servitude; [14] for on seizing power he began himself to enslave the people he had championed against foreign domination. [15] He was a man of low birth, but he was called to royal power by divine authority. [16] He had annoyed King Nandrus by his outspokenness; he was sentenced to death by him, and had relied on his swiftness of foot to escape. [17] He was lying down, having fallen asleep from exhaustion, when a huge lion approached him as he slept; with its tongue it cleaned the sweat that was pouring from him and, then, when he awoke, calmly left him. [18] It was this strange occurrence that first inspired Sandrocottus to hope for royal power. He then gathered a band of outlaws and incited the Indians to revolution. [19] Later, as he was preparing for hostilities against Alexander's governors, a wild elephant of immense size came up to him of its own accord and, just as if it were tame, let him get on its back. It became his guide in the war and showed remarkable prowess in battle.

[20] Having gained the throne in this manner, Sandrocottus was ruler of India at the time that Seleucus was laying the foundations for his future greatness. [21] Seleucus made a truce with him, settled matters in the East and returned to the fight with Antigonus.[12] [22] The allies combined their forces, and a battle was fought in which Antigonus was killed and his son Demetrius put to flight. [23] But the war against their enemy terminated, the allies turned their weapons on one another once again. Unable to reach agreement on the division of plunder,[13] they split once more into two factions, [24] with Seleucus allied to Demetrius and Ptolemy to Lysimachus. Cassander died, and his son Philip succeeded him. [25] So it was that wars started all over again for Macedon, as if from the very beginning.

---

11. Chandragupta Maurya, ruler of the kingdom of Magadha c.322–291.

12. The Peace with Chandragupta was perhaps made in 303. Justin has moved to the battle of Ipsus in Phrygia in 301, at which Cassander and Ptolemy were not in fact present; Diod. 21.1.4; Plut. *Demetrius* 29ff.

13. That is, Coele-Syria, claimed by Seleucus, but annexed by Ptolemy. Cassander died in 297; his sons, Philip, Antipater and Alexander, ruled less than four years altogether.

BOOK 16

1 [1] King Cassander's death was soon followed by that of his son Philip,[1] and not long afterwards Queen Thessalonice, Cassander's wife, was murdered by her son Antipater, even though she pleaded for her life by the breasts which had suckled him. [2] The motive for the killing was that, after her husband's death, she appeared to have favoured Alexander during the partition of the kingdom between the brothers. [3] Everyone considered the crime all the more heinous because there was no evidence of foul play on the mother's part, [4] although when a crime involves killing a parent no sufficient justification can be offered in its defence. [5] Following this, Alexander intended to make war on his brother to avenge his mother's murder, and he sought assistance from Demetrius. [6] Demetrius, who hoped to overrun the kingdom of Macedon, did not hesitate to comply. [7] Fearing his coming, Lysimachus persuaded his son-in-law, Antipater, to be reconciled with his brother instead of allowing his father's enemy into Macedonia. [8] Demetrius now realized that the brothers had begun to settle their differences, and he treacherously killed Alexander, seized the throne of Macedon and called an assembly of the army to justify the murder.

[10] At the assembly Demetrius claimed that it was he who had been attacked by Alexander first, that he had not set a trap but anticipated one. [11] He had more right to be king of Macedon, he said, whether by virtue of his age and experience or for other cogent reasons. [12] For, he continued, his father had been companion to King Philip and Alexander the Great on all their campaigns.[2] [13] Subsequently he had been guardian of Alexander's children, and he had also been responsible for hunting down the rebels. [14] Antipater, on the other hand, the grandfather of these young men, had always shown himself a harsher governor of the kingdom than the kings themselves had been, [15] while their father, Cassander, who had wiped out the royal family, had shown no mercy to women or children and did not stop until he had destroyed every

---

1. See 15.4.24. Continuing sources are Diod. 21.7ff.; Plut. *Demetrius* 36ff.; Plut. *Pyrrhus* 6ff. In this chapter we reach the year 294. For events from Ipsus to the Roman conquest see *A History of Macedonia* vol. III (Oxford 1988), 199ff. (F. W. Walbank).

2. Not really true: Antigonus had remained in Asia Minor in 333 and became Alexander's satrap of Greater Phrygia. For the rest of his exploits see Books 14–15.

last descendant of the royal line. [16] Since he had been unable to exact vengeance for these crimes from Cassander himself, said Demetrius, he had transferred the punishment to the latter's children. [17] So, he concluded, if the spirits of the dead had any awareness, Philip and Alexander would surely prefer to see their avengers, rather than those who murdered them and their family, as the rulers of Macedon. [18] This appeased the people, and Demetrius was declared king of Macedon. [19] Under pressure from a war with Dromichaetes, a king of the Thracians, and fearing that he might be obliged to fight Demetrius at the same time, Lysimachus also ceded to Demetrius the other part of Macedonia which had fallen to his son-in-law Antipater, and concluded a peace with him.

2 [1] Equipped with the entire might of the kingdom of Macedon, Demetrius now decided to seize Asia. However, Ptolemy, Seleucus and Lysimachus, who had learned from their experience in the previous conflict the strength that could come from cooperation, once more formed an alliance, joined forces and shifted the theatre of war against Demetrius to Europe. [2] For the war they found a companion and ally in Pyrrhus, king of Epirus, who was hoping that Demetrius could lose Macedonia as easily as he had acquired it. [3] And this was no futile hope: Pyrrhus bribed Demetrius' army, put Demetrius himself to flight and seized the throne of Macedon.[3]

[4] While this was going on, Lysimachus murdered his son-in-law, Antipater, who was protesting that the throne of Macedon had been taken from him by the treachery of his father-in-law, and imprisoned his own daughter, Eurydice, for joining Antipater in his complaints. [5] Thus it was that the entire house of Cassander paid the penalty to Alexander the Great by their murder, torture or parricide, whether for his assassination or for the extinction of his line. [6] And Demetrius, cut off by so many armies, preferred a dishonourable capitulation to Seleucus when he might have died with honour.[4]

[7] When the war was over, Ptolemy died with a glorious record of achievements to his credit. Breaking with the established law of nations, he had, before he became infirm, passed on the crown to the youngest of his sons,[5] and had even succeeded in justifying his action

3. In the year 287.
4. Cf. 12.14. He was captured in Cilicia and drank himself to death in 283 after three years in captivity.
5. Probably not the youngest, Ptolemy II Philadelphus reigned from 282 to 246.

to the people, [8] who were as enthusiastic about accepting the son's rule as the father had been in bestowing it on him. [9] Amongst all the many demonstrations of affection of father and son for each other, the following had especially won the young man the love of his people: after publicly passing the crown to his son the father had, as an ordinary subject, served the king as a member of his bodyguard and had declared that to be the father of the king was a finer thing than ruling any kingdom.

3 [1] Discord, which inevitably plagues equal partners, had by now precipitated war between Lysimachus and Pyrrhus, allies a short while before. [2] In this Lysimachus had prevailed and seized control of Macedonia, driving out Pyrrhus. [3] After that Lysimachus had gone on to attack Thrace and then Heraclea, a city whose early history and that of its final days are both fascinating.[6] [4] The Boeotians, afflicted with a plague, had been told by the oracle at Delphi to found a colony consecrated to Hercules in the area of Pontus. [5] However, because they were alarmed at the prospect of a long and dangerous voyage and all preferred to die in their own country, the matter had been disregarded. Then the Phocians attacked them, [6] and the Boeotians, after suffering a number of defeats, had recourse to the oracle once more, only to receive the response that the remedy for the war was the same as for the plague. [7] They therefore assembled a band of colonists, who sailed to Pontus and founded the city of Heraclea. And since they had put in at that spot at the bidding of the Fates, they quickly acquired great wealth. [8] Then the city became embroiled in many wars with its neighbours and was also much troubled by strife within. In the rich history of Heraclea the following episode is particularly remarkable.

[9] During their ascendancy after the defeat of the Persians, the Athenians had assessed the tribute to be paid by Greece and Asia for the maintenance of a fleet. All the states contributed eagerly in order to guarantee their own security, all but the people of Heraclea, who had refused a contribution because of their friendship with the Persian kings. [10] Consequently, Lamachus was sent with an army by the Athenians to wrest from them by force the contribution which they refused, but

---

6. For what follows see S. M. Burstein, *Outpost of Hellenism: The Emergence of Heraclea on the Black Sea* (Berkeley and Los Angeles 1976). The founding of the city, most of whose colonists were Megarian, probably took place shortly after 570. It had a native historian named Nymphis, who was perhaps Trogus' source.

while he was laying waste the land of the Heracleans after leaving his ships off shore, he lost his fleet when it was wrecked by a sudden storm, along with the greater part of his army.[7] [11] He could not make the return journey by sea—his ships were gone—and he dared not go by land through all the savage tribes of the region with his small band of men. But the people of Heraclea, considering it more honourable to see in this an opportunity to show kindness than to exact revenge, gave the Athenians supplies and military assistance before sending them on their way, [12] and thought themselves well recompensed for the destruction of their land if they had turned former enemies into friends.

4 [1] Heraclea suffered many hardships, including a tyranny.[8] [2] For when the commons made irresponsible demands for a cancellation of debts and a redistribution of the land owned by the wealthy, the matter was long debated in the senate, [3] but no solution to the problem could be found. Finally, the people of Heraclea sought help against their lower classes, who were turning their idle hands to political mischief—first from Timotheus, general of the Athenians, and then from Epaminondas, general of the Thebans. [4] When both men refused, they turned to Clearchus, whom they had themselves driven into exile. [5] Such was the urgency of their situation that they were summoning to protect their country a man whom they had barred from it. [6] Clearchus, however, whom exile had made even more villainous, looked on the rift amongst the people as an opportunity to make himself tyrant. [7] First he conferred in secret with Mithridates, the enemy of his fellow-citizens, and made a pact with him to betray the city to him when he was recalled, provided that he be appointed governor. [8] But then he directed against Mithridates himself the treachery which he had devised for his citizens. [9] For after he had returned from exile (ostensibly to arbitrate the Heracleans' civil discord), at the prearranged time that he was supposed to hand over the city to Mithridates, Clearchus arrested the king along with his retinue of friends and set him free only after the king had paid a large ransom.

[10] Thus, from being Mithridates' ally, Clearchus had abruptly turned himself into his foe; similarly, after being defender of the cause of the senate, he suddenly emerged as champion of the commons. [11] He not

7. Lamachus' expedition was in 424; see *AO* 132. Thuc. 4.75 makes no mention of the kindness of the Heracleans.

8. See Diod. 15.81.5f., under 364/3, and for Clearchus' death 16.36.3, under 353/2, which account does not square with Justin's on the setting and names Clearchus' successor as his son Timotheus; Memnon *FGH* 434 F 2.1 agrees with Justin. For Timotheus see *AO* 262.

only incited the lower classes against the men responsible for his rise to power, the men by whom he had been brought home and established in the citadel, but he also inflicted on the latter all the atrocities characteristic of a ruthless tyranny. [12] He summoned the commons to a meeting and declared that he would no longer support the repression of the people by the senators, that in fact he would intervene if they persisted in their previous brutality. [13] However, should they, the people, feel that they could hold their own against the cruelty of the senators, he would leave with his troops and not interfere in their civil disputes; [14] but if they lacked confidence in their own strength, he would not fail to defend his fellow-citizens. [15] So let them decide, he said, and either order him to leave, if that was what they wanted, or else stay behind as a supporter of the people's cause. [16] Won over by these words, the people conferred supreme power on Clearchus, and their resentment at the power of the senate led them to deliver themselves, along with their wives and children, into subjection to a despotic tyranny. [17] Clearchus then arrested sixty senators—the others having fled in all directions—and placed them in irons. [18] The lower orders were overjoyed that the senate was being destroyed by its very own leader, that the tables had been turned and that the help the senators had anticipated proved to be their undoing. [19] Clearchus indiscriminately threatened all the senators with execution and then increased the price of their ransom; for he took large sums of money to rescue them secretly from the threats of the commons, but after robbing them of their fortunes he also robbed them of their lives.

5 [1] The tyrant then learned that preparations for a war against him were being made by the senators who had escaped, with a number of city-states prompted by compassion to come to their assistance. He therefore freed the slaves of those senators [2] and, in order that the respectable families in their distress should be spared no cruelty whatsoever, he forced their wives and daughters to marry their former slaves, threatening with execution any refusing to comply. He did this to increase the slaves' loyalty to himself and their antipathy towards their masters. [3] The married women, however, considered these doleful marriages worse than sudden death, [4] and many of them took their own lives before the ceremony or during the nuptials themselves (after first killing their new husbands), thus saving themselves from a dismal fate by a heroic act of moral probity. [5] There followed a battle in which the tyrant prevailed, after which he dragged the captive senators before the faces of their fellow-citizens, as in a triumph. [6] Returning to the city, he imprisoned some of them, tortured others, and yet others he put to death. No spot in the city was

exempt from the tyrant's brutality. [7] But his callousness was combined with insolence, and his brutality with arrogance. [8] His unbroken run of success at times made him forget that he was a man; at times he called himself the son of Jupiter. [9] When he went out in public a golden eagle was borne before him as a symbol of his lineage, [10] and he put on purple clothes, the boots worn by kings in tragedy and a golden crown. [11] Moreover, he named his son Ceraunus,[9] making a mockery of the gods in his selection of names as well as in his own pretensions.

[12] Two very well-bred young men, Chion and Leonides, were shocked by his behaviour and conspired to assassinate the tyrant in order to liberate their country. [13] They were students of the philosopher Plato, who were eager to display to their native land the virtue in which they trained themselves each day, following their master's precepts. They took on fifty of their relatives under their personal guardianship and set them in ambush, [14] while they themselves made haste, like two men with a dispute, to the tyrant in the citadel, as though to a king. [15] They were admitted because of their ties of friendship with Clearchus, and while the tyrant was preoccupied with listening to the one who spoke first, he was struck down by the other. [16] Because their associates were late in bringing help, however, the young men were themselves overwhelmed by the bodyguard [17] and so it was that, although the tyrant was assassinated, the country was not liberated. [18] For Clearchus' brother Satyrus seized the tyranny as Clearchus had done, and through many years, as the power passed down by succession, the people of Heraclea remained under the rule of tyrants.

BOOK 17

1 [1] At about the same time[1] the areas of the Hellespont and the Chersonese were struck by an earthquake, [2] but the worst devastation overtook the city of Lysimachia (founded twenty-two years earlier by King Lysimachus), which was totally destroyed. [3] This was an omen which predicted a grim future for Lysimachus and his descendants, and ruin for his kingdom along with the destruction of the afflicted areas. [4] Nor would these portents remain unfulfilled: a short while afterwards Lysimachus developed for his own son Agathocles a hatred

---

9. Which means "thunderbolt," signifying the power of Zeus.
1. We return to the late 280s, where Justin left off at 16.3.3.

that was abnormal not just in a father but in any human being, and had him poisoned by his stepmother, Arsinoë,[2] although Lysimachus had appointed him successor to the throne and through him won many victories in war. [5] For Lysimachus this was the first step towards disaster, the beginning of his impending ruin. [6] For the murder was followed by the massacre of the most prominent citizens, who thus paid the price for expressing sorrow over the young man's killing.   [7] As a result the survivors of the blood-bath and the army officers eagerly defected to Seleucus [8] and induced him to attack Lysimachus, a move which he was already contemplating out of jealousy of the king's reputation. [9] This was the final struggle between the comrades of Alexander;[3] this particular pair had been virtually kept in reserve to demonstrate the vagaries of Fortune. [10] Lysimachus was seventy-four, Seleucus seventy-seven, [11] but at such an age both were still young in spirit and both had an insatiable craving for power. [12] The two between them had the world in their hands, but they felt themselves confined and restricted, measuring the terms of their lives not by the passage of years but by the extent of their empires.

2   [1] In that war Lysimachus, who had previously lost 15 children from a variety of causes, met his own end fighting bravely, and thus provided the final touch to the downfall of his family. [2] Seleucus was overjoyed by such a great victory and by the thought (which he considered more important than the victory) that he was now the sole survivor of the circle of Alexander, and that he was the conqueror of conquerors. This was not the achievement of a human, but the gift of a god, he boasted, [3] little realizing that he would soon himself be an example of the frailty of the human condition. [4] Some seven months later he was trapped and killed by Ptolemy,[4] whose sister had been Lysimachus' wife, [5] and along with his life he lost the kingdom of Macedon, which he had wrested from Lysimachus. [6] Ptolemy, eager to exploit the memory of his father, Ptolemy the Great, amongst the people and to gain favour for having avenged Lysimachus, at first determined to win over Lysimachus' sons. [7] He therefore asked for the hand in marriage of Arsinoë, who was his own sister and their mother, with a promise to adopt the boys. [8] The reasoning behind this was that, once he had

2. The daughter of Ptolemy I, on whom see further below.
3. The end was the battle of Corupedium in 281. See Appian *Syr.* 62ff.
4. Ptolemy Ceraunus ("Thunderbolt") was the half-brother of Arsinoë; his full brother Philadelphus had the succession in Egypt.

taken their father's place, the boys would not venture to work against him, either out of respect for their mother or because he was, in name at least, their father.

[9] He also wrote to seek the cooperation of his brother, the king of Egypt, claiming that he was putting aside his resentment over the seizure of their father's kingdom, and no longer would he seek from a brother what he had more honourably gained from the enemy of his father. [10] He used all manner of flattery on the king to prevent his joining Antigonus, son of Demetrius, and Antiochus, son of Seleucus, with whom Ptolemy was about to go to war; he did not want a third enemy.[5] [11] Nor did he overlook Pyrrhus, king of Epirus, a man who would be a great asset to whichever side he joined [12] and who, since he himself wanted to prey on each of them individually, was trying to ingratiate himself with all the parties involved. [13] On the point of assisting the people of Tarentum against the Romans, Pyrrhus asked Antigonus to lend him some ships to ferry his army to Italy, while at the same time he asked Antiochus, who had more wealth than troops, for a loan of money and Ptolemy for Macedonian auxiliary forces. [14] Ptolemy, who could not justify holding back on the grounds that his forces were too weak, granted him 5,000 infantry, 4,000 cavalry and 50 elephants, but for a limited term of two years.[6] [15] In return for this, Pyrrhus married Ptolemy's daughter and left Ptolemy to safeguard his realm, after having established peaceful relations with all his neighbours, in order not to leave the kingdom prey to his enemies when he took his prime troops to Italy.

3 [1] Since I have mentioned Epirus, I should say something about the beginnings of this kingdom.[7] [2] Originally it was the Molossians who were dominant in the region, [3] but subsequently Pyrrhus, son of Achilles, settled in the area after losing his father's kingdom while absent from it during the Trojan War. His people were initially called Pyrrhidae, and later Epirotae. [4] Pyrrhus came to the temple of Jupiter at Dodona to consult the oracle and there abducted Lanassa, granddaughter of

5. The rule of Antigonus II Gonatas in Macedonia began in 276 and ran to (probably) 239. Antiochus I Soter ruled from 281 to 261. For Pyrrhus, who crossed to Italy in 281/0, see Plut. *Pyrrhus* 13ff. Though the Latin uses the spelling "Pyrrus," we retain the familiar form of the well-known name in the translation.

6. Different numbers at Plut. *Pyrrhus* 15.1. For the marriage cf. 24.1.8, though there is no evidence it ever took place, perhaps because Ceraunus died in 279. Pyrrhus' wives are recorded at Plut. *Pyrrhus* 9.

7. Cf. Plut. *Pyrrhus* 1ff.

Hercules, whom he married and by whom he had eight children. [5] A number of the girls he gave in marriage to neighbouring monarchs, and he acquired great wealth with the help of these family ties. [6] To King Priam's son Helenus, in recognition for outstanding service, he awarded the kingdom of Chaonia and he also gave him the hand of Hector's widow, Andromache, to whom he had himself been married after being awarded her in the distribution of the Trojan spoils. [7] Shortly afterwards he was waylaid at Delphi by Orestes, son of Agamemnon, and died there amongst the altars of the god. [8] His successor was his son Piales.

[9] Subsequently the crown descended in regular succession to Thary-bas. [10] Since he was not yet of age and was the last survivor of a noble line, Tharybas' welfare and education were accordingly all the more important to the entire population, who therefore appointed guardians for him. [11] He was also sent to Athens for schooling, and the more he surpassed his ancestors in learning, the more he won the approval of his people. [12] He was the first to create a legal system, a senate, annual magistracies and a regular constitution, [13] so that, while the country may have been founded by Pyrrhus, its culture was established by Tharybas. [14] His son was Neoptolemus, who became the father of Olympias, Alexander the Great's mother, and of the Alexander[8] [15] who succeeded him on the throne of Epirus and who died amongst the Bruttii after fighting a war in Italy. [16] After his death, Alexander was suc-ceeded by his brother Aeacides,[9] whose incessant military clashes with the Macedonians exhausted the people and made him unpopular with his fellow-citizens. [17] He was therefore driven into exile, leaving on the throne his son Pyrrhus, who was a mere infant, just two years old. [18] Because his father was so hated by the people, they also sought out the child to put to death; but he was spirited away and taken to the Illyrians, [19] where his upbringing was entrusted to Beroa, wife of King Glaucias, herself of Aeacid descent.[10] [20] Glaucias was either moved to pity by the boy's circumstances or won over by his infant charms; at all events the king long protected him against Cassander, king of Macedon (who added threats of war to his demands for his return), to the point of adopting the child to help keep him safe. [21] This had a profound effect on the Epirotes, whose hatred softened to pity. When Pyrrhus was eleven years

8. Justin has omitted Tharybas's son Alcetas from the genealogy. For Neop-tolemus, Olympias, and her brother Alexander see 7.6.10ff.; 8.6.4ff.; 9.6.1; 9.7.3ff.; 12.1.4; 12.2.1ff.

9. Actually his cousin.

10. On the claimed lineage of the Molossian royal house see 11.4.5; 12.16.3.

old, they recalled him to the throne, and he was given guardians who were to look after his kingdom until he reached manhood. [22] Then, as a young man, he fought many wars, and his successes brought him such a great reputation that he alone seemed capable of defending the people of Tarentum against the Romans.[11]

BOOK 18

1 [1] To resume:[1] when the people of Tarentum sent a second delegation to Pyrrhus, king of Epirus, and he also received appeals from the Samnites and the Lucanians, who likewise needed his assistance against the Romans, he promised to come to their aid with an army (though, in fact, he was induced to do so less by the entreaties of his petitioners than the prospect of seizing an empire in Italy). [2] He was already disposed to such a move, but what had prompted him to act was the precedent set by his ancestors, for he did not wish to appear a lesser man than his uncle Alexander, in whom the Tarentines had already found a champion against the Bruttii, or to be seen to have displayed less courage than Alexander the Great, who brought the East into subjection in a campaign fought far from home. [3] Accordingly, he left his fifteen-year-old son Ptolemy in charge of the kingdom and landed his forces in the harbour of Tarentum. To cheer him on this remote campaign he took with him his two young sons, Alexander and Helenus.

[4] On hearing of Pyrrhus' arrival, the Roman consul, Valerius Laevinus, made haste to encounter him before the auxiliary forces of the king's allies could unite, and he led out his army into the field. [5] Nor did the king hold back from the fight, despite his numerical inferiority. [6] The Romans were carrying the day when the hitherto unfamiliar sight of elephants baffled them initially, and then made them give ground; and the victors were suddenly vanquished by these strange monsters of the Macedonians. [7] But for the enemy it was no bloodless victory; Pyrrhus himself suffered a serious wound, and most of his men were killed, with

11. Suffice it to say that Pyrrhus' career was not as smooth as Justin's last sentence suggests.
  1. Continued from 17.2. The story goes on in Plut. *Pyrrhus* 16ff.; other sources at *MRR* 1.191ff.; P. Valerius Laevinus was consul in 280; C. Fabricius Luscinus' embassy occurred in 279. Pyrrhus' final defeat in Italy came in 275. For his uncle Alexander see 12.2.1ff.

the result that he gained more glory than joy from that particular victory. [8] Many cities which had waited to see the result of the fight surrendered to Pyrrhus, [9] and the Locrians were not the only ones to betray their Roman garrison and defect to him. [10] From the spoils of the battle Pyrrhus sent two hundred captured soldiers to Rome without asking for ransom, so that the Romans, already aware of his valour, would also become aware of his generosity. [11] Then, a few days later, after the arrival of the troops of his allies, he engaged the Romans a second time, but with the same result as in the earlier battle.

2 [1] Meanwhile, the Carthaginian general Mago had been sent with 120 ships to support the Romans.[2] He came to the senate and declared that the Carthaginians were distressed that the Romans were being subjected to a war in Italy by a foreign king. [2] The object of his mission, he said, was to see that the Romans, under attack from an enemy from without, should also receive support from outside. [3] The Carthaginians were thanked by the senate, but their help was declined. [4] Mago, however, in keeping with his Punic character,[3] waited a few days and then secretly approached Pyrrhus, ostensibly on a peacemaking mission from the Carthaginians, but really to find out his plans with regard to Sicily, to which, it was rumoured, the king was being invited. [5] For that had also been the reason for the Carthaginians' sending help to the Romans—to keep Pyrrhus in Italy, engaged in a war with the Romans, so that he could not cross to Sicily.

[6] In the meantime Fabricius Luscinus, sent as an ambassador by the Roman senate, concluded a peace treaty with Pyrrhus. [7] To ratify this, Cineas was sent to Rome with sumptuous gifts from Pyrrhus, but he found no household whose doors would open to his largesse. [8] This instance of Roman integrity is paralleled by another which occurred at about the same time. [9] A delegation which had been sent to Egypt by the senate rejected the rich gifts offered it by King Ptolemy.[4] A few days later its members, invited to dinner, were sent golden wreaths. These they accepted as being a good omen for their mission, but the following day they set them on the statues of the king. [10] So when Cineas brought back the news that the treaty with the Romans had been rejected by Appius Claudius and was asked by Pyrrhus for his impression

---

2. Polybius 3.25 marks a treaty between Rome and Carthage at this time.

3. The notion that Carthaginians could not be trusted resounds through Roman writings; see also below 18.6.2.

4. Ptolemy II Philadelphus; *MRR* 1.197 places this in 273.

of Rome, he replied that he thought it a city of kings. [11] After this, ambassadors from Sicily arrived on the scene to give Pyrrhus control over the entire island, which had been continually troubled by wars with the Carthaginians. [12] Pyrrhus left his son Alexander at Locri, strengthened the cities of his allies with powerful garrisons and transported his army to Sicily.[5]

3 [1] Since we have now mentioned the Carthaginians, I must give a brief account of their beginnings, going somewhat further back into the history of the people of Tyre, whose fortunes were equally lamentable.[6] [2] The people of Tyre owe their origin to the Phoenicians [3] who left their native land after suffering an earthquake. They settled first at the Syrian lake and subsequently on the coastline, [4] where they established a city which they called Sidon because of the abundance of fish in the area ("sidon" being Phoenician for "fish"). [5] Many years later they were defeated by the king of Ascalon, after which they took to their ships and founded the city of Tyre the year before the fall of Troy.[7] [6] There they were long embroiled in wars against the Persians, with mixed success. They did emerge victorious but their strength was exhausted, and they were subjected to atrocious treatment by their own slaves, whose numbers had become excessive. [7] The latter hatched a conspiracy and murdered the entire free population, including their own masters. Gaining control of the city, they then seized their masters' homes, assumed control of the government, took wives and fathered what they had not been themselves, free children.[8]

[8] Among the many thousands of slaves involved was one who was of such a humane disposition as to be moved to pity by the plight of his aging master and his young son. He looked on his masters not with a ruthless hostility but with a compassionate devotion. [9] He got them out of harm's way and pretended they had been killed. The slaves then discussed the constitution of their state and decided that one of their number should be made king, specifically the man who was the first to see the rising sun (for he would seem to be the one most favoured

5. The account is resumed at 23.3.
6. Justin is an important source for Carthaginian history. Trogus derived much from Timaeus for this episode. See in general B. H. Warmington, *Carthage* (London 1960).
7. The traditional date for which equates to 1194.
8. There is a play on words here: the Latin "liberi" can mean either "free men" or "children." It is, of course, evident that they had murdered only the free *male* population.

by heaven).[9] Our slave reported the matter to his master Strato—for that was his name—who lay in hiding. [10] In the middle of the night everybody proceeded to the same open space and, while all the others looked east, the slave, who had been briefed by Strato, alone fixed his gaze in a westerly direction. [11] At first the others thought it was madness to look for the sunrise in the west. [12] When, however, dawn began to break and the rising sun started to gleam on the highest points of the city, the other slaves kept watching to catch a glimpse of the sun itself, and so it was this one who was the first to point out to all of them the sun catching the highest roof in the city. [13] His reasoning seemed uncharacteristic of a slave, and when the others asked who was responsible for it, he confessed about his master. [14] Then it was understood how far the free intellect surpassed the servile, and that slaves were superior in wickedness, not intelligence. [15] The old man and his son were spared, and the slaves, thinking they had been protected by some deity, made Strato king. [16] After his death the throne passed to his son and then his grandsons.

[17] The atrocity of the slaves gained notoriety and was a frightful example the world over. [18] So when some years later Alexander the Great was campaigning in the East, he stormed their city as though in general vindication of law and order and, in memory of the old massacre, crucified all survivors of the battle.[10] [19] The only family which he left unimpaired was that of Strato, to whose descendants he restored the throne. He also gave to the island settlers of free birth who had had no involvement in the crimes, so that the population of the city could be reestablished after the eradication of its servile stock.

4 [1] Founded in this manner under the auspices of Alexander, Tyre quickly gained strength through its thrift and enterprise. [2] Before the massacre of the masters, when they had a strong economy and a large population, its people had sent some young men to Africa and founded Utica. [3] Meanwhile King Mutto died in Tyre, appointing as his heirs his son, Pygmalion, and his daughter, Elissa, a girl of exceptional beauty.[11]

9. An interesting parallel with the story at 1.10.3ff. of how Darius I gained the throne.

10. This was not mentioned at 11.10.10ff. Perhaps we should assume that Strato's family lost the throne at this point, as Trogus may have specified.

11. Elissa, a genuine Phoenician name, was immortalized as Dido in Vergil's *Aeneid*; it may be noted that Aeneas does not appear in Justin's version. Elissa is mentioned in a quotation from one Menandros of Ephesus provided by Josephus *Against Apion* 1.18, where the date corresponds with that of the Timaean

[4] The people consigned the throne to Pygmalion, though he was still a boy, [5] while Elissa married her uncle Acherbas, the priest of Hercules, a position ranking next to that of king. [6] Acherbas had great wealth but he kept it concealed; and out of fear of the king he had entrusted his gold not to his house but to the earth. [7] Although people were not aware of this, rumour of it still got out. [8] This excited Pygmalion who, in total disregard of human rights, put to death the man who was both his uncle and brother-in-law, with no thought for family obligations.

[9] The crime turned Elissa against her brother for a long time. Finally, concealing her hatred and assuming a conciliatory demeanour, she secretly prepared her escape, taking into her confidence a number of the more prominent citizens who she thought hated the king as much as she did and were just as eager to get away. [10] Then she outwitted her brother: she pretended that she wished to move in with him so that her husband's home would no longer revive within her, when she wished to forget, the painful memory of her grief for him, and so that bitter reminders of him would no longer meet her eyes. [11] Pygmalion was not displeased when he heard his sister's words, for he thought that along with her would come the gold of Acherbas. [12] At the start of the evening, however, when men were sent by the king to help her with her moving, Elissa had them embark on some ships along with all her possessions and, setting out to sea, forced them to throw overboard some bags weighted with sand, pretending it was money. [13] Then, shedding tears, she called on Acherbas in a mournful voice, begging him to accept graciously her wealth, which he had left to her, and to take as his funerary offerings the things that had been the cause of his death. [14] Then she turned to the helpers. As for herself, she had long been wishing to die, she told them; but they were now threatened with cruel torture and agonizing punishments for having cheated the greedy tyrant of the riches of Acherbas, for which he had committed murder. [15] In this way she terrified them all, and then took them on as companions in her escape. She was also joined by groups of senators who had prepared themselves for that night, and so, after gathering the sacred objects of Hercules, whose priest Acherbas had been, they all proceeded on their search for a home in exile.

---

tradition (cf. Dionysius of Halicarnassus *Roman Antiquities* 1.74) for the foundation of Carthage, 814, a date not too far away from the archaeological estimate. See also below 18.6.9. Hercules in the next sentence stands for the Phoenician Melkart.

5 [1] Their first landfall was the island of Cyprus. [2] Here, prompted by the gods, the priest of Jupiter offered himself to Elissa as a companion and associate in her quest along with his wife and children, making a condition that the position of priest remain his and his descendants' in perpetuity. [3] The compact was accepted as being a clear omen of good fortune. [4] It was a custom in Cyprus to send young girls down to the sea-shore on specific days before their marriage to earn money for their dowry by prostitution, and to offer Venus libations for the preservation of their virtue in the future. [5] Elissa had some eighty of these girls abducted and taken aboard so that her young men might have wives and her city a posterity. [6] In the meantime Pygmalion had learned of his sister's escape and had been preparing to hound her in her flight with an impious war. He was with difficulty persuaded to take no action by his mother's entreaties and by warnings from the gods; [7] for inspired soothsayers predicted that he would not go unpunished if he impeded the growth of a city that had enjoyed the most auspicious foundation in the world. Thus it was that the fugitives gained some respite.

[8] Elissa sailed into a gulf of Africa and here made overtures of friendship to the natives, who were themselves happy at the arrival of these foreigners with whom they could conduct trade by barter. [9] Then she bought some land, just as much as could be covered by a cow's hide, where she could give some recreation to her men, weary from the long sea-journey, until the time of her departure. She next gave orders for the hide to be cut into very fine strips, and in this way she took possession of a greater area than she had apparently bargained for. From this the place was afterwards called the Byrsa.[12] [10] Then neighbouring peoples flooded in, bringing with them many goods to sell to the foreigners in the hope of making money, [11] and established their homes there; and something resembling a city developed from this mass of humanity. [12] Further, ambassadors from the people of Utica brought the Tyrians gifts, recognizing them as their cousins, and urged them to found a city in that place where they had settled by chance. [13] The Africans, too, were eager to have them stay. [14] As a result, with the agreement of all, Carthage was founded, and an annual tax assessed for the land on which the city stood. [15] When the foundations were first being laid, an ox's head was found, an omen that, while the city would be prosperous, it would face hardships and always be enslaved. The city was therefore moved to another location. [16] There, too, a head was found, that of a

12. The citadel of Carthage, now known as the hill of St Louis.

horse, indicating that the people would be warlike and mighty; and so it provided for the city an auspicious site. [17] Then, as various tribes converged on it, drawn by the new town's reputation, both people and city quickly attained greatness.

6 [1] Its successful enterprises brought material prosperity to Carthage. Then Hiarbas, king of the Maxitani, summoned ten of the leading Carthaginians and asked for Elissa's hand in marriage, threatening war if they refused. [2] The ambassadors, afraid to report this to the queen, dealt with her with typical Punic ingenuity. They announced that the king was requesting someone to teach him and his Africans a more refined way of life—[3] but who could possibly be found willing to leave blood relatives for barbarians who lived like animals? [4] The ambassadors were then taken to task by the queen for refusing to accept a harsher life for the good of the fatherland to which they owed their very lives, should circumstances demand. Whereupon they revealed to her the errand given them by the king, adding that she should herself follow the course of action which she recommended for others, if she had the interests of the city at heart. [5] Caught in this trap, Elissa long called out the name of her husband, Acherbas, with streaming tears and sorrowful lamentation, finally replying that she would go where her destiny and that of her city called her. [6] To carry out this undertaking she set aside a period of three months. She built a pyre on the outskirts of the city and sacrificed many animals, as if to placate the spirit of her dead husband and send him offerings before her marriage. Then, taking a sword, she mounted the pyre. [7] She looked back at her people and declared that she was departing to join a husband, just as they had directed, and ended her life with the sword. [8] As long as Carthage remained unconquered, Elissa was worshipped as a goddess.

[9] This city was founded seventy-two years before Rome.[13] [10] While the valour of Carthage in warfare was much acclaimed, her domestic stability was riven by dissensions of various kinds. [11] When amongst other misfortunes the Carthaginians were beset by a plague, they resorted to a bloodthirsty and unconscionable form of religious ceremony to avert it—[12] they offered human sacrifice and brought to their altars children of an age that arouses pity even in one's enemies, seeking the indulgence of the gods by shedding the blood of those beings for whose lives the gods are most frequently invoked.

---

13. See above n. 11.

7 [1] Such iniquitous behaviour turned the gods against the Carthaginians. They had long fought with success in Sicily, but when the theatre of war was transferred to Sardinia, they lost most of their army and were defeated in a critical battle. [2] Because of this they ordered into exile their general Malchus,[14] under whose leadership they had conquered part of Sicily and also achieved great success against the Africans, and with him they sent the portion of the army which had survived the campaign. [3] The soldiers were incensed at this, and they sent a deputation to Carthage, first to beg for their return from exile and a pardon for the unsuccessful campaign, and then to give notice that what they could not gain by entreaty they would achieve by armed force. [4] When both the appeals and threats of the deputation were rebuffed, they allowed a few days to pass and then boarded their ships and arrived under arms at the city. [5] They called gods and men to witness that they were coming not to storm their native land but to recover it, and to show their compatriots that what they had lacked in the previous war was not courage but good fortune. [6] They then cut supplies to the city and laid siege to it, reducing the Carthaginians to the depths of despair. [7] Meanwhile, Carthalo, son of Malchus, the leader of the exiles, was passing by his father's camp on his way back from Tyre—he had been sent there by the Carthaginians to bring to Hercules tithes from the Sicilian plunder taken by his father. He was summoned by his father, but he replied that he would discharge the religious obligations of the state before turning to his personal duties. [8] The father took this ill, but he dared not do anything that violated religious observance.

[9] A few days later, Carthalo requested a leave of absence from his people and returned to his father, parading himself before the eyes of all his people, dressed in the purple robes and fillets of his priesthood. [10] His father took him aside and said: "Have you the effrontery, you miserable scoundrel, to come into the presence of all these pitiable citizens dressed in your purple and gold, to enter a camp full of sadness and dejection decked with the insignia of peace and happiness and almost beside yourself with joy? Couldn't you have done your flaunting somewhere else, before other people? [11] Was there not somewhere more appropriate than the place where your father was in disgrace and suffering the miseries of a painful banishment? [12] More than that, I summoned you a short while ago and you arrogantly disregarded your— I won't say 'your father,' but at least the leader of your fellow-citizens.

14. Possibly not a true personal name, as the Phoenician "melek" means "king." The date seems to be in the 580s.

[13] What do you think you are showing off in that purple and those crowns if not the renown of my victories? [14] Accordingly, since you recognize in your father nothing but an exile, I too shall consider myself your commander rather than your father and set a precedent with you so that no one hereafter may mock a father's unhappy circumstances." [15] With that Malchus ordered that he be crucified, dressed in his finery, on a towering cross visible to the whole town. [16] A few days later Malchus took Carthage. He called the people to an assembly where he complained of the injustice of his exile, argued that the war had been unavoidable, and declared that, satisfied with his victory, he would punish only those responsible for the wrongful exile of their unfortunate compatriots but would otherwise grant a general amnesty. [17] He thereupon put ten senators to death and returned the city to constitutional rule. [18] Shortly afterwards Malchus himself was accused of aspiring to become king, and paid the penalty for his twofold crime, committed both against his son and against his country. [19] He was succeeded as general by Mago, whose energy promoted Carthage's wealth as well as its territorial boundaries and military renown.

BOOK 19

1 [1] The Carthaginian general Mago was the very first to organize military discipline and thereby to establish a Punic empire; and he built up the strength of his state as much by his tactical skills as by his personal courage.[1] He died leaving two sons, Hasdrubal and Hamilcar. [2] These followed in the footsteps of their courageous father and were successors to him in greatness as well as by pedigree. [3] It was under their leadership that an attack was launched on Sardinia, and a war also fought against the Africans who were demanding the payment of many years' tribute on the city. [4] The Africans, however, had not only the better cause, but superior fortune as well, [5] and the war with them ended with a financial settlement rather than on the field of battle. [6] Also, in Sardinia, Hasdrubal was seriously wounded, and he died after transferring his command to his brother, Hamilcar. [7] His passing was regarded as a historical landmark, both because of the extent of the city's mourning for him and also because of his eleven dictatorships and four triumphs.

---

1. We are at the end of the sixth century.

[8] The death also raised the morale of the enemy, as though the strength of the Carthaginians had perished with their leader. [9] And so, because of the injustices which they had continually suffered at the hands of the Carthaginians, the peoples of Sicily sought the assistance of Leonidas, brother of the king of Sparta; and a savage war erupted which lasted a long time and in which victory fluctuated between the two sides.[2]

[10] Meanwhile, ambassadors came to Carthage from Darius, king of Persia, bearing an edict. The Carthaginians were forbidden to make human sacrifices or to eat the flesh of dogs. [11] Moreover, they were told by the king to burn rather than bury the bodies of their dead. [12] The ambassadors also requested assistance against Greece, on which Darius was about to make war. [13] The Carthaginians refused their help on the grounds that they were continually at war with their neighbours, but they readily complied with the other instructions so as not to appear thoroughly recalcitrant.

2 [1] In the meantime, Hamilcar was killed in the war in Sicily. He left three sons: Himilco, Hanno and Gisgo.[3] [2] Hasdrubal had the same number of sons as Hamilcar, these being Hannibal, Hasdrubal and Sapho, [3] and it was in their hands that the government of Carthage lay at this time. [4] An attack was made on the Mauretanians,[4] while there was also war with the Numidians; and the Africans were forced to refund to the Carthaginians the tribute that had been paid for the founding of the city. [5] Then, since such a powerful family of generals posed a threat to the liberty of the state, and since these men took decisions and action in everything on their own, a judicial body of a hundred senators was appointed, [6] which was to require accountability from commanders returning from war. This was to instill fear in them and make them frame their orders in the field in such a way as to respect the judicial processes and laws which existed at home.

[7] In Sicily, Himilco replaced Hamilcar as general.[5] Himilco had fought many successful battles on land and sea and had captured many towns, but now he lost his army to a sudden epidemic of the season.

2. This seems to refer to the Spartan Dorieus, as at Her. 5.43, 46ff.; Diod. 4.23.3. Leonidas became king after the death of Dorieus and Cleomenes (Her. 7.205).

3. The battle of Himera was thought to have occurred on the same day as Salamis in 480/79: Her. 7.165ff.; Diod. 11.20ff.

4. Mid-fifth century; cf. Pliny *NH* 2.169.

5. See Diod. 13.8off. (the year 406/5) and for what follows, in the summer of 396, 14.70ff.

[8] When this was reported in Carthage, the city went into mourning; every corner resounded with lamentation—it was just as if the city had been captured. [9] Private houses were shut; shut, too, were the temples of the gods. All religious activity was suspended, all private business cancelled. [10] Then the people converged in a body on the harbour and, as the few survivors of the catastrophe disembarked, they asked them for news of their relatives. [11] They began with diffident hope, anxious fear, the uncertain anticipation of loss; but when the fate of their kin became clear to the unhappy citizens, the lamentations of mourners and the cries and tearful complaints of bereaved mothers could be heard all along the shore.

3 [1] Meanwhile, the general who had lost his men left his ship dressed in the dirty tunic of a slave, and the sorrowing Carthaginians came together in droves to catch sight of him. [2] He, too, holding his hands up to heaven, shed tears, at one moment over his own lot, at the next for the fortunes of the state. [3] He then reproached the gods for having taken away from him the great military honours and the many trophies which they themselves had given him for his victories; for wiping out his victorious army, which had captured so many cities and had so often defeated its enemies in land and naval battles; and for destroying it not in combat but with a plague. [4] Even so, he declared, he brought to his fellow-citizens not inconsiderable solace in that, while their enemies might feel happy at the Carthaginians' misfortunes, they could not pride themselves on them, [5] since they could not claim that the Carthaginian dead had fallen at the hands of the foe or that those who had returned had been put to flight in the field. [6] Further, the booty which the enemy had captured when the Carthaginians had abandoned camp was not such as they could display as spoils from a defeated foe; it was what they had seized after title to it had been relinquished, when the accidental deaths of its owners left it without inheritors. [7] As regards the enemy, the Carthaginians had withdrawn as winners; as regards the plague, as losers. [8] But nothing caused him greater distress, he said, than not having been able to die amongst the bravest of his men, and instead to have been preserved not to derive pleasure from life but to be the plaything of misfortune. [9] And yet, after bringing back the pitiful remnants of his troops to Carthage, he was now going to follow those comrades of his; [10] and he would show his fatherland that the reason for his surviving to that day was not that he wanted to stay alive but so that he should not, by dying, fail the men whom the loathsome plague had spared, abandoned amidst the armies of their

enemy. [11] Loudly declaring this, he entered the city and, when he arrived at the threshold of his house, he dismissed the crowd which had been attending him with, as it were, his final address. [12] He locked his doors, let no one in to see him, not even his sons, and took his own life.

BOOK 20

1 [1] When Dionysius had driven the Carthaginians from Sicily and seized control of the entire island, he took his forces across to Italy.[1] He thought that inactivity was hazardous to his rule and that to keep such a large army in idleness was dangerous; [2] at the same time he wanted his soldiers' strength honed by unremitting toil and the boundaries of his realm pushed forward. [3] His first campaign was against the Greeks who held the coastal areas of the Italian Sea closest to him, [4] and after defeating them he attacked all their neighbours, designating as his enemies any inhabitants of Italy who were of Greek blood. [5] At that time these nations had settled not just a part of Italy but virtually all of it. [6] In fact, many cities to this day exhibit traces of Greek culture despite the passage of time. [7] The Tuscan peoples living on the coast of the Lower Sea came from Lydia, [8] and the Veneti, whom we find today inhabiting the Upper Sea, were sent to that place, under the leadership of Antenor, by Troy after its capture and defeat.[2] [9] Adria, too, which stands close to the Illyrian Sea and which also gave its name to the Adriatic Sea, is a Greek city; [10] while Arpi was founded by Diomedes, after the destruction of Troy, when he was shipwrecked in the region. [11] Pisae, in Liguria, also had Greek founders, and Tarquinii in Etruria and Spina in Umbria derive from the Thessalians, Perusia from the Achaeans. [12] I have no need to mention the city of Caere, or the Latin peoples deemed to be founded by Aeneas. [13] The Falisci and the peoples of Nola and

1. While Trogus' prologue tells us that Dionysius I was mentioned in Book 19, he has not yet appeared in Justin. While Timaeus again looms as the source in the present book, Diodorus (15.89.3) notes the history of Dionysius by the contemporary Philistus. A modern treatment is L. J. Sanders, *Dionysius I of Syracuse and Greek Tyranny* (London 1987). The events here are interspersed in Diodorus from 13.90 onward, beginning in the year 405 and ending in 367.

2. For the alleged Lydian origin of the Etruscans see Her. 1.94. The Lower Sea is the Tyrrhenian, the Upper Sea the Adriatic. On the Veneti see Livy 1.1.2 with R. M. Ogilvie, *A Commentary on Livy Books 1–5* (Oxford 1965), 35f.

Abella are clearly colonists from Chalcis. [14] Then there is the whole length of Campania, the Bruttii and the Sabines, the Samnites, [15] and the Tarentines, who, we are told, came from Sparta and were called the Illegitimates.[3] [16] They say that Philoctetes founded the city of Thurii; and to this day visits are made there to his tomb, and likewise, in the temple of Apollo, to the arrows of Hercules which sealed the fate of Troy.

2 [1] The people of Metapontum also have on display, in the temple of Minerva, the iron tools used for the construction of the Trojan horse by Epeos, their founder. [2] This explains why all that area of Italy was called "greater Greece".[4]

[3] At the very beginning, however, the people of Metapontum, in league with those of Sybaris and Croton, determined to drive the other Greeks from Italy. [4] First they captured the city of Siris, but in storming it they put to the sword, amidst the very altars, 50 young men who were clinging to the statue of Minerva, along with the priest of the goddess, dressed in his vestments. [5] For this reason they were beset by a plague and by internal dissensions both, and the people of Croton took the initiative and approached the Delphic Oracle. [6] The reply they were given was that their tribulations would cease if they placated the goddess Minerva, whom they had wronged, and the spirits of the men they had killed. [7] They therefore proceeded to construct life-sized statues for the young men and especially for Minerva; but the Metapontines found out about the oracle of the gods and decided to forestall the people of Croton in securing the favour of the dead souls and of the goddess—they set up smaller statues of stone for the young men and appeased the goddess with sacrificial cakes. [8] And so the plague was halted for both peoples, with the competition between them characterized by grandeur on the one side and speed on the other.

[9] Restored to health, the people of Croton did not remain inactive for long. [10] Angry that during their assault on Siris the town had been given support against them by the Locrians, they now opened hostilities with the latter. [11] Alarmed, the Locrians had recourse to the Spartans, whom they begged for help as suppliants. [12] The Spartans, however, were vexed at the prospect of a distant campaign and told them to ask Castor and Pollux for help. [13] The Locrian ambassadors did not disregard an answer given by an allied city and, setting off for the nearest

3. See 3.4.
4. "Maior Graecia" rather than the more usual "Magna Graecia," i.e. "Great Greece."

temple, they offered sacrifice and prayed for divine assistance. [14] The sacrifice proceeded auspiciously, and the Locrians, who imagined that they had obtained what they had been requesting, were as delighted as if they were going to be taking the gods away with them. They set down cushions for the deities in their ship and, setting off with favourable omens, brought to their countrymen words of consolation rather than assistance.

3 [1] When the people of Croton learned of these events, they too sent ambassadors to the oracle at Delphi asking how they could gain a victory and a successful conclusion to the war. [2] The answer given was that victory over their enemy was to be sought by prayer rather than weapons. [3] They therefore made a pledge of a tenth of their prospective spoils to Apollo, but the Locrians found out about their enemies' vow and the oracle of the god, and they themselves promised a ninth of any spoils taken, keeping the matter secret so as not to be outbid in pledges to the god. [4] They then marched forth to battle where 120,000 men of Croton had taken up their positions under arms. When the Locrians considered their own numerical inferiority—they had a mere 15,000 men in the field—they abandoned all hope of victory and agreed to meet the death that was surely theirs; [5] their desperate situation fired them individually with such fervour that they considered themselves victorious if they did not die unavenged. [6] But in seeking merely to die with honour, they succeeded in gaining a victory, and it was only their desperation that brought them their success. [7] While the Locrians were fighting, an eagle constantly hovered over their battleline, and kept flying around them until they prevailed. [8] Moreover, two young men were sighted fighting on the wings of the army; they bore arms different from all the others, were of extraordinary size and had white horses and scarlet cloaks.[5] They were no longer to be seen after the battle. [9] The wonder which this provoked was amplified by the unbelievable speed with which news of the battle was reported: on the very day on which the engagement took place in Italy, the victory was announced in Corinth, Athens and Sparta.

4 [1] After this the people of Croton gave up training in physical prowess and paid no further attention to warfare.[6] [2] They developed a positive

---

5. Evidently Castor and Pollux; see 2.12 above.
6. Athletes of Croton enjoyed remarkable success at the Olympic games from 588 to 484, after which not a single victor is known from that city. Whether this had anything to do with Pythagoras is another matter; it seems chronologically

aversion to that which they had taken up unsuccessfully, and they would have transformed their life-style into one of outright hedonism had it not been for the philosopher Pythagoras. [3] He was born on Samos, the son of Maratus[7], a wealthy merchant, and after making great progress in a philosophical education there, he had set out first for Egypt and then Babylonia to learn astronomy and examine the question of the origins of the universe, ultimately attaining the heights of learning. [4] On his return he had gone to Crete and Sparta to familiarize himself with the legal systems of Minos and Lycurgus,[8] which were famous at that time. [5] Endowed with all this learning he came to Croton where he succeeded by his personal authority in reconverting to the practice of frugality a population which had lapsed into luxurious living. [6] He made a point of praising virtue every day, and of listing the ills of profligacy and the disasters which had struck states ruined by this malaise; [7] and he rallied the common people to such an enthusiastic espousal of the simple life that it came to appear incredible that any of them had ever been profligate. [8] It was a frequent practice of his to give instruction to married women apart from their husbands, and to children apart from their parents. [9] To the former he would teach chastity and obedience to their husbands, to the latter decorum and literary studies, [10] and he continually impressed upon all of them the importance of temperance as the parent of the virtues. [11] And by reiterating his arguments he achieved such success that the married women cast off their gold-embroidered robes and the other finery of their rank as being the promoters of extravagance, took them to the temple of Juno and consecrated them to the goddess herself, [12] thus declaring publicly that the real finery of married women was chastity, not clothes. [13] How far he succeeded with the young people can clearly be gauged from his triumph over the recalcitrant female temper.[9] [14] However, when three hundred of the young men formed an association by swearing an

---

impossible. See W. K. C. Guthrie, *A History of Greek Philosophy* vol. 1 (Cambridge 1971), 173ff.

7. The text is a problem here; according to Her. 4.95, Pythagoras' father was called Mnesarchus.

8. For the latter see 3.2.5ff. The Spartan and Cretan systems had much in common and tradition spoke of the latter as a model for the former.

9. Such is the traditional interpretation of the Latin (see Lewis and Short, *A Latin Dictionary* s.v. "profligo"), but the following has been suggested by Professor A. MacGregor: "How profligate the character of the youth had become can clearly be gauged from the stubborn depravity that he overcame among the women."

oath of fraternity and began to live apart from the other citizens, they turned the entire community against them; it suspected them of banding together to form some secret conspiracy. [15] Thus, when they had assembled in a single house, the citizens decided to burn them alive. [16] In the commotion some sixty of them died, and the others went into exile.

[17] After twenty years in Croton Pythagoras moved to Metapontum, where he died, [18] and such was the admiration felt for him that the citizens made his house a temple and worshipped him as a god.

5 [1] As I observed above,[10] the tyrant Dionysius had transported an army from Sicily to Italy and launched an attack on the Greeks. He defeated the Locrians and went on to attack the people of Croton, who were now barely regaining their strength in the long peace which followed the disastrous outcome of their previous war. [2] However, with their small numbers the people of Croton put up stouter resistance to Dionysius' huge army than they had with all their thousands to the diminutive force of Locrians. [3] Such is the valour that poverty can find in the face of insolent riches; and unexpected victory is, on occasion, so much more certain than the one that was expected.

[4] While Dionysius was fighting the campaign he was approached by legates from the Gauls who had burned Rome some months before. They sought an alliance and friendly relations with him, [5] observing that their nation was situated amidst his foes and would therefore be of great use to him, either fighting with him in the actual battle or else operating at the rear when the enemy was preoccupied with the engagement. [6] Dionysius was pleased with the embassy. He confirmed the alliance and, now that his strength was augmented with Gallic auxiliaries, recommenced the war as if beginning afresh. [7] What brought these Gauls to Italy in search of a new home was internal dissension and incessant strife in their homeland. [8] Tired of this, they entered Italy, drove the Etrurians from their homes and founded Mediolanum, Comum, Brixia, Verona, Bergomum, Tridentum and Vicentia. [9] The Etrurians for their part, after losing their ancestral homes, seized the Alps under the leadership of Raetus and founded the Raetian people, so named after their leader.

[10] However, Dionysius was recalled to Sicily by the coming of the Carthaginians. They had rebuilt their army and were now renewing

10. 20.1.1. Events here are recounted in Diod. 14–15; the attack on Croton is at 14.100ff. under the years 390/89 and 389/8; for the Gauls see 14.113ff. (387).

with increased vigour the war which they had abandoned.[11] [11] The Carthaginian general in the campaign was Hanno, [12] whose personal enemy was Suniatus, at that time the most powerful man in Carthage. Out of hatred for Hanno, Suniatus had written a letter in Greek telling Dionysius, as if confiding in him, of the coming of the Carthaginian army and the inertia of its general. The letter was intercepted and Suniatus was condemned for treason; and a decree was passed in the senate [13] forbidding any Carthaginian thereafter to study Greek literature or language, to ensure that no one be able to communicate with the enemy orally or in writing without an interpreter. [14] Not long afterwards Dionysius, the man whom neither Sicily nor Italy had been able to contain a short time before, was defeated and broken by constant warfare, and finally murdered by a conspiracy of his own kin.[12]

BOOK 21

1 [1] When the tyrant Dionysius was killed in Sicily, his soldiers replaced him with the eldest of his sons, who was also called Dionysius.[1] [2] They were thus following the dictates of nature, but they also thought the kingdom would be stronger for remaining in the hands of one man than if it were split up and divided among a number of sons. [3] At the start of his reign, however, Dionysius dearly wished to eliminate the uncles of his brothers, whom he saw as competitors for his power and also as men who would urge the other children of the elder Dionysius to partition the kingdom. [4] For a short time he veiled his intentions and concentrated first on winning popular support; for, if he gained general approval in advance, the action on which he had decided would be more pardonable. [5] He therefore released from prison 3,000 convicts, granted a three-

---

11. In some manuscripts the word "lue" occurs, which could be correct. If it is, then the translation would be "abandoned because of the plague."

12. Diod. 15.73f. (the year 368/7) says he died of illness.

1. Dionysius II, who ruled for twelve years from 367, was treated by Philistus in two books down to 363/2 (Diod. 15.89.3), though again Trogus' immediate source will have been Timaeus. The succession occurs at Diod. 15.74 and events thereafter are interwoven in Diodorus' account through Book 16. Though expelled in 356, Dionysius regained the tyranny in 347, only to be ousted again in 343, at which time he went to Corinth. Justin omits the part played by Dion and Timoleon, both of whom enjoy biographies by Plutarch. See R. A. Talbert, *Timoleon and the Revival of Greek Sicily* (Cambridge 1974).

year remission of taxes to the people and resorted to all possible kinds of seductive measures to win over the hearts of all his subjects. [6] He then turned to the crime on which he was intent, putting to death not only the relatives of his brothers but his brothers themselves. [7] Thus he left to the people to whom he owed a share of his rule not even a share in this life, inaugurating with his own kin his despotic rule before inflicting it on others.

2 [1] With his rivals eliminated, Dionysius now lapsed into inertia; from his self-indulgence he developed obesity and an eye-disease which rendered him sensitive to sunshine, dust and even daylight. [2] Thinking he was regarded with contempt because of this, he began an orgy of cruelty, not, like his father, filling the prisons with convicts, but the city itself with blood, [3] which made him an object of abhorrence rather than contempt. [4] The people of Syracuse accordingly declared war on him and he deliberated for a long time whether to abdicate or put up armed resistance, [5] but he was forced into battle by his soldiers who were hoping to gain plunder and to pillage the city. [6] He was defeated, and when he tried his luck a second time with no more success, he sent an embassy to the Syracusans promising to lay down his tyranny if they sent him men with whom he could conclude a peace treaty. [7] Some leading citizens of Syracuse were sent to him for this purpose. Dionysius put them in prison and, when the Syracusans were off their guard and had no fear of an offensive move, sent his army to destroy their city. [8] Thus a critical battle was fought inside the city itself, but the townspeople overwhelmed their foes by their numbers and Dionysius was driven back. He was afraid he would be besieged in the citadel, and so he took all his royal possessions and slipped furtively away to Italy. [9] He was accepted as a refugee by his allies, the Locrians, and then, as if he were their legitimate ruler, he seized the acropolis and subjected them to his characteristic ruthlessness. [10] He ordered the arrest of the wives of leading citizens so he could ravish them; he abducted virgins before their marriage and gave them back defloured to their betrothed; he either banished from the state or had executed all the richest citizens, confiscating their property.

3 [1] Then, since he lacked an excuse for plunder, he played a crafty trick on the entire community. [2] Once, when the Locrians were hard pressed in a war with Leophron, tyrant of Rhegium, they had made a vow to prostitute their unmarried women on the festival of Venus if they were victorious. [3] This vow had gone unfulfilled, and now the Locrians were fighting an unsuccessful war with the Lucanians. Dionysius called them to a meeting and urged them to send their wives and daughters to the temple of Venus dressed in all their finery. [4] From these women a hundred would be selected by lot to discharge the communal vow and, to satisfy the religious requirements, spend a month on show in a brothel, but all the men would have previously sworn not to touch any of them. [5] So that this should not work to the disadvantage of the young women who were to release the state from its vow, they would issue a decree that no girl should marry until these women were given husbands. [6] Dionysius' plan was approved—it respected both the religious obligations and the virtue of the young women—and all the women, decked out in their expensive robes, made haste to assemble at the temple of Venus. [7] Dionysius sent in his soldiers, stripped all the women and made the jewelry of the matrons his personal booty. [8] Some of the ones with richer husbands saw them put to death; others the tyrant tortured to make them reveal the fortunes of their spouses. [9] By employing such tactics he reigned for six years, after which, driven from the city by a conspiracy of the Locrians, he returned to Sicily. There he used a stratagem to retake Syracuse, where everyone had felt secure after a long interval of peace.

4 [1] Such were the events in Sicily. In Africa, meanwhile, the leading Carthaginian citizen, Hanno, used his personal fortune, which surpassed the resources of the state, to seize power and tried to make himself king by a massacre of the senate.[2] [2] For this crime he chose the day appointed for his daughter's marriage in order that his wicked schemes could be more easily concealed behind the veil of religious practice. [3] He put on one banquet in the public porticoes for the common people, and another in his own home for the senate, so that he could, in greater secrecy and without witnesses, kill the senators by poisoning their cups and the more easily attack a state bereft of protection. [4] Although the affair was divulged to the magistrates by Hanno's servants, the crime was merely forestalled, not punished; it was feared that, when such a powerful man was involved, a judicial inquiry might do more damage than the initial plot. [5] Satisfied with having checked him, the magistrates merely imposed by decree a limit to what one might spend on a wedding and ordered that this be observed by the whole state, not just one man, so that they should not seem to be singling out an individual rather than correcting a general fault.

[6] Baffled by this ploy, Hanno next incited a slave uprising, and again fixed a day for the assassinations. But once more he saw that he had been betrayed and, fearing a trial, he seized one of the forts with 20,000

2. For this episode Justin is the prime source.

slaves. [7] While he was attempting to induce the Africans and the king of the Mauretanians to join him, he was captured. First he was flogged, then his eyes were gouged out, and his arms and legs broken, as though punishment were being inflicted on every part of his body; finally he was put to death before the eyes of his people, and his body, mutilated by the lash, fixed to a cross. [8] His sons, too, and all his relatives, innocent though they were, were put to death to prevent any member of such an iniquitous family surviving either to imitate his crime or to avenge his death.

5 [1] Meanwhile, Dionysius, reinstated in Syracuse, was day by day becoming more repressive and savage towards his citizens, and was as a result beset by another conspiracy. [2] On this occasion he abdicated, surrendered the acropolis along with his army to the Syracusans and, taking with him only his personal effects, set off for exile in Corinth. [3] Thinking that the greatest security lay in the lowest levels of society, he there lapsed into the most degrading style of life. [4] Not satisfied with lounging about the public places, he would drink there too; not content with merely being seen in the taverns and whore-houses, he stayed in them for days on end. [5] He would hold the most trivial discussions with the lowest of the low, and wander around filthy and dressed in rags. [6] He even preferred to be laughed at than to laugh at someone else. He would haunt the marketplace and devour with his eyes what he could not afford. He would wrangle with pimps before city officials. [7] And he did all that to appear contemptible rather than fearsome. [8] Finally he took up the profession of schoolteacher, teaching his boys at the street-corners, so that he would be continually seen in public by those who feared him, or else more easily despised by those who did not. [9] For though tyrants are always well-endowed with such vices, in his case the vices were simulated and not a reflection of his nature; he did these things from design rather than because he had lost his regal dignity—he knew from experience how hated the name "tyrant" was, even in the absence of power. [10] So he struggled to erase the resentment felt for his past actions by making his present ones the object of disdain, seeking a safe rather than respectable course of action. [11] Yet while he resorted to these deceptions, he was three times charged with aspiring to tyranny, and he was acquitted only because he was regarded with contempt.

6 [1] Meanwhile the Carthaginians were alarmed by the enormous success of Alexander the Great and feared that he intended to add Africa to his Persian empire. They therefore sent Hamilcar, who had the surname "Rodanus," a man particularly remarkable for his ingenuity and eloquence, to investigate Alexander's intentions.[3] [2] The anxiety of the Carthaginians was further increased by the capture of Tyre, the city of their original founders,[4] [3] and also by the founding of Alexandria, a potential rival to Carthage, on the borders of Africa and Egypt, [4] as well as by the success of a king whose ambition and good fortune knew no bounds. [5] Accordingly, Hamilcar, who used Parmenion to gain an audience with the king, pretended that he had come to seek refuge with the king after being expelled from his country, and he offered his services as a common soldier on the campaign. [6] After finding out Alexander's plans in this way, he gave a full account to his fellow-citizens, written on wooden tablets with fresh wax poured over them.[5] [7] But when he returned to his country after the king's death, the Carthaginians executed him—demonstrating as much ruthlessness as ingratitude—on the grounds that he had tried to sell out the city to the king.

BOOK 22

1 [1] Agathocles, tyrant of Sicily, who rose to an eminence equal to that of Dionysius the Elder, achieved sovereignty from a mean and lowly background.[1] [2] He was born in Sicily, the son of a potter, and his boyhood was no more respectable than his beginnings [3] for, thanks to his remarkable good looks, he long supported himself by submitting to sexual perversions. [4] Then, as he passed the years of puberty, he transferred his immoral ways from men to women, [5] after which, having gained a reputation with both sexes, he turned his hand to larceny. [6] After a while Agathocles came to Syracuse, where he was admitted to the citizenship, but he was long without credit [7] because he had neither property to lose nor honour to tarnish. [8] He finally enrolled as a common soldier, but his life became as turbulent now as it had been disreputable before and he was ready to put his hand to any villainy. [9] Certainly, he was recognized as being both a man of action and a very able speaker in debate. [10] And so he became, in short order, a centurion

3. Cf. Diod. 17.113.2; Arrian 7.15.4; Frontinus *Strategems* 1.2.3 (from Trogus).
4. See 18.3ff.
5. A trick reminiscent of Demaratus' at 2.10.13ff.
1. Timaeus seems to remain Trogus' source (cf. Pol. 12.15), if not that of other writers. There are, nonetheless, similarities with the account of Diodorus, which begins with Book 19 in 317/6.

and then a military tribune. [11] In his first campaign, against the people of Aetna, he gave a good account of himself to the Syracusans, [12] and in the next, against the Campanians, he inspired all his fellows with such optimism as to his capabilities that when their general, Damascon, died Agathocles was selected to replace him. [13] He also married Damascon's wife (with whom he had already had an affair), on her husband's death.[2] [14] Not satisfied with his sudden rise from poverty to riches Agathocles also practiced piracy against his country, [15] and was saved only by the fact that, when his accomplices were captured and tortured, they denied his involvement. [16] He twice tried to gain power in Syracuse, and twice was driven into exile.

2 [1] Agathocles went into exile amongst the Murgantini,[3] by whom, because of their hatred for the Syracusans, he was first made praetor, then general. [2] In the ensuing war he captured the city of Leontini and also laid siege to the city of Syracuse, his own fatherland. [3] The Syracusans appealed for help to the Carthaginian general Hamilcar, who laid aside his animosity towards them and sent military support. [4] Thus, at one and the same time, Syracuse was being defended by an enemy with the devotion of a citizen and also attacked by a citizen with the hatred of an enemy. [5] But when Agathocles saw that the defence of the city was more spirited than the attack, he sent messengers to Hamilcar and prevailed on him to undertake negotiations for peace between himself and the Syracusans, privately promising him some favours in return. [6] Filled with such hopes, Hamilcar made a pact with him that each lend his support to the other, on the understanding that Hamilcar receive from Agathocles as much military support to increase his authority at home as he should lend Agathocles in order to face the Syracusans. [7] Consequently, Agathocles not only gained a peace treaty through the negotiations but was also appointed praetor in Syracuse, [8] whereupon he swore an oath to Hamilcar, taking forth and handling the cult-objects of Ceres, that he would be loyal to the Carthaginians. [9] Then, given 5,000 Africans by Hamilcar, he killed all the most powerful members of the nobility [10] and, creating the impression that he was going to establish a constitution, had the commons summoned to a meeting in the theatre, having already convened the senate in the gymnasium as though he were going to conduct some preliminary business with them. [11] These measures taken, he sent in his soldiers, cordoned off the commons and

2. In Diod. 19.3 Agathocles marries the widow of his lover Damas.
3. The people of Morgantina.

massacred the senate. [12] When the slaughter was over, he also put to the sword the richest and most energetic of the common people.

3 [1] Next, Agathocles drafted troops and levied an army.[4] Thus equipped, he made a sudden attack on the neighbouring cities, who feared no hostile move against themselves, [2] and he also persecuted in a shameful manner the allies of the Carthaginians, with the acquiescence of Hamilcar. As a result, the allies lodged complaints at Carthage, not so much about Agathocles as about Hamilcar, [3] accusing the one of being a despotic tyrant and the other of being a traitor for making a pact which sacrificed the fortunes of the allies to the most vicious of enemies. [4] From the start, they said, Syracuse—a city which had always been an adversary of the Carthaginians and Carthage's rival for power in Sicily— had been delivered to Agathocles to secure his alliance with Hamilcar. And now, in addition, the city-states of their allies had been sacrificed to the same man, ostensibly to keep the peace. [5] They were accordingly making a formal declaration to the Carthaginians that these measures would shortly recoil upon them, and that the Carthaginians would soon realize the extent of the damage they had done, as much to Africa itself as to Sicily.

[6] These protests set the senate against Hamilcar, but since he still held his command they conducted a vote on him in secret. They had the senators' ballots cast into an urn, without being read out, and sealed until the return from Sicily of a second Hamilcar, the son of Gisgo. [7] In fact, this clever manoeuvre of the Carthaginians with the untallied ballots was thwarted by the death of Hamilcar, and thanks to the workings of destiny a man was delivered from punishment after being wrongfully condemned without a fair hearing by his fellow-citizens. [8] This episode provided Agathocles with a motive for opening hostilities against the Carthaginians.[5] [9] His first encounter was with Hamilcar, son of Gisgo; defeated by him, Agathocles withdrew to Syracuse to renew the struggle with increased strength. [10] But his fortunes in the second battle were the same as in the first.

4 [1] The victorious Carthaginians now laid siege to Syracuse.[6] Agathocles could see he was no match for them in military strength and also that he was ill equipped to withstand a siege; moreover, he had been deserted by his allies, who had been shocked by his brutality. He therefore

4. 314/3: Diod. 19.65, 70ff.
5. 312/11 and 311/10: Diod. 19.102ff, 106ff.
6. 310/09: Diod. 20.3ff.

decided to transfer the theatre of war to Africa, [2] displaying thereby an incredible bravado, since he was carrying the war to the city of men for whom he was no match in front of his own city, attacking the territory of others when he was unable to defend his own, and insulting his conquerors after he had been conquered. [3] The secrecy which surrounded this plan was as astonishing as the original idea. All he told his people was that he had found a way to victory, and he asked them only to strengthen their resolve to face the siege, which would be of short duration, saying that he gave anyone dissatisfied with the current state of affairs complete freedom to leave; [4] 1,600 left and Agathocles provided the rest with grain and funds to face the pressures of the siege. He took with him just 50 talents for immediate needs, intending to obtain the rest from his enemy rather than from his allies. [5] He then freed all slaves of an age suitable for military service, swore them in and embarked them on vessels with what constituted the majority of his armed forces, believing that a complete leveling of social class would lead to competition amongst them in heroism. All the rest he left to defend the fatherland.

5 [1] Thus, in the seventh year of his reign, Agathocles set a course for Africa, accompanied by his two grown sons, Archagathus and Heraclides, and with none of the soldiers aware of his destination—[2] they all believed they were on a marauding expedition to Italy or making for Sardinia. It was only when he had disembarked his army on the coast of Africa that he revealed his strategy to them all. [3] He pointed out to them the difficulties in which Syracuse found herself, having no other recourse but to inflict on the enemy what the Syracusans themselves were suffering. [4] War, he said, was fought in one fashion at home and in another abroad. At home one's resources consisted entirely of what the strength of the country could supply; abroad, an enemy could also be defeated by his own strength, as allies defected and, out of resentment over their long subjugation, cast about for outside assistance. [5] The Syracusans had a further advantage, he said, in that the cities and strongholds of Africa were not walled and not situated on mountains, but lay in open plains and had no fortifications, so they could all be easily enticed into joining his campaign from fear of being destroyed. [6] Thus a greater war was going to flare up against the Carthaginians from Africa itself than from Sicily; support for the Syracusans would come together from all quarters against a single city, whose reputation was greater than its power, and from this source he would derive the might he had not brought with him. [7] Sudden panic amongst the Carthaginians would

also be of no little importance for their victory, he added; alarmed at
the great daring of their enemy, they would be thrown into confusion.
[8] Then there would be the burning of farms, the pillaging of defiant
cities and fortresses, and finally the siege of Carthage itself, [9] all of
which would make the enemy realize that they had no monopoly on
offensive warfare, but that others could also make war on them. [10] By
such means not only could the Carthaginians be beaten, but Sicily too
could be liberated, for their enemies would not persist in the siege when
there was pressure on their own territory. [11] Consequently, he said,
an easier campaign could not be found anywhere else, nor a richer booty,
for, after the capture of Carthage, all of Africa and Sicily would be the
prize of the victors. [12] And certainly the renown of such a distinguished
campaign would last forever and be so great that it could never fade
into oblivion; it would be said that the Syracusans were unique amongst
mortals in that they exported to enemy territory a war they could not
sustain at home, actually went on the offensive against their conquerors
and laid siege to those who were besieging their own city. [13] Thus,
he concluded, they should all go into the campaign with fortitude and
enthusiasm because no other could give them a richer prize if they were
victorious or a more illustrious memorial if they lost.

6 [1] Although the spirits of his men were raised by these words of
encouragement, they were unnerved by superstition because of an omen:
during the sea-voyage there had been an eclipse of the sun. [2] Agathocles
was as careful in explaining the phenomenon as in explaining his tactics;
he claimed that, if the eclipse had occurred before their departure, he
would have considered it a portent of evil for those embarking, but since
it occurred after they left, it was a sign for those against whom they were
sailing. [3] At all events, he said, an eclipse of any of the planets[7] always
signified an alteration in the current state of affairs, and it was certain that
this meant change both for the prosperity of the Carthaginians and for the
Syracusans' own trials and tribulations. [4] His men were reassured by
this, and with the agreement of the army he ordered that all the ships be
burned, so that everyone would know that, with the possibility of escape
removed, their prospects were limited to victory or death. [5] Then, as
they advanced, they laid waste everything in their path and set fire to
fortresses and country-houses, until Hanno came to meet them with a

---

7. The Latin expression here, "naturalium siderum" ("natural stars"), seems
to be unique to Justin and probably refers to the planets, including the sun and
the moon, which can be said to govern nature (so Gronovius).

levy of 30,000 peasants. [6] But when battle was joined, 2,000 Sicilians fell and 3,000 Carthaginians, along with their leader.[8] [7] By this victory the spirits of the Sicilians were raised, those of the Carthaginians crushed.

[8] With his enemies defeated, Agathocles now proceeded to reduce cities and fortresses, carrying off enormous plunder and massacring many thousands of the enemy. [9] He then pitched camp five miles from Carthage so that its inhabitants might observe, from the walls of the city itself, the loss of their dearest possessions, the destruction of their land and the burning of their farms. [10] Meanwhile, word spread far and wide throughout Africa that the army of the Carthaginians had been destroyed and their cities seized. [11] There was universal amazement and wonder that so great an empire could be so suddenly under attack, and from an already defeated enemy at that. Then, little by little, the wonder turned into contempt for the Carthaginians, [12] and shortly afterwards not only the Africans but the most famous cities, too, accepted these revolutionary developments and defected to Agathocles, whom they supplied with grain and funds.

7 [1] These reversals of the Carthaginians were aggravated by an event which came virtually as the climax of their misfortunes: the loss in Sicily of an army along with its commander.[9] [2] News arrived that, after Agathocles left Sicily, the Carthaginians became less energetic in prosecuting the siege of Syracuse and were massacred by Antandrus, brother of King Agathocles. [3] Hence, since the Carthaginians were experiencing the same fortune at home and overseas, it was not just the tribute-paying cities which began to abandon them but also the allied princes, who measured their obligations of friendship not by loyalty but by success.

[4] Amongst the latter was the king of Cyrene, Ophellas, who entertained the outrageous ambition of dominating the whole of Africa.[10] He had formed an alliance with Agathocles through legates and had reached an agreement with him that, should the Carthaginians be vanquished, control of Sicily would go to Agathocles, control of Africa to himself. [5] Ophellas now came in person with a large army to join

8. An interesting case of variation in numbers: according to Diod. 20.13.1, 200 Greeks fell and 1000 Carthaginians (noting that some put the latter figure as high as 3000), while Orosius 4.6.25 puts the figure at 2000 Carthaginians and 2 Sicilians!

9. 309/8: Diod. 20.29ff.

10. 308/7: Diod. 20.38ff.

the struggle and Agathocles plied him with unctuous remarks and abject flattery—they had often dined together, and Agathocles' son had
been adopted by Ophellas.   Then, once Ophellas was off his guard,
Agathocles murdered him, [6] took over his army, and defeated the
Carthaginians (who were renewing their war-effort with all their might)
in a momentous battle which spilled much blood in both armies. [7] The
Carthaginians were struck with such despondency after this critical encounter that Bomilcar, their leader, would have gone over to Agathocles
with his troops but for a mutiny in the latter's army.   [8] Bomilcar
was then crucified for his crime by the Carthaginians in the centre of
the forum, so that the place which had in the past served to crown
his honours might now also witness his torment. [9] Bomilcar, however, bore the cruelty of his fellow-citizens with fortitude, to the extent of haranguing the Carthaginians on their wrongdoings from the
top of his cross as though from a court bench, [10] accusing them
of having destroyed Hanno with a groundless and malicious charge
of aspiring to kingship, of exiling the innocent Gisgo, and of cast-
ing votes secretly against his own uncle, Hamilcar, for having wished
to make Agathocles their ally rather than their enemy.   [11] After
shouting out these charges before a crowded assembly of the people,
he expired.

8 [1] Meanwhile, once his business in Africa was finished, Agathocles
entrusted his army to his son, Archagathus, and returned to Sicily, thinking that nothing had been accomplished in Africa if Syracuse remained
under siege.[11] [2] For after the death of Hamilcar, son of Gisgo, a fresh
army had been sent there by the Carthaginians.   [3] As soon as he
arrived, all the cities of Sicily immediately raced to surrender to him,
since they had heard of his achievements in Africa, and so, driving the
Carthaginians from Sicily, Agathocles made himself master of the entire
island. [4] He then returned to Africa, where he was confronted by a
mutiny amongst the troops, whose pay had been withheld by the son until
the father returned. [5] Agathocles summoned the men to a meeting and
calmed them with conciliatory remarks, saying that they should get their
pay from the enemy, not keep dinning him about it, that they would share
the victory and also share the spoils. [6] Let them but make a little effort,
he urged, until what was left of the war was terminated; for well they
knew that the capture of Carthage would fulfil the hopes of them all.
[7] The mutiny was quelled, and a few days later Agathocles led his army

---

11. 307/6. Cf. Diod. 20.54ff., which does not quite square in detail.

towards the enemy encampment, where he incautiously joined battle and lost most of his troops. [8] He fled back to his camp, but he could see that there was resentment felt against him for joining battle recklessly, and he was also worried by the men's earlier rancour over not being paid. In the dead of night he slipped away from camp accompanied only by his son Archagathus.

[9] On learning of this, Agathocles' soldiers panicked no less than if they had been taken by the enemy. They declared that they had now been forsaken twice over in the midst of their enemies by their king, a man who had abandoned their safety when he had an obligation not to neglect even their burial. [10] They wanted to pursue their king, but when they were attacked by the Numidians, they returned to camp. Archagathus, however, was caught and brought back; he had lost his way during the night and become separated from his father. [11] Agathocles sailed to Syracuse on the ships with which he had returned to Africa from Sicily, along with the men who had looked after them—[12] a superlative illustration of unprincipled behaviour: a king deserting his own army, and a father betraying his sons. [13] In Africa, meanwhile, after the flight of their king, the Sicilian soldiers made a pact with the enemy, killed Agathocles' children and surrendered to the Carthaginians. [14] Archagathus, at the moment he was being put to death by Arcesilaus, his father's erstwhile friend, asked what he thought Agathocles would do to the children of the man who was now rendering him childless, to which Arcesilaus replied that he was satisfied with knowing that they had outlived the children of Agathocles. [15] After this the Carthaginians sent generals to Sicily to pursue the war to a finish, and Agathocles made peace with them on even terms.[12]

BOOK 23

1 [1] After making peace with Carthage, the Sicilian king Agathocles subdued by force of arms a number of city-states which, overconfident in their strength, had been rebelling against him.[1] [2] Now he felt restricted by the narrow confines of the island over which he had entertained no hope of gaining even partial control at the beginning of his career,

12. 306/5: Diod. 20.77ff.
    1. For Agathocles' crossing to Italy in the 290s see Diod. 21.3f., 8, then 16 for his death in 289. For Dionysius see 20.1.1ff., 5.1ff.

and he crossed to Italy, following the example of Dionysius, who had reduced many of the city-states in Italy. [3] There his first opponents were the Bruttii, since they appeared to be the strongest and richest of the Italian tribes at that time, and they were, moreover, ready to seize opportunities to hurt their neighbours. [4] They had driven from Italy many communities of Greek origin, [5] and had also defeated in battle the Lucanians, who were their founders, making peace with them on even terms. [6] So savage was their temperament that they did not even keep their hands off those from whom they were descended.

[7] The Lucanians had employed the same system of education for their children as the Spartans. [8] As soon as they reached puberty, the children were kept in the woods among the shepherds, with no slaves to serve them and no garments to wear or to sleep on, the aim being to condition them from their earliest years to hardship and deprivation, having no contact with city life. [9] Their food was what they caught by hunting, their drink milk or spring-water. Thus were they toughened for the hardships of war. [10] Now fifty of these children used to make frequent raids on their neighbours' fields but, when many others flooded in to join them, and the attractions of the spoils swelled their numbers, they threw the whole region into turmoil. [11] Accordingly, Dionysius, tyrant of Sicily, plagued by complaints from his allies, had sent 600 Africans to stop the marauders. [12] The youths, however, stormed the Africans' stronghold, which had been betrayed to them by a woman called Bruttia and, when shepherds quickly came in droves to join them at the rumour of a new city being established, founded there a city-state, calling themselves Bruttii after the woman. [13] Their first war was with the Lucanians, to whom they owed their beginnings; [14] encouraged by victory over them, they made peace on even terms and proceeded to subdue all their other neighbours through armed struggle, acquiring in a short time such power that they were considered dangerous even to monarchs. [15] Then, when Alexander king of Epirus came into Italy with a large army to help the Greek city-states, he was destroyed by them along with all his forces.[2] [16] And so their aggressiveness, inflamed by this success, long struck terror into their neighbours. [17] Finally, Agathocles received an appeal for assistance and crossed from Sicily to Italy in the hope of expanding his domain.

2 [1] The Bruttii, shaken by the report of his coming, at first sent a deputation to him requesting an alliance and a compact of friendship.

2. See 12.2.1ff.; 18.1.2.

[2] Agathocles invited the ambassadors to dinner so they would not see his army being transported; then, fixing their audience for the next day, he boarded ship and eluded them. [3] But the stratagem had no happy outcome for Agathocles: a virulent disease forced him to return to Sicily a few days later. [4] The disease racked his whole frame, as the noxious fluid made its way through all his sinews and joints, and he was assailed by what seemed to be a civil war amongst the various parts of his body. [5] There was no hope for him, and war broke out between his son and his grandson, who were already claiming his kingdom as though he were dead. The son was killed and the grandson seized the throne.

[6] Now Agathocles' anxiety over his disease and the illness itself both grew worse as each exacerbated the other. In despair, he put his wife Theoxena and the two young children he had had by her on board ship, together with all his money, his slaves and his royal furniture (in which no king was richer than he), and sent them back to Egypt, the country from which he had received his wife.[3] His fear was that they would find an enemy in the man who had usurped his throne. [7] His wife begged for a long time not to be torn from her sick husband's side; she did not want her leaving to compound the wrong of the grandson's parricide and make her seem as heartless in abandoning her husband as the grandson had been in attacking his grandfather. [8] In marrying Agathocles, she said, she had bound herself to all his fortunes, not merely the good ones, and she would be willing to buy at the risk of her own life the chance of receiving her husband's last breath and of meeting her obligation to bury him, thus discharging the solemn duty owed to a spouse, which no other would undertake if she left. [9] As they were departing, the little children clung to their father's embrace, lamenting tearfully, while the wife, who was never again to see her husband, smothered him with kisses; and the old man's tears were just as pitiful. [10] They were weeping for a dying father, he for his children's exile; they bemoaned the loneliness which their father, a sick old man, would feel after their departure, he that his children, born to the prospect of a throne, should be left destitute. [11] Meanwhile the entire palace echoed throughout with the weeping of those who were witness to such a cruel separation. [12] Finally their tears were brought to an end by their enforced departure, and the king's death closely followed his sons' leaving. [13] While these events were taking place, the Carthaginians had learned of what was happening in

3. A daughter of Ptolemy I Soter.

Sicily.[4] Thinking that they had been presented with an opportunity to seize the entire island, they crossed to it in strength and brought many city-states into subjection.

3 [1] Moreover, Pyrrhus was now at war with the Romans.[5] [2] His support had been sought by Sicily, as noted above, and when he came to Syracuse he was hailed as king of Sicily as well as of Epirus. [3] Elated by this good fortune, he designated Sicily as the kingdom of his son Helenus (his family estate, so to speak, since Helenus was the son of King Agathocles' daughter) and Italy as that of Alexander. [4] After this Pyrrhus fought many successful battles against the Carthaginians, [5] but in a short while legates came to him from his Italian allies telling him that resistance to the Romans was impossible and that they would surrender unless he came to their aid. [6] Troubled by the danger on two fronts, and at a loss what to do or whom to help first, Pyrrhus took time to reflect on the matter, since he was pulled in both directions at once. [7] For with the Carthaginian threat on one side and the Roman on the other, it seemed risky not to transport his army to Italy, riskier still to take it away from Sicily: the one party might be lost through his failure to bring help, the other through being abandoned by him. [8] In this sea of troubles the safest haven, strategically speaking, appeared to be to use all his strength to finish the fight in Sicily and, after disposing of the Carthaginians, to transport his victorious army to Italy. [9] Pyrrhus therefore joined battle and won another victory; because he was leaving Sicily, however, he appeared to be running away in defeat. [10] Accordingly, his allies defected from him and the speed with which he lost control of Sicily matched the ease with which he had gained it. [11] His luck in Italy was no better and he returned to Epirus. The outcome of both campaigns served marvellously as an object lesson. [12] Earlier, he had success beyond his wildest dreams, and good fortune had brought him dominions in Italy and Sicily and many victories over the Romans; now bad fortune, destroying all that he had amassed, as though to point out the frailty of the human condition, added to the Sicilian disaster a shipwreck at sea, an ignominious battle against the Romans and withdrawal in disgrace from Italy.

---

4. Cf. Diod. 21.18.
5. Continued from 18.2; sources are indicated at 18.1. The continuing account is at Plut. *Pyrrhus* 22ff.

4 [1] After Pyrrhus' departure from Sicily, Hiero was made chief magistrate.[6] [2] Hiero was a man of such moderation that, with the unanimous support of all the city-states, he was first made general in the war against Carthage, and then king. [3] His upbringing as a child virtually presaged the sovereignty that lay in store for him. [4] His father was Hieroclitus, a nobleman whose lineage derived from Gelon, former tyrant of Sicily, [5] but on his mother's side his family was lowly, even shameful. [6] Born of a slave-girl, he had been exposed by his father as a disgrace to his family. [7] But the baby, deprived of any human succour, was for many days fed by bees who heaped their honey round him where he lay. [8] And so, on the advice of the soothsayers, who predicted the child was marked out for kingship, the father took back the infant and made every effort to train him for the prospective sovereignty which he was promised. [9] Furthermore, when Hiero was at his lessons in school with his schoolmates, a wolf suddenly appeared amongst the crowd of boys and seized his writing-tablet. [10] Also, when he was a young man and beginning his first military campaigns, an eagle settled on his shield and an owl on his spear, [11] a portent which signified that he would be a prudent politician, a courageous fighter and a king. [12] Finally, he often fought against men who challenged him to single combat, and he always emerged the winner. [13] He was given many military awards by King Pyrrhus. [14] He was possessed of extraordinary good looks as well as a strength that was amazing for a mere mortal. [15] He had an engaging way of speaking, was fair in his business dealings and prudent in his exercise of authority, so that the only regal attribute he seemed to lack was a kingdom.

BOOK 24

1 [1] While these events were taking place in Sicily, in Greece the kings Ptolemy Ceraunus, Antiochus and Antigonus were at war with each other, [2] and almost all the city-states of Greece, perceiving this as an opportunity for themselves, were encouraged to hope for freedom.[1]

---

6. Cf. Pol. 1.8f.; Diod. 22.13. The date is in the first half of the 260s.

1. Book 24 picks up from 17.2.15; the year is 280/79. Plut. *Pyrrhus* continues to cover events; cf. also Diod. 22.3f., 9, and for the Gallic incursions Pausanias 10.19.4ff. Hieronymus of Cardia remains a likely source for events up to the death of Pyrrhus.

Following the lead of the Spartans, they sent each other embassies to cement alliances amongst themselves and plunged into the fray. [3] To avoid seeming to have initiated hostilities with Antigonus, under whose rule they lay, they proceeded to attack his allies the Aetolians, [4] giving as a pretext for the war that the Aetolians had forcibly occupied the plain of Cirrha which, as all Greece had agreed, had been consecrated to Apollo.[2] [5] As general for this campaign they selected Areus, who, with their combined forces, raided the Aetolian cities and the crops planted in their fields, burning what could not be carried off. [6] Aetolian shepherds caught sight of this from their mountains. Some 500 of them came together, mounted an attack on the enemy—who were dispersed and unaware of their aggressors' numbers because panic and the smoke from the fires had obstructed their vision—and chased off the marauders, cutting down about 9,000. [7] The Spartans then sought to renew hostilities, but many city-states refused them support in the belief that their goal was to dominate rather than liberate Greece. [8] Meanwhile the war between the kings came to an end, with Ptolemy putting Antigonus to flight and seizing control of all Macedonia. Ptolemy then made peace with Antiochus and entered into a family alliance with Pyrrhus by giving him his daughter in marriage.[3]

2 [1] With the removal of external threats, Ptolemy now turned his impious and villainous thoughts towards domestic crimes, and hatched against his own sister Arsinoë[4] a plot for depriving her sons of their lives and Arsinoë herself of control of the city of Cassandrea. [2] His first scheme was to feign love for his sister and request her hand in marriage, for he had no means of getting at his sister's sons, whose throne he had seized, other than by affecting friendly relations with her. [3] But Ptolemy's penchant for evildoing was well known to his sister,[5] [4] and when she refused to believe him he sent word that he wished to share his throne with her sons, and that in going to war with them his intention had not been to wrest the kingdom from them but merely to enable him to give it back to them as a gift. [5] He told her to send a witness to his oath in the matter, saying that he would, in the man's presence, bind himself with any pledges she wished before their ancestral gods. [6] Arsinoë did not know what to do; she was afraid of being duped by perjury if she sent

2. For the sacred plain cf. 8.1.4 n.
3. See 17.2.15.
4. See 17.2.4ff.
5. Or perhaps: "Ptolemy's criminal intent was recognized by his sister."

someone, and of provoking her brother's insane cruelty if she did not. [7] She was more afraid for her children than for herself, and thought she would protect them by marriage to him; so she sent Dion, one of her friends. [8] Ptolemy took him to the holy temple of Jupiter which the Macedonians had venerated from days of old.[6] There he grasped the altar with his hands and, touching the very statues and cushioned seats of the gods, used bizarre and extravagant oaths to swear [9] that it was in total sincerity that he sought the hand of his sister, that he would name her his queen, that he would not insult her by taking another wife or recognizing children other than hers as his sons. [10] Arsinoë was filled with hope and delivered from her fear. She talked with her brother face to face, and his expression and melting eyes promised as much good faith as did his oath, whereupon she agreed to marry her brother despite the loudly voiced objection of her son, also named Ptolemy, that treachery was afoot.

3 [1] The wedding was celebrated with great pomp and universal rejoicing. [2] Ptolemy also summoned the army to an assembly where he set a diadem on his sister's head and addressed her as queen. [3] Receiving this title, Arsinoë was beside herself with joy, believing that she had recovered what she had lost with the death of her previous husband, Lysimachus, and she ventured to invite her spouse to her own city of Cassandrea—the city which, because of Ptolemy's lust for it, had occasioned the plot. [4] Arsinoë preceded her husband and declared the day of his arrival a holiday for the whole city, ordering that houses, temples and everything else be decorated and altars and sacrificial victims set in place in all quarters. [5] She also sent her sons to meet Ptolemy wearing garlands—Lysimachus who was sixteen, and Philip who was three years his junior, both of them strikingly good looking.[7] [6] To conceal his treachery, Ptolemy hugged them enthusiastically, too eagerly for the affection to be real, and for a long time showered kisses on them. [7] When he reached the gate, he ordered the citadel seized and the boys killed. They ran to their mother for protection and were butchered in her arms while Arsinoë kissed them [8] and all the while cried aloud, asking what dreadful crime she had committed either by the marriage or by her subsequent actions. Time and again she offered herself to the assassins in

6. This ought to refer to the temple of Zeus at Dium, which, since its Greek form is "Dion," casts suspicion on the reality of Arsinoë's friend.

7. We are left to conclude that the third son, Ptolemy, refused to go (see above 24.2.10).

place of her sons; often she took the boys' bodies in her arms to shield them with her own, trying to deflect to herself the blows aimed at her children. [9] Eventually, denied even the right to bury her sons, she was dragged off from the city attended by two slaves, her clothes torn and her hair dishevelled. She went into exile on Samothrace, her misery all the more intense for not having been permitted to die with her sons. [10] But Ptolemy's crimes did not go unpunished. A short time afterwards, the immortal gods exacted vengeance for all his treacherous actions and his bloody murders—he was stripped of his throne by the Gauls and taken prisoner, to perish by the sword, as he deserved.

4 [1] The Gauls had become so numerous that the lands that bred them could not hold them all; so they sent off 300,000 men, as a "sacred spring,"[8] in search of new homes. [2] Of these a number settled in Italy, capturing and burning the city of Rome, [3] and others, led by birds (for the Gauls are superior to everyone in the craft of augury), made their way into the recesses of Illyria, massacring the barbarians as they went, to settle in Pannonia.[9] [4] They were a violent, reckless, warlike people who were the first after Hercules to cross the impassable heights of the Alps and regions made uninhabitable by the cold (a feat which had, indeed, earned Hercules respect for his valour and belief in his immortality). [5] There the Gauls vanquished the Pannonians and spent many years in a succession of wars with their neighbours. [6] Then, heartened by their success, they divided their armies, some of which headed for Greece, others for Macedonia, laying waste with the sword everything in their path. [7] Such was the terror inspired by the name "Gaul" that kings would actually try to buy peace from them with huge sums of money even when they were not under attack.

[8] Only Ptolemy king of Macedon heard of the approach of the Gauls without trepidation. Driven on by the Furies that punish parricide, he went to meet them with a small number of poorly organized troops, as if wars could be fought as easily as crimes committed. [9] He even rejected an offer, brought by an embassy of the Dardanians, of 20,000 armed men to assist him, adding the insulting comment that all was over for Macedon if, after singlehandedly vanquishing the entire East, its people now needed Dardanians to defend its frontiers. [10] The

8. The "sacred spring" (Latin "ver sacrum") was an Italic practice of marking out children born at a certain time to be sent to form a new settlement when they became adult.
9. In what is roughly modern Hungary.

soldiers under his command, he said, were the sons of the men who had served victoriously under Alexander the world over. [11] When this was reported to the Dardanian king, he declared that the renowned kingdom of Macedonia would soon fall because of the foolhardiness of a callow youth.

5 [1] To test the mood of the Macedonians, the Gauls sent ambassadors to Ptolemy, under the leadership of Belgius, offering him a chance to buy peace. [2] Ptolemy, however, boasted among his subjects that the Gauls were seeking peace out of their fear of war, [3] and he was no less arrogant in his bluster before the ambassadors than he was amongst his friends, telling them that he would grant them peace on the sole condition that they hand him their leaders as hostages and lay down their arms—for he would not trust them unless they were disarmed, he said. [4] When the report of the embassy was brought back, the Gauls burst into laughter, declaring openly that Ptolemy would soon be aware of whether their offer of peace was made for their own good or for his. [5] A few days passed, battle was joined, and the Macedonians were defeated and cut to pieces. [6] Ptolemy was captured after he had received many wounds. He was decapitated, and his head was fixed on a lance and paraded all over the battlefield to strike terror into the enemy.[10] [7] Flight proved the salvation of a small number of Macedonians; the rest were either taken prisoner or killed.

[8] When this was reported throughout Macedonia, city gates were closed and the whole country was filled with lamentation. [9] People grieved for the loss of their sons, were fearful that their cities faced destruction, or called out the names of their kings Alexander and Philip, imploring their aid as if they were deities. [10] Under them, they said, they had not merely been secure; they had also been the conquerors of the world. [11] Prayers were raised to them to protect the fatherland, which by their illustrious achievements they had raised to the skies, and to bring aid to the afflicted, whom King Ptolemy's mad recklessness had brought to ruin. [12] While all others were in despair, Sosthenes, one of the Macedonian generals,[11] thought they should not be resorting to prayers.

10. This occurred in 279, after he had reigned one year and five months (Porphyry of Tyre *FGH* 260 F 3.9).

11. From Porphyry *FGH* 260 F 3.10f. we learn that between Ptolemy Ceraunus and Sosthenes Macedon was ruled for two months by Ceraunus' brother Meleager and for 45 days by Antipater, son of Philip and grandson of Cassander; there were also periods of anarchy, but Sosthenes was in power from 278/7 to 276/5.

He mobilized the young men, checked the Gauls who were still gloating over their victory and kept Macedonia from being pillaged by the enemy. [13] Because of these courageous services to his country, Sosthenes was, despite his lowly birth, favoured above the many noblemen who aspired to the throne of Macedon, [14] and though he was hailed as king by the army, he made his soldiers take their oath to him as "commander in chief" rather than "king."

6 [1] One contingent of Gauls, led by Brennus, had poured into Greece. When Brennus heard of the success of his countrymen who had been led by Belgius to victory over the Macedonians, he was angry that, once the victory was won, a rich plunder, swollen with the spoils of the East, had been so lightly abandoned. He therefore brought together an army of 150,000 infantry and 15,000 cavalry and invaded Macedonia. [2] In the process of pillaging fields and farms he was met by Sosthenes with an army of Macedonians disposed for battle; but these were few, and the Gauls many, the Macedonians apprehensive and the Gauls powerful, so that the former were easily defeated. [3] Beaten, the Macedonians then hid within the walls of their cities, and the triumphant Brennus proceeded to pillage all the Macedonian countryside, with no one standing in his way. [4] Then, as if the spoils of this world were now of little account, he turned his attention to the temples of the immortal gods, joking like a fool that the gods were rich and should be generous to men. [5] He immediately changed course for Delphi, setting plunder before religion, and gold before any fear of offending the immortal gods. The latter, he declared, needed no riches since it was their practice to squander them on mankind.

[6] The temple of Apollo at Delphi is set on Mt Parnassus, above a precipice sheer on every side. Here a community was established by the large numbers of people who came together from all quarters in admiration for the grandeur of the place and who settled on the rocky height. [7] Thus, temple and community are protected by cliffs rather than walls, and by natural rather than manmade fortifications, so that it is debatable which commands more wonder, the place's defences or the god's majestic presence. [8] The central portion of the cliff recedes to form the shape of a theatre. As a result, the noise of raised human voices and any concomitant flourish of trumpets is multiplied and magnified beyond the original volume as the rocks resound and echo, a phenomenon which, when people are unaware of the cause, generally increases their awe for the grandeur of the place and adds bewilderment to their wonder. [9] In this rocky hollow, some halfway up the hill, there is a narrow

plateau; and here there is a deep aperture in the ground which is left open for the delivery of oracles. A chill gust of air is driven up from this by a force like a wind, and this deranges the priests and impels them, now under the spell of the god, to give his response to those consulting him. [10] There are to be seen here many rich gifts from monarchs and peoples, their splendour bearing witness to the gratitude of worshippers repaying their vows and to the reliability of the gods' responses.

7 [1] When he was in sight of the temple, Brennus long reflected on whether he should set to work immediately or give his travel-weary troops a night's respite for recuperation. [2] The generals of the Aenianes and the Thessalians, who had joined him to share the plunder, urged him to brook no delay while the enemy were ill prepared and the panic inspired by his arrival was fresh. [3] Allow a night to pass, they said, and the enemy would regain their spirits, and perhaps get reinforcements, too, while the roads which now lay open would be blockaded. [4] But the rank and file of the Gauls had experienced long deprivation, and on discovering that the countryside was well stocked with wine and other provisions, they had been as delighted with the abundance of supplies as they would have been with victory. They had spread out through the fields [5] and, breaking ranks, were wandering around, as though they were victorious, to seize everything they could. This gave the people of Delphi a breathing space. [6] The story goes that, at the first rumour of the Gauls' coming, the peasants were forbidden by the oracle to transport their harvested crops and wine from their farms. [7] The salutary nature of this injunction was not understood until the large quantities of wine and other provisions had served to delay the Gauls and allowed reinforcements to arrive from Delphi's neighbours. [8] Consequently, once their allies' strength was added to their own, the Delphians fortified their city before the Gauls, who were lingering over their wine as if it were their plunder, could be brought back to their standards. [9] Brennus had a select force of 65,000 infantry, chosen from the entire army, while the Delphians and their allies had a mere 4,000 soldiers. [10] Full of contempt for such numbers, Brennus, to whet the spirit of his men, pointed out to them all the opulence of their prospective booty. The statues and the chariots which could be seen in large numbers in the distance were cast in solid gold, he said, and the weight of this plunder was greater than it appeared.

8 [1] Excited by this claim, and at the same time the worse for wear from yesterday's drinking, the Gauls charged into battle heedless of the dangers. [2] The Delphians for their part counted more on the god than on their own strength. Full of contempt for their enemy, they fought back

vigorously and, using rocks or weapons, hurled down from the mountain top the Gauls who were clambering up. [3] While the two sides were thus locked in combat, the priests from all the temples, together with the priestesses themselves, suddenly came rushing to the front line of the combatants. Their hair was dishevelled, they were wearing their insignia and fillets, and they were trembling and distracted. [4] They cried out that there had been an epiphany of the god, that they had seen him leaping down into his temple through the aperture in the roof [5] while they were all supplicating his aid, that he was young and possessed of a remarkable beauty, surpassing that of mortals. Accompanying him were two virgins in armour who had come to meet him from the two neighbouring temples of Diana and Minerva. [6] They had not just seen this with their eyes, said the priests, but they had also heard the twang of a bow and the clang of weapons. [7] So, adding the most earnest entreaties, they cautioned the Delphians not to hesitate to massacre the enemy and participate in the victory of the gods, who stood before their very standards.

[8] Fired by these declarations, the Delphians all rushed enthusiastically into battle. [9] They, too, immediately felt the presence of the god, for an earthquake sheared off a section of the mountain, which crushed the army of the Gauls; and their densely packed phalanxes scattered under the blows of the enemy and came to ruin. [10] Next a storm arose to finish off the wounded with freezing hail. [11] Brennus himself, their leader, unable to tolerate the pain of his wounds, took his own life with a dagger; [12] and his second in command left Greece at a rapid pace with 10,000 men, casualties all, after punishing those who had advocated the campaign. [13] But Fortune was no kinder to the fugitives; terrified, they had not one night under shelter, not one day free of hardship and peril, [14] while incessant rain, frost-hardened snow, hunger, exhaustion and, worst of all, lack of sleep continually ground down the pitiful remnants of the ill-starred campaign. [15] Moreover, the peoples and tribes through which their route led hounded the straggling force as their prey. [16] And thus it turned out that from this huge army, which shortly before had felt such confidence in its strength as to hold even the gods in contempt, none survived to tell the tale of this terrible debacle.

BOOK 25

1 [1] The two kings Antigonus and Antiochus had made peace, and Antigonus was returning to Macedonia, when a new enemy suddenly arose against him: [2] the Gauls left behind by Brennus to defend their country's frontiers when the latter was marching into Greece.[1] Not wishing to appear the only lazy ones, these put under arms 15,000 infantry and 3,000 cavalry, [3] routed the forces of the Getae and Triballi and, hovering over Macedonia, sent an embassy to the king to offer him peace at a price, and at the same time to spy out his camp. [4] In keeping with the generosity befitting a king, Antigonus invited them to dinner, for which he put on a magnificent feast. [5] But the Gauls, impressed by the great masses of gold and silver that were on display, and tempted by the opulence of the available booty, left more eager for war than when they had arrived. [6] To intimidate them, the king ordered that they be shown his elephants (he assumed that they were a type of animal never seen by the barbarians) and also his well-equipped fleet, [7] not realizing that, by showing off his strength, he was exciting them with the anticipation of rich booty rather than striking fear into them. [8] Thus, when they returned to their people, the ambassadors exaggerated everything and stressed the king's wealth, as well as his unwariness. [9] His camp was full of gold and silver, they said, but it was not defended even by a ditch or a rampart; and the Macedonians had abandoned the performance of all the normal military duties as though they had sufficient protection in their riches. [10] Evidently they believed that they had no need of the help of iron,[2] since they had gold in abundance.

2 [1] The Gauls were a covetous people, and this report was enough to spur them to seize the plunder; there was also the example of Belgius, [2] who not long before had slaughtered a Macedonian army together with its king. [3] And so they all agreed to a night attack on the camp of the king. The latter, however, saw this storm on the horizon and had on the previous day given the word for his men to remove everything from the camp and hide themselves in the nearest wood. All that protected the camp was the fact that it was deserted. [4] For when they saw it was completely empty, devoid not only of defenders but even of guards, the Gauls suspected trickery rather than flight on the enemy's part and for a long time feared to enter the gates. [5] Finally, leaving the fortifications undamaged and intact, they occupied the camp, which they could only search, not plunder. [6] Carrying off what they could find, they converged on the beach. Here, while they were pillaging the ships without due caution and while they had no fear of such a thing happening, they were

1. The year is 276; cf. Diod. 22.4.
2. I.e. weapons made of the metal.

cut to pieces by the oarsmen and a part of the army which had sought shelter there with their wives and children. [7] Such was the slaughter of the Gauls that the report of this victory secured peace for Antigonus, not only with the Gauls but also with his barbarous neighbours.

[8] Yet at that time the Gauls had such an abundance of manpower that they filled the whole of Asia like a swarm. [9] Eventually, eastern kings fought no wars without a Gallic mercenary force, and if they were expelled from their kingdoms, they sought refuge with none but the Gauls. [10] So great was the terror inspired by the Gallic name, and such their unbroken record of success in war, that these kings believed that they could not safeguard their regal power, or recover it if it were lost, without the prowess of the Gauls. [11] Their assistance was called for by the king of Bithynia, and when the victory was won, they partitioned his kingdom with him, calling that region Gallograecia.

3 [1] In the meantime, while these events were taking place in Asia, Pyrrhus had been defeated in a naval engagement in Sicily by the Carthaginians.[3] He sent an embassy to request reinforcements from Antigonus, king of Macedonia, [2] declaring that if Antigonus failed to send them he, Pyrrhus, would be obliged to fall back on his own kingdom, and that he would seek from Antigonus himself the territorial expansion he had wanted to gain at the expense of the Romans. [3] When the ambassadors returned with a refusal, Pyrrhus arranged for a sudden departure, without revealing his plans. [4] He instructed his allies to prepare for war in the meantime and transferred the defence of the citadel of Tarentum to his son Helenus and his friend Milo. [5] On his return to Epirus he immediately invaded Macedonia. Antigonus came to meet him with an army, but was defeated in battle and took flight. [6] Pyrrhus accepted the surrender of Macedon and, as if he had made up for the loss of Sicily and Italy by the acquisition of the kingdom of Macedon, sent for the son and the friend whom he had left at Tarentum. [7] Thus rudely stripped of the ornaments of his position, Antigonus retired to Thessalonica with a few cavalrymen who accompanied him in his flight, there to observe such events as would follow the loss of his throne and to renew preparations for war along with a troop of Gallic mercenaries which he had hired. [8] But he was again decisively beaten, by Pyrrhus' son Ptolemy,[4] and he fled with seven companions. He no

3. Plut. *Pyrrhus* 26ff. takes us to his death in 272. For events thereafter Phylarchus of Athens is a suggested source; his work extended to 220/19.
    4. See 18.1.3.

longer cherished hopes of recovering his kingdom but only hunted for a hiding place to save his life and wilderness for his escape.

4 [1] Pyrrhus was thus placed in a position of supreme power, but he could not now be content with what previously he could hardly have wished for. His thoughts turned to dominion over Greece and Asia. [2] He took as much pleasure from warfare as he did from being king, and none could resist him wheresoever he directed his territorial aspirations. [3] But while he was regarded as the unconquerable conqueror of kingdoms, he quickly lost what he had conquered and gained—so much more did he pay attention to acquiring supremacy than to keeping it. [4] He moved his troops to the Chersonese, where he was met by deputations from the Athenians, the Achaeans and the Messenians. [5] Indeed, struck with admiration for his reputation and also for his exploits against the Romans and the Carthaginians, the whole of Greece was awaiting his arrival. [6] His first campaign was against the Spartans. In this he faced greater courage from the women than the men, losing his son Ptolemy along with the strongest part of his army; [7] for when he attacked the city, so many women ran forward to defend their native land that he fell back, defeated more by shame than by military strength.

[8] His son Ptolemy was so energetic, they say, and so good a fighter that he took the city of Corcyra with sixty men; again, in a naval battle, he jumped aboard a quinquireme from a small boat, accompanied by seven men, took the vessel and held on to it; [9] and in the attack on Sparta he rode his horse right to the centre of the city where he was killed when a crowd converged on him. [10] When his body was brought to his father, Pyrrhus is reported to have said that his death had come later than he had himself feared, or than Ptolemy's recklessness had deserved.

5 [1] Driven back by the Spartans, Pyrrhus made for Argos. Here he attempted to capture Antigonus, who had shut himself up in the city, but while he furiously fought in the thick of the fray, he was fatally struck by a stone hurled from the walls. [2] His head was brought to Antigonus. The latter showed clemency in victory, and when Pyrrhus' son Helenus surrendered to him with his Epirotes, Antigonus sent him back to his kingdom and gave him the remains of his father (who was as yet unburied) to take home.

[3] There is general agreement amongst the sources that no monarch of the day, or of previous times, could be compared with Pyrrhus, and that there had rarely appeared in history anyone of a purer life or a more transparent honesty—not merely among royalty but even among famous men of any station. [4] And such, they say, was this man's grasp

of military science that he consistently remained undefeated in his campaigns against the mighty kings Lysimachus, Demetrius and Antigonus; [5] while in those against the Illyrians, the Sicilians, the Romans and the Carthaginians he was never the loser and very often emerged the victor. [6] It is certainly true that the fame of his achievements and the glory surrounding his name brought worldwide renown to his hitherto small and insignificant country.

BOOK 26

1 [1] After the death of Pyrrhus there were great military upheavals not only in Macedonia, but in Asia and Greece as well. [2] The Peloponnesians were treacherously delivered up to Antigonus. [3] Elsewhere there was either dismay or jubilation, as the various states had either hoped for assistance from Pyrrhus or had lived in fear of him, and these accordingly allied themselves with Antigonus or else, driven by their mutual animosities, rushed into war with each other.

[4] While these convulsions were shaking the provinces, Aristotimus, a prominent citizen, seized the tyranny in Elis.[1] [5] He executed many of the leaders of the community and drove more into exile. Then the Aetolians sent an embassy to ask him to restore the wives and children of the exiles, a request which he initially refused. [6] Later, however, apparently relenting, he granted all the married women permission to rejoin their husbands and fixed a day for their departure. [7] The women, presuming they were going to live with their husbands in permanent exile, took all their most precious possessions and assembled at the gate, intending to set off in a single column, as it were. They were stripped of everything and thrown into prison, with infants murdered in the bosoms of their mothers and young girls dragged away to be violated.

[8] All were dumbfounded by this despotic act of cruelty. The leading Elian citizen was one Hellanicus (an old man who had already lost his children and who, accordingly, had nothing to fear, because of his age and lack of close family). He gathered at his house the most loyal of his friends and encouraged them to reclaim their country's liberty. [9] The

---

1. The text is a problem, but Elis is historically correct. Justin is the major source; cf. Plut. *Mor.* 249 F, 250 F, 253 B; Pausanias 5.5.1. The time is around 270. The anachronistic use of the word "provinces" reveals the later Roman perspective.

friends hesitated to put an end to the danger they faced in common by risking any danger as individuals, and they requested time to consider the problem. Hellanicus at once summoned his slaves, ordered the doors locked and had a message sent to the tyrant that he should send men to arrest conspirators at his house; at the same time he told each of his friends in harsh tones that since he could not be the man responsible for the liberation of their native land, he would have his revenge for their desertion of the cause. [10] Faced with danger on both sides, the friends then chose the honourable course and swore to kill the tyrant. So Aristotimus was brought down, four months after seizing the tyranny.

2 [1] Meanwhile Antigonus was facing war on several fronts both from King Ptolemy and from the Spartans; and he had also to face a fresh enemy, an army flooding in from Gallograecia.[2] He therefore set out with all his forces against the Gauls, leaving only a small contingent to face his other foes and maintain the appearance of a regular camp. [2] The Gauls learned of this and while they, too, were preparing themselves for battle, they slaughtered sacrificial animals to take the auspices about the engagement. Great carnage and total destruction were foretold for them by the entrails, but the Gauls were infuriated rather than frightened by this. Hoping that the threats from heaven could be averted by shedding the blood of their own kin, they butchered their wives and children, thus making parricide the start of so inauspicious a war. [3] Such fury had possessed their savage hearts that they showed no mercy to those of an age that even their enemy would have spared, and they inflicted all the ferocity of war on their children and the mothers of their children—those for whom wars are usually undertaken. [4] Thus, assuming that they had ransomed their lives and victory by their crime, they went into battle as they were, still bloody from the recent massacre of their families, and the result was no happier than the omen. [5] As they fought, they were surrounded first by the avenging Furies of parricide, and only then by the enemy; and, as the spirits of their victims danced before their eyes, they were annihilated. [6] So great was the carnage that it looked as if gods and men had made a pact to wipe out the parricides.

[7] On hearing the result of this encounter, Ptolemy and the Spartans avoided contact with the victorious army of their enemy and retired

2. That is, Antigonus II Gonatas (276–239) and Ptolemy II Philadelphus (282–246). We enter the obscurities of what is known as the Chremonidean War (after the mover of an Athenian decree), which probably began in 268 and for which the other main source is Pausanias 3.6.4ff.; cf. Diod. 20.29; Plut. *Agis* 3.7. The Gauls were Antigonus' mercenaries, who revolted at Megara in 266.

to safer territory. [8] As for Antigonus, when he saw them retreat he attacked the Athenians, while his men were still in high spirits after their last victory. [9] While he was thus engaged Alexander, king of Epirus, anxious to avenge the death of his father, Pyrrhus, pillaged the land of Macedonia.[3] [10] Antigonus came back from Greece to face him, but he was deserted by his soldiers and lost, along with his army, the kingdom of Macedon. [11] His son, Demetrius, was a mere boy, but in his father's absence he rebuilt the army and not only recovered Macedonia, which Antigonus had lost, but also wrested control of Epirus from Alexander. [12] Such was the unreliability of the soldiers, such the fickleness of Fortune that, in turn, kings found themselves exiles and exiles found themselves kings. 3 [1] Thus Alexander, who had sought refuge in exile with the Acarnanians, was restored to his throne, as much by the wish of the people of Epirus as by the assistance of his allies.

[2] During the same period King Magas of Cyrene died.[4] Before his illness Magas had betrothed his only daughter Berenice to his brother Ptolemy's son in order to end his quarrel with Ptolemy. [3] After the king's death, however, the girl's mother, Arsinoë, wished to annul the marriage, which had been arranged against her wishes. She sent a deputation to summon from Macedonia Demetrius, brother of King Antigonus, to marry the young woman and assume the throne of Cyrene, Demetrius being himself the son of a daughter of Ptolemy. [4] Demetrius wasted no time. The winds in his favour, he came swiftly to Cyrene; but from the start he behaved arrogantly through confidence in his good looks, with which his mother-in-law had already started to become infatuated. He was overbearing in his dealings with the royal family and the military; and he had also turned his attempts to ingratiate himself from the girl to her mother. [5] This first made the girl suspicious, then it provoked the animosity of the people and the soldiers. [6] Consequently, the support of the entire population veered towards the son of Ptolemy, and a plot was hatched against Demetrius. Assassins were dispatched to deal with him when he had come to the bed of his mother-in-law. [7] Arsinoë, however, heard her daughter's voice as the latter stood at the door giving orders for her mother to be spared, and for a little while she protected her lover by shielding him with her body. [8] But killed he was, and Berenice, while

3. Probably in 262/1. Alexander II had succeeded Pyrrhus some ten years earlier. The details of Justin's account are suspect as to Antigonus' defeat and Demetrius' role, though the latter became co-regent with Antigonus in 257.
4. He was, in fact, Ptolemy's half-brother. Demetrius the Fair died in 250.

satisfying her filial duty, at one stroke punished her mother's scandalous conduct and also complied with her father's judgment in her choice of a husband.

BOOK 27

1 [1] When King Antiochus of Syria died, he was succeeded by his son Seleucus.[1] Urged on by his mother, Laodice, who should have restrained him instead, Seleucus inaugurated his reign with a murder, [2] putting to death his stepmother Berenice, sister of Ptolemy, king of Egypt, along with his little half-brother, who was Berenice's son. [3] By committing this crime he tainted himself with ignominy; he also became embroiled in a war with Ptolemy. [4] Learning that men had been sent to kill her, Berenice barricaded herself at Daphina,[2] [5] and when it was reported to the cities of Asia that she was under siege there with her little boy, they all sent help to her, remembering as they did the authority wielded by her father and her forefathers, and feeling pity for this undeserved turn of fortune. [6] Her brother Ptolemy, too, alarmed at the danger facing his sister, left his kingdom and rushed to her at the head of all his troops. [7] But before help arrived Berenice, who could not be taken by storm, succumbed to treachery and was murdered.[3] Everyone was outraged. [8] Accordingly, all the cities[4] went over to Ptolemy, appalled by this example of ruthlessness and at the same time wishing to avenge the woman they had intended to defend. [9] Had he not been recalled to Egypt by civil disorder there, Ptolemy would have taken possession of Seleucus' entire kingdom.[5] [10] So much hatred had the crime of parricide engendered for the one, so much support a sister's undeserved death for the other.

---

1. Antiochus II Theos had ruled from 261 to 246; his son Seleucus II Callinicus then reigned until 225. Laodice was Antiochus' sister and wife. Berenice was sister to Ptolemy III Euergetes, who also came to the throne in 246. The conflict is the so-called Laodicean War.
2. Daphne, a suburb of Antioch.
3. Cf. Val. Max. 9.10 ext. 1; Polyaenus 8.50.
4. At this point in the manuscripts the phrase "which had seceded put together a huge fleet and suddenly" occurs, but this seems to be an intrusion, since it appears in much the same form at 2.1, where it is more appropriate.
5. See Burstein nos. 98 and 99.

2 [1] After Ptolemy's departure Seleucus put together a large fleet to combat the cities which had deserted him, but suddenly, as though the gods themselves were avenging the murder, a storm arose and he lost the fleet by shipwreck. [2] From this great armada Fortune left him nothing beyond his naked body, his life and a few companions who had survived the wreck. [3] It was an unlucky turn of events, yet one which Seleucus might well have wished for, since the city-states which had defected to Ptolemy from hatred of him now had a change of heart, as though in the gods' eyes sufficient atonement had been made to them. They began to pity him, and they put themselves under his authority once more. [4] Thus, rejoicing in his misfortunes and enriched by his losses, Seleucus assumed he could match Ptolemy's strength and attacked him. [5] But it was as if he had been born just to be the plaything of Fortune, as if he had regained his royal power only in order to lose it again. Defeated in battle and finding himself with no more of a retinue than he had enjoyed after his shipwreck, he fled in panic to Antioch.

[6] From there Seleucus wrote a letter to his brother, Antiochus, begging for his assistance and offering as remuneration for his aid the portion of Asia within the boundaries of the Taurus range. [7] Although Antiochus was only fourteen, he had a lust for power beyond his years, and he grasped this opportunity, but not with the brotherly love with which it was being offered. Instead, he harboured a larcenous desire to take everything from his brother; and, boy though he was, he was possessed of the villainous audacity of a man. [8] This is why he was given the nickname "Hawk"—he resembled a bird of prey more than a human being, making his living by preying on the possessions of others.[6] [9] In the meantime, Ptolemy had learned that Antiochus was coming to Seleucus' aid and, to avoid fighting both at the same time, he made a ten-year peace treaty with Seleucus. [10] But the peace which the latter was granted by his enemy was broken by his brother, for Antiochus hired an army of Gallic mercenaries, and the man whose help he had sought brought Seleucus not assistance but war, and behaved not as a brother but as a foe. [11] In the ensuing battle Antiochus was, indeed, the victor, thanks to the valour of the Gauls;[7] but then the Gauls, thinking that Seleucus had fallen in the engagement, turned their weapons against Antiochus himself, expecting to have a freer hand in pillaging Asia if they wiped out the royal line entirely. [12] When Antiochus realized this, he paid them a ransom for himself as one would to bandits, and made an alliance with his own hired soldiers.

6. His name "Hierax" is the Greek word for hawk.
7. Trogus' prologue tells us the battle was fought near Ancyra.

3 [1] Meanwhile, since the brothers were estranged and exhausted by their violent feuding, King Eumenes of Bithynia attacked the victorious Antiochus and his Gauls in order to take possession of Asia while it was untenanted, as it were.[8] [2] Since they were still weak from their last campaign, while Eumenes' strength was intact, he had no difficulty in defeating them. [3] In fact, all wars undertaken at that time had as their goal the destruction of Asia; anyone who became relatively powerful would seize Asia like so much booty. [4] The brothers Seleucus and Antiochus were at war over Asia, while Ptolemy, king of Egypt, though ostensibly wishing to avenge his sister, was really lusting after Asia. [5] Thus Asia was being ransacked by the Bithynian Eumenes, on one side, and by the Gauls, ever the force hired by the weaker camp, on the other; and while she was beset by all these brigands, no one could be found to defend her.

[6] After defeating Antiochus, Eumenes had seized most of Asia, but not even then could the brothers come together, although the prize for which they were at war was lost. Ignoring the enemy from without, they revived hostilities in order to destroy each other.

[7] In these hostilities Antiochus was once more defeated. Exhausted by a flight which lasted many days, he came finally to his father-in-law, Ariamenes, king of Cappadocia.[9] [8] At first he was given a cordial welcome by Ariamenes; but within a few days he discovered that a plot was being hatched against him and he fled to save himself. [9] Finding no safe haven in his flight, he went to his enemy Ptolemy, whom he thought he could rely on more than his brother (for he had in mind either what he had intended to do to his brother or what he had deserved to suffer at his brother's hands). [10] But Ptolemy was no more sympathetic towards Antiochus when he surrendered than when he was a declared enemy, and he had him placed under close arrest. [11] Antiochus escaped from here, too, with the help of a courtesan he had come to know a little too well; he gave his guards the slip, but in his flight he was killed by bandits. [12] At about the same time Seleucus also lost his kingdom and died after being thrown from his horse. Thus the brothers were also subject to

---

8. Eumenes I was King of Pergamum from 263 to 241; the ruler here, as Trogus correctly has it in his prologue, was his successor Attalus I (241–197). The battle took place soon after that at Ancyra, around 235, near Pergamum.

9. Ariamenes of Cappadocia was the father-in-law of Antiochus' sister Strato-nice.

twin fates, as it were: both of them exiles after being kings, both paid the penalty for their crimes.[10]

BOOK 28

1 [1] After losing her husband Alexander, who was also her full brother, Olympias, daughter of Pyrrhus, king of Epirus, assumed the guardianship of Pyrrhus and Ptolemy, the sons whom she had had by him, as well as the management of the kingdom. The Aetolians wanted to wrest from her a part of Acarnania which the father of her boys had been given for his contribution to the war, so she appealed for help to King Demetrius of Macedonia.[1] [2] Although Demetrius already had a wife—the sister of Antiochus, king of Syria—Olympias gave him the hand of her daughter, Phthia, in marriage, in order to secure by family ties the assistance she could not gain from his compassion. [3] The wedding was duly celebrated; but while Demetrius gained influence through the new marriage, he faced hatred from his earlier one. [4] His first wife, feeling herself divorced, left of her own accord for the court of her brother Antiochus, whom she pushed into war with her husband.

[5] Having no confidence in the Epirots, the Acarnanians also took the step of appealing to the Romans for help against the Aetolians. From the Roman senate they gained a commitment that a delegation would be sent [6] to tell the Aetolians to remove their garrisons from the cities of Acarnania, and leave independent the only people who did not, in days of old, send help to the Greeks against the Trojans, founders of their race.

2 [1] The Aetolians, however, listened to the Roman embassy with disdain. They made taunting references to the Carthaginians and the Gauls, by whom the Romans had been cut to pieces in so many wars, [2] and advised them that, before transferring their arms to Greece, they should open up their gates, now closed by fear of a Punic war, to face the Carthaginians. [3] They then told them to remember who was threatening whom. [4] The Romans, they said, had been unable to

10. These deaths occurred in 226–225. Antiochus Hierax was killed in Thrace (Pol. 5.74).
1. From this point a parallel account is Pol. 2.2ff.; the time is the late 230s. As for Trogus' source, Timagenes is suggested. One can, however, detect in section 2 the overblown arrogance of the Aetolians which is so much a part of Polybius' portrayal.

protect their own city against the Gauls and, when it was captured, had
not defended it with cold steel but paid a ransom for it in gold.[2] [5] But
when the same people invaded Greece with a somewhat larger force,
they added, the Greeks had totally annihilated them, not only unaided
by troops from abroad but without even using all their domestic forces,
and where the Gauls had intended to establish cities and the seat of their
empire the Greeks had given them a burial ground. [6] Italy, on the other
hand, with the Romans still quaking after the recent burning of their city,
had been almost completely overrun by the Gauls. [7] So the Romans
should drive the Gauls from Italy before threatening the Aetolians, and
defend their own territory before attacking that of others.

[8] And what manner of men were these Romans, anyway, they
asked. Mere shepherds occupying land purloined from its rightful owners;
[9] men who could not find wives because of their disreputable origins and
who had therefore used state terrorism to seize them;[3] [10] men who, in a
word, had founded their city on a murder and smeared the foundations of
its walls with the blood of fratricide.[4] [11] The Aetolians, conversely, had
always been the leaders of Greece; they had outshone all other Greeks
in courage as well as authority. [12] In fact, they alone had continually
shown contempt for the Macedonians when these were prosperous and
ruling the world; they alone had shown no fear of King Philip and had
disregarded the edicts of Alexander the Great after his conquest of Persia
and India, when everyone shivered at his name. [13] So, they said, they
had a word of advice for the Romans: they should be satisfied with their
present fortunes and not challenge that warlike might which, as they
well knew, had slaughtered the Gauls and looked with scorn upon the
Macedonians. [14] Dismissing the Roman deputation with these words
and wishing to avoid appearing braver in words than in action, they laid
waste the territory of Epirus and of Acarnania.

3 [1] Olympias had now passed on her kingdom to her sons, and Ptolemy
had succeeded his dead brother, Pyrrhus. [2] Ptolemy, however, after
setting out to engage the enemy with an army drawn up for battle, fell
sick and died on the march. [3] Olympias was grief-stricken by the two
deaths, life became a burden to her and she, too, did not long survive her
sons. [4] Of the royal family there now remained only Nereis, a young

2. See 6.6.5; 20.5.4; 43.5.9; the sentiment is repeated in Mithridates' speech at
38.4.8. For the Gallic invasion of Greece see Books 24 and 25.
3. The taking of Sabine women; see Livy Book 1 and below 43.3.2.
4. Romulus' elimination of Remus.

girl, and her sister, Laodamia. Nereis married Gelon, son of the tyrant of Sicily; [5] Laodamia was killed in a riot of the people after she had sought refuge at the altar of Diana. [6] This was a crime which the immortal gods punished by inflicting one disaster after another on the people of Epirus and almost entirely annihilating its inhabitants. [7] For after suffering crop failure and famine, and after being torn by civil dissension, the Epirots were finally almost wiped out by foreign wars. [8] Milo, too, the man who murdered Laodamia, went insane and mutilated his own flesh, now with a sword, now with a stone, and finally with his own teeth, to die eleven days later.

[9] After these events in Epirus, King Demetrius died in Macedonia leaving a son, Philip, who was still a mere boy.[5] [10] Antigonus, appointed his guardian, married his ward's mother and endeavoured to have himself made king. [11] After a time an ominous insurrection arose among the Macedonians, keeping Antigonus for a time shut up in the palace. Nevertheless, he ventured out in public without bodyguards, [12] hurled his diadem and purple robe into the crowd and told them to give these to another who would not know how to rule them, or else whom they knew how to obey. [13] Hitherto, he said, he had experienced no pleasures which could have made the throne enviable, only hardships and dangers. [14] He then listed his services to them: his punishment of the rebellious allies; his suppression of the Dardanians and Thessalians jubilant over the death of King Demetrius; and, finally, not only his defense, but also his advancement, of the prestige of Macedon. [15] If they were unhappy with this record, he concluded, then he was laying down his command and returning to them his office, because they were looking for a king to whom they could give orders. [16] Ashamed, the people told him to take back his royal power, but he refused to do so until the ringleaders of the insurrection were handed over for execution.

4 [1] Following this, Antigonus opened hostilities with the Spartans, the only people to have shown contempt, during the wars with Philip and Alexander, both for the empire of Macedon and its armed might, feared by everyone else.[6] [2] Between these two famous peoples a war now arose to which both committed all their strength, the one side for the age-old

5. Demetrius died in 229, defeated by Dardanians. Antigonus III Doson ruled until 221. We are at Pol. 2.44f.; his castigation of Phylarchus at 2.56 makes the latter a possible source for Trogus, directly or not. We also have Plut. *Aratus* (Aratus himself wrote of the period); *Cleomenes* 7ff., esp. 16ff.; *Philopoemen* 5ff.

6. The author's opinion, with some justification, is, in the word "only," at odds with the claims of the Aetolians at 28.3.12.

glory of Macedon, the other not just for its unbroken independence but for its very survival. [3] The Lacedaemonians went down in defeat, but bore their misfortune stoutheartedly, not only the men, but their women and children, too. [4] In the battle no one begrudged his life; no woman wept for a lost husband; old men paid tribute to the death of their sons; sons expressed joy for fathers who were killed in action; all the survivors lamented their lot, at not having themselves fallen for the freedom of the fatherland. [5] Everybody opened their doors to the casualties, tended their wounds, revived the exhausted, [6] and all the while there was no confusion, no panic in the city, and each person lamented the common misfortune rather than his own.

[7] Meanwhile, after dispatching a large number of the foe, King Cleomenes appeared, his entire body soaked with his own and the enemy's blood. [8] On entering the city he did not drop to the ground, did not ask for food or drink, did not even lay down the burden of his arms. [9] Instead, he leaned against a wall and, when he saw that only 4,000 had survived the battle, encouraged the men to save themselves for more propitious times which their state would see. [10] Then he left with his wife and children for the court of Ptolemy in Egypt where, given a dignitary's welcome by Ptolemy, he long lived in the king's highest regard. [11] Finally, after the death of Ptolemy, he and all his family were killed by the king's son.[7]

[12] After the wholesale slaughter of the Spartans, Antigonus felt sympathy for the fortunes suffered by this great city. He forbade his men to plunder and he pardoned all the survivors, [13] declaring that his war had been with Cleomenes, not the Spartans, and that with Cleomenes' flight his anger was entirely at an end. [14] Nor would his glory be at all diminished, he said, if it went down in history that Sparta had been saved by him, the only man by whom it had ever been captured. [15] Accordingly, he added, he was sparing the land and buildings of the city since men had not survived for him to spare. [16] Shortly afterwards Antigonus himself died, passing on his throne to Philip, his ward, who was fourteen years old.

---

7. For the successions on the deaths of Ptolemy and Antigonus see the beginning of Book 29.

BOOK 29

1 [1] At about the same time almost the whole world was experiencing changes in government as new kings succeeded old.[1] [2] In Macedonia, Philip, at the age of fourteen, ascended to the throne on the death of Antigonus, who was both his guardian and his stepfather; [3] in Asia, when Seleucus was killed, Antiochus was made king when no more than a child; [4] the kingdom of Cappadocia likewise had been transferred to Ariarathes, who was still a boy, by his father; [5] and Ptolemy had seized control of Egypt after murdering his mother and father, earning himself by this criminal act the sobriquet "Philopator." [6] The Spartans, too, had replaced Cleomenes with Lycurgus. [7] And to complete the number of changes at this time, Hannibal was made general among the Carthaginians at a young age, not because older men were unavailable, but because of the hatred of the Romans which the Carthaginians knew had been bred into him since boyhood, but which was to prove disastrous, not so much for Rome as for Africa itself. [8] These boy-kings had no men of riper years to guide them, but in their enthusiasm to follow in the steps of their forefathers, they all revealed great natural abilities. [9] The sole exception was Ptolemy; villainous in seizing his realm, he was also inefficient in administering it.[2] [10] As for Philip, he was constantly being harassed by the Dardanians and all the other neighbouring peoples— who lived on terms of inveterate hostility to the Macedonian kings in any case—because they were contemptuous of his age. [11] Philip, on the other hand, after driving back his enemies, was not satisfied with having defended his own territory but yearned to take the initiative and attack the Aetolians.

2 [1] While Philip was considering this, Demetrius, king of Illyria, approached him with abject entreaties.[3] He had recently been defeated by Paulus, the Roman consul, [2] and he was complaining about his

---

1. Cf. Pol. 2.71. The successors are Philip V (221–179); Antiochus III ("the Great"; 223–187); Ariarathes IV Eusebes (220–c.162); Ptolemy IV Philopator (222–205). Lycurgus was king of Sparta from 219 to c.212. On Hannibal see Pol. 3.8ff.

2. See Pol. 5.34ff., 79ff. and below Book 30.

3. The defeat was by L. Aemilius Paulus in 219; Pol. 3.16, 18f.; *MRR* 1.236. Events in this book were covered in Pol. 4–5, 7–11; Livy treats the period of the war with Hannibal in Books 21–30. Polybius was Livy's main source for Greek affairs.

ill-treatment at the hands of the Romans, who, he said, dissatisfied with being confined within the boundaries of Italy, and harbouring the unconscionable ambition of dominating the whole world, were now at war with every monarch. [3] Aiming at the domination of Sicily, Sardinia, Spain and, indeed, the whole of Africa, they had undertaken a war against the Carthaginians and Hannibal; [4] and he himself had been attacked, Demetrius said, only because he seemed to be their neighbour—as though it were a crime for any king to be next to the borders of their empire. [5] Philip, continued Demetrius, should be on his guard, having his example before him; his kingdom being more accessible and of greater renown, he would have the Romans as even more ferocious enemies. [6] Moreover, he declared, he was ceding to Philip the rights to his kingdom, which the Romans had seized; he would find it more agreeable seeing an ally rather than his enemies in possession of his realm. [7] With talk like this Demetrius persuaded Philip to forget the Aetolians and make war on the Romans instead, which Philip thought would be less difficult now that he had heard of their defeat by Hannibal at Lake Trasimene.[4] [8] To avoid being simultaneously involved in a number of wars, Philip made peace with the Aetolians, creating the impression that his intention was not to transfer the war elsewhere but rather to maintain the tranquillity of Greece. This, he claimed, had never been in greater danger, [9] for to the west the new empires of Carthage and Rome were in the ascendant, and all that held these back from attacking Greece and Asia was their duel for supremacy. The victors in this conflict, he said, would lose no time in crossing to the East.[5]

3 [1] He could see arising in Italy, he continued, the cloud of fierce and bloody war; he saw a storm coming from the west with thunder and lightning, a storm destined to stain everything with a torrential rain of blood, in all the parts of the world to which the squall of victory transported it. [2] Greece had often experienced violent upheavals in wars fought at different times with the Persians, the Gauls or the Macedonians, but they would think all of that insignificant should the troops which now were clashing in Italy spill over the borders of that land. [3] He could see the bloody and murderous wars the two peoples were fighting against each other, throwing into the fray their military might and their generals' tactical skills. Such frenzy, Philip said, could

4. In 217.
5. This speech, including the storm image that follows, echoes that which Pol. 5.104 attributes to Agelaus of Naupactus.

not be terminated merely by the demise of one of the adversaries and without engulfing neighbours in the destruction. [4] So, he concluded, while it may be true that Macedonia had less to fear than Greece from the truculent spirit of the victors of this struggle (Macedonia being more remote and more capable of defending itself), [5] he was nevertheless certain that men who clashed with such might would not be content to stop at victory; he himself was bound to feel apprehensive of having to fight those who emerged the winners.

[6] Using this excuse, Philip terminated his war with the Aetolians and, concentrating exclusively on the Romano-Carthaginian conflict, proceeded to assess carefully the strengths of each side. [7] Though they had the Carthaginians and Hannibal at their throats, the Romans, too, were apparently not free from fear of Macedon, [8] for they stood in awe of the longstanding renown which the Macedonians enjoyed as the conquerors of the East, as well as of Philip's burning passion to emulate Alexander; they knew that Philip was ready to fight and that he was an enterprising man.

4 [1] When Philip learned that the Romans had once more been defeated by the Carthaginians,[6] he openly declared himself Rome's enemy and began to build ships to transport an army to Italy. [2] He then sent an ambassador with a letter to Hannibal to form an alliance with him. [3] The legate was captured, however, and brought before the senate, which released him unharmed, not out of regard for the king but to prevent an undecided enemy being made a committed one.[7] [4] Later, however, when news was brought to Rome that Philip was going to transport his forces to Italy, the Romans sent the praetor Laevinus with a fleet of men-of-war to prevent his crossing. [5] After sailing to Greece, Laevinus made a number of promises to the Aetolians and pushed them to undertake a war against Philip. Philip, for his part, induced the Achaeans to make war on the Romans.

[6] Meanwhile, the Dardanians began to raid Macedonian territory, and after taking 20,000 captives they forced Philip to withdraw from his Roman campaign to defend his kingdom. [7] While this was happening, the praetor Laevinus made an alliance with King Attalus[8] and began pillaging Greece; whereupon the city-states, reeling from these blows,

---

6. At Cannae in 216.

7. Livy 23.33. M. Valerius Laevinus was praetor in 215 and was concerned with Greece until 211.

8. And the Aetolian League, in 212 or 211: Livy 26.24ff.; Sherk no. 2.

repeatedly sent deputations to Philip to ask for his assistance. [8] All the while, the Illyrian kings were dogging his steps demanding with persistent entreaties that he make good his promises; and, in addition, the Macedonians who had been the victims of the raids clamoured for revenge. [9] Beset by all these urgent problems, Philip was at a loss which to address first; yet he promised all the petitioners that he would send help promptly, not because he was able to keep his promises but to fill them with hope and thereby keep them loyal to their alliance to him. [10] His first campaign was against the Dardanians, who, waiting for him to leave his kingdom, threatened Macedonia with force greater than his own. [11] He also made peace with the Romans, who were happy enough to postpone for the moment a war with Macedon;[9] and he set a trap for the leader of the Achaeans, Philopoemen, who, he had learned, was trying to win over the hearts of Macedon's allies to the side of the Romans. Philopoemen, however, learned of the trap and avoided it, subsequently using his influence to make the Achaeans abandon Philip.

BOOK 30

1 [1] While Philip applied himself to his urgent problems in Macedonia, the conduct of Ptolemy in Egypt was of a different character.[1] [2] After gaining his throne by parricide and adding to the murder of both his parents the assassination of his brother, he had surrendered himself to a life of luxury, apparently believing that his record was one of accomplishment, and the entire palace had adapted itself to the character of the king. [3] The corruption and apathy arising from his inactivity and indolence was not confined to Ptolemy's friends and provincial governors; it also spread throughout the army, which lost its enthusiasm for military service. [4] When Antiochus, king of Syria, learned of this, he was goaded on by the inveterate hatred which existed between the two kingdoms to make a swift attack, overrunning a large number of Ptolemy's cities and mounting an assault on Egypt itself. [5] Ptolemy became alarmed and, sending deputations, tried to delay Antiochus until he could ready his forces. [6] He then levied a great army in Greece, fought a successful battle against Antiochus and would have wrested his kingdom from him

---

9. The Peace of Phoenice in 205; Livy 29.12. For Philopoemen see Plut. *Philopoemen* 12.

1. See Book 29 n. 2. Cf. Pol. 14.11 for Agathoclia.

had he but aided fortune with a display of courage. [7] Instead, satisfied with recovering the cities which he had lost, Ptolemy made peace with Antiochus and eagerly seized an opportunity for further idleness. He relapsed into prodigality, put to death his wife, Eurydice, who was also his sister, and fell victim to the charms of the courtesan Agathoclia. [8] With no thought for the greatness of the name Ptolemy and forgetting his royal dignity, he spent his nights in whoring and his days in feasting. [9] To this were added the instruments of debauch, drums and the tambourines, and the king himself, now turned conductor, no longer a mere spectator at the orgy, accompanied them on his own stringed instrument. [10] Such, at the start, was the disease, veiled in silence, the unseen malady that beset the tottering palace.

2 [1] As the licentiousness grew ever more rampant, the whore's effrontery could no longer be confined within the palace walls, [2] and she was made all the more presumptuous by the king's daily debaucheries, which he shared with her brother, Agathocles, a good-looking boy who prostituted himself to gain advancement. [3] Things were made even worse by their mother, Oenanthe, who used the allurements of her two children to keep the king in her clutches. [4] Not satisfied with having the king in their power, these three now proceeded to take over his kingdom as well, appearing in public, receiving salutations and being attended by a retinue. [5] Agathocles stayed close to the king's side and governed the state, while the women dispensed tribunates, governorships and military commands. Nobody had less authority than the king himself in his own kingdom. [6] Then he died, leaving a five-year-old son, his child by his sister Eurydice.[2] His death was long kept secret as the women plundered the royal treasury and, allying themselves with totally unscrupulous individuals, tried to seize control of the realm. [7] The matter came to light, however, and there followed mob rioting in which Agathocles was killed and the women crucified in punishment for the death of Eurydice. [8] With the demise of the king and the execution of the whores, the people of Alexandria felt that the disgrace of their kingdom had been expiated. They sent an embassy to the Romans with the request that they assume the protection of the orphaned prince and safeguard the kingdom of Egypt; for, they said, Philip and Antiochus had already made a pact and divided it between themselves.

2. In 205. His successor was Ptolemy V Epiphanes (204–180); see Pol. 15.20, 25ff., and below the beginning of Book 31. For the Roman involvement see Sherk no. 3.

3 [1] The Romans welcomed the deputation, looking as they were for reasons to make war on Philip, who had plotted against them during the Punic war. [2] Besides, now that the Carthaginians and Hannibal were defeated, there was no one whose forces they feared more, for they reflected on the chaos Pyrrhus had caused in Italy with a small contingent of Macedonians and on the Macedonian achievements in the East. [3] Ambassadors were accordingly dispatched to tell Philip and Antiochus to keep their hands off Egypt, [4] and Marcus Lepidus was sent to Egypt to administer the orphan prince's kingdom as his guardian.

[5] While this was happening, embassies reached Rome from King Attalus and from the people of Rhodes complaining of wrongs suffered at the hands of Philip.³ It was this that removed from the senate any hesitation over war with Macedon. [6] Under the pretext of aiding their allies, the Romans immediately declared war on Philip and sent some legions with a consul into Macedonia. [7] Shortly afterwards, through confidence in the Romans, all Greece made war on Philip, inspired to confront him by the hope of regaining its erstwhile independence. Under pressure on all sides, the king was obliged to sue for peace. [8] Then, when the terms of the peace had been set forth by the Romans, Attalus, the Rhodians, the Achaeans and the Aetolians all began to reclaim their former territory. [9] Philip, for his part, admitted that he could be brought to meet the Romans' conditions; but he added that it was a disgrace that the Greeks, who had been defeated by his ancestors Philip and Alexander and sent beneath the yoke of Macedon, should be dictating terms of peace to him like victors—they should be giving an account of how they had come to be his subjects, he said, rather than trying to claim their freedom. [10] Finally, however, Philip was granted his request of a two-month truce so that a peace which could not be negotiated in Macedonia could be requested from the senate in Rome.

4 [1] That same year there was an earthquake between the islands of Thera and Therasia, at a point equidistant from the coastline of the two. [2] Here, to the astonishment of sailors, an island suddenly emerged from the ocean depths amid an eruption of boiling waters. [3] Also on that day, in Asia, the same earthquake struck Rhodes and many other cities, causing catastrophic damage as it levelled buildings and swallowing some cities whole. [4] The prodigy evoked universal alarm, and the soothsayers

---

3. In 201. For the following see Pol. 16 and 18; Diod. 28.5ff.; Livy 31–33; Plut. *Flamininus*.

predicted that the rising empire of Rome would devour the old empire of Greece and Macedonia.

[5] Meanwhile, refused a peace treaty by the senate, Philip incited the tyrant Nabis[4] to join him in the war. [6] Then, having brought out his army in order of battle opposite the enemy line, he proceeded to exhort his men by reminding them of the Macedonian conquest of the Persians, the Bactrians, the Indians and all Asia to the limits of the East. [7] This war, he said, was to be prosecuted with much more fortitude than those others, liberty being so much more precious a possession than empire. [8] Flamininus, the Roman consul, was also inspiring his troops to battle, commenting on their most recent achievements and pointing to the lands crushed by Roman prowess: Carthage and Sicily on the one side, Italy and Spain on the other. [9] Hannibal should not be considered inferior to Alexander the Great, he said; but the Romans had driven him from Italy and conquered Africa itself, which constituted a third of the world. [10] The Macedonians, too, should not be judged on the basis of their reputation of old, but on their current strength; [11] for the Romans were at war not with Alexander the Great, who they were told was invincible, and not with an army which had conquered all of the East, [12] but with Philip, an immature boy who had difficulty protecting his frontiers against his neighbours, and with the Macedonians of today, who not so long ago had been the prey of the Dardanians. [13] The Macedonians, he said, recounted the glorious exploits of their forefathers, but Flamininus those of his own men; [14] for it was by no other army that Hannibal, the Carthaginians and practically all of the West had been brought into submission, but by these very men whom he now had under his command.

[15] Such exhortations inspired the soldiers on both sides, and they now clashed in combat, one side priding itself on its eastern empire, the other on its western, the one carrying into the war the old and worn-out glory of its ancestors, the other the freshly blossoming renown of recent achievements in the field. [16] The Macedonians fell before the fortunes of Rome. [17] Defeated in battle, Philip sued for peace with Flamininus. He kept the title of king, but lost all the cities of Greece (which represented the portions of his realm outside his ancient domain), retaining Macedonia alone. [18] The Aetolians, however, were displeased; Macedonia had not also been taken from the king, as they had suggested, and given to them as a prize of war. So they sent an

4. Of Sparta. T. Quinctius Flamininus was sent to Greece as consul in 198 and arranged the peace treaty with Philip in 196, after defeating him at Cynoscephalae in 197. Cf. Sherk nos. 4–6.

embassy to Antiochus to flatter him on his greatness and urge him into war with the Romans by raising the prospect of a pan-Hellenic alliance.

BOOK 31

1 [1] On his death, King Ptolemy Philopator of Egypt had left a young son who he had hoped would succeed him, but the boy's age gained him scant respect, so that he fell prey even to his servants.[1] Antiochus, king of Syria, therefore decided to invade Egypt. [2] He overran Phoenicia and the other settlements which were on Syrian soil but under Egyptian jurisdiction, after which the senate sent ambassadors to him to warn him to keep his hands off the kingdom of its ward, who had been entrusted to its safe-keeping by his father's last request. [3] To these Antiochus paid no attention. After a while another deputation arrived which, omitting all mention of the ward, demanded that the city-states which had fallen to the Roman people by the rules of war be restored to their former status. [4] Antiochus' refusal precipitated a declaration of war, a war which he lightly accepted but unsuccessfully conducted.

[5] In this same period the tyrant Nabis had seized control of a large number of the city-states of Greece.[2] [6] To avoid having the strength of Rome simultaneously occupied on two fronts, the senate wrote to Flamininus to tell him to liberate Greece from Nabis just as he had liberated Macedonia from Philip, if it seemed like a good plan to him. [7] To this end his command was extended. What made the prospect of war with Antiochus alarming was the name of Hannibal, who, according to allegations made to the Romans by his rivals in secret reports, had made an alliance with Antiochus. [8] Hannibal, these men claimed, was not content to live under the rule of law because he had become used to power and the unlimited licence of a military career—his intolerance of a peaceful life in the city kept him on the lookout for fresh reasons to go to war. [9] These reports were false, but they were taken to be true by their nervous recipients.

---

1. See 30.2.6ff. For the contents of this book see Pol. 18.49ff., 20 and 21; Diod. 28 and 29; Livy 33.38 through Book 37; Plut. *Flamininus*. For Flamininus see *MRR* 1.341, 344.
2. See 30.4.5.

2 [1] Eventually, stricken with fear, the senate sent Cnaeus Servilius as ambassador to Africa to keep an eye on Hannibal's movements, with secret instructions to arrange his assassination by his rivals, if he could, and so finally free the people of Rome from the dread of his hated name.[3] [2] But the matter was not long kept secret from Hannibal, who was a man quick to foresee and forestall danger, and as ready to anticipate failure when things were going well as success when they were going badly. [3] Hannibal now spent the whole day in the forum of Carthage before the eyes of the leading Carthaginian citizens and of the Roman ambassador. At the end of it, as evening drew on, he mounted a horse and rode to an estate which he had near the city and close to the coast; his slaves were kept ignorant of his movements and had been instructed to await his return at the city gate. [4] On the estate he had been keeping some ships manned by oarsmen hidden in a concealed bay. He also had in readiness on the property a large sum of money so that, when the situation demanded, his flight would not be delayed by the lack of opportunity or of money. [5] He now chose some young slaves (augmenting their number with several Italian prisoners-of-war), boarded a ship and set a course to join Antiochus. [6] The next day the city awaited in the forum its leading citizen, who was also at that time a consul. [7] When word was brought that he was gone, there was universal panic, just as if their city had been captured; and everyone predicted that Hannibal's flight spelled their ruin. [8] As though war had already been declared on Italy by Hannibal, the Roman ambassador discreetly returned to Rome with the disturbing news.

3 [1] In Greece, meanwhile, Flamininus formed alliances with a number of cities, conquered the tyrant Nabis in two consecutive battles and left him virtually exhausted in his kingdom, broken by the severe terms of the peace. [2] But after the independence of Greece had been restored, the garrisons withdrawn from the cities, and the Roman army taken back to Italy, Nabis was excited by what he saw as territory open for the taking; and he made a sudden attack on a large number of states.[4] [3] This alarmed the Achaeans. To prevent the trouble next door from spreading to themselves, they declared war on Nabis and appointed as their leader their praetor Philopoemen, a man of remarkable energy. [4] In that war Philopoemen's courage was so conspicuous that

---

3. In 195; *MRR* 1.341.
4. Cf. Plut. *Philopoemen* 14f.

he merited comparison, in the view of all, with the Roman general Flamininus.[5]

[5] At this time Hannibal, who had reached Antiochus, was welcomed by him as a gift from heaven, and [6] his arrival so inspired the king's confidence as to focus his thoughts less on the war than on the prizes of victory. [7] Hannibal, however, was well acquainted with Roman valour and kept telling him the Romans could be conquered only in Italy. [8] For such a campaign he made a request for 100 ships, 10,000 infantry and 1,000 cavalry, promising that with this force he would resume war in Italy as effectively as he had fought it before, [9] and bring to the king as he sat in Asia either victory over the Romans or peace terms favourable to the king. [10] The Spaniards, he said, were burning for war and only needed a leader, while Italy was now better known to Hannibal himself than in the past. Furthermore, he concluded, Carthage would not remain inactive but would immediately make herself his ally.

4 [1] The king liked his plan, and one of Hannibal's companions was dispatched to Carthage to encourage the war party there and announce that Hannibal would soon be at hand with his troops, adding that their side lacked nothing but the energetic support of the Carthaginians, that Asia would supply their troops for the war and also defray their expenses. [2] When this message was taken to Carthage, the messenger himself was captured by Hannibal's personal enemies, brought before the senate and asked to identify the person to whom he had been sent. With typical Carthaginian ingenuity, the messenger replied that he had been sent to the entire senate, since this was a matter concerning not merely individuals but the whole community. [3] The Carthaginians then spent many days considering whether they should send the man to Rome to clear themselves, as a people, of complicity; but during this time he secretly boarded a ship and returned to Hannibal. On discovering this, the Carthaginians took action and had the matter reported to Rome by an ambassador. [4] For their part, the Romans sent ambassadors to Antiochus.[6] In the guise of an official delegation, these were to spy out the state of the king's preparations and either assuage Hannibal's hostility towards the Romans or else arouse against him Antiochus' suspicion and displeasure by frequent conversations with him. [5] The ambassadors accordingly met Antiochus at Ephesus and delivered the dispatches from

5. The comparison continued to the extent that Plutarch paired the biographies of the two men.

6. In 193; *MRR* 1.348f.

the senate. [6] While they were awaiting his reply, they were, every day, constantly at Hannibal's side assuring him that he had been overcautious in leaving his country, since the Romans could be completely relied upon to keep a peace made not so much with his state as with Hannibal himself. [7] Hannibal, they said, had gone to war less from hatred of the Romans than from love of his own country, for which every decent man should be prepared to sacrifice even his life; the causes of the war were public and determined by their respective nations, rather than private and determined by the generals. They went on to praise his exploits. [8] Pleased with such topics of conversation, Hannibal talked too often and too enthusiastically with the ambassadors, unaware that his familiarity with the Romans was provoking the king's animosity. [9] For Antiochus assumed from these frequent conversations that Hannibal was reconciled with the Romans. He therefore broke with his former practice and now disclosed nothing to him; excluding him from all his deliberations, he began to hate him as an enemy and traitor. It was this that wrecked the great preparations for the war, for what they lacked was skilful leadership. [10] The senate's dispatch had told Antiochus to be satisfied with his territory in Asia so that he would not oblige the Romans to enter his country. Antiochus ignored this and decided on an offensive rather than defensive war.

5 [1] It is said that, after holding numerous councils of war in the absence of Hannibal, Antiochus finally had him summoned, not intending to follow his advice on a course of action but to avoid the appearance of having entirely disregarded him, and that after questioning the others in turn he eventually came to Hannibal. [2] Hannibal took in the situation and declared that he understood that he had been invited not because the king needed his advice but merely to complete the number of opinions. Even so, he said, from hatred for the Romans as well as from affection for the king—for only at Antiochus' court had he been left a secure place of exile—he would explain the strategy for fighting the war. [3] Then, asking their pardon in advance for his frankness, he said he approved of none of their current policies or procedures, and that he was against Greece being the theatre of war when Italy provided richer opportunities. [4] The Romans, he explained, could be beaten only by their own arms, and the only way Italy could be conquered was by Italian forces; for they were a different kind of men from other mortals, with a different way of waging war. [5] In other wars it was most important to have been the first to gain a territorial or temporal advantage, to have plundered farmland and taken cities; as for the Roman, whether one has preempted him in seizing territory or defeated him in battle, one still has to grapple with him even when he is beaten and down. [6] Thus if someone attacks them in Italy, he can use the Romans' own resources, their own strength and their own arms to defeat them, as Hannibal himself had done. [7] But one would be mistaken to leave them Italy as the source of their strength, as mistaken as someone wishing to divert a river without starting at the headwaters, but trying instead to turn its course and dry it up when the waters had already increased to a flood. [8] This had been his advice to the king in private, he said, and he had actually offered his services to execute the plan; and he had now repeated his counsel in the presence of the king's friends so they might all know how a war should be fought against the Romans and be aware that, while the latter were invincible abroad, they were vulnerable at home. [9] For, he continued, they could be divested of their city before they could be divested of their empire, of Italy before their provinces. In fact, they had been captured by the Gauls and almost annihilated by himself; and he had never been beaten by them before he left their territory, whereas on his return to Carthage the fortunes of war had immediately changed with the change of theatre.

6 [1] The king's courtiers opposed Hannibal's suggestion. Not that they gave any thought to the expediency of the policy; they simply feared that, if his advice were accepted, he would gain first place in the king's favour. [2] As for Antiochus, it was not the strategy but its author which displeased him; he was afraid that credit for victory would go to Hannibal rather than himself. [3] So the entire enterprise began to fall apart because the courtiers slavishly agreed with every whim of the king; no plan was devised on the basis of strategic or rational considerations. The king himself lapsed into self-indulgence over the winter and every day was occupied with some new marriage. [4] In contrast, the Roman consul, Acilius,[7] who had been sent out to conduct the campaign, was making every effort to organize troops, weapons and all the other things needed for war; he was strengthening his ties with allied states and making overtures to those which were undecided. Nor was the outcome of the war at variance with each side's preparedness. [5] At the first clash the king could see his men giving way, and rather than bring assistance to those in difficulties he set himself as leader of the fugitives, leaving to his conquerors a rich camp. [6] Then, while the Romans were preoccupied with the plunder, Antiochus fled to Asia. Beginning now to regret that he had rejected Hannibal's advice, he resumed friendly relations with him and followed

---

7. M'. Acilius Glabrio, consul 191; *MRR* 1.352; cf. Sherk no. 12.

his recommendations in everything. [7] In the meantime word was brought to Antiochus that the Roman general Livius was approaching,[8] sent by the senate to conduct the war at sea with eighty warships, news which gave the king hopes of reviving his fortunes. [8] He decided to fight a sea battle before the city-states allied to him could go over to the enemy, in the hope that the defeat he had suffered in Greece could be effaced by the glory of a fresh victory. [9] Hannibal was therefore entrusted with his fleet and the battle got under way. But the Asian soldiers were no match for the Romans, nor their vessels for the Roman men-of-war, though the margin of the defeat was lessened by the skill of their admiral.

[10] Word of the victory had not yet reached Rome, and the city was accordingly still undecided over its selection of consuls.   7 [1] But to face the leadership of Hannibal no better choice could be made than the brother of Africanus, since it was the special task of the Scipios to conquer Carthaginians.[9] [2] Thus Lucius Scipio was made consul and given as his assistant his brother, Africanus, so that Antiochus might be made aware that his confidence in the vanquished Hannibal was no greater than the Romans' confidence in the victorious Scipio. [3] While the Scipios were transporting their army to Asia, news reached them that the war was virtually at an end on all fronts; they found that Antiochus had been defeated in battle on land, and Hannibal at sea. [4] As soon as they arrived, Antiochus sent ambassadors to them to ask for peace, bringing for Africanus a very personal gift—his son, whom the king had taken prisoner as he crossed the sea in a small boat. [5] Africanus, however, said that private benefactions lay outside his official cognizance, and that the obligations of a father were of one sort, those of the country another—and the latter took precedence not only over children but over life itself. [6] Thus while he welcomed the king's gift with gratitude, he would repay the kindness from his personal resources but, as far as peace and war were concerned, he answered, there could be no allowance for private interests and no curtailment of his country's authority. [7] In fact, at no time did he negotiate his son's ransom in the senate nor did he allow the senate to debate the matter; he had said he would, as befitted his honour, reclaim him by force of arms. [8] After this the terms of peace were specified: Asia would come under Roman control; Antiochus was to be satisfied with the throne of Syria; he was to surrender all ships, captives

8. C. Livius Salinator, praetor 191; *MRR* 1.353.
9. In the latter stages of the war with Hannibal, P. Cornelius Scipio (Africanus) had led the Romans to victory. Now his brother became consul for 190; *MRR* 1.356, 358; cf. Sherk no. 14.

and deserters; and he was to repay the Romans all their expenditures on the war. [9] When this was reported to Antiochus, he replied that he was not yet so utterly defeated as to allow himself to be stripped of his kingdom, and the terms were incitements to war rather than inducements to peace.

8 [1] Preparations for war were therefore made by both sides, and the Romans entered Asia and reached Ilium. Here the people of Ilium and Rome met each other joyfully, the former recalling Aeneas and the other chieftains who had set off from their land, the latter their descent from these heroes. [2] The happiness they all displayed was as intense as would be normal between parents and children reunited after a long interval. [3] The Trojans were pleased that their descendants had conquered the West and Africa and were now claiming Asia as their hereditary empire; they said the fall of Troy was an event to be welcomed so that the city could be so auspiciously reborn. [4] For their part, the Romans were filled with an insatiable desire to see their ancestors' home, the cradle of their forefathers and the temples and statues of their gods.

[5] After the Romans left Ilium, they were met by King Eumenes with some auxiliary forces, and soon afterwards a battle was fought with Antiochus.[10] [6] In this a Roman legion was driven back on the right wing, and the men began to run back to their camp, in greater disgrace than danger. Then the military tribune, Marcus Aemilius, who had been left in charge of the camp, told his men to arm themselves, march out beyond the rampart and threaten those in flight with drawn swords, adding that the fugitives would be killed if they did not return to the fight and that they would find their own camp more dangerous than that of the enemy. [7] Frightened by this twofold danger, the legion returned to the battle, accompanied by the comrades who had stopped them fleeing; they wreaked great havoc and thus paved the way for victory. Of the enemy 50,000 were killed and 11,000 captured. [8] When Antiochus sued for peace, nothing was added to the earlier conditions, for Africanus declared that as defeat did not diminish the Roman spirit so, in victory, success did not make it insolent. [9] The Romans then divided up the captured states among their allies, because they considered Asia more fitting to be given away as a gift of Rome than kept as a possession for the pursuit of pleasure; the glory of victory was to be claimed for the Roman name, and extravagant riches left to the allies.

10. Eumenes II Soter (197–160); see Sherk nos. 7 and 13. Antiochus was defeated at Magnesia in 190 and the peace settlement was finalized in 188.

BOOK 32

1 [1] It was the Aetolians who had pushed Antiochus into his wars against Rome, and now that he was defeated they were left alone before the Romans, no match for them in strength and bereft of all support.[1] [2] Shortly afterwards they were defeated, losing the independence which they alone among so many Greek city-states had preserved intact in the face of Athenian and Spartan sovereignty. [3] Their plight was all the more distressing for arriving so late in their history, as the Aetolians reflected on the days when they had, with their own forces alone, withstood the colossal might of Persia and, in the war of Delphi, broken the ferocity of the Gauls which had struck terror into Asia and Italy. And their reflection on their past glory made them regret their lost liberty all the more.

[4] In the meantime a dispute over supremacy, and then open warfare, broke out between the Messenians and the Achaeans. [5] In this war the famous Achaean general Philopoemen was taken prisoner, not because he did not dare to risk his life but because, while he was rallying his men to the fight, he was thrown from his horse as he crossed a ditch and overpowered by a crowd of the enemy. [6] While he lay on the ground, the Messenians, either from fear of his courage or out of respect for his dignity, dared not kill him. [7] As though by taking him they had concluded the entire war, they happily paraded their captive throughout the city, as in a triumph, while the people streamed out to meet him, as if it were their general and not the enemy's who was coming. [8] The Achaeans would have shown no more fervour at seeing him as victor than their enemy did now at seeing him in defeat. The Messenians had him brought to the theatre so they could all have a look at the man whose capture they each thought beyond belief. [9] He was then taken to prison where, out of regard for his eminence, the Messenians gave him poison. This he took with the joy of a victor, having first asked if Lycortas, the lieutenant of the Achaeans whom he knew to be second to himself as a military tactician, had escaped without harm. On hearing that Lycortas had got away Philopoemen expired, saying that things had not gone entirely ill for the Achaeans. [10] Shortly afterwards the war recommenced, the Messenians were defeated and they paid the penalty for putting Philopoemen to death.

---

1. This continues events from 189. Other sources are Pol. 21.25ff., 40ff. and 22–25; Diod. 29.11ff.; Livy 38–40; Plut. *Philopoemen* 18ff. Philopoemen died in 183.

2 [1] Meanwhile, in Syria, King Antiochus had been defeated by the Romans and subjected to a heavy tribute as a condition of peace.[2] Forced by financial difficulties, or else motivated by greed, he now entertained hopes that, under the pretext of his obligation to pay the tribute, he would be the more easily forgiven for sacrilege, and so he took an army and made an attack at night on the temple of Jupiter of Elymais. [2] When news of this got out, the local people rushed to the scene and Antiochus was killed, along with his entire force.

[3] In Rome, a large number of the Greek city-states had come to complain about wrongs they had suffered at the hands of Philip, king of Macedon, and there was a debate in the senate between Philip's son Demetrius, sent by his father to exonerate him before the senate, and the ambassadors of the city-states.[3] Bewildered by the number of complaints, the young Demetrius suddenly fell silent. [4] The senate was impressed by his modesty, which had previously won general approval when he had been a hostage at Rome, and decided the case in his favour. Thus by his own restraint Demetrius secured pardon for his father, not through the regular defence procedure but with his own decency pleading his case for him. [5] This was indicated in the senatorial decree, which made it clear that it was less a case of the king being absolved as of the father being presented as a gift to the son. [6] The episode earned Demetrius malicious criticism instead of gratitude for his negotiations. [7] For jealousy provoked the ill will of his brother, Perseus, and Demetrius also fell into disfavour with his father when the latter learned the reason for his pardon—Philip was annoyed that the figure cut by his son should weigh more with the senate than the father's authority and kingly dignity. [8] When Perseus discerned his father's chagrin, he made a daily practice of slandering the absent Demetrius before him, making the king at first resent, and finally suspect, him. For he would reproach Demetrius at one time with being a friend of the Romans, at another of betraying his father. [9] In the end he made up a story that a plot had been hatched against his own life by Demetrius, and to corroborate this he produced informers, suborned witnesses and committed the crime of which he was accusing his brother. [10] By these means Perseus pushed his father into the murder of a son, and cast a pall of gloom over the entire palace.

2. See 31.8.5ff. Antiochus' death came in 187.
3. The year is 185. The death of Demetrius occurred in 181, that of Philip in 179.

3 [1] With Demetrius killed and his rival removed, Perseus became not only more neglectful but even offensive towards his father, behaving as though he were king rather than heir to the throne. [2] Philip was affronted by this conduct, and every day he began to regret more bitterly the death of Demetrius. Then, suspecting that Demetrius had been the victim of a plot, he proceeded to interrogate witnesses and informers under torture. [3] When he came to learn of the foul play, he was tormented as much by the crime of Perseus as by the unwarranted death of Demetrius, and he would have exacted vengeance had he not been forestalled by death. [4] For, a short while afterwards, he died of a malady brought on by his remorse, leaving behind great preparations for a war against the Romans, which Perseus subsequently put to use. [5] Philip had, in fact, also prevailed upon the Scordiscan Gauls to join him in the war, and would have brought a serious war on the Romans had he not died.

[6] After their unsuccessful attack on Delphi—in which they had felt the power of the god more than that of the enemy—the Gauls had lost their leader Brennus and taken flight as outcasts, some to Asia and some to Thrace.[4] [7] Then they retraced their steps and moved back towards their original homeland. [8] One group of them settled at the confluence of the Danube and the Save, choosing the name Scordisci for themselves. [9] The Tectosagi, however, reached their old homeland of Tolosa, but here they were struck by a deadly plague and did not regain their health until they followed the advice given in the prophetic utterances of their soothsayers and sank in the lake of Tolosa the silver and gold which they had taken in war and by sacrilege. [10] Long afterwards the Roman consul, Caepio, removed all this—110,000 pounds of silver and one and a half million pounds of gold—[11] and this sacrilege was later the cause of Caepio and his army being wiped out.[5] The Romans also fell prey to a violent war with the Cimbri, which seemed a punishment for the accursed money. [12] Large numbers of the Tectosagi, attracted by the lure of booty, headed back to Illyricum; and these, after plundering the Istrians, settled in Pannonia.

[13] They say that the Istrian people are descended from the Colchians who were sent by King Aëtes to pursue the Argonauts who had abducted his daughter. [14] The Colchians entered the Ister from the Black Sea, and sailed far inland up the river Save, tracking the Argonauts. Then

---

4. See 24.6ff.; 25.2.
5. Q. Servilius Caepio, consul 106, proconsul 105, when he suffered the defeat; *MRR* 1.553, 557.

they transported their ships on their shoulders over the mountain ranges right to the coast of the Adriatic Sea, aware that the Argonauts had done this before them because of the large dimensions of their ship. [15] The Argonauts, however, had sailed off and the Colchians, failing to find them, were either so frightened of their king or so weary of their long sea-journey that they settled near Aquileia and were called Istrians after the name of the river by which they had left the sea.

[16] The Dacians are descendants of the Getae, who had shown cowardice when fighting under King Oroles against the Bastarnae. As punishment for their cowardice, they were compelled by order of the king to sleep with their heads placed where they normally put their feet and to perform for their wives the services previously done by the wives for them. This state of affairs did not alter until they wiped out the ignominy incurred in the war by a display of valour.

4 [1] To resume: Perseus had succeeded his father Philip on the throne, and now he began to entice all the aforementioned nations to join him in his war against the Romans.[6] [2] Meanwhile, war broke out between King Prusias (with whom Hannibal had sought refuge after Antiochus had been granted a peace treaty by the Romans) and Eumenes, the aggressor being Prusias, who had broken the peace treaty through his confidence in Hannibal's abilities. [3] Since the Romans included amongst their conditions for peace the demand that Antiochus surrender him, Hannibal, warned by the king, fled to Crete. [4] There, despite leading a tranquil life, he could see that he was resented because of his excessive wealth. He therefore filled some wine-jars with lead and deposited them in the temple of Diana as if to give protection to his fortune; [5] now that the community was no longer concerned about him, since it had his wealth in its possession as a guarantee, he made off to Prusias, after first filling with his gold some statues which he carried with him, so that his riches might go unseen and not pose a threat to his life. [6] Prusias, defeated by Eumenes in a battle on land, transferred the struggle to the sea, where Hannibal engineered a victory by a novel strategem. He had all manner of snakes put into earthenware jars, and in the midst of the fighting hurled these onto the enemy ships. [7] At first, the Pontic soldiers thought it laughable that an enemy incapable of using the sword should be fighting a battle with earthenware pots but, when

6. Perseus ruled from 179 until the defeat of 168. Prusias is Prusias II of Bithynia (c.182–149). For Hannibal see Livy 39.51, for the Roman embassy *MRR* 1.380 (the year 183).

the ships began to fill with snakes and they faced danger from two sides, they conceded victory to the enemy. [8] After news of this was brought to Rome, ambassadors were sent by the senate to force the two kings into a peace treaty and demand the surrender of Hannibal. But when Hannibal learned of this, he took poison and cheated the embassy by suicide.

[9] This year was marked by the deaths of the three greatest generals in the world: Hannibal, Philopoemen and Scipio Africanus.[7] [10] Of Hannibal it is generally regarded as true that not even when Italy trembled before him as he thundered in the war with Rome, and not even when he held the highest command on his return to Carthage did he recline to take a meal or permit himself more than a pint of wine; [11] and, surrounded though he was by so many female captives, he was so continent as to make one deny that he was born in Africa. [12] At all events, so restrained was his behaviour that, though he was at the head of armies made up of different peoples, he was never the object of conspiracy amongst his own men and never treacherously betrayed, despite the fact that his enemies had often tried to use both approaches against him.

BOOK 33

1 [1] The war which the Romans fought with Macedon created less upheaval than the Punic War, but it was more celebrated since the Macedonians were more famous than the Carthaginians; for they were aided first by their glorious reputation of having conquered the East, and then by the support of all the kings.[1] [2] The Romans accordingly enrolled more legions and also sent for assistance from Masinissa, king of Numidia, and all their other allies; Eumenes, king of Bithynia, was also instructed to assist their campaign with all his might. [3] On Perseus' side, apart from the Macedonian army, reputed to be invincible, there were also reserves in the treasury and the granaries, laid up by

7. The coincidence was irresistible; see also Pol. 23.12ff.; Diod. 29.18ff.; Livy 39.50.10f.
1. The friction between Rome and Macedon began in 174, but war broke out in 171, ending with Perseus' defeat at Pydna in 168. Other sources are Pol. 27–30; Diod. 29.33f., 30–31.14; Livy 41.22ff. through to the end of Book 45. That Perseus had "the support of all the kings" is not the only overstatement here—the Macedonian army could hardly claim invincibility.

his father, sufficient to sustain a ten-year war. Overconfident because of these resources and forgetting the fate of his father, Perseus kept telling his men to bear in mind Alexander's glory of old. [4] A cavalry engagement came first. Perseus emerged victorious, thus drawing to his side all who had been wavering and awaiting the result. [5] He nevertheless sent ambassadors to the Roman consul to ask for the terms of peace which the Romans had granted his father even in defeat, and he declared himself ready to indemnify the expenses of the war like a defeated combatant. Nevertheless, the consul Licinius set terms as severe as if Perseus had actually been defeated.[2] [6] The Romans, in the meantime, fearing a dangerous campaign, made Aemilius Paulus consul and gave him an extraordinary command of operations against Macedon.[3] When Paulus reached his army, he lost little time in engaging the enemy. [7] The night before the battle was to be fought, there was an eclipse of the moon, which all took to be a bad omen for Perseus, interpreting it as a portent of the end of the kingdom of Macedon.

2 [1] In that engagement Marcus Cato, son of the orator,[4] fell from his horse while putting up a remarkable fight in the thick of the enemy, and proceeded to do battle on foot. [2] When he fell, a troop of the enemy had surrounded him with a bloodcurdling yell, intending to kill him where he lay; but Cato recovered too quickly, and inflicted great carnage on them. [3] The enemy swooped down from all sides to fell this one man, and as he lunged at a tall Macedonian his sword slipped out of his hand and fell amongst a company of the enemy. [4] Protecting himself with his shield, Cato plunged amidst the swords of the foe, as both armies looked on, in order to retrieve the weapon. Recovering it, and after receiving many wounds, he returned to his comrades as shouts arose from the enemy. The others imitated his daring and so won the day. [5] In his flight, King Perseus sailed to Samothrace with 10,000 talents. Cnaeus Octavius,[5] dispatched by the consul to hunt him down, captured him along with his two sons, Alexander and Philip, and brought him as a prisoner to the consul.

[6] From the time of Caranus,[6] the first to rule it, down to Perseus, Macedon had thirty kings. It was under their rule for 924 years, but

2. P. Licinius Crassus, consul in 171; *MRR* 1.416.
3. L. Aemilius Paulus, consul in 168; *MRR* 1.427.
4. *MRR* 1.431.
5. Praetor in 168; *MRR* 1.428.
6. See 7.1.7.

its hegemony lasted only 152 years.[7] [7] When it fell under Roman control, it was made free, with magistracies established in each of its cities, and it received from Paulus a legal system which it employs to this day. [8] Senators of suspect loyalty from all the cities of the Aetolians were sent to Rome with their wives and children and kept there for a long time to prevent them from fomenting unrest in their country. Only after the senate was repeatedly entreated, over many years, by deputations from their city-states were they grudgingly sent back to their various homes.[8]

BOOK 34

1 [1] The Carthaginians and Macedonians had now been brought to heel and the strength of the Aetolians enfeebled by the detention of their leaders.[1] In the whole of Greece at that time only the Achaeans still seemed too powerful to the Romans, not because the resources of their constituent states were too great but because all these states acted in concert with each other. [2] For though divided into states—into separate limbs, as it were—the Achaeans are nevertheless a single body and a single realm, and they repel threats to individual cities by pooling their strength. [3] The Romans were therefore seeking a pretext for war; and Fortune opportunely provided them with a protest from the Spartans, whose territory the Achaeans were plundering at that time because of their mutual animosity. [4] The answer given to the Spartans by the senate was that the Romans would send an embassy to Greece to look into the affairs of their allies and eradicate any injustice.[2] [5] In fact, the ambassadors were given secret orders to break up the Achaean League and make each of the cities autonomous, so they might be the more easily forced into submissiveness and any recalcitrant cities transplanted. [6] The ambassadors therefore summoned the leading citizens of all the states to Corinth, where they read out the decree of the senate and explained its policy, [7] saying that it was in the interests of all that individual states have their own political and legal systems. [8] When this became public knowledge, the Achaeans

---

7. A curious figure, leaving one to wonder what Trogus felt to be the limiting dates of Macedonian control.

8. In 150; Pol. 35.6.

1. Carthage had been overcome in 147/6 and the Macedonian pretender Andriscus dealt with in 148. See Pol. 36, 38–39.

2. In 147; *MRR* 1.464.

in a fit of lunatic rage killed all the foreigners in the city. [9] They would even have killed the ambassadors of Rome themselves, had not the latter fled in panic when they heard the uproar begin.

2 [1] When news of this was brought to Rome, the senate immediately assigned the conduct of a war against Achaea to the consul Mummius.[3] He swiftly transported his army to the scene, energetically made all necessary preparations and then gave the enemy the opportunity to do battle. [2] The Achaeans, however, behaved as though a war with Rome were a matter of no importance, and everything on their side was left in neglect and disorder. [3] Their minds on plunder rather than battle, they brought up wagons to haul off the spoils from their enemies, and also stationed their wives and children on hill-tops to view the contest. [4] But when battle was joined, they were cut down before the eyes of their families, providing them with a doleful spectacle and leaving them a grim and piteous memory. [5] The wives and children now became part of their enemy's booty, transformed from spectators into prisoners. [6] The city of Corinth itself was destroyed and its entire population sold into slavery to provide an object lesson to the other cities and deter them from insurrection.

[7] While this was happening, King Antiochus of Syria launched an attack on his sister's eldest son, Ptolemy, king of Egypt.[4] The latter was extremely lethargic and so enfeebled by his daily excesses that he not only neglected the duties of the crown but, because of his obesity, lacked even normal human feelings. [8] Driven from his throne, he took refuge in Alexandria with his younger brother, also named Ptolemy. Making the latter a colleague in his kingship, he sent an embassy to the senate in Rome asking for its assistance and appealing to the obligations of their alliance. The brothers' entreaties swayed the senate.

3 [1] Popilius was now sent out as an ambassador to Antiochus to tell him to leave Egypt alone, or withdraw from it if he had already invaded.[5] [2] He found Antiochus in Egypt, and when the king made to kiss him (for Popilius was one of the people whose friendship Antiochus had cultivated while a hostage in Rome), Popilius said that their personal friendship had

---

3. L. Mummius, consul in 146; *MRR* 1.465f.

4. Affairs begin in 170 with Pol. 27.19. The monarchs are Antiochus IV Epiphanes (175–c.164) and Ptolemy VI Philometor (180–145). The latter exercised joint rule with Ptolemy VIII and Cleopatra II from 170 and was expelled in 164 (Pol. 31.10, 17ff.).

5. In 168; *MRR* 1.430.

to be in abeyance for the time being since the demands of his fatherland stood in its way. [3] He then produced and handed over the decree of the senate. He saw Antiochus hesitate and refer the matter to his friends for discussion. Using the staff which he was carrying in his hand, Popilius then traced a circle around the king large enough to include the friends, and told them to discuss the matter and not leave the circle until Antiochus gave the senate his answer as to whether he would be at peace or war with the Romans. [4] This toughness of resolve broke the will of the king, making him reply that he would comply with the senate's orders.

[5] On returning to his kingdom, Antiochus died, leaving a son who was just a child, to whom [6] guardians were assigned by the people.[6] The boy's uncle Demetrius, who was a hostage at Rome, now approached the senate when he learned of the death of his brother Antiochus. He said that his brother was still alive when he had come as a hostage but, now that that brother was dead, he did not know for whose good behaviour he was standing hostage. [7] He therefore thought it fair, he continued, that he be released to claim the throne; after all, since he had followed international convention in ceding it to his elder brother, that throne was now his due inasmuch as he was older than the orphan. [8] When he realized he was not gaining his release from the senate (which secretly judged that the kingdom would be safer with the orphan than with him), he left the city on the pretence of going hunting and covertly boarded ship at Ostia with some accomplices in his flight. [9] He sailed to Syria, where he was welcomed with universal acclaim and, after he had put the orphan and his guardians to death, awarded the throne.

4 [1] At about the same time Prusias, king of Bithynia, conceived the idea of assassinating his son Nicomedes, whom he had kept at a distance, in Rome, because he favoured the younger sons whom he had had by Nicomedes' stepmother.[7] [2] But his plan was disclosed to the young man by those who had undertaken to implement it. They urged the son, since he had become a target of his father's ruthlessness, to anticipate the trap and turn the crime back against its author. It was not hard to convince him. [3] Thus when he arrived in the kingdom of his father, summoned by Prusias, he was straightaway proclaimed king. [4] Deprived of his throne by his son and made a private citizen again, Prusias was even

6. Antiochus V Eupator (163–162); Demetrius I Soter (162–150). See Pol. 31.2, 9, 11ff.; Appian *Syr.* 46f.

7. For Prusias see 32.4.2. His successor is Nicomedes II Epiphanes (149–c.127). See Diod. 32.20f.; Zonaras 9.28.

deserted by his slaves. [5] While he lived in hiding, he was assassinated by his son—a crime as heinous as the father's order for the murder of the son.

BOOK 35

1 [1] Once he had ascended the throne of Syria, Demetrius, thinking inactivity might be dangerous for him as a newcomer, decided to increase the territory of his kingdom, and his power, by making war on his neighbours.[1] [2] Since he had a grudge against Ariarathes, king of Cappadocia, for having rejected the hand of his sister in marriage, he welcomed the appeal from Ariarathes' brother Orophernes, who had been unjustly dethroned by him. Happy with being given an honorable pretext for war, Demetrius decided to restore Orophernes to the throne. [3] Orophernes, however, in a display of ingratitude, made a pact with the people of Antioch, who were hostile to Demetrius and determined to dethrone the very man by whom he was in the process of being restored. [4] When Demetrius learned of this, he still spared Orophernes' life, so that Ariarathes would not be released from the fear of a war with his brother; but he had him arrested and kept prisoner at Seleucia. [5] As for the people of Antioch, they were not deterred from their revolt by the betrayal of the plot. [6] Under attack from Demetrius, they received assistance from Ptolemy, king of Egypt, from Attalus, king of Asia, and from Ariarathes of Cappadocia; and they recruited a certain Bala, a young man of the lowest station, to reclaim by force the kingdom of Syria, on the grounds that it had belonged to his father. [7] To complete the insult to Demetrius, Bala was given the name Alexander, and it was put forth that he was the son of King Antiochus. [8] So intense was the hatred for Demetrius amongst the whole population that his rival was by common consent ascribed not just royal power but noble birth as well. [9] Thus, by an amazing turn of events, Alexander, forgetting his former humble rank and equipped with the strength of the East almost in its entirety, made war on Demetrius, defeated him, and deprived him at once of his life and his throne. [10] Nevertheless, Demetrius did not lack

1. See 34.3.5ff. Other sources are Pol. 31.33ff.; Diod. 31.32–32.10. Besides Demetrius and Ptolemy VI, the monarchs involved are Ariarathes V Eusebes Philopator of Cappadocia (c.163–c.130); Attalus II of Pergamum (160–139); Alexander Balas (150–145); Demetrius II Nicator (145–140, and see 36.1).

courage in his own defence. In the first battle he routed his enemy; and when the kings renewed the war, he killed many thousands in pitched battle. [11] In the end, however, his spirit still unbroken, he fell fighting valiantly in the thick of the fray.

2 [1] At the start of the war Demetrius had entrusted his two sons, along with a large sum of gold, to a friend of his on Cnidus, to remove them from the dangers of the war and keep them safe to avenge their father's death, if matters so turned out. [2] The elder of these was Demetrius, who had passed the age of puberty. When the boy heard of the dissipation of Alexander, whom unexpected wealth and the trappings of another man's success kept a virtual prisoner in the palace, lounging amidst his bevies of concubines, he gained support from the Cretans and attacked Alexander, who felt secure and free from fear of enemy attack. [3] Moreover, the citizens of Antioch threw in their lot with Demetrius, wishing, by fresh services to him, to make amends for the old wrong they had done his father. His father's soldiers also transferred their allegiance to him, fired with enthusiasm for the young man and preferring the commitment of their former oath of allegiance to the arrogance of the new king. [4] So it was that Alexander was brought down by a stroke of fortune as spectacular as that by which he had been elevated. He was defeated and killed in the first engagement, paying a penalty both to Demetrius, whom he had killed, and to Antiochus, whom he had falsely claimed as his father.

BOOK 36

1 [1] On recovering his father's throne, Demetrius himself became corrupted by success.[1] Succumbing to the failings of youth, he lapsed into idleness and everywhere incurred as much contempt for his inertia as his father had incurred hatred for his arrogance. [2] And so cities in all districts rebelled against his rule; and to remove the stigma of indolence he decided to attack the Parthians. [3] The peoples of the East were not unhappy to see him come, because of the ruthlessness of Arsacides, king

1. Posidonius took up where Polybius finished and may have been an ultimate source for Trogus, even if mixed with others and mediated by another writer (Timagenes?). We have, in general, Diod. 33–34/5; Appian *Syr.* 67ff. Demetrius II Nicator was a Parthian prisoner from 139 to 129. Antiochus VI Epiphanes was killed in 142 and Antiochus VII Sidetes ruled from 138 to 129.

of the Parthians, and also because, after growing used to the old empire of the Macedonians, they found the high-handedness of their new rulers difficult to bear. [4] Assisted by reinforcements from the Persians, the Elymaeans and the Bactrians, Demetrius put the Parthians to flight in a series of battles. [5] In the end he was tricked by a false offer of peace and taken prisoner. He was put on public display before the cities and made a spectacle for their rebellious populations, to ridicule the support of these peoples for him. [6] He was then sent off to Hyrcania where he was given kind treatment in keeping with his former status.

[7] Meanwhile in Syria Trypho, who had taken pains to be installed by the people as the new guardian of Antiochus, Demetrius' stepson, killed his ward and seized the kingdom of Syria. [8] He held the throne for a time, but eventually enthusiasm for the new regime began to fade and he was defeated in battle by Demetrius' brother, Antiochus, a mere boy who was being brought up in Asia. The kingdom of Syria then reverted to the line of Demetrius.[2] [9] Antiochus well remembered that his father had been hated for his arrogance and his brother despised for his idleness. To avoid falling into the same vices himself, he married Cleopatra, his brother's widow, and took vigorous action against the cities which had defected at the start of his brother's reign. He subdued them and added them once more to the territory of his kingdom. [10] He also conquered the Jews. These had been part of the Macedonian empire under Antiochus' father, Demetrius, but had regained their independence by force of arms.[3] So great was their strength that they subsequently would tolerate no Macedonian king. They enjoyed political independence and tormented Syria with major wars.

2 [1] The Jews came originally from Damascus, the most renowned city of Syria, from which came also the kings of Assyria, who were descended from Queen Semiramis.[4] [2] The city was named after King Damascus, in whose honour the Syrians venerate as a temple the tomb of his wife Atarathe, regarded by them since her time as a goddess of great sanctity. [3] Azelus followed Damascus as king, and soon after him came Adores, Abraham and Israhel. [4] Israhel, however, gained greater fame than his forebears because he was fortunate enough to have ten sons born to him. [5] He therefore split his people into ten kingdoms and committed them to his sons, calling them all Jews (Judaei) after Juda, who had died

2. That is, Demetrius I.
3. Diod. 34/35.1 (the year 134); Josephus *AJ* 13.8.2f.
4. See 1.2.

just after the division, and commanding that his memory be cherished by all since his portion had been distributed amongst them all. [6] The youngest of the brothers was Joseph. Joseph's brothers, fearful of his outstanding abilities, waylaid him and sold him to foreign merchants, [7] by whom he was taken into Egypt, where he mastered the art of magic by his quick intelligence and soon became a great favourite of the king. [8] For he was very shrewd with omens, and originated the interpretation of dreams. It seemed that no aspect of divine or human order was beyond his knowledge, [9] so that he foretold barrenness in the fields many years before the event, and all Egypt would have perished in the resulting famine had not the king issued an edict on Joseph's advice and ordered crops to be stored up over a number of years. [10] So successful was he when put to the test that his predictions seemed to be made by a god rather than a man.

[11] Joseph's son was Moses, who not only inherited his father's knowledge but also had good looks to recommend him. [12] When the Egyptians were beset by mange and leprosy, however, they heeded the advice of an oracle and drove him from the borders of Egypt, along with those afflicted, to prevent the further spreading of the plague. [13] Moses became the leader of the exiles and stole objects of worship belonging to the Egyptians. The latter tried to recover these by force of arms but were forced by bad weather to return home. [14] Moses then moved back towards Damascus, the ancient homeland, and occupied Mt Sinai. When he finally reached this point with his people, exhausted after seven days without food in the Arabian desert, he established for all time the seventh day (traditionally called the Sabbath by that people) as a holy day of fasting since that was the day which had marked the end of their hunger and wandering. [15] Moreover, because they remembered that it was from fear of contagion that they had been expelled from Egypt, and so as not to incur disfavour with the natives of the area, the Jews avoided social contacts with strangers. This was done for a specific end, but by degrees it developed into religious practice. [16] After Moses his son, Arruas, was made priest in charge of the Egyptian objects of worship, and soon afterwards king. And ever after that it was the practice amongst the Jews for their kings to be their priests as well. This integration of their judicial and religious systems made the Jews unbelievably powerful.

3 [1] The wealth of the nation accrued from taxes on balsam, a product exclusive to those regions. [2] There is a valley enclosed by an unbroken mountain range, as though by a wall, to form the shape of a camp; it has an area of 200 acres, and is called Aricus. [3] In it is a forest notable

both for its lushness and its attractiveness, for it is studded with clumps of palm and balsam trees. [4] Balsam trees are shaped like pine trees, only they are shorter, and are cultivated like vines. At a certain season of the year they secrete balsam. [5] The area is as remarkable for its sunny climate as its lushness, for, though the sun in this part of the world is hotter than anywhere else on earth, in that spot a mild breeze produces a kind of natural and sustained relief from it. [6] In that region there is a wide lake called the Dead Sea because of the extent and the stillness of its waters. [7] It is not set in motion by the wind because of its bitumen, which makes its waters viscous even in the face of a whirlwind, and it is unnavigable because all lifeless objects sink to the bottom. It will keep no wood afloat except that which is daubed with alum.[5]

[8] It was Xerxes, king of Persia, who first conquered the Jews. Afterwards they, along with the Persians themselves, came under the rule of Alexander the Great and long remained under the sway of the Macedonian empire as a people subject to the throne of Syria. [9] When they rebelled against Demetrius, they sought the friendship of the Romans and were the very first of the peoples of the East to accept their independence from the Romans, who found it easy to be lavish with other people's property.[6]

4 [1] During the changes of regime in Syria, as the throne passed from one new king to another, in Asia King Attalus[7] was, by the murder of his friends and the execution of his kinsmen, defiling the flourishing kingdom which he had received from his uncle Eumenes. He falsely claimed first that his aged mother, then that his wife Berenice had been killed by villainy on the part of his victims. [2] After this insane outburst of violence, he assumed shabby clothing, let his beard and hair grow long as people on trial do, and no longer went out in public or appeared before the people or held cheerful dinners in the palace or, indeed, gave any other indication of being a balanced human being—to the extent that he seemed to be paying his penalty to the shades of those whom he had killed. [3] Then, with no regard for the administration of his kingdom, he began to cultivate gardens, planting various herbs and mixing together the poisonous with the harmless. He would then send assortments of all these, shot through with the sap of the poisonous ones, as special presents

---

5. So the text, but the variant "bitumine" ("daubed with pitch") seems to give better sense.

6. In 161; 1 Maccabees 8; Josephus *AJ* 12.417ff.; *MRR* 1.444 n. 1.

7. Attalus III of Pergamum (139–133); Diod. 34/35.3f.

for his friends. [4] From this pastime he moved on to bronzeworking, and took pleasure in wax-modelling and pouring and forging bronze. [5] He then began constructing a tomb for his mother but, while he was busy with this, he fell ill from sunstroke and died six days later. In his will the Roman people were named as his heirs.

[6] There was, however, a son of Eumenes, Aristonicus, born not from a legitimate marriage but from a mistress, Ephesia, the daughter of a lyre-player. After Attalus' death Aristonicus took possession of Asia, claiming it as his father's kingdom.[8] [7] He fought many successful battles against the cities which refused to yield to him from fear of the Romans, and now seemed to be established as king when Asia was assigned to the consul Licinius Crassus.[9] [8] Crassus, however, had his mind more on the treasure of Attalus than on the conduct of the war. As the year closed, he joined battle with his army in disorder, suffered defeat, and paid with his blood for his reckless greed. [9] The consul Perpenna,[10] sent out as Crassus' replacement, defeated Aristonicus in their first engagement and took him prisoner. The treasure of Attalus, the inheritance of the people of Rome, he loaded on ships and dispatched to Rome. [10] Displeased with this, his successor, the consul M'. Aquilius,[11] hastened with all possible speed to snatch Aristonicus from Perpenna, considering that the prisoner should rather adorn his own triumph. [11] The rivalry between the consuls, however, was cut short by the death of Perpenna. [12] So it was that Asia, made now the property of the Romans, transmitted to Rome its vices along with its riches.[12]

BOOK 37

1 [1] The senate had given orders for the destruction of the city and entire people of the Phocaeans because they had borne arms against the Roman people both in this war and, earlier, in the war fought with Antiochus; and after Aristonicus had been taken prisoner, the people of Massilia, since the Phocaeans were their founders, sent a deputation to Rome to make an appeal on their behalf, and succeeded in gaining a

---

8. As Eumenes III (133–129).
9. P. Licinius Crassus Dives Mucianus, consul 131; *MRR* 1.500, 503.
10. M. Perpenna, consul 130; *MRR* 1.501f., 504.
11. Consul 129; *MRR* 1.504; Perpenna was now proconsul.
12. See Sherk nos. 44 and 45.

pardon from the senate.[1] [2] After this, rewards were paid to the kings who had brought the Romans help against Aristonicus: Mithridates of Pontus was given Greater Syria, and the sons of Ariarathes, king of Cappadocia (who had fallen in the war), were given Lycaonia and Cilicia. [3] The Roman people showed greater loyalty to the sons of their ally than the boys' mother did to her children; by the former the youngsters had their kingdom extended, by the latter their lives taken away. Laodice had had six children of male sex by King Ariarathes; she feared that she would not long remain in control of the kingdom once any of them grew up, so she resorted to murder, killing five of them by poison. [5] Only one young boy was rescued from his mother's villainy by the vigilance of relatives and after Laodice was killed—the people put her to death for her cruelty—he became the sole occupant of the throne.[2]

[6] Mithridates, who met a sudden end, also left a son, and he, too, was called Mithridates. [7] Such was his subsequent eminence that he eclipsed all monarchs in grandeur, not only those of his own day but all those before him as well, and he fought wars with the Romans over a period of 46 years, with intermittent success. [8] He did, indeed, go down in defeat before the greatest generals—Sulla, Lucullus and the rest, and especially Cnaeus Pompeius[3]—but he did so only to rise again greater and more glorious than before in renewing the struggle, and to return all the more redoubtable from his losses. [9] In the end he died an old man in the kingdom of his fathers, not through the violence of an enemy but from suicide. He left a son as his heir.

2 [1] The greatness that was to be his had been foretold even by strange celestial phenomena. [2] On two occasions, both in the year of his birth and in the year he began his reign, a comet burned so brightly for 70 days that the entire sky seemed to be on fire. [3] In its greatness it filled a quarter of the heavens, and with its brilliance it outshone the sun, while its rising and setting each took a period of four hours. [4] As a boy, Mithridates faced treasonous plots on the part of his guardians, who set him on an unbroken horse and made him ride and throw javelins at the same time. [5] Their attempts came to nothing because Mithridates rode

1. See 36.4.6ff. The triumphal records show Aquilius was still in Asia in 126 and the settlement was perhaps not made until 123; *MRR* 1.509, 513. Mithridates V Euergetes was king of Pontus c.150–121/0 and was succeeded by Mithridates VI Eupator, who ruled until 63.

2. Ariarathes VI Epiphanes Philopator (c.120–c.111).

3. For Sulla (whose name is spelt Sylla in Seel's text) see *MRR* under the years 88–84; for Lucullus under 74–67; for Pompey under 66–63.

the horse with a mastery beyond his years; so they had to poison him next. [6] Fearing this very thing, the king took frequent doses of antidote, and so immunized himself against their plots, taking exotic preventive agents in ever stronger amounts, that when he was an old man, he could not die by poison even when he wanted to. [7] Afraid then that his enemies might succeed with the sword where they had failed with poison, he feigned a passion for hunting and in this way avoided being under a roof, either in town or the country, for seven years. [8] Instead he would roam the forests and pass the night in different areas of the mountains. Everyone was kept ignorant of the locations, and Mithridates meanwhile became used to escaping from, or chasing, wild beasts at a run, even pitting his strength against some of them. [9] By doing this, he both avoided attempts on his life and also hardened his physique to endure any test of courage.

3 [1] When he assumed control of his kingdom, Mithridates' first thoughts were not for governing it but for extending it. [2] He turned, therefore, to the hitherto invincible Scythians, who had wiped out Zopyrion, general of Alexander the Great, and his 30,000 soldiers; who had massacred the Persian king Cyrus and 20,000 men; and who had put to flight Philip, king of Macedon.[4] These he succeeded in completely vanquishing. [3] With his strength thus increased, he went on to seize Pontus, too, and then Cappadocia. [4] His thoughts now moving to Asia, he set off in secret from his kingdom with some friends and roamed all over that country, with none aware of his presence, familiarizing himself with the location of all its cities and the geography of the land. [5] He then went on to Bithynia where, as though he were already master of Asia, he surveyed all the areas that would favour his victory. [6] After this he returned to his kingdom, where it was already believed that he had perished, to discover there a baby boy to whom his sister and wife, Laodice, had given birth during his absence.[5] [7] But while Mithridates was being congratulated on his return from his long expedition and on the birth of his son, he ran the risk of being poisoned. His sister Laodice, since she believed him dead, had begun sleeping with his friends and, thinking that she could conceal her wrongdoing by an even greater crime, she prepared a poison for him on his return. [8] Mithridates learned of this from serving-women and exacted punishment for the crime from those responsible for it.

---

4. See 1.8; 2.3.1ff.; 9.1.9ff.; 12.2.16f.
5. Around the year 112.

4 [1] Winter was drawing on and Mithridates was spending his time on the open plains rather than at the dinner-table, in training rather than in relaxation, and with his brothers-in-arms rather than with his cronies, competing in horse- or foot-racing and tournaments of strength. [2] Moreover, he was toughening his army by daily exercise to endure hardship as well as he did; invincible himself, he had also created an unbeatable force. [3] He then made an alliance with Nicomedes,[6] overran Paphlagonia, conquered it and partitioned it with his ally. [4] When word was brought to the senate that Paphlagonia was occupied by the two kings, it sent ambassadors to both with orders that the country be restored to its former status. [5] Mithridates, believing that he was now a match for the greatness of Rome, gave the arrogant reply that the kingdom had come to his father as an inheritance; he was surprised, he said, that he should face difficulties in this regard when his father had not. [6] Undaunted by Roman threats, he also seized Galatia. [7] Nicomedes, unable to offer any such justification, replied that he would restore the country to its legitimate ruler. [8] He then renamed his own son, calling him Pylaemenes, a traditional name of Paphlagonian kings, and, as though he had restored the throne to the royal line, held on to it by means of a false name. [9] Ridiculed in this manner, the ambassadors returned to Rome.

BOOK 38

1 [1] Mithridates had begun a succession of murders with the killing of his wife, and he now decided to eliminate the sons of his other sister, Laodice—it was her husband, Ariarathes, king of Cappadocia, whom he had treacherously killed using the services of Gordius; for he thought the death of the father would have served no purpose if the young men gained possession of their father's throne, which he passionately coveted.[1] [2] While he was preoccupied with such schemes, Nicomedes, king of Bithynia, overran Cappadocia, which its king's death had left without a ruler. [3] When news of this was brought to Mithridates, he

6. Nicomedes III Euergetes of Bithynia (c.127–c.94); the year is 104.
1. For general consideration of Mithridates and the early first century see Memnon *FGH* 434 F 22 (Sherk no. 56); also Appian *Mith.* 10ff. For Nicomedes see 37.4.3. In Cappadocia Ariarathes VII Philometor was monarch c.111–c.100; then Mithridates installed his son as Ariarathes Eusebes Philopator.

used the excuse of family obligation to his sister to send her help in driving Nicomedes from Cappadocia. [4] But by that time Laodice had made a treaty with Nicomedes and married him.

[5] In anger over this, Mithridates expelled the garrisons of Nicomedes from Cappadocia and restored the kingdom to his sister's son, a highly commendable action had not treachery followed in its wake. [6] For, some months later, Mithridates pretended that he wished to restore to his native land Gordius, the man whose services he had used for the murder of Ariarathes. His hope was that if the young prince objected he would have a pretext for war; on the other hand, if he agreed, the son could also be removed by the same agent whom Mithridates had used to kill the father. [7] When the young Ariarathes discovered what Mithridates was trying to achieve, he was incensed that his father's assassin was being brought out of exile by, of all people, his uncle, and he amassed a mighty army. [8] Even though Mithridates led into battle 80,000 infantry, 10,000 cavalry and 600 scythed chariots, Ariarathes' troops were no less numerous, thanks to the support of neighbouring kings. Mithridates, afraid that the outcome of the war was in doubt, changed tactics and resorted to subterfuge. [9] He invited the young man to a meeting at which he carried a dagger concealed in his undergarment. A man was sent over by Ariarathes to search him, as is the convention amongst royalty, and this man began to feel the lower part of Mithridates' abdomen somewhat too attentively. Mithridates told him to be careful that he not find a weapon different from the one he was looking for. [10] His plot thus cloaked by a witticism, he took Ariarathes aside from his courtiers as though to talk with him in private and killed him as both armies looked on. He then handed the kingdom of Cappadocia to his own eight-year-old son, giving him the name Ariarathes and making Gordius his regent.

2 [1] The Cappadocians, however, galled by the inhumanity and caprice of their governors, rebelled against Mithridates and recalled the brother of their late king, also called Ariarathes, from Asia, where he was being brought up.[2] [2] Mithridates renewed the fight, defeated Ariarathes and expelled him from the kingdom of Cappadocia. Not long afterwards the young man died from a disease brought on by grief. [3] After the boy's death Nicomedes was afraid that Mithridates, having acquired Cappadocia, would also overrun its neighbour, Bithynia, and he therefore bribed a strikingly good-looking boy to claim his "father's kingdom" from the Roman senate, alleging that Ariarathes had had three children rather

2. Ariarathes VIII (c.96).

than two. [4] He also sent his wife, Laodice, to Rome to corroborate the story of the three sons born to Ariarathes. [5] When Mithridates heard of this, he displayed just as much impertinence himself. He sent Gordius to Rome to make the claim before the senate that the boy to whom Mithridates had delivered the throne of Cappadocia was a son of the Ariarathes who had died bringing aid to the Romans in the war with Aristonicus. [6] The senate, however, recognizing the ambition of the two kings, who were concocting fictitious claims to steal the thrones of others, took Cappadocia from Mithridates and, to appease the latter, Paphlagonia from Nicomedes. [7] To avoid insulting the kings by depriving them of something only to give it to others, both populations were given their independence. [8] The Cappadocians, however, refused the gift of freedom and said their nation could not survive without its king. Accordingly, Ariobarzanes was appointed their king by the senate.[3]

3 [1] At that time the king of Armenia was Tigranes,[4] who, long before, had been given as a hostage to the Parthians and who had recently been sent back to occupy the throne of his father. Mithridates was eager to entice this man to join him in the war against Rome which he had long had in mind. [2] Using the services of Gordius, therefore, he induced Tigranes, who had no idea that he might offend the Romans, to attack the indolent Ariobarzanes; and in order to avoid the impression that there was duplicity involved, he gave Tigranes his daughter Cleopatra in marriage. [3] At the first approach of Tigranes, Ariobarzanes took his wealth and hastened to Rome. Thus, thanks to Tigranes, Cappadocia proceeded to fall once more under the domination of Mithridates. [4] At the same time, on the death of Nicomedes, his son, himself called Nicomedes, was also driven from his kingdom by Mithridates; and he, too, came as a suppliant to Rome. A decree was then passed in the senate that both the kings be restored to their thrones, and Manius Aquilius and Mallius Malthinus were sent out as the senate's representatives to enforce the order.[5]

[5] On learning this, Mithridates formed an alliance with Tigranes to prosecute the war against the Romans, and they struck a bargain between them that the cities and land would belong to Mithridates, the captives

3. Ariobarzanes I Philoromaios (c.95–c.62).
4. Tigranes II ("the Great"; c.95–55).
5. The new king is Nicomedes IV Philopator (c.94–74). See *MRR* 2.35f., 43 (the years 89 and 88).

and all movable goods to Tigranes. [6] Aware of the magnitude of the war
he was fomenting, Mithridates then sent embassies to the Cimbri to solicit
support, as well as to the Gallograeci, the Sarmatae and the Bastarnae.
[7] For when he had previously been considering war with Rome, he had
already courted all these peoples by various gifts and favours. He also
ordered an army to come from Scythia, and he armed the whole of the
East against the Romans. [8] Thus he had little difficulty in defeating
Aquilius and Malthinus, whose army was made up of Asian soldiers.
When these were put to flight along with Nicomedes, Mithridates was
given a wholehearted welcome by the cities. [9] There he found large
quantities of gold and silver, which had been carefully amassed by former
kings, and a great deal of military equipment. Taking possession of all
this, he remitted to the cities all debts public and private, and granted
them exemption from taxes for five years. [10] He then summoned his
men to a meeting and used various methods of exhortation to incite them
to the Roman or rather the "Asian" wars. [11] I have considered this
speech worthy of inclusion in my abridgement just as it was originally
written. Pompeius Trogus presented it in indirect discourse, since he was
critical of Livy and Sallust for having transgressed the proper bounds
of history by inserting into their work speeches in direct discourse, but
composed in their own style.[6]

4 [1] It would have been desirable, said Mithridates, to have had the
opportunity to consider whether they should be at war or at peace with
the Romans, [2] but not even people with no hope of victory doubted the
need to resist an aggressor—for all men draw the sword against a robber,
to retaliate at least, even if they cannot save themselves. [3] It was no
longer a question of whether they could remain at peace, for they had
gone beyond mere feelings of hostility to come to grips in battle; now
they must consider how and with what prospects they were to prosecute
a war already begun. [4] He was confident of victory, he said, if they
would but take courage; they knew as well as he that the Romans could
be beaten, for they had put Aquilius to flight in Bithynia and Malthinus in
Cappadocia. [5] If the examples of others would be more impressive than
their own experience, he continued, he had been told that the Romans
had been routed in three battles by Pyrrhus, king of Epirus, who had with

6. Or possibly "instead of using their own words." Contrary to general
opinion and despite the possible indication of the translation "just as it was
originally written," there is nothing in Justin's words to show necessarily that he is
reproducing verbatim what he found in Trogus.

him no more than 5,000 Macedonians.[7] [6] He had heard that Hannibal remained as a victor in Italy for 16 years, and that what had stopped him from taking the city of Rome was not the strength of the Romans but the bitter rivalry and jealousy of his own people. [7] He had heard, too, that the peoples of Transalpine Gaul invaded Italy and occupied it by settling in most of its largest cities; that they had seized considerably more territory there than the same race of Gauls had taken in Asia, a so-called unwarlike country. [8] Rome had not only been conquered by the Gauls, he was told, but also captured by them, so completely that the Romans were left only the top of a single hill; and the enemy had been removed not by warfare but by payment of a ransom. [9] The Gallic name had always terrified the Romans, and he could himself count it as part of his strength. For the Gauls living in Asia differed from those who had settled in Italy only geographically; [10] they had the same origin, valour and style of fighting. Further, the Asian were all the more spirited than the Italian Gauls, having made their way through Illyricum and Thrace on a longer and more difficult journey, and very nearly devoting more effort to travelling over those territories than to occupying the points where they settled.

[11] Ever since Rome was founded, he had heard, Italy had never been completely subdued by her, but had for years on end carried on perpetual wars with her, with some peoples fighting for independence and others even to challenge her leadership, [12] and it was claimed that the armies of Rome had been wiped out by many cities and by some even sent under the yoke as a novel form of insult.[8] [13] But we should not linger over old examples, he said; at this very moment the whole of Italy had arisen in the war begun by the Marsi, demanding not independence but a share in the government and the rights of citizenship.[9] [14] And the city was also beset by internal strife amongst its leading men, as violent as the war with her neighbours in Italy; and civil war was much more dangerous than war with the Italians. [15] At the same time the Cimbri—innumerable thousands of savage, barbarous peoples— had, like a whirlwind, overrun Italy from Germany.[10] [16] Even if

---

7. Here and elsewhere in the speech is demonstrated the rhetorical advantage of referring to the past with less than accuracy; cf. the Aetolians at 28.2.

8. See Livy 9.1ff. The humiliation of being paraded under the enemy yoke was inflicted on the Roman army defeated by the Samnites at the Caudine Forks in 321 B.C.

9. The Social War of 91–89.

10. And had been defeated by Marius in 101.

the Romans could sustain individual wars against these enemies, they would be overwhelmed by their collective assault, which led him to think that they would not even have their hands free for a war with him.

5 [1] So, he continued, they should seize this opportunity and swiftly build up their strength; if they remained inactive when the Romans were preoccupied, they might have more trouble dealing with them later when they were disengaged and at peace. [2] It was not a question of whether they should take up arms, but whether to do so at a time which favoured themselves or the enemy. [3] For a war was started against him by the Romans from the moment when they took from him, while he was still a child, Greater Phrygia (which they had granted to his father as a reward for helping them against Aristonicus), a country which Seleucus Callinicus had given his great-grandfather Mithridates as dowry.[11] [4] And was not their ordering him to leave Paphlagonia another form of war? That country had not come to his father through violence or warfare, but as an inheritance, through adoption in a will and the extinction of the royal line of the country.

[5] In the face of these harsh decrees,[12] his acquiescence did not mollify the Romans, nor had he stopped them from becoming more oppressive with every day that passed. [6] For, he asked, in what respect had he not complied with their wishes? Had he not relinquished Phrygia and Paphlagonia? Had he not removed his son from Cappadocia which he had taken as victor in conformity with international convention? [7] But his right to the victory had been wrested from him by men who had acquired nothing except by warfare. [8] And Chreston, king of Bithynia, on whom the senate had decided to make war—had not Mithridates killed him to gratify the Romans? In spite of all that, he was made personally accountable for any action taken by Gordius or Tigranes. [9] Just to insult him, the senate had even awarded Cappadocia its independence— something the Romans normally took away from everyone else. And then, when the population of Cappadocia had earnestly asked for Gordius as their king instead of the independence which they were offered, the sole reason for their not gaining their wish was that Gordius was his friend. [10] Nicomedes had attacked him, he said, at the bidding of the Romans, and because he had proceeded to defend himself they had come to obstruct him. Now their reason for going to war with him would be

11. Seleucus II Callinicus (246–225).
12. See 38.3.4.

that he had not allowed himself to be torn to pieces, without lifting a finger, by Nicomedes, son of a dancing-girl.

6 [1] For what the Romans struck out at was not the wrong-doing of kings but rather their strength and their majesty; nor was it against Mithridates alone that they had employed such violent tactics—they had done so often against everybody else as well. [2] One example was their treatment of his grandfather Pharnaces,[13] who had been made successor to Eumenes, king of Pergamum, after a formal inquiry into the matter. [3] Another was that of Eumenes, whose fleets the Romans had used to make their first crossing to Asia and on whose army they had relied more than upon their own to crush Antiochus the Great and the Gauls in Asia, and later King Perseus in Macedonia.[14] [4] Even Eumenes had been formally deemed an enemy and forbidden access to Italy; and because the Romans had felt it unseemly to fight a war with him directly, they had done so with his son Aristonicus.[15] No one, they thought, had rendered them greater service than Masinissa, king of Numidia: [5] it was Masinissa who was credited with the defeat of Hannibal, the capture of Syphax and the destruction of Carthage; and along with the two famous Africani he was hailed as the third saviour of the city.[16] [6] And yet the Romans had recently fought so merciless a war with his grandson that, even when he was defeated, they made no concession to the memory of his grandfather, to spare him the ordeal of imprisonment and being put on display in a triumph.[17]

[7] Such was the principle of hatred towards all monarchs that they had established, evidently because they themselves had had kings who were such that even their names made them blush: shepherds from amongst the Aborigines, soothsayers from the Sabines, exiles from Corinth, slaves from Etruria, captured or bred at home, or—the most distinguished name of them all—the Superbi.[18] And by their own account their founders were

13. Pharnaces I (c.185–c.170).
14. See 31.8; 33.
15. See 36.4.6ff.
16. Masinissa contributed to the Roman victory in 202, but died in 149, before the destruction of Carthage, even though he had played a part in the resumption of hostilities. The "two Africani" are the conqueror of Hannibal and Scipio Aemilianus.
17. A reference to the defeat of Jugurtha in 105.
18. "The Proud," a sobriquet applied usually only to the last Tarquin king, expelled at the end of the sixth century. The founders are, of course, Romulus and Remus.

suckled at a she-wolf's teats! [8] That is why their entire population had the temperament of wolves, with an insatiable thirst for blood and a ravenous hunger for power and riches.

7 [1] Suppose, he continued, that he were compared with the Romans in terms of breeding. He was superior to that motley rabble of refugees since he could trace his line back on his father's side to Cyrus and Darius, the founders of the Persian empire, and on his mother's to Alexander the Great and Seleucus Nicator, founders of the Macedonian empire. Again, if their population were compared with his, he belonged to races[19] who were not just a match for the power of Rome but who had also stood up to that of Macedonia. [2] Not one of the peoples subject to him had experienced foreign domination, he said; never had they been ruled by kings not of their own race—whether they looked at Cappadocia or Paphlagonia, or else Pontus or Bithynia, and likewise Greater and Lesser Armenia. None of these peoples had even been reached by the famous Alexander who subdued the whole of Asia, nor by anyone who succeeded or preceded him. [3] As for Scythia, only two kings before Mithridates, Darius and Philip, had ventured to enter, much less subdue, it; and they had barely made good their escape from the part of the world from which Mithridates himself was drawing most of his strength against the Romans. [4] He had been far more apprehensive and diffident in embarking on his Pontic wars: he was merely a raw novice, while Scythia, apart from its military strength and courage, also enjoyed the protection of desert wastes and a freezing climate, all of which presaged a campaign involving great risk and hardship. [5] And as he faced those obstacles, he could not even hope for booty from the enemy, nomads lacking not only money but even a fixed habitation.

[6] Now, however, he was embarking on a war of a different nature. There was no climate milder than that of Asia, no soil more fertile, no place more appealing because of its numerous cities; most of their time they would spend as though on festivities rather than on campaign, in a war no one knew whether to call easy or enriching. [7] For they had surely heard of the wealth of the neighbouring kingdom of Attalus, or of the long-established riches of Lydia and Ionia; and rather than storming them they were simply going to occupy them. [8] So impatiently was Asia awaiting him that she was even calling upon him to come—such hatred for the Romans had been hammered into its peoples by the rapacity of

19. Or possibly "he was the king of races . . .", if, as has been argued, the word "regem" has been lost between "se" and "gentium."

the proconsuls, the public auctioning of property by the tax-gatherers, and the fraudulence of their litigation.[20]

[9] All they needed to do was follow him, and realize what such a great army could achieve under his command, a leader whom they had seen capture Cappadocia, after killing its king, on his own initiative and without the help of any of his men, and the only man in the world to have subdued all Pontus and Scythia, which none before him was able to pass through in safety or even enter. [10] As for his fairness and generosity, he did not object to his own soldiers being called as his witnesses, and he had this fact as evidence of these qualities in himself, that he was the only king in possession not merely of the kingdoms of his forefathers, but of foreign kingdoms as well, inherited as a result of his own munificence, namely Colchis, Paphlagonia and the Bosphorus.

8 [1] Having thus aroused the fervour of his men, Mithridates began his series of wars with Rome, 23 years after assuming the crown.[21]

[2] In Egypt, King Ptolemy had died, and an embassy was sent to the Ptolemy who was king of Cyrene to offer him the throne, along with the hand of Queen Cleopatra, his own sister.[22] [3] This thought alone brought joy to Ptolemy: without a struggle he had gained his brother's kingdom, for which he knew his brother's son was being groomed both by his mother, Cleopatra, and by the leading citizens, whose support he enjoyed. Ptolemy turned on them all, and as soon as he entered Alexandria he ordered the boy's supporters to be butchered. [4] As for the boy himself, on the day of the wedding at which the king was taking his mother in marriage, Ptolemy killed him in his mother's arms amidst the arrangements for the banquet and the rites of the marriage, and entered his sister's bed still dripping with the gore of her son. [5] After this he was no more gentle with his subjects, who had invited him to take the throne; his foreign troops were given authority to kill them, and blood flowed daily in every quarter. Ptolemy also divorced his sister, raping her virgin daughter and then marrying her. [6] Appalled by these atrocities, the people slipped away in various directions, leaving their country as exiles in fear of their lives. [7] Left alone in the great city with none but his entourage, Ptolemy saw that he was the ruler of empty buildings rather than people and he therefore issued an edict to encourage immigration.

20. In 97, the proconsul in Asia, Q. Mucius Scaevola, and his legate, P. Rutilius Rufus, had taken steps to curtail abuses, but suffered at the hands of the offended interest group; *MRR* 2.7f.
21. The actual figure should be 33 years.
22. We go back to the accession of Ptolemy VIII Euergetes Physcon (145–116).

[8] As the immigrants poured in, Ptolemy went out to meet the Roman ambassadors, Scipio Africanus, Spurius Mummius and Lucius Metellus, who were coming to inspect the condition of the kingdoms of the Roman allies.[23] [9] To the Romans, however, he was as ludicrous a figure as he was a cruel one to his fellow-citizens. He had an ugly face, and was short in stature; and he had a distended belly more like an animal's than a man's. [10] The repulsiveness of his appearance was heightened by his dress, which was exceedingly fine-spun to the point of transparency, just as if he had some motive for putting on display what a decent man should have made every effort to conceal. [11] By now Ptolemy had made himself hated by the immigrant population, as well, and after the departure of the ambassadors (one of whom, Africanus, had become himself a spectacle for the Alexandrians while he inspected their city) he feared a plot against his life and so slipped away into exile with the son whom he had had by his sister, and with his wife, the rival of her own mother. Next he levied a mercenary army and launched an attack at once on his sister and his country. [12] He then summoned his eldest son from Cyrene and put him to death so that the Alexandrians could not make him king in opposition to himself.[24] At this point the people tore down Ptolemy's statues and busts. [13] Thinking this had been done from affection for his sister, Ptolemy killed the son he had had by her, dismembered the body, set it in a basket and had it presented to the mother at a banquet on her birthday. [14] The incident brought revulsion and grief to the entire city as well as the queen, and cast such gloom over the joyous feast that the entire palace was suddenly ablaze with sorrow. [15] The attention of the leading citizens was thus turned from a feast to a funeral. They displayed the mangled limbs to the people and made them see from the murder of his son what they could expect from their king in future.

9 [1] When she was done with grieving for her loss, and because she could see that she was threatened with outright war against her brother, Cleopatra sent a deputation to seek help from King Demetrius of Syria, whose own fortunes were erratic and remarkable. [2] As noted above,[25] Demetrius had attacked the Parthians and had emerged the victor in numerous engagements, but he was suddenly caught in an ambush and taken prisoner, with the loss of his army. [3] The Parthian king, Arsacides,

---

23. Diod. 33.28.1ff. This embassy seems to belong about 140; *MRR* 1.480f.
24. Possibly late 131; Diod. 34/5.14.
25. 36.1. Demetrius returned in 129 and ruled until 125. Phraates II was king of Parthia from 139 to 129.

displayed a kingly magnanimity and sent him to Hyrcania, where he not only provided him with the mode of life of a king but also gave him the hand of his daughter in marriage, promising to restore to him the throne of Syria which Trypho had seized in his absence.

[4] After Arsacides' death, Demetrius despaired of ever returning. He could not bear his captivity, he was weary of the life of a commoner, luxurious though it was, and he secretly planned an escape to his kingdom. [5] He was encouraged and accompanied by his friend Callimander, who, after Demetrius' capture, had hired guides and come from Syria to Babylon, through the Arabian deserts, dressed as a Parthian. [6] However, Arsacides' successor, Phrahates, took a shorter route along minor roads and, thanks to the speed of his horsemen, overtook the fugitive Demetrius and brought him back. [7] Brought before the king, Callimander was not only pardoned but even rewarded for his loyalty, while Demetrius was severely reprimanded by Phrahates and sent back to his wife in Hyrcania, with orders that he be kept under stricter guard. [8] Time passed, and the fact that he now had children earned him some trust. Demetrius took the same friend and ran off once more, only to meet with the same ill fortune as on the previous occasion; he was caught almost at the frontier of his kingdom and brought back to the king who, in his displeasure, had him removed from his sight. [9] On that occasion, too, he was restored to his wife and children, sent back to Hyrcania, the country which was to serve as his punishment, and presented with golden dice as a reproof for his childish flightiness. [10] The Parthians' humane and lenient treatment of Demetrius was not prompted by innate compassion or by a regard for family ties, but rather by their designs upon the throne of Syria. They intended using Demetrius against his brother Antiochus,[26] as circumstances, the occasion or the fortunes of war required.

10 [1] When he heard of this, Antiochus, thinking he should strike the first blow in the war, led out against the Parthians an army which he had tempered in numerous wars against his neighbours.[27] [2] But there was as much provision in it for luxurious living as for fighting a campaign; 80,000 men-at-arms were attended by 300,000 camp-followers, most of whom were cooks and bakers.[28] [3] Certainly there was so much silver

26. Antiochus VII Sidetes.
27. See Diod. 34/5.15ff.
28. In the manuscripts the word "scaenicorum" ("[and] entertainers") appears, deleted by Seel.

and gold that even the common soldiers used hobnails of gold in their boots, and trod underfoot the substance people so love that they fight over it with cold steel. [4] Cooking vessels, too, were of silver—as though they were proceeding to a dinner rather than a war. [5] On Antiochus' approach, many eastern princes came to meet him, surrendering their persons and their thrones with curses on the arrogance of the Parthians. The first encounter took place forthwith. [6] Victorious in three battles, Antiochus seized Babylon and began to be dubbed "the Great." Thus, as all the peoples were defecting to him, the Parthians were left with nothing but the lands of their fathers. [7] Phrahates then dispatched Demetrius to Syria with a Parthian escort to seize the throne, so that Antiochus would be brought back from Parthia to defend his own territory. In the meantime, Phrahates everywhere tried to catch Antiochus by subterfuge, since he could not beat him by force.

[8] Because of the large numbers of his men, Antiochus had distributed his army in winter quarters throughout the cities, and it was this that brought about his downfall. The cities could see that they were burdened by having to supply provisions and tolerate the offensive behaviour of the soldiers. They therefore defected to the Parthians and, on a prearranged day, they made a surprise attack on the part of the force quartered with them, so that the various divisions could not reinforce each other. [9] When word of this came to Antiochus, he advanced with the contingent which was wintering with him in order to assist those who were closest at hand, only to meet while on the march the king of the Parthians, against whom he put up a braver fight than did his forces. [10] Finally, however, the enemy's valour prevailed and Antiochus, deserted by his craven troops, was killed. Phrahates gave him a funeral befitting a king and took as his wife (for he had fallen in love with the girl) the daughter of Demetrius, whom Antiochus had brought with him. [11] He then began to regret having let Demetrius go, and promptly sent some cavalry squadrons to bring him back. Demetrius, however, had been afraid of this very move on his part; and the men sent after him found him already ensconced in his kingdom. After trying all manner of expedients with no success, they returned to their king.

BOOK 39

1 [1] After Antiochus and his troops were annihilated in Parthia, all Syria was in mourning for the loss of the army. [1] Nevertheless, released from confinement among the Parthians and restored to his throne, Antiochus' brother Demetrius [2] decided to make war on Egypt—as if the Parthian wars conducted by his brother and himself had been successful, wars in which one brother had been taken prisoner and the other killed! For his mother-in-law, Cleopatra, promised him the throne of Egypt as the reward for his assistance against her brother. [3] In trying to acquire another's property, however, he lost his own, as often happens, when Syria rebelled. It started with the people of Antioch, led by Trypho, who deplored the king's tyrannical behaviour, which had now become unbearable through his exposure to the brutality of the Parthians; then the Apameni and all the other cities followed their example and defected from Demetrius during the king's absence. [4] Moreover, Ptolemy, king of Egypt,[2] who was also under attack from Demetrius, now learned that his sister Cleopatra had set the treasures of Egypt on board ship and sought refuge in Syria with her daughter and her son-in-law Demetrius. He therefore sent a young Egyptian, the son of the merchant Protarchus, to launch an attack on the kingdom of Syria. [5] A story was fabricated to the effect that the young man had been taken into the royal family through adoption by King Antiochus, and since the Syrians, in order to escape Demetrius' tyrannical behaviour, would not reject any king whatsoever, he was given the name Alexander and considerable assistance was sent to him from Egypt.

[6] In the meantime there arrived the body of Antiochus, who had been killed by the king of Parthia. Set in a silver casket and sent back to Syria for burial, it was received with great emotion by the cities and, in order to give credence to his own story, by King Alexander. This scene won him great support amongst the people, everyone thinking his tears were not forced but genuine. [7] Demetrius, for his part, was defeated

---

1. See 38.9f. This book, along with Book 40, is the only reasonably coherent narrative to survive for the events it covers. It has been concluded that the ultimate source was quite good, though again the mediation of Timagenes is suggested. See also Diod. 34/5.24, 28f., 34, 39a; Appian *Syr.* 68ff. The Syrian succession is Demetrius II Nicator, restored 129–125; Seleucus V 125; Antiochus VIII Grypos 125–96 (with Cleopatra Thea 125–121); Antiochus IX Cyzicenus 115–95.

2. Ptolemy VIII Euergetes Physcon (145–116).

by Alexander and, with misfortune besetting him on all sides, he was finally abandoned even by his wife and children. [8] Left with a few slaves, he made for Tyre, intending to use the sanctity of the temple to protect himself; but as he disembarked from his ship he was killed on the orders of the governor. [9] One of his sons, Seleucus, assumed the crown without his mother's permission, and as a result was assassinated by her. The other, who was nicknamed Grypos because of the size of his nose,[3] was established as king by the mother but only to the extent that the title "king" remained with the son, while all the power of the throne rested with the mother.

2 [1] After seizing the throne of Syria, Alexander was flushed with pride over his success, and began to show disdain even for Ptolemy himself, the man who had engineered his accession to the throne.[4] [2] Ptolemy accordingly settled his differences with his sister and proceeded to devote his entire strength to the destruction of Alexander's kingdom, which the latter had acquired by Ptolemy's resources solely because of his hatred for Demetrius. [3] He therefore sent assistance to Grypos on a massive scale and also gave him the hand of his daughter, Tryphaena, in marriage, in order to encourage the various peoples to support his grandson by establishing family ties as well as a military alliance with him. [4] It was not an unsuccessful manoeuvre. When everyone saw Grypos equipped with the resources of Egypt, they began little by little to defect from Alexander. [5] Then came the battle between the kings, following which the defeated Alexander fled to Antioch. There, finding himself short of money and the troops without pay, he ordered the removal of the solid gold statue of Victory in the temple of Jupiter, cloaking his sacrilege with a witticism to the effect that "Victory was on loan to him from Jupiter." [6] Some days later he ordered the gold statue of Jupiter himself, which was of enormous weight, to be dragged off in secret, but he was surprised in his sacrilegious act and forced to flee when a crowd converged on the spot. Overtaken by a violent storm and deserted by his men, he was captured by bandits. He was brought to Grypos and put to death.

[7] After recovering his father's throne and being freed from threats from abroad, Grypos became the target of his mother's treachery. Through her lust for power she had already betrayed her husband, Demetrius, and killed her other son; now she took it ill that her prestige was diminished by Grypos' victory, and so she set before him a cup

---

3. The word is the Greek for "hook-nosed."
4. The year is 122.

of poison when he was returning from exercise. [8] Grypos, however, had been forewarned of the plot and, pretending to challenge his mother on a point of courtesy, bade her drink it herself. She refused, and he insisted. Finally, he brought forward his informant and openly accused her, declaring that the only means that remained to her of clearing herself of the crime was to drink what she had offered her son. So the queen was beaten by a crime that recoiled on its author, and died by the poison which she had prepared for another. [9] His throne thus secured, Grypos gained for himself and his kingdom eight years of tranquillity. [10] After that, a rival for the throne came on the scene in the person of his brother Cyzicenus, born of the same mother as he, but the son of Grypos' uncle Antiochus.[5] Grypos tried to remove him by poison, but only provoked him to contest the throne by arms all the sooner.

3 [1] While the kingdom of Syria was being convulsed by these murderous rivalries, King Ptolemy of Egypt died, leaving the Egyptian throne to his wife and whichever of their two sons she should choose.[6] He was acting as if matters would be more settled in Egypt than in Syria, when the mother in choosing one of the sons was sure to make an enemy of the other. [2] The mother leaned towards the younger son, but she was forced by the people to select the elder. Before giving him the throne, however, she deprived him of his wife, forcing him to divorce his sister Cleopatra, whom he loved dearly, and ordering him to marry his younger sister Selene—an unmotherly decision to make with respect to her daughters, in that she was taking a husband from one and giving him to the other. [3] Cleopatra, who was thus not so much repudiated by her husband as dismissed by her mother with the divorce, married Cyzicenus in Syria and, so as not to bring him merely the bare title of wife, she also came to her husband with a dowry in the form of the garrison of Cyprus, which she inveigled into defecting. [4] Now equal to his brother Grypos in military strength, Cyzicenus opened hostilities against him, only to be defeated and put to flight. [5] Then Grypos proceeded to besiege Antioch, the city where Cyzicenus' wife Cleopatra was to be found, and when it was captured Tryphaena, the wife of Grypos, ordered that highest priority be given to hunting down her sister Cleopatra. Not that she wished to help her when taken prisoner; rather it was to ensure that she escape none of the miseries of captivity. For Tryphaena believed that it was from feelings of jealousy towards herself

5. Antiochus VII Sidetes, 138–129.
6. Cleopatra III and Ptolemy IX Soter II (Lathyros) ruled 116–107.

that Cleopatra had entered this kingdom rather than any other, and that she had declared herself her sister's enemy by marrying her sister's foe. [6] She then accused Cleopatra of introducing foreign armies into the dispute between the brothers, and also of marrying outside Egypt against her mother's wishes, after she had been repudiated by her brother. [7] For his part, Grypos begged Tryphaena not to force him to do so dreadful a deed. None of his ancestors, he said, amidst so many wars domestic and foreign, had ever unleashed his wrath on women after a victory; their sex itself sufficed to spare them the perils of war and the cruelty of the victors. [8] And in the case of this particular woman there was also, apart from the code of ethics observed by all combatants, a blood relationship, for the woman who was the object of her vindictive fury was her own sister, his cousin, and the aunt to the children whom they shared. [9] To all these family ties he added his reverence for the temple in which Cleopatra had sought refuge, saying that he needed to be all the more respectful of the gods since his victory derived from their favour and support. Furthermore, by killing Cleopatra Grypos would in no way impair Cyzicenus' strength, nor indeed would he bolster it by giving her back to him. [10] But the more stubbornly Grypos refused to give way, the more the sister was fired with a womanly doggedness, for she thought all these words derived not from human compassion but from sexual attraction. She therefore summoned some soldiers and sent a group of them to kill her sister. [11] They entered the temple; unable to drag her out, they hacked off her hands while she clung to the statue of the goddess. Then, cursing her assassins, Cleopatra expired, enjoining revenge for her death on the deities who had been violated. [12] Shortly afterwards another engagement found Cyzicenus victorious. He captured Grypos' wife Tryphaena, who had just murdered her sister and, by executing her, appeased the shades of his late wife.

4 [1] In Egypt, Cleopatra was exasperated with sharing the throne with her son Ptolemy and incited the people against him. She also took his wife Selene from him—an act all the more cruel because Ptolemy had already had two children by her—and forced him into exile, summoning her younger son, Alexander, and making him king in his brother's place.[7] [2] Not content with having driven her son from his throne, Cleopatra then hounded him while he was in exile in Cyprus. This drove him from

7. Cleopatra III and Ptolemy X Alexander ruled 107 to 101; the latter ruled with Cleopatra Berenice from 101 to 88; then Ptolemy IX Soter II returned and ruled until 81.

Cyprus, and so she put to death the general of her own army for having let Ptolemy escape alive; yet, in fact, Ptolemy had withdrawn from the island because he was ashamed to fight his mother, not because he was militarily weaker. [3] Terrified by this ruthlessness on his mother's part, Alexander likewise abandoned her, preferring a secure and stable life to a throne fraught with danger. [4] Cleopatra was now afraid that her elder son, Ptolemy, might receive assistance from Cyzicenus to recover Egypt; she therefore sent considerable help to Grypos, along with Selene to be his wife, and thus married to the enemy of her former husband. [5] She also sent legates who succeeded in recalling her son Alexander to the kingdom, but she was caught plotting against his life and executed by him, surrendering her last breath not to fate but to parricide. [6] She richly deserved her infamous death—she had driven her own mother from her marriage bed, made two daughters husbandless by marrying them to their brothers in turn, made war on one son after driving him into exile and treacherously plotted the death of the other after robbing him of his throne.[8]

5 [1] Nor was Alexander spared punishment for so unspeakable a murder. As soon as word got out that it was the son who was guilty of killing the queen, there was rioting amongst the people and he was driven into exile. Ptolemy was recalled and restored to the throne because he had been unwilling either to go to war with his mother or to use armed force to recover from his brother what he had formerly possessed.

[2] Meanwhile, Ptolemy's brother died. The son of a concubine, this brother had been left the kingdom of Cyrene in his father's will, and now he made the Roman people his heirs.[9] [3] For already the fortunes of the Romans, displeased at being confined to Italy, had begun to reach out for the kingdoms of the East. So it was that this part of Libya also became a province, to be followed by Crete and Cilicia, conquered in the war against the pirates, and also turned into regular provinces. [4] When this happened, the kingdoms of Syria and Egypt both felt restricted by the proximity of the Romans. They had regularly sought to extend their territories by wars with their neighbours but, now that their freedom to manoeuvre was removed, they turned their respective strength to destroying each other, [5] to such an extent that, exhausted by constant hostilities, they were regarded with contempt by their neighbours and

8. In addition to the immediately preceding narrative see 38.8.5, 11.

9. In 74. Crete and Cilicia were part of Pompey's settlement of the East in 63, ratified in 59.

fell prey to the Arabs, formerly an unwarlike people. [6] Their king, Herotimus, had confidence in the 700 sons whom he had had by his concubines. He split up his forces, overran Egypt at one time, Syria at another, and thus, draining the strength of his neighbours, brought greatness to the Arab name.

BOOK 40

1 [1] The mutual hatred of the brothers, and then of sons who inherited their parents' antagonisms, left the kings and the kingdom of Syria exhausted by implacable conflict. The people accordingly sought assistance from abroad and began to look around for foreign kings to succeed to their throne. [1] [2] Some were in favour of inviting Mithridates of Pontus, others Ptolemy from Egypt; but they were also aware that Mithridates was embroiled in a war with Rome, while Ptolemy had always been Syria's enemy. [3] Thus they unanimously settled on Tigranes, king of Armenia, who, apart from his own domestic strength, had the additional advantage of being an ally of the Parthians and a relative of Mithridates. [4] Tigranes was therefore summoned to take over the throne of Syria, which he occupied peacefully for eighteen years, during which time he was obliged neither to open hostilities against anyone nor defend himself against an aggressor.

2 [1] However, if Syria was secure against its enemies, it nonetheless fell prey to an earthquake in which 170,000 people and many of its cities perished. The soothsayers declared this to be an omen portending a change of regime. [2] And, in fact, Tigranes was defeated by Lucullus; and Antiochus, son of Cyzicenus, was summoned by the same Lucullus to the throne of Syria. [3] But what Lucullus had given, Pompey later took away. When Antiochus made a request for the throne, Pompey replied that he would not install him as king even if Syria wanted him, and he certainly would not if she were opposed to him, because, during

1. See Book 39 n. 1. The brothers are Grypos and Cyzicenus (39.1ff.); no fewer than six claimants followed their deaths in 96 and 95 until Tigranes (Bickerman 160). Tigranes II was king of Armenia c.95–55, ruler of the Syrian kingdom 83–69; then Lucullus replaced him with Antiochus XIII Asiaticus (*MRR* 2.133). He experienced varying fortunes until Pompey removed him in 64 (*MRR* 2.163f.). For Mithridates see above Book 38. The Egyptian monarch was still (until 81) Ptolemy IX Soter II. See Appian *Syr.* 48f.

the eighteen years that Tigranes was king of Syria, Antiochus had lurked in a corner of Cilicia. It was only now that Tigranes had been defeated by the Romans that Antiochus came seeking the rewards that the efforts of others had won. [4] He had not, said Pompey, taken away from Antiochus a throne that was his; nor would he give him a kingdom that he had ceded to Tigranes and which he could not defend, for fear that Antiochus would render it once more susceptible to the marauding of Jews and Arabs. [5] Accordingly, Pompey reduced Syria to a province and, little by little, the East, through the quarrels of its kings, who were all of the same blood, became the territory of Rome.

BOOK 41

1 [1] Today the Parthians rule the East, the world being partitioned, as it were, between them and the Romans; but originally they were exiles from Scythia.[1] [2] Evidence for this comes from the name of the people, for in Scythian the word for exiles is "Parthi." [3] In the days of the Assyrians and the Medes, these were the most obscure of the peoples of the East, [4] and later on, when power in the East passed from the Medes to the Persians, they fell to the victors as booty, like a nameless rabble. [5] Finally, they were subject to Macedon, after the conquest of the East, [6] so that one may well feel surprise that they should, through their valour, have achieved such success as to rule the nations in whose empires they had been like a herd of slaves.

[7] The Parthians were also beset by the Romans in three wars, during which they faced the greatest generals of Rome when she was at the height of her power; and of all the people in the world they alone emerged not just on equal terms but as victors. [8] Greater glory is theirs, however, for having been able to raise themselves amidst the once-renowned kingdoms of Assyria, Media and Persia and the opulent Bactrian empire, with its thousand cities, than for having prevailed in wars against a distant foe, [9] especially when they were constantly

1. It is supposed that Trogus' sources for Parthian (and Indian) history were Timagenes, Posidonius and Apollodorus of Artemita. Romans of the late Republic and Augustan era had particular reason to be interested in the Parthians, who continued to be a concern through the following centuries. For previous mention of the Parthians see 2.1.3, 3.6; 11.15.2; 12.4.12; 13.4.23; 36.1.2ff.; 38.9.2ff.; 39.1.1ff.

plagued by serious conflicts with the Scythians and other neighbours, and were faced with all manner of trials and perils. [10] Driven from Scythia by internal feuds, they stealthily settled in the deserts bordered by Hyrcania, the Dahae, the Arei, the Sparni[2] and the Margiani. [11] They then advanced their borders—initially without interference from their neighbours, and afterwards despite their efforts to stop them—to such an extent as to encompass not only the vast, low-lying plains, but also steep hills and towering mountain ranges. [12] This is why most of Parthia experiences either extremes of heat or cold, since the mountains are beset by snow and the plains by heat.

2 [1] Government of the nation, after its secession from the Macedonian empire, lay with a monarchy. [2] Next in rank to the kings is a class of councillors, from which the Parthians draw generals in war and magistrates in peacetime. [3] Their language is halfway between Scythian and Median, and is a blend of the two. [4] Once they had their own style of clothing, but with the coming of prosperity their dress became transparent and loose, like that of the Medes. As for arms, their fashion is partly native, partly Scythian. [5] Their army differs from that of other races in being composed mostly of slaves rather than free men; and the slave-population increases daily, since no one is allowed to manumit and all slave children are therefore born into a lifetime of slavery. The Parthians bestow as much care on these children as they do on their own, taking great pains to teach them horse-riding and archery, [6] and it is the extent of an individual's wealth which determines the number of horsemen he supplies to the king for service in war. In fact, when Antony launched his attack on the Parthians, he was met by 50,000 cavalry, of whom only 400 were free men.[3]

[7] The Parthians know nothing of hand-to-hand combat or besieging and storming cities. For them strategy consists in alternate charge and retreat by the cavalry; and they often pretend to flee to put the pursuing enemy off guard against their weapons.[4] [8] In battle the signal is given on a drum, not a trumpet. They cannot fight over a long period; but if their stamina were the equal of the violence of their attack, they would be irresistible. [9] They usually quit the engagement in the very heat of the fight and soon afterwards come back from their retreat to renew the

2. Or "Apartani": the text is uncertain.
3. In 36 (cf. 42.5.3).
4. The proverbial "Parthian shot" derives from this practice of firing while in apparent retreat.

battle, so that the critical moment has to be faced just when one thinks he has won. [10] Armour for themselves and their horses consists of corselets covered with scales, which completely cover the bodies of both. Gold and silver they use for their weapons and for nothing else.

3 [1] For the pleasure of sexual variety, the Parthians each have several wives; and they punish no crime more seriously than adultery. [2] For this reason they prohibit their women not only from dining amongst men but even from being seen by them. [3] The only meat in their diet is that which comes from the hunt. [4] They ride horses constantly, using them to go to war and to feasts, and for all private and public functions. On them they travel, halt, conduct business and hold conversations. In fact, the only clear difference between slaves and free men is that slaves travel on foot, free men invariably on horseback. [5] Disposal of the dead normally involves the corpse being torn apart by birds or dogs, and the bones are finally buried when they are bare. [6] The Parthians are all very devout with regard to religion and the worship of the gods. [7] Their national character is impetuous, truculent, devious and insolent; they consider violence appropriate for males, and passivity for females. [8] They are always restless and ready to create trouble, either at home or abroad; and they are naturally taciturn, more given to action than words, keeping a veil of silence over success as well as failure. [9] They obey their leaders from fear rather than respect. [10] They are unrestrained in their sexual pleasures, but sparing with food; and no reliance can be placed on their word or their promises, except when keeping them is in their own interest.

4 [1] When, after the death of Alexander the Great, the kingdoms of the East were being split up amongst his successors, no Macedonian thought the Parthian kingdom important enough for him, and it was given to a foreign ally, Staganor.[5] [2] Later, when the Macedonians were divided in civil war, the Parthians joined the other peoples of Upper Asia in support of Eumenes, transferring their allegiance to Antigonus after Eumenes' defeat.[6] [3] After the time of Antigonus they fell under the power of Seleucus Nicator, and then Antiochus and his successors. It was against Antiochus' great-grandson Seleucus, that they first revolted, in the time of the first Punic War, during the consulship of L. Manlius Vulso and M. Atilius Regulus.[7] [4] They could revolt with impunity because of the wrangling

---

5. So the text; his name was in fact Stasanor (see above 13.4.23).
6. At Diod. 19.29, they appear in 317 fighting with Antigonus against Eumenes.
7. The year is 256.

of the two royal brothers Seleucus and Antiochus, who were so eager
to wrest the kingdom from each other that they neglected to suppress the
rebellion. [5] At this same time Theodotus, governor of the thousand Bactrian cities, also rebelled and had himself declared king. The populations
all over the East followed his example and defected from Macedonia.

[6] At that time there lived Arsaces, a man of obscure origins but
proven courage. [7] He had been making a living by robbery and
banditry, and when he heard the news of Seleucus' defeat by the Gauls in
Asia, Arsaces, freed from fear of the king, entered Parthia with a band of
robbers. Here he defeated the Parthian governor, Andragoras, put him
to death and assumed command of the people.[8] [8] Not long afterwards
he also seized the throne of Hyrcania and, bolstered by his power over
the two peoples, proceeded to raise a large army, fearing as he did both
Seleucus and Theodotus, king of Bactria. [9] Theodotus' death, however,
soon delivered him from that fear; and he made a peace treaty with the
late king's son, who was also named Theodotus. Shortly afterwards
he fought a battle with King Seleucus, who had come to suppress the
rebellion, and emerged the victor. [10] The Parthians have ever since
commemorated that day as being the start of their independence.

5 [1] Seleucus was then recalled to Asia by fresh troubles, and Arsaces
was thus given a respite. He used this to settle the affairs of Parthia, levy
troops, build fortresses and strengthen the cities. [2] He also founded
a city called Dara on Mount Apaortenon. Such are the features of the
site that no place could be either more secure or more attractive. [3] It
is totally encircled with sheer cliffs so that no troops are needed to protect
it, while the soil around it is so fertile that the city is amply supplied by
local produce. [4] There are springs and woodland in such abundance
that there is a plentiful water supply and it is also well provided for the
pleasures of the hunt. [5] Having won the kingdom and consolidated
it, too, Arsaces died at an advanced age, as renowned a figure for the
Parthians as Cyrus is for the Persians, Alexander for the Macedonians
and Romulus for the Romans. [6] The Parthians revered his memory
by giving all their subsequent kings the name Arsaces. [7] His son,
who succeeded to the throne, was thus also called Arsaces.[9] He fought
with admirable gallantry against Antiochus, son of Seleucus, who was
equipped with a force of 100,000 infantry and 20,000 cavalry, and finally

8. His regnal dates are c.238–215.
9. He died c.190 and was succeeded by Phriapitius, who ruled until 176;
Phraates I reigned c.176–171, Mithridates I c.170–139 (cf. Diod. 33.18).

was accepted by him as an ally. [8] The third king of the Parthians was Priapatius; but he was also called Arsaces (for, as was observed above, the Parthians gave all their kings this name, as the Romans use the names Caesar and Augustus). [9] This Arsaces died after a reign of fifteen years, leaving two sons, Mithridates and Phrahates. After the custom of his people, the elder of these, Phrahates, inherited the throne. He vanquished in war the Mardi, a powerful nation, but died shortly afterwards, leaving several sons. [10] Phrahates passed over all of these, however, preferring to leave the kingdom to his brother Mithridates, a man of renowned integrity. He thought that the obligations he had as king outweighed those he had as a father, and that his country's interests should take precedence over his children's.

6 [1] At about the same time that Mithridates was beginning his rule in Parthia, Eucratides was beginning his in Bactria,[10] both of them great men. [2] But the fortunes of the Parthians prevailed, carrying them to the zenith of their power under this king. [3] The Bactrians, for their part, were buffeted in various conflicts and lost not just their empire but their liberty as well. Worn down by wars with the Sogdians, Arachosians, Drancae, Arei and Indians, they finally fell, virtually in a state of exhaustion, under the power of the Parthians, a weaker people than themselves. [4] Eucratides nevertheless conducted many wars with great valour. Weakened by these, he found himself facing a siege by Demetrius, king of the Indians,[11] but by making repeated sorties he was able to defeat 60,000 of the enemy with 300 men. Delivered from the siege after four months, he then brought India under his sway. [5] During the return journey from India, he was murdered by his son, whom he had made partner in his royal power. The son did not conceal his parricide and, as though he had killed an enemy rather than his father, drove his chariot through his blood, ordering the corpse to be cast aside unburied.

[6] Meanwhile, as this was taking place in Bactria, war arose between the Parthians and the Medes. Both enjoyed intermittent success, but final victory lay with the Parthians. [7] Bolstered by this extra strength, Mithridates appointed Bocasis governor of Media while he himself made for Hyrcania. [8] On his return from there, he went to war with the king of the Elymaeans. Defeating him, he also added this nation to his realm and advanced the empire of the Parthians from the Caucasus mountain

10. Eucratides I (c. 171–155).
11. Demetrius I may have reigned around 200–185, Demetrius II around 180–165, but they may be one and the same person.

right to the River Euphrates, bringing many peoples under his sway. [9] He then succumbed to illness and died with glory at an advanced age, as great a man as his great-grandfather Arsaces.

BOOK 42

1 [1] On the death of Mithridates, king of Parthia, his son Phrahates was made king.[1] Phrahates had determined to open hostilities with Syria to avenge Antiochus' attack on the kingdom of Parthia, but he was recalled to the defence of his own territory by unrest among the Scythians. [2] These had been induced by an offer of pay to come to the aid of the Parthians against Antiochus, king of Syria; but, since they arrived on the scene only when the battle was over and were cheated of their pay on the pretext that they had arrived too late with their support, they regretted having made such a long journey for nothing and demanded either compensation for their inconvenience or another enemy to fight. Receiving a disdainful response, the Scythians took offence and proceeded to lay waste Parthian territory. [3] Phrahates accordingly marched out to meet them, leaving the charge of his kingdom to a certain Himerus who, in the bloom of his youth, had been his lover. Himerus behaved with the cruelty of a tyrant, forgetting both the manner of his former life and the fact that he was a mere deputy, and severely maltreated the Babylonians and many other communities. [4] Phrahates himself led into battle an army of Greeks which he had captured in the war against Antiochus and had then treated in an offensive and brutal manner, forgetting that captivity had not diminished their hostility towards him and that, indeed, the humiliating mistreatment they had suffered at his hands had further exacerbated it. [5] Thus it happened that, when they saw the Parthian line give ground, the Greeks went over to the enemy and took long-desired revenge for their captivity with a bloody massacre of the Parthian army along with King Phrahates himself.

2 [1] Phrahates was replaced as king by his uncle Artabanus.[2] The Scythians, satisfied with their victory, merely ravaged Parthia and went back home. [2] Artabanus then made war on the Tocharii, but received

---

1. Phraates II ruled 139–129. Cf. Diod. 34/35.15. For Antiochus' attack see above 38.10.
2. Artabanes I (c.128–124); Mithridates II (c.124–88).

a wound to the arm from which he immediately died. [3] He was succeeded by his son Mithridates, whose achievements earned him the sobriquet "the Great"—burning with ambition to rival the valour of his forebears, he actually surpassed them in renown by his greatness of spirit. [4] He conducted many wars against his neighbours with great courage and added many peoples to the Parthian empire. [5] He also fought a number of successful campaigns against the Scythians, and avenged the injury inflicted on his ancestors. [6] Finally, he made war on Artoadistes, king of Armenia.[3]

[7] Now, since we are making a transition to Armenia, we should go back a little and look into its beginnings. [8] There is no justification for passing over such a great kingdom in silence when its territory is, after Parthia, greater than that of all other realms, [9] stretching, as it does, 1100 miles from Cappadocia all the way to the Caspian Sea, with a breadth of 700 miles. [10] It was founded by Armenius, companion of Jason the Thessalian, the man whom King Pelias wanted killed because his remarkable courage posed a threat to his rule. Pelias ordered Jason to undertake a military expedition to Colchis and bring back the ram's fleece, famous the world over. Pelias was hoping that he would perish either in the perils he would face on such a long voyage or in a war with barbarians so far inland. [11] Jason therefore spread the word of his glorious expedition and, when the finest young men virtually from all over the world came racing to join him, he assembled an army of the world's most courageous warriors, who were given the name "Argonauts." [12] He brought his army home safe and sound after great exploits, but was again driven from Thessaly with considerable violence by the sons of Pelias. He then took with him the throngs who had been flocking to him every day from all the nations of the world because of reports of his valour, and made for Colchis once more, accompanied by his wife, Medea, whom he had divorced but taken back again out of pity for her in her exile, and by Medus his stepson, whom Medea had borne to King Aegeus of Athens. In Colchis Jason restored to the throne his father-in-law, Aeëtes, who had been deposed.

3 [1] He then fought momentous wars with his neighbours, adding a number of cities which he captured to his father-in-law's realm (to make amends for the wrong he had done Aeëtes on his earlier expedition, when he had taken his daughter Medea and killed his son Aegialeus) and allotting others to the peoples which he had brought with him. [2] After

3. Artavasdes, who died c.95.

Hercules and Liber, who were, according to tradition, kings of the East, Jason is said to have been the first human being to have conquered that part of the world. [3] To certain peoples he assigned as chieftains Erygius[4] and Amphistratus, the charioteers of Castor and Pollux. [4] He struck an alliance with the Albani who supposedly followed Hercules from Mount Alba in Italy at the time when the latter was taking his cattle through Italy after killing Geryon. During the war with Mithridates[5] these people remembered their Italian origins and greeted the army of Pompey as their brothers. [5] Thus almost all of the East accorded to Jason, as their founder, divine honours and temples (which, years later, Parmenion the general of Alexander the Great had torn down so that no one's name should be more venerated in the East than Alexander's). [6] After Jason's death, Medus, who was his father's equal in valour, founded the city of Media in honour of his mother and established the kingdom of the Medes, whom he named after himself. It was with this kingdom that control of the East subsequently lay. [7] The Albani have as their neighbours the Amazons, whose queen Thalestris, according to numerous sources, asked to sleep with Alexander.[6]

[8] Further, Armenius, himself a Thessalian and one of Jason's officers, founded Armenia by bringing together the throngs who were wandering aimlessly after the death of Jason, their king. [9] It is in the mountains of Armenia that the River Tigris rises, its initial flow being quite small. After some distance it plunges underground, to re-emerge after 25 miles in the region of Sophene as a mighty river, and in that form it enters the marshlands of the Euphrates.

4 [1] To resume: after the war with Armenia King Mithridates was driven from the kingdom of Parthia by the senate because of his cruelty.[7] [2] His brother Orodes assumed the vacant throne and for a long time laid siege to Babylon, where Mithridates had sought refuge, finally starving the townspeople into submission. [3] Mithridates, however, relying on his kinship with Orodes, voluntarily put himself in his hands; [4] but Orodes considered him an enemy rather than a brother and ordered

---

4. This is Seel's emendation; the manuscripts read, among other things, "frigium/phrygium."

5. Of Pontus.

6. See 12.3.5.

7. There is evident confusion. The actual succession after Mithridates runs Gotarzes I (c.90–c.80), Orodes I (c.80–78), Sinatruces (c.77–70), Phraates III (c.70–58), Orodes II (c.58–39). The last named defeated Crassus at Carrhae in 53 (*MRR* 2.230).

him butchered before his eyes. After this, Orodes fought a war with the Romans, wiping out the entire Roman army along with its general, Crassus, and Crassus' son. [5] Orodes' son Pacorus was sent to prosecute what remained of the war with Rome, but despite great successes in Syria he was recalled to Parthia because he had roused his father's suspicions; in his absence the Parthian army left in Syria was cut to pieces with all its officers by Cassius, quaestor of Crassus.[8] [6] Not long after these events, the civil war between Caesar and Pompey broke out among the Romans. In this the Parthians took the Pompeian side, because they had been allies of Pompey during the war with Mithridates, and also because of the death of Crassus; for they had heard that a son of Crassus was a supporter of Caesar, and they were in no doubt that he would avenge his father if Caesar prevailed.[9]

[7] Thus when the Pompeian cause was defeated, the Parthians sent help to Cassius and Brutus against Augustus and Antonius.[10] At the end of the war, when Pacorus was again their general, they made an alliance with Labienus, laid waste Syria and Asia and launched a massive attack on the camp of Ventidius, who had routed the Parthian army during Pacorus' absence, as Cassius had done before him. [8] Ventidius, however, pretending to be afraid, long held back from the fight and allowed the Parthians to insult him for a time. Eventually, when the Parthians were feeling secure and jubilant, he unleashed some of his legions against them, and the shock scattered the Parthians, who made off in different directions. [9] Pacorus believed that his men in their flight had drawn the Roman legions away with them, and he attacked Ventidius' camp, assuming it to be defenceless. [10] At that juncture Ventidius sent forth the remainder of his legions and wiped out the contingent of Parthians along with the prince Pacorus himself. In no war did the Parthians ever receive a greater blow. [11] Pacorus' father, Orodes, had a short while before heard of the devastation of Syria and the occupation of Asia by the Parthians, and he had been boasting of Pacorus' victory over the Romans; now, when this news reached Parthia and the king was suddenly apprised of his son's death and the destruction of his army, his grief mounted to frenzy. [12] For days on end he refused to speak to anyone, or to eat, or to utter a sound—it was as if he had been

8. *MRR* 2.229, 237, 242 (the latter in the year 51).

9. Dio 42.2.5 insists on Parthian hatred for Pompey. Caesar was planning a Parthian campaign at the time of his death.

10. For what follows through to 36 see the account in Dio 48–49. For P. Ventidius Bassus see *MRR* 2.388, 393. Pacorus died in 38.

struck dumb. [13] Then, many days later, when his grief had set free his tongue again, all he did was call out Pacorus' name. He thought he saw Pacorus; he thought he heard Pacorus; he thought he was talking with him and standing next to him; then at other times he would tearfully grieve for him as lost. [14] After a long period of mourning a further cause for concern came to vex the pitiful old man, namely which of his thirty sons he should make heir to the throne in place of Pacorus. [15] His many concubines, on whom he had fathered so many sons, kept trying to cajole the old man, each of them concerned for her own children. [16] But the destiny of Parthia, which had parricides for its kings almost as a matter of course, saw to it that the most vicious one of them all, who also bore the name Phrahates, should be made king.[11]

5 [1] Phrahates immediately killed his father, as if he were refusing to die, and butchered all thirty of his brothers. Nor did his parricides stop short of his sons. [2] When he saw that he had antagonized the upper class by his repeated atrocities, he ordered his grown son put to death so there could be no other candidate for the throne. [3] Antonius attacked him with sixteen mighty legions for having assisted the effort against Caesar and himself but fled from Parthia after sustaining heavy losses in numerous battles.[12] [4] The victory made Phrahates even more despotic, but even as he planned many further cruelties he was driven into exile by his people. [5] He long importuned neighbouring states with entreaties for help, turning finally to the Scythians, and it was with Scythian aid in particular that he was restored to the throne.

[6] In Phrahates' absence the Parthians had appointed as king a certain Tiridates.[13] When he heard of the approach of the Scythians, Tiridates fled with a large group of his courtiers to Caesar, who at that time was at war in Spain. He brought to Caesar as a hostage Phrahates' youngest son, whom he had managed to seize because the boy was insecurely guarded. [7] On learning of this, Phrahates immediately sent an embassy to Caesar demanding the return of "his slave Tiridates" and the son.[14] [8] Caesar listened to the delegation from Phrahates and also took note of Tiridates' requests—for Tiridates himself also wished to be restored to the throne, claiming that Parthia would be under Roman jurisdiction if the throne

11. Phraates IV reigned until 2 B.C., when he in turn was murdered by Phraates V.

12. In the year 36; *MRR* 2.400.

13. He lasted from about 30 to 25. See Dio 51.18.2f. Caesar is, of course, Augustus.

14. Dio 53.33 under the year 23; Augustus *Res Gestae* 32.

were his as a gift of the Romans. He then declared that he would not surrender Tiridates to the Parthians, but neither would he assist Tiridates against the Parthians. [9] Nevertheless, to avoid the impression that nothing had been gained from Caesar throughout the negotiations, he both restored the son to Phrahates without ransom and also ordered that Tiridates be afforded a life of luxury for as long as he wished to remain among the Romans. [10] Later, once the war in Spain was over, Caesar came to Syria to arrange a settlement of the East and filled Phrahates with fear that he might be intending to make war on Parthia. [11] As a result, Roman captives were rounded up from all over Parthia, those from Crassus' army as well as from Antonius', and returned to Augustus along with the military standards.[15] [12] Furthermore, both the children and the grandchildren of Phrahates were given to Augustus as hostages, and Caesar accomplished more by the greatness of his reputation than any other general could have done by force of arms.

BOOK 43

1 [1] Having dealt with the history of Parthia, the East and virtually the whole world, Trogus now returns home, as if after a long trip abroad, to the early years of the city of Rome. He thought he would be behaving like an ungrateful citizen if, after elucidating the achievements of all other nations, he remained silent about his native land alone. [2] He therefore touches briefly on the early period of the Roman Empire, in such a manner as not to exceed the scope of his projected work, but so as not to pass over in total silence the origins of the city which is now the capital of the entire world.

[3] The first inhabitants of Italy were the Aborigines.[1] Their king, Saturnus, is reputed to have been a man so just that there was no slavery

15. In 20; Dio 54.8; Augustus *Res Gestae* 29.2. The hostages, for whom see *Res Gestae* 32.2, came to Rome around 10 B.C.

1. Rome's origins were of great interest in the Augustan period, an interest evident above all in Vergil's *Aeneid*. Two other contemporaries wrote histories still extant which began with legendary origins and the kingship, Livy and Dionysius of Halicarnassus. There is, of course, no reason why Trogus should use a Greek source for this section, and there was Roman historical writing to draw upon, going back especially to Cato's *Origines*. It is not to be expected that there would be complete agreement between versions. The word "aborigines" simply means "original inhabitants," from the Latin *ab origine*, "from the beginning."

during his reign and no private ownership of property; instead, everything was held in common, undivided, as if all men shared a single family estate. [4] It was to commemorate the example of this man that those measures were taken which permit slaves throughout the land to recline with their masters at the Saturnalia, with all enjoying a position of equality. [5] And so Italy was first called Saturnia after its king, and the hill on which he lived was called Mount Saturnius, where the Capitol is today, as if Saturnus has been evicted from his own home by Jupiter.[2] [6] Third to reign after Saturnus,[3] they say, was Faunus, and it was when he was king that Evander came to Italy with a small group of his countrymen from the Arcadian city of Pallanteum. Faunus generously allotted him some land and the hill which Evander subsequently named the Palatium. [7] At the foot of this hill Evander established a temple for Lycaeus, whom the Greeks call Pan and the Romans Lupercus.[4] The cult-statue of the god is naked and is cloaked with the skin of a goat, the dress worn now for the ceremonial race through Rome at the Lupercalia. [8] Faunus had a wife called Fatua. She was possessed by a divine spirit and would foretell the future, to all appearances in a fit of frenzy, which is why, to this day, the word used of the speech of those divinely inspired is *fatuari*.[5] [9] Latinus was conceived and born of a liaison between Faunus' daughter and Hercules, who, at that time, after the killing of Geryon was driving through Italy the cattle that were the spoils of his victory.

[10] It was when Latinus was king that Aeneas came to Italy from Ilium, after Troy had been taken by the Greeks. Aeneas was immediately faced with war; but when he led his army into the field of battle he was invited to parley, and he so impressed Latinus that Aeneas was accepted by him as co-ruler and also adopted as his son-in-law, with Latinus' daughter, Lavinia, given to him in marriage. [11] After this they both made war together on Turnus, king of the Rutulians, who had been cheated of the hand of Lavinia; and in this campaign both Turnus and Latinus lost their lives. [12] Aeneas' victory entitled him to sovereignty over both peoples, and he founded Lavinium, named after his

2. In historical times the Capitol was the site of the temple of Jupiter Optimus Maximus.

3. The second has been omitted; he was Picus, father of Faunus (Vergil, *Aeneid* 7.48).

4. The Lupercalia remain mysterious. There seems a likely connection with wolves (the Latin for wolf is *lupus*), but the existence of a deity called Lupercus is thought to be a late invention.

5. Etymological speculation is common among Roman antiquarians, and this one is unique; the verb occurs nowhere else in this sense.

wife. [13] He next fought a war against Mezentius, king of the Etruscans, in which Aeneas himself perished. His son, Ascanius, succeeded him. Ascanius left Lavinium and founded Alba Longa, which remained the capital of the realm for 300 years.

2 [1] After a succession of kings in this city, finally Numitor and Amulius ascended the throne. [2] Numitor had the prerogative by virtue of his age; but Amulius overthrew him and forced his daughter Rea into a life of perpetual virginity to prevent any male claimant to the throne emerging from the family of Numitor. He cloaked his wrongdoing with a hollow honour, giving the impression that Rea had been chosen to be a priestess, rather than sentenced to punishment. [3] Shut away in the grove sacred to Mars, she gave birth to two boys; whether they were begotten of an illicit liaison or by Mars is not known. [4] When Amulius learned of this, his fears were multiplied by the birth of the two. He ordered the boys to be exposed and he clapped the girl in irons, an indignity which brought about her death. [5] Fortune, however, keeping a watchful eye on Rome's beginnings, gave the boys to a she-wolf to be suckled; the animal had lost her cubs and, wishing to empty her distended teats, offered herself as the infants' nurse. [6] Since the wolf returned regularly to the babies as though to her cubs, the herdsman Faustulus became aware of what was going on, removed the children from the animal and brought them up in a rustic way of life amidst his cattle. [7] The boys were believed to be the sons of Mars on the basis of apparently incontrovertible proofs—either because they were born in the grove of Mars, or because they had been suckled by a wolf, which is under Mars' protection. One boy's name was Remus and the other's Romulus. [8] Once they were grown, daily contests of strength amongst the herdsmen increased both the stamina and the agility of the boys. [9] Now, since they were often engaged in the arduous task of keeping bandits from raiding their animals, Remus was captured by those very bandits, and was presented to the king as himself doing precisely what he had been trying to prevent others from doing; he was charged with having made a practice of plundering the herds of Numitor. He was then handed over to Numitor by the king for punishment. [10] Numitor felt compassion because of the boy's tender years and was led to suspect that he was his grandson who had been exposed. He was disturbed by the resemblance of the lad's features to those of his daughter, and by the fact that his age was consistent with the date of the exposure; then Faustulus suddenly arrived with Romulus, and Numitor learned from him the early history of the boys. They thereupon formed a conspiracy. The young men armed themselves to avenge their mother's death, and Numitor did likewise to reclaim the throne of which he had been robbed.

3 [1] After Amulius was killed, the throne was restored to Numitor, and the city of Rome was founded by the young men.[6] [2] After that a senate comprising a hundred older men, called "fathers," was established, and the Sabine maidens were seized, since the neighbouring peoples would not deign to intermarry with herdsmen.[7] Surrounding peoples were crushed in war and Roman rule was established, first over Italy and soon over the world.

[3] In those days the kings still had spears, called "sceptres" by the Greeks, instead of the diadem; for from the early period of their history the Romans worshipped ancient spears as immortal gods, and it is in memory of this veneration that statues of the gods are to the present day equipped with spears.

[4] In the time of King Tarquin[8] some young Phocaeans sailed from Asia into the mouth of the Tiber and made an alliance with the Romans, after which they set off in their ships for the most remote inlets of Gaul, founding Massilia between the Ligurians and the wild Gallic tribes. Their exploits were impressive, as they defended themselves against the barbarous Gauls or themselves went on the attack against those by whom they had been attacked.

[5] The Phocaeans, constricted by territory which was limited and barren, had in fact turned their attention more to the sea than the land, and had been making their living from fishing, trading and often even from piracy, which in those days was considered a noble occupation. [6] Thus it was that as they were venturing to the farthest shores of the ocean, the Phocaeans arrived in the gulf of Gaul at the mouth of the Rhone. [7] They were captivated by the beauty of the spot and, when they returned home and recounted what they had seen, they inspired more to join them. [8] The commanders of the fleet were Simos and Protis. These visited the king of the Segobrigii, whose name was Nannus—it was in his territory that they wished to build their city—and requested an alliance.

6. The traditional date was around 754/3.
7. See above 28.2.8ff.
8. Tarquinius Priscus, who was held to have reigned from 616 to 578. Massilia (Marseilles) was founded around 600. Cf. 37.1.1.

[9] It so happened that on that particular day the king was busy with arrangements for the wedding of his daughter Gyptis; in accordance with the tradition of his people, he was preparing to give her in marriage to a son-in-law who would be chosen at the wedding-feast. [10] All Gyptis' suitors had been invited to the ceremony, and the Greek visitors were also summoned to the banquet. [11] The girl was then brought in and told by her father to hand some water to whomsoever she chose as her husband. Passing by everyone else, she turned to the Greeks and handed the water to Protis who, becoming a son-in-law instead of a visitor, was given by his father-in-law a site on which to build his city. [12] And so Massilia was founded, in a remote bay near the mouth of the River Rhone, in a sequestered nook of the sea, as it were. [13] The Ligurians, however, kept a jealous eye on the city's growth and harassed the Greeks with continuous warfare, but the Greeks so distinguished themselves in repelling the dangers that they crushed their enemy and established numerous colonies in the captured territory.

4 [1] It was from these Greeks that the Gauls learned to live in a more civilized manner, abandoning or modifying their barbarous ways; they learned to practice agriculture and encircle their cities with walls. [2] Then they became used to a life governed by law rather than armed might, to cultivating the vine and planting the olive-tree; and so brilliantly successful was the society and its affairs that, instead of Greece emigrating to Gaul, it looked as if Gaul had been moved to Greece. [3] On the death of Nannus, king of the Segobrigii (the man by whom the Greeks had been given the site for their city), his son Comanus succeeded to the throne. One of the local chieftains now asserted that sooner or later Massilia would prove to be the ruin of her neighbours and should be crushed at birth so that she could not overwhelm Comanus later on when she was stronger.[9] [4] He added the following story. There once was a pregnant bitch which begged a shepherd for a spot in which to give birth. Granted this, she made the further request that she be permitted to bring up her pups in the same place. Finally, when the pups were grown and she had the support of her family to rely on, she demanded title to the place for herself. [5] Just so, said the prince, the people of Massilia, who now seemed to be mere squatters, would one day dominate the whole region. [6] This upset the king, who set a trap for the Massilians. On the day of the festival of the Floralia, he took advantage

---

9. There is a lacuna in the text at this point, since the sentence lacks a main clause; but the sense is clear enough.

of his ties of hospitality with them to send into the city a large number of brave and powerful warriors, and he ordered still more carried in on wagons, hidden behind the wickerwork of the carts and covered with branches. [7] Comanus himself hid with his army in the mountains next to the city so that, when the gates would be opened at night by the men mentioned above, he could arrive at just the right moment for the assault and with his army fall upon a city buried in sleep and wine.[10] [8] But the plot was divulged by a woman who was a relative of the king and who had been having an affair with a young Greek. While in his arms, the woman took pity on his charms and revealed the plot, telling him to avoid the danger. [9] The young man immediately reported the matter to the magistrates and, when the conspiracy came to light, all the Ligurians were arrested and those in hiding dragged from the wickerwork. [10] All were put to death, and a trap was laid for the king while he was laying his own. Seven thousand were slaughtered, along with the king himself. [11] From that day forward the people of Massilia have shut their gates on feast-days, stood on guard, posted look-outs on the walls, challenged foreigners, maintained security and in times of peace maintained the city in a state of war. [12] Thus a good institution has there been preserved, not simply when circumstances demand it, but from a habit of acting prudently.

5 [1] Later, the Massilians fought great wars with the Ligurians[11] and great wars with the Gauls. This both magnified the renown of their city and also, after a number of victories, made the valour of the Greeks celebrated amongst their neighbours. [2] They also routed Carthaginian forces on many occasions, when a war arose over the seizure of some fishing boats, and granted the Carthaginians peace after defeating them. [3] They formed an alliance with the Spaniards and were absolutely loyal to the treaty made with the Romans almost at the original foundation of Massilia, energetically supporting their allies in all their wars. This both increased their confidence in their strength and also guaranteed them peace with their enemies.

[4] Massilia was flourishing, with its exploits famous, its wealth abundant and its strength renowned when, suddenly, the peoples around her united to wipe out the Massilian people, as though to extinguish a fire

10. The phrase "a city buried in sleep and wine" ("urbemque somno ac vino sepultam") almost reproduces Vergil *Aeneid* 2.265, "urbem somno vinoque sepultam," which itself is a variant on Ennius *Annales* 292, "nunc hostes vino domiti somnoque sepulti."
11. E.g. in 154; *MRR* 1.154.

that menaced them all. [5] The chieftain Catumandus was unanimously chosen as leader of these peoples. He laid siege to the city of his enemies with a mighty army of elite warriors; but as he slept he was terrified by a dream of a fierce-looking woman who told him that she was a goddess. Catumandus therefore took the initiative to make peace with the Massilians. [6] He asked permission to enter the city and worship their gods; and when he came to the acropolis of Minerva, he caught sight of the cult-statue of the goddess in the portico—the woman he had seen in his dream. He suddenly exclaimed that she was the one who had frightened him in the night, that it was she who had ordered him to raise the siege. [7] He congratulated the people of Massilia on the protection which he could see the immortal gods afforded them, presented a golden necklace to the goddess and made a permanent treaty with the people of Massilia.

[8] So peace was gained and Massilian security established. Subsequently, some of the ambassadors of the Massilians who were returning from Delphi (where they had been sent with gifts for Apollo) heard that the city of Rome had been captured and burned by the Gauls.[12] [9] When the news was brought home, it was met with public mourning by the people of Massilia, who contributed gold and silver from both public and private sources to make up the total weight demanded by the Gauls, from whom, they had learned, the Romans had bought peace. [10] In return for this benefaction it was decreed that the Massilians be exempted from taxation, granted seats amongst the senators for public shows and given a treaty putting them on an equal footing with Romans.

[11] At the end of this book Trogus tells us the following. His forefathers were of Vocontian origin,[13] his grandfather, Pompeius Trogus, had received Roman citizenship from Gnaius Pompeius in the war against Sertorius [12] and his uncle had been a cavalry squadron leader under the same Pompeius in the war with Mithridates. He adds that his father served under Gaius Caesar and was responsible for his correspondence, his diplomatic missions and his official seal.

12. In 387; see 6.6.5; 20.5.4; 24.4.3; 28.2.4; 38.4.8.
13. I.e. from Gallia Narbonensis (see the Introduction). Pompey fought against Sertorius in Spain in the years 76–72. On Pompey and Mithridates see 37.1.8. Those granted citizenship took their Roman name from their patron, hence Trogus becomes Pompeius.

BOOK 44

1 [1] As Spain represents the bounds of Europe, so will it also mark the end of this work. [2] The ancients originally called this country Hiberia, after the River Hiberus, and subsequently Hispania after Hispalus. [3] Situated between Africa and Gaul, it is bounded by the waters of the Ocean and the mountains of the Pyrenees. [4] Smaller than both lands mentioned above, it is also more fertile than either. It is not subjected to intense heat like Africa, nor is it constantly buffeted by winds like Gaul. Rather, since it lies between the two, its temperate climate and its salutary seasonal rains make it prolific in all manner of crops, to the extent that its abundant production of the entire range of foodstuffs meets the needs not only of its own people but those of Italy and the city of Rome, as well. [5] From Spain, in fact, come large quantities not only of wheat, but also of wine, honey and oil. The country has not only deposits of iron of high quality,[1] but also herds of swift horses. [6] Moreover, it is admirably provided not just with produce from its surface soil—there is also abundant wealth of metals hidden beneath. There is flax and Spanish broom in abundance,[2] and certainly no land is richer in red lead. [7] In Spain the rivers are not so violent or swift flowing as to cause damage; rather, they flow gently, irrigating vineyards and plains, and at their estuaries are well stocked with fish, most of them in addition being rich in gold, which they carry along as gold dust. [8] Spain touches Gaul only at the mountain range of the Pyrenees; everywhere else it is encircled by the sea. [9] The country is more or less square-shaped, except for a narrowing at the Pyrenees where the shoreline compresses it. The range of the Pyrenees extends for 600 miles. [10] The climate is uniformly healthy throughout Spain because the air is nowhere infested with noxious marsh vapours. There is the additional factor of the sea-breezes, which blow continuously on all sides of the country. These make their way throughout the province, ventilate the air rising from the land and so provide a wholesome environment for its inhabitants.

2 [1] The inhabitants of Spain are able to endure hunger and fatigue; they are courageous to the point of death. All are given to a strict and

---

1. This is odd, as in § 6 wealth of metals is mentioned and at 3.8 the same words as here recur.
2. Ruehl wished to transpose these words to the end of the first sentence in § 5 so as to keep the mentions of crops and metals separate.

rigorous frugality. [2] They prefer war to peace; lacking an enemy from without, they will look for one at home. [3] They have often died under torture to protect secrets confided to them; they have a stronger will to maintain confidentiality than to live. [4] There is a famous story of the fortitude of a slave in the Punic War who, having avenged his master, broke into triumphant laughter when being tortured, and overcame the cruelty of his torturers with his serene cheerfulness. [5] They are a nimble and agile race, with a restless spirit; to most Spaniards their war-horses and weapons are more precious than their own blood. [6] They prepare no banquets for feast-days; the practice of taking hot baths they learned from the Romans after the second Punic war.

[7] Over the many epochs of their history, the Spaniards had no great leader apart from Viriatus, who harassed the Romans for ten years with mixed success;[3] so far are their natures more akin to those of wild beasts than human beings. Viriatus himself was not formally elected by a vote of the people; the Spaniards simply followed him because he knew how to take precautions and was skillful at avoiding danger. [8] Such was his integrity and restraint that, although he often defeated the armies of Roman consuls, he did not change the style of his arms or his dress, or even his diet, despite his great successes, but maintained the same appearance as when he first started fighting, so that any of the rank and file appeared more wealthy than the general himself.

3 [1] In Lusitania, close to the River Tagus, mares are impregnated by the wind, according to many sources. Such myths arise because of the fertility of these mares and the large number of the herds of horses, which in Gallaecia and Lusitania are evidently so great and so swift that they might well be thought to have been conceived by the wind itself. [2] The Gallaecians lay claim to Greek ancestry. After the Trojan War, they maintain, Teucer had fallen into disfavour with his father, Telamon, because of his brother Ajax's death and was not welcomed back to his kingdom. He went to Cyprus; there he founded a city which he called Salamis after his former country . Then, when he received word of his father's death, Teucer made again for his fatherland, [3] but was prevented from putting in there by Eurysaces, the son of Ajax. Instead he landed on the coast of Spain and occupied the region where New Carthage is situated today; from there he moved on to Gallaecia, where he settled and gave the people of the area their name.

3. See Diod. 33 and *MRR* 1 under the years from 147 until the victory of Q. Servilius Caepio in 138.

[4] Part of Gallaecia is inhabited by a people called the Amphilochi. It is an area with abundant resources of copper and lead, as well as red lead, which has also brought about the naming of a river in the region.[4] [5] It is also very rich in gold, so much so that its inhabitants often break up clods of gold with the plough. [6] In the territory of this people stands a sacred mountain, the violation of which with iron implements is forbidden by religious scruple; but whenever its soil is split by lightning (a regular phenomenon in the region) and gold is unearthed, collection of the gold is permitted on the grounds that it is a gift from a god. [7] Women are responsible for domestic matters and the cultivation of the land; men take charge of warfare and plunder. [8] The iron of the Amphilochi is of high quality, but their water is harder even than their iron; for the iron is sharpened when tempered in it, and no weapon is approved by those people unless it has been first dipped in either the River Birbilis or the Chalybs. [9] Hence the people living along the second river are called Chalybes, and they are reputed to have better iron than anyone else.

4 [1] The woodlands of the Tartessii, in which, tradition has it, the Titans made war on the gods, were once inhabited by the Curetes whose earliest king, Gargoris, was the first to discover how to gather honey. [2] When a grandson was born to him as a result of his daughter's illicit love affair, Gargoris was ashamed of the girl's scandalous conduct and tried to have the child killed by various methods; when, with the aid of some good fortune, the boy survived all his trials, the grandfather felt compassion because of all the dangers he had faced, and the boy finally succeeded to the throne. [3] Gargoris had first ordered him to be exposed and, some days later, had sent someone to look for the corpse of the child who had been exposed; but he, it was discovered, had been nourished by the milk of various wild animals. [4] When the child was brought home, Gargoris then ordered him thrown on a narrow pathway on which cattle passed to and fro, truly the act of a heartless man, who preferred to see his grandson trampled underfoot rather than killed by a single stroke. [5] Here, too, the boy remained unharmed and did not lack for nourishment; whereupon the king cast him first to starving dogs, which had been tormented by being kept from food for many days, and then even to swine. [6] Not only was the infant unhurt, but he was also fed at the teats of some of these animals, and finally the king gave orders for him to be thrown in the

---

4. The Minius, modern Minho; the Latin for red lead (cinnabar) is "minium."

ocean. [7] Now it became perfectly clear that the child enjoyed the protection of some divinity: amid the surging tides and the ebb and flow of the waters, he was carried along as though on a ship rather than on a wave, and deposited by a gentle current on the shore. [8] Shortly afterwards a hind arrived to offer her udders to the infant. From consorting with this nurse the boy gained outstanding swiftness of foot; and joining the herds of deer he long traversed the mountains and the forests with a speed as great as theirs. [9] Finally he was caught in a snare and presented as a gift to the king, who recognized him from the familiarity of his features and from marks branded on his body in infancy. [10] The boy was then designated as successor to the throne by Gargoris, full of wonder at all the trials and dangers which he had faced.

[11] He was given the name Habis and, when he ascended the throne, his greatness was such that his rescue from so many dangers was clearly due to the magnanimity of the gods. He constrained a barbarous people to live according to law, and was the first to teach them to break in oxen for ploughing and to grow grain from planting; and, loathing the foods to which he himself had been subjected in the past, he forced them to abandon their primitive diet and live on more refined fare. [12] His adventures would seem mere myth but for the reports that the founders of Rome were suckled by a wolf and Cyrus, king of Persia, nourished by a dog.[5] [13] It was by Habis, too, that the people were forbidden to engage in servile occupations, and the population was divided by him into seven cities. [14] After the death of Habis, the realm remained in the hands of his successors for many ages.

In another area of Spain, one made up of islands, royal power lay with Geryon. In this region the pasture is so lush that animals would burst if there were no enforced pause in their feeding. [15] This accounts for the cattle of Geryon (in those days cattle were regarded as the only form of wealth) which were so famous as to lure Hercules from Asia in the hope of great spoils. [16] As for Geryon himself, they say that he was not triple-bodied, as in the myths, but that there were three brothers who enjoyed such concord that they always seemed to be of one mind about everything; and that they did not of their own volition attack Hercules but, after seeing their cattle being stolen, had merely tried to recover in battle what they had lost.

5. See 1.4.

5 [1] After the Spanish dynasties it was the Carthaginians who first gained control of the country.[6] [2] Following instructions given in a dream, the people of Gades brought the cult of Hercules to Spain from Tyre (also the country of origin of the Carthaginians) and founded a city there, but the neighbouring peoples in Spain, envious of the progress made by the new city, made war on them. The Carthaginians therefore sent assistance to their cousins. [3] The expedition met with success; the Carthaginians both defended the people of Gades from aggression and also, by even greater aggression on their part, added an area of the country to their own empire. [4] Later, encouraged by the success of their first expedition, they also sent their general Hamilcar[7] with a large force to seize the entire country but, after achieving great success at first, he was drawn into an ambush, as he followed up his good fortune too recklessly, and killed. [5] Hamilcar's son-in-law, Hasdrubal, was sent out to replace him, and he, too, lost his life, killed by the slave of a certain Spaniard, who meant to avenge the unjust execution of his master. [6] These were followed by a general greater than either, Hannibal, son of Hamilcar; for Hannibal surpassed the exploits of both his predecessors and conquered all of Spain. He went on to attack the Romans and wore down Italy with various defeats over a period of sixteen years. [7] Meanwhile, the Romans, who sent the Scipios to Spain, first drove out the Carthaginians from the country and then fought bitter wars with the Spaniards themselves. [8] Complete subjection of the country, however, and the Spaniards' acceptance of the Roman yoke could not be achieved until Caesar Augustus,[8] having conquered the rest of the world, turned his victorious arms on them and, bringing a wild and barbarous people to a more civilized way of life under the rule of law, gave them a regular provincial administration.

6. In fact, the word used is "province," reflecting the status of Spain in the Roman Empire. For the founding of Carthage see 18.3ff. Gades is Cadiz.

7. Hamilcar Barca. He, Hasdrubal and Hannibal can be followed through Pol. 1–3 and Rome's war with Hannibal through Livy 21–30. The brothers P. and Cn. Cornelius Scipio went out to Spain in 218 and remained there until their deaths in 211, to be succeeded in 210 by the son of the former, the future Africanus, who expelled the Carthaginians in 206.

8. As Augustus himself noted at *Res Gestae* 26.2. There was campaigning in Spain from 27 to 19.

Prologues to
the Philippic History of Trogus

---

1. The contents of the first volume are as follows.[1] The empire of the Assyrians from King Ninus down to Sardanapallus, after whom sovereignty was transferred by Arbaces to the Medes, where it remained until their last king, Astyages. Astyages was driven from the throne by his grandson, Cyrus, and the Persians assumed power. Then an account of Cyrus' attack on King Croesus of Lydia, whom he defeated and captured. At this point there is a digression on the geography of the Aeolic and Ionian cities and on the early history of the Lydians and of the Etruscans in Italy. After Cyrus, his son Cambyses conquered Egypt. Then comes the early history of the Egyptian cities. After the death of Cambyses, Darius killed the Magi, acquired the throne of Persia and, after capturing Babylon, embarked on his Scythian wars.

2. The geography of Scythia and Pontus, and the early history of Scythia up to the war in which Darius was driven from the country. After being routed from there Darius made war on Greece, using the services of Datis and Tissaphernes. Only the Athenians put up any resistance. Then comes the early history of Athens and an account of its kings down to the tyranny of Pisistratus. After wiping out the tyranny, the Athenians defeated the Persians at Marathon. The early history of Thessaly is traced. After the expulsion of Xerxes from Greece, the war was carried into Asia by the Athenians, where it continued until Xerxes' death.

3. After Xerxes' death, his son Artaxerxes' vengeance on his father's murderer, Artabanus, and his war with the man responsible for the seccession of Egypt; how, at first, his general Achaemenes was defeated, and how Egypt was again retaken by Bagabaxus. Then how the Greeks fought among themselves after making peace with the king. There follows the early history of the Peloponnesians, telling how their country was

---

1. As the prologue to each book begins with much the same rubric, after Book I it is omitted.

occupied by descendants of Hercules, a Dorian people. Next the Argolic and Messanian wars and the alliance between the tyrants of Sicyon and Corinth. Then the war of Crisa and the war which the Athenians fought first with the Boeotians and afterwards with the Peloponnesians.

4. An account of Sicilian history from its very beginnings down to the destruction of the Athenian fleet at Syracuse.

5. The so-called Decelian War between the Athenians and the Spartans up to the capture of Athens. How the 30 tyrants were driven from Athens. The war which the Spartans waged with Artaxerxes in Asia because of the assistance they gave Cyrus. There follows a digression on the history of the war fought with his brother by Cyrus and the Greeks who served under him.

6. The war fought in Asia by the Spartans, led by Dercylides and Agesilaus, against the Persian satraps, down to the naval battle at Cnidus, in which the Spartans were defeated and the Athenians regained their empire. This is followed by the Corinthian War and the Boeotian War, in which the Spartans lost their empire when they were defeated at Leuctra and Mantinea. Then, in Thessaly, the establishment of the hegemony of Jason of Pherae, and of Alexander of Pherae after him, and its dissolution. Then comes the war of the allies, fought against the Athenians by the people of Chios, Rhodes and Byzantium. At this point there is a transition to Macedonian history.

7. An account of the early history of Macedonia and its kings, from Caranus, founder of the race, down to Philip the Great, and of the exploits of Philip himself to the capture of the city of Mothone. The early history of the Illyrians and the Paeonians is also presented in a digression.

8. An account of Philip the Great's exploits after the capture of the city of Mothone, from the commencement of the Phocian War, called the Sacred War, to its end. Inserted into this section is the war which Philip fought with the cities of Chalcidice, the most famous of which, Olynthos, he destroyed. There follows Philip's defeat of the Illyrian kings, his subjection of Thrace and Thessaly, his appointment of Alexander as king at Epirus after deposing Arybbas, and his unsuccessful attack on Perinthos.

9. How Philip was repulsed from Perinthos. The early history of Byzantium, the siege of which Philip was forced to abandon before his attack on Scythia. Then the history of Scythia is traced from the period at which the earlier account had broken off down to the war which Philip fought with Atheas, king of Scythia. Returning from there Philip invaded Greece and defeated the Greeks at Chaeronea. He was preparing for hostilities against Persia and had sent ahead a fleet with his generals aboard when he was assassinated by Pausanias (who cornered him at his daughter's wedding[2]) before he could commence his Persian campaign. Persian history is then retraced to Darius Nothus, who was succeeded by his son, Artaxerxes, nicknamed Mnemon. The latter, after defeating his brother, Cyrus, and using Conon to rout the Spartan fleet at Cnidos, waged war with Evagoras, king of Cyprus. Then the author goes back to the early history of Cyprus.

10. Persian history. How Artaxerxes Memnon made peace with the Cypriot king, Evagoras, and made preparations for his war with Egypt in the city of Acre; how he was himself defeated amongst the Cadusi, but went on to punish his officials who were in revolt in Asia, starting with Dotames, satrap of Paphlagonia. The early history of the Paphlagonians is given, followed by Artaxerxes' punishment of the satrap of the Hellespont, Ariobarzanes, and then, in Syria, of the satrap of Armenia, Orontes. After vanquishing all these, Artaxerxes died, to be succeeded by his son, Ochus. Ochus then put the nobles to death and captured Sidon. He made war on Egypt three times. After Ochus' death, Arses was king, and after him Darius, who clashed with Alexander, king of Macedon.

11. The history of Alexander the Great down to the death of King Darius of Persia, with a digression on the origins and kings of Caria.

12. Alexander the Great's Bactrian and Indian campaigns down to the time of his death, with digressions on the activities of his general Antipater in Greece, and those of the Spartan king Archidamus and Alexander the Molossian in Italy, where both were destroyed with their armies. Additional information is given on the beginnings in Italy of the Apulians, the Lucanians, the Samnites, and the Sabines, and on how Zopyrion perished with his army in the Pontus.

13. How on Alexander's death his chief officers distributed among themselves the governorships of the provinces, and how the veterans

---

2. This translation of the words "occupatis angustiis nuptiarum filiae" follows Seel's note that "angustiis" can refer to a dense crowd (which Pausanias then took advantage of). However, the use of the phrase "occupatis angustiis" at Justin 9.6.4 seems clearly to indicate the taking up of a position in a narrow tunnel. Hence here we might expect a translation such as "caught him in a narrow passage."

selected by Alexander to man colonies left them and tried to return to Greece, only to be wiped out by Pithon. The Lamian war which Antipater fought in Greece. The war in which Perdiccas killed King Ariarathes, and how Perdiccas was killed. The war in which Eumenes killed Neoptolemus and Crateros. There is also a digression on the origins and kings of the Quirenae.

14. The war fought between Antigonus and Eumenes; Antigonus' expulsion of Eumenes from Cappadocia and of Arridaeus and Clitos from Lesser Phrygia, after they were defeated in a naval battle in the Hellespont. Then the renewal of the war by Eumenes, who employed the Argyraspids but lost his life when he was defeated by Antigonus. Then how, in Macedonia, Cassander, after defeating Polyperchon and recovering Munichia from the defector, Nicanor, besieged Alexander's mother, Olympias, at Pydna and put her to death.

15. How Demetrius, son of Antigonus, was defeated at Gaza by Ptolemy, and how, in Macedonia, Cassander killed one son of King Alexander and how Polyperchon killed the other. How Demetrius defeated Ptolemy with his fleet off Cyprus but was nevertheless forced to raise the seige of Rhodes. The early history of the Rhodians is traced in a digression. Leaving Rhodes, Demetrius liberated Greece from Cassander. Then his father, Antigonus, waged war with Lysimachus and Seleucus. There follows a history of Seleucus, and of the Indian king, Sandrocottus. How Antigonus died after being defeated in battle and the remnants of his empire were gathered up by his son. Next come the exploits of the Spartan Cleonymus in Corcyra, Illyricum and Italy, and his loss of Corcyra. Then the death of King Cassander.

16. How, on Cassander's death, disagreements arose amongst his sons and Demetrius, called to the support of one of them, killed him and assumed the throne of Macedonia. He was soon deposed by Pyrrhus, king of Epirus, after which he transferred the theatre of war to Asia, where he died after being captured by Seleucus. Then comes the death of Ptolemy, who had named his son Philadelphus as his successor, and a description of how Lysimachus, captured in Pontus and released by Dromichaetes, once more seized control of the city-states in Asia formerly in the power of Demetrius and of Heraclea in Pontus. There follows an account of the early history of Bithynia and Heraclea, and of the tyrants of Heraclea: Clearchus, Satyrus and Dionysius. Lysimachus put the sons of these to death and seized the city.

17. How Lysimachus had his son Agathocles murdered by his step-mother, Arsinoë, and how he fought a war with King Seleucus, in which he was defeated and lost his life. That was the last conflict between the comrades of Alexander. There follows an account of how Seleucus lost his troops, along with Diodorus, in Cappadocia and was subsequently killed by Ptolemy, the brother of Lysimachus' wife, Arsinoë, and of how Ptolemy, surnamed Ceraunus, was made king in his place by the army and seized Macedonia. Ceraunus brought the wars with Antiochus and Pyrrhus to an end, giving support to Pyrrhus so that he could go to the defence of Tarentum against the Romans. Next comes an investigation of the early history of the kings of Epirus down to Pyrrhus, and of Pyrrhus' own achievements before his expedition to Italy.

18. The exploits of Pyrrhus of Epirus against the Romans in Italy, and his expedition to Sicily after this war to face the Carthaginians. There follows a digression on the early years of the Phoenicians, Sidon and Velia, and on the history of Carthage.

19. The achievements of the Carthaginians in Africa, thanks to Sabellus Anno,[3] and in Sicily, when they captured Selinus, Acragas, Camerina and Gela. In this war Dionysius the Syracusan seized control of Sicily. There is an account of the war which the Carthaginians fought against him under Himilco, who in besieging Syracuse lost his army and his fleet.

20. The history of Dionysius the elder of Sicily, of how he drove off the Carthaginians and undertook campaigns in Italy. Then comes an investigation of the origins of the Veneti, the Greeks and the Gauls who live in Italy. The career of Dionysius is followed up to the time of his death, and the exploits of Anno the Great in Africa are recounted.

21. How, in Sicily, Dionysius the younger administered the empire which his father had lost. Driven out by Dion, Dionysius battled with the Sicilians until he lost his children and his brothers, and then retired to Corinth. The narrative continues with the liberation of Sicily from war with Carthage by Timoleon. After the latter's death, there was a second revolt and Sosistratus called in the Carthaginians, who then blockaded Syracuse. In this war Agathocles came to power.

22. The history of Agathocles. How he gained power thanks to the Carthaginians, and afterwards waged war against them, in Sicily first of

---

3. So Seel's text, but the conjecture "Sabellus" which he adopts means "Sabine," which makes no sense; Hanno is Carthaginian.

all; then, defeated by them, he crossed to Africa, seized the country and killed Ophellas, king of Cyrene. He returned to Sicily once more and took control of the whole island, but went back to Africa and there lost his troops, after which he fled, alone, to Sicily. There, under attack again, he both made peace with the Carthaginians and also brought to heel the Sicilians who had revolted from him.

23. Agathocles' conquest of Sicily and his war against the Bruttii in Italy, followed by an examination of the beginnings of the Bruttii. After crushing all his foes, the king lost his life in a conspiracy hatched by his son, whom he had disinherited, and his grandson. War then broke out between Agathocles' foreign troops and the native Sicilians, and this brought Pyrrhus, king of Epirus, to Sicily, where he went to war with the Carthaginians and the Mamertini. Returning to Sicily from Italy, Pyrrhus was defeated in battle by the Romans and he returned to Epirus.

24. The war fought in Asia between Antigonus Gonatas and Antiochus, son of Seleucus, and that waged in Macedonia by Ptolemy Ceraunus against Monunius the Illyrian and Ptolemy, son of Lysimachus; and an account of how Ptolemy stripped his sister Arsinoë of her rule over the cities of Macedonia and of how he himself lost his life in a clash with Belgius, leader of the Gauls. There follows an investigation of the early history of the Gauls who took possession of Illyricum. Then comes their invasion of Greece under the leadership of Brennus and their defeat and destruction at Delphi.

25. Antigonus' destruction of the Gauls, then the war which he fought with Apollodorus, tyrant of Cassandrea. The Gauls' expedition into Asia and their war with King Antiochus and with Bithynia, areas taken over by the Tyleni. Then an account of how, on his return from Italy, Pyrrhus deprived Antigonus of the throne of Macedonia, blockaded Lacedaemon and died at Argos, and how his son Alexander went to war in Illyria with King Mitylus.

26. A catalogue of the Greek cities in which Antigonus Gonatas established his leadership, followed by a description of his destruction of the mutinous Gauls at Megara, his killing of the Lacedaemonian king, Areus, at Corinth, and then his war with Alexander, son of his brother Craterus. Then an account of how the leader of Achaea, Aratus, seized Sicyon, Corinth and Megara; how King Antiochus, surnamed Soter, died in Syria, after killing one of his sons and appointing the other one, Antiochus, as heir to the throne; how in Asia the son of King Ptolemy allied himself with Timarchus and rebelled against his father; how Antigonus' brother Demetrius died after assuming the rule of Cyrene; and how, on the death of King Antiochus, his son Seleucus Callinicus ascended the throne.

27. Seleucus' war in Syria against Ptolemaeus Trypho, and likewise in Asia against his own brother, Antiochus Hierax, a war in which he was defeated by the Gauls at Ancyra; this followed by the report of the Gauls' killing of Zielas of Bithynia after they were defeated at Pergamum by Attalus. Then an account of how Ptolemy captured Adaeus for the second time and had him put to death; how Antigonus defeated Sophron in a naval battle at Andros; and how Antiochus, put to flight in Mesopotamia by Callinicus, escaped the clutches of Ariamenes, who was plotting against him, and subsequently escaped from the guards of Trypho. Antiochus was then killed by the Gauls; his brother, Seleucus, also died; and Apaturius killed the eldest of Seleucus' sons.

28. How the people of Epirus killed Laodamia after the death of Alexander, king of Epirus, and a digression on the upheavals amongst the Basterni. Then the history of the rout of King Demetrius of Macedon by the Dardani. On Demetrius' death, the guardianship of his son, Philip, was assumed by Antigonus, who reduced Thessaly and Caria in Asia, helped the Achaeans against the Spartan king, Cleomenes, and captured Sparta. After losing his throne, the Spartan Cleomenes sought refuge in Alexandria and died there. The Illyrian War which the Romans fought with Teuta is dealt with in a digression.

29. The exploits of King Philip against the Dardani and the Aetolians, then an account of the early history of Crete. After forming an alliance with this island, Philip clashed with the Illyrians, the Dardani and, once more, with the Aetolians, the latter receiving assistance from the Romans. When the war was finished, Philip attacked Attalus.

30. How, on the death of Ptolemy Tryphon, his son Philopator defeated King Antiochus at Raphia, and how Philopator himself died from his desperate love for Agathoclea, leaving a son who was still a minor (against whom Antiochus conspired with Philip, king of Macedon). Then come Philip's operations in Asia after he commenced hostilities with Attalus. Returning from there he fought with the Roman generals, Sulpicius and Flamininus, by whom he was defeated. Peace followed. Then there is a transition to the history of Antiochus who, after ascending the throne, pursued the rebels Molon and Achaeus, the former into Media, the latter into Asia. Achaeus he besieged in Sardis and then entered into his wars with Rome, after subduing Upper Asia as far as Bactria.

31. The war which Titus Flamininus and Philopoemen, the leader of the Aetolians, fought with the Lacedaemonian Nabis; also the war fought against Antiochus in Achaea under the consul Acilius and in Asia under Scipio, and Hannibal's eventual flight to the king from Carthage. Then the war with the Aetolians prosecuted by the same Acilius who had driven Antiochus from Greece.

32. The defection of the Spartans and the Messenians from the Achaeans, during which Philopoemen lost his life. Then the war in Asia against the Gauls, conducted by the Romans under the leadership of Manlius. Next the hostility of King Philip towards the Romans because of the cities taken from him, which led to his putting to death one of his sons, Demetrius, and his incitement of the Basternae, who attempted to cross to Italy. There follows a digression on Illyria, on how the Gauls who had seized Illyricum returned once more to Gaul, and on the beginnings of Pannonia and the progress made by the Dacians thanks to King Burobustes. Then comes the war fought in Asia by King Eumenes against the Gaul, Ortiagontes, against Pharnaces of Pontus and against Prusias, during which the Carthaginian Hannibal gave aid to Prusias. Then come the exploits of Hannibal after the defeat of Antiochus, and Hannibal's death. On the death of Seleucus, son of Antiochus the Great, his brother Antiochus succeeded to the throne.

33. The war which the Romans fought against the king of Macedon, Perseus, son of Philip, on whose capture Epiros was destroyed. The collapse of the solidarity of the Achaean city-states when antagonism arose between the Achaeans and the Spartans. Then the resumption of the war in Macedonia by the Romans against the false Philip.

34. The Achaean War, which the Romans prosecuted under the leadership of Metellus and Mummius and in which Corinth was destroyed, followed by the war of King Eumenes with the Gallograeci and, in Pisidia, with the Selegenses. Then the exploits of King Antiochus of Syria and King Ptolemy Epiphanes of Egypt. There follows an account of the wars fought by Philometor and Euergetes, the two sons left by Ptolemy when he died, first against Antiochus (a war finished by the Romans), and then between themselves. In the latter the elder brother was driven out but restored by the Romans, who divided the kingdom between the two. Next comes the secret flight of Demetrius, surnamed Soter (who had been a hostage in Rome), after the death of Antiochus, king of Syria, his seizure of Syria and his hostilities with Timarchus, king of the Medes, and Ariarathes, king of Cappadocia. Then the early history of Cappadocia, with the quarrels of Ariarathes and Orophernes over the throne and an account of how, on the death of Eumenes, king of Asia, Attalus replaced him and went to war with the Selegenses and King Prusias.

35. The pirate-war beteween the peoples of Crete and Rhodes, and the rebellion of the people of Cnidus against the Ceramenses. Then an account of how Alexander was suborned to challenge Demetrius Soter, claiming to be the son of Antiochus Epiphanes, this leading to war in which Demetrius was defeated and lost his life. Next a description of how his elder son, Demetrius, with the help of Ptolemy Philometor (who died in the campaign), defeated Alexander, who had become hated because of his stupidity, and how war then broke out between Demetrius and Diodotus Trypho, resulting in Demetrius being driven from the throne of Syria by Trypho. The author then retraces the history of the upheavals in Upper Asia caused by Araetheus and the Parthian Arsaces.

36. Trypho's war with Antiochus, surnamed Sidetes, the brother of Demetrius, after Demetrius had been driven from Syria and taken prisoner by the Parthians. Then Antiochus' killing of Hyrcanus and his crushing of the Jews. There follows a digression on the beginnings of the Jews. Next, how Attalus, king of Asia, crushed the Thracian Caeni and left as successor to his empire Attalus Philometor. Finally, on the death of King Philometor, his brother Aristonicus seized the throne and fought a war with the Romans in which he was taken prisoner.

37. After the early history of the Pontic kings, there is an account of the succession of power in Pontus down to its last king, Mithridates Eupator, and then of how, on assuming the throne, Mithridates subdued Pontus and Paphlagonia before entering his wars with Rome. There is a digression on the beginnings and the exploits of the kings of the Bosphorus and Colchis.

38. Mithridates Eupator's seizure of Cappadocia, after he killed Arathes, and of Bithynia, after he defeated Nicomedes and Maltinus. Then an account of how, on the death of Ptolemy Philometor, his brother Physcon assumed the throne of Egypt and faced, first, rebellions amongst his people and then war with his sister, Cleopatra, and with Demetrius, king of Syria. There follows a digression on Demetrius' capture by the Parthians and how his brother, after defeating Trypho in Syria, made war on the Parthians, only to be destroyed along with his army.

39. How, when Antiochus Sidetes was killed by the Parthians, his brother Demetrius was released and subsequently recovered the throne of Syria, losing his life when Alexander Zabinaeus was bribed to make war on him. Demetrius' son Antiochus Grypos defeated Zabinaeus and seized the throne, and fought a war in Syria and Cilicia with his brother Antiochus Cyzicenus. Then how, on the death of King Ptolemy Physcon, his son Ptolemy Lathyros assumed the throne but was driven from Alexandria to Cyprus by his mother, and how he was later attacked by her in Syria, after she had replaced him on the throne with his brother, Alexander, until eventually the mother was killed by Alexander and Ptolemy recovered the throne of Egypt. Next comes the history of the reign of Alexander's son, who followed Lathyrus, and his expulsion and replacement by Ptolemy Nothus. There follows a narrative on the Jews' and Arabs' harassment of Syria with overland marauding, and the Cilicians' instigation of a pirate-war at sea, a war which the Romans fought in Cilicia under Marcus Antonius. Then comes Heracleo's seizure of power in Syria after the death of the king.

40. How, on the death of King Grypos, Cyzicenus lost his life in armed conflict with Grypos' sons, and how the latter were then wiped out by Eusebes, the son of Cyzicenus. Then the recommencement of civil war, the demise of the royal house of the Antiochi, and the seizure of Syria by the Armenian Tigranes, who was soon afterwards defeated and deprived of it by the Romans. Then the report of how, at Alexandria, Ptolemy Lathyrus was replaced on his death by his sons. One of the latter was given Cyprus, which the Romans took from him following the proposal of P. Clodius; the other fled to Rome when his arrest was called for during an uprising in Alexandria, and he later regained his throne thanks to the war fought by Gabinius. On his death he was succeeded by his son who, quarreling with his sister, Cleopatra, murdered Pompey the Great and also went to war with Caesar at Alexandria. Then there is an account of how his sister, Cleopatra, succeeded him on the throne, how she embroiled M. Antonius in a love affair with her and how, with the conclusion of the battle of Actium, she brought the reign of the Ptolemies to an end.

41. Parthian and Bactrian history. The establishment of the empire in Parthia by King Arsaces, followed by his successors Artabanus and Tigranes, surnamed the Divine, by whom Media and Mesopotamia were brought into subjection. There is a digression on the geography of Arabia. Next comes Bactrian history, with a description of the founding of the empire by King Diodotus and then, during his reign, the occupation of Bactra and Sogdiana by the Scythian tribes, the Saraucae and the

Asiani. There is also some Indian history, namely the achievements of the Indian kings Apollodotus and Menander.

42. Parthian history. There is an account of Himerus' war on the Meseni after he was made governor of Parthia by Phrates and of his brutal treatment of the people of Babylon and Seleucia. Then how Phrates was succeeded on the throne by King Mithridates, surnamed The Great, who made war on the Armenians. There follows a review of the beginnings of Armenia and its geography. Then an account of how, after a succession of several different kings in Parthia, Orodes came to the throne, how he destroyed Crassus and how he gained control of Syria thanks to his son Pacorus. Orodes was succeeded by Phrates, who went to war both with Antonius and with Tiridates. There is also a section on Scythian history, then one on the Asian kings of the Tochari, and on the demise of the Saraucae.

43. The beginnings of the ancient Latins, the topography of the city of Rome and its history down to Tarquinius Priscus. Then come the beginnings of Liguria and the history of Massilia.

44. The history of Spain and Carthage.

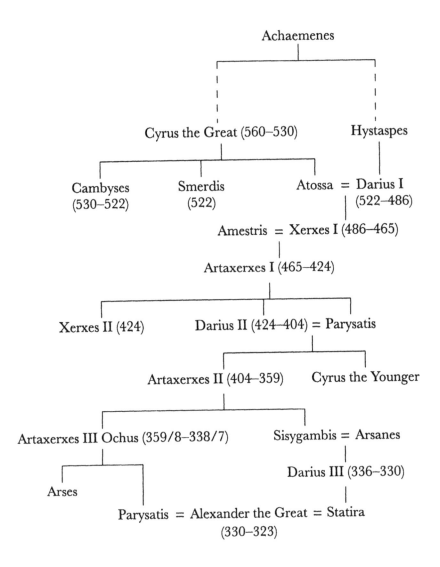

1. ACHAEMENID RULERS OF PERSIA

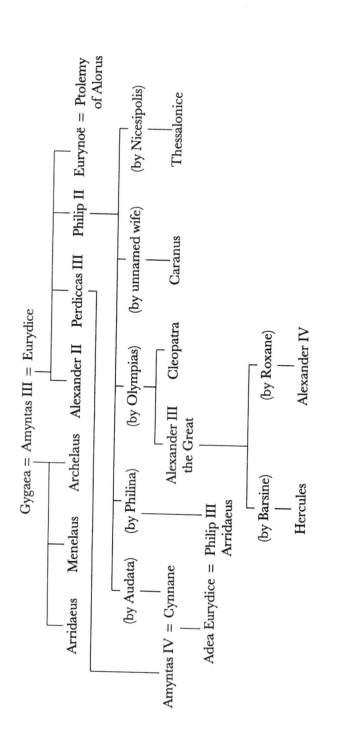

STEMMA 2.   THE MACEDONIAN ROYAL HOUSE FROM AMYNTAS III TO ALEXANDER IV

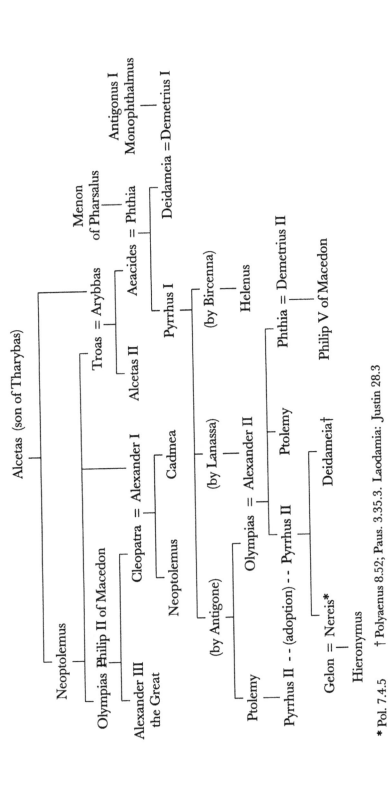

STEMMA 3. THE ROYAL HOUSE OF EPIRUS

* Pol. 7.4.5   † Polyaenus 8.52; Paus. 3.35.3. Laodamia: Justin 28.3

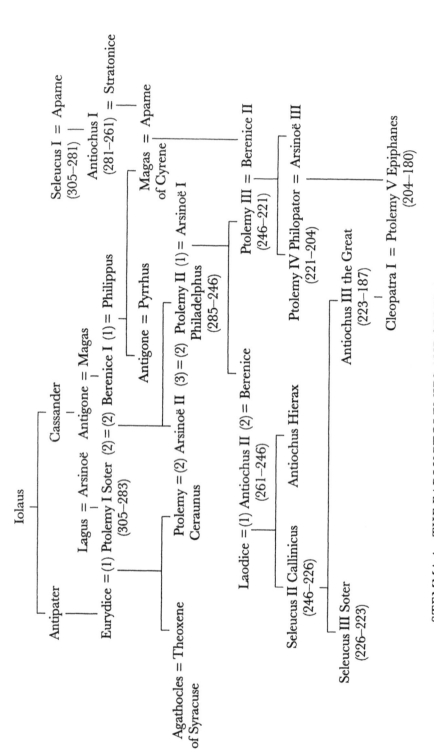

STEMMA 4. THE EARLY PTOLEMIES AND SELEUCIDS TO c. 180 B.C.

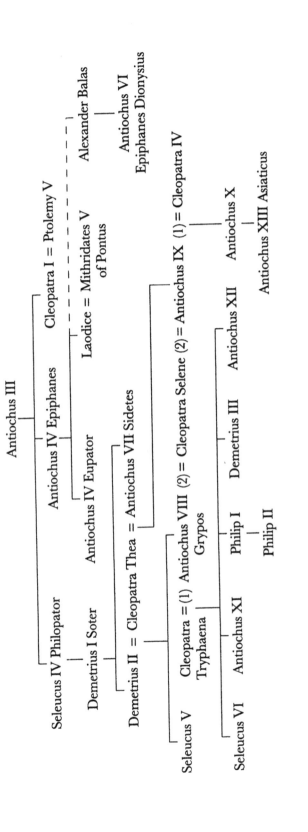

STEMMA 5. THE LATER SELEUCIDS

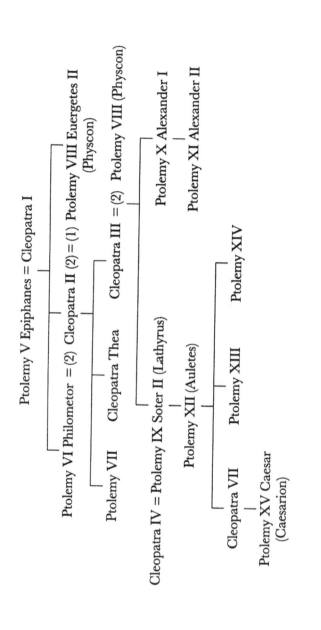

STEMMA 6.   THE LATER PTOLEMIES

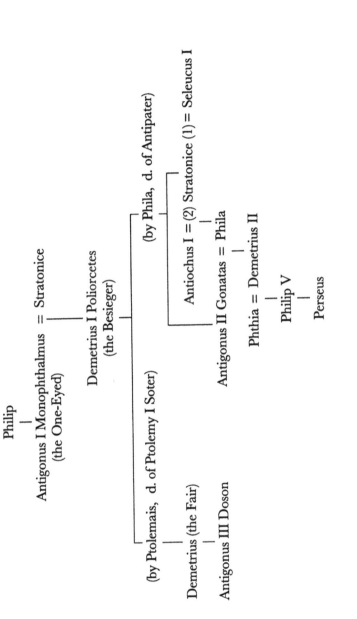

STEMMA 7. THE ANTIGONID RULERS OF MACEDON

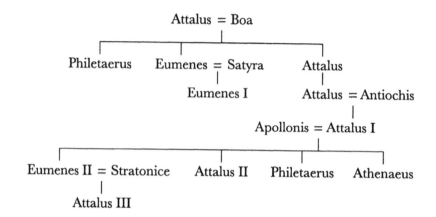

STEMMA 8. THE ATTALIDS OF PERGAMUM
(following the stemma of R. E. Allen)

Index to the Epitome

This index follows that of Seel, with considerable correction and adaptation so as to be an index to the English translation. Romans are listed according to family name; elements of nomenclature given in parentheses do not appear in the text of Justin.

24.4.3, 32.3.12, 38.4.10
India: attacked by Semiramis, 1.2.9;
subjugated in part by Alexander,
1.2.9, 12.7ff.; colonies founded
by Alexander in, 13.4.21; former
governors of retained upon the
death of Alexander, 13.4.19; liberated, but regained by Seleucus,
15.4.12ff.; King Sandrocottus of,
15.4.13ff.; seized by Eucratides,
41.6.4
Indians: under Alexander, the son of
Cleophis, 12.7.10; at war with
the Bactrians, 41.6.3. *See also*
Cleophis; Porus; Sandrocottus;
Demetrius
Indus, 12.10.5, 13.4.20
Iollas, 12.14.6ff.
Ionia, 5.4.17, 5.5.1, 38.7.7
Ionians: defeated by Darius, 2.5.12;
in the war at Salamis, 2.12.1ff.,
2.12.25; desert the Athenians,
5.2.9; again subjugated, comply
with the Persians, 5.5.1
Iphicrates, 6.5.2
Ismenias, 5.9.8
Israhel, 36.2.3f.
Ister (river), 2.5.10, 9.2.11, 32.3.14
Istrians, 32.2.12ff.
Italians: allies of Pyrrhus, 23.3.5;
captives of Hannibal, 31.2.5
Italy: torn from Sicily, 4.1.1; inhab-
ited by the Aborigines, 43.1.3;
first called Saturnia after King
Saturnus, 43.1.5; crossed by
Hercules, 43.1.9; reached by
Aeneas, 43.1.10; held by the
Greeks, 20.1.3; part of called
Greater Greece, 20.2.2; invaded
by Dionysius, 20.1.1ff.; invaded
by the Gauls, 20.5.8ff., 24.4.2,
28.2.6, 38.4.7; perpetually at war
with the Romans, 38.4.12; gets
wheat from Spain, 44.1.4; cities
of send deputations to Alexander,
12.13.1
(C. Iulius) Caesar, 43.5.12; wages

war against Pompey, 42.4.6
(M. Iunius) Brutus, opponent of
Octavian and Antonius, 42.4.7

Jason: leader of the Argonauts,
42.2.10ff., 42.3.1ff.; temples of,
42.3.5
Jews: beginnings of up to Demetrius,
the king of Syria, 36.2f.; regain
independence, 36.1.10; conquered by Antiochus Sidetes,
36.1.10; torment Syria with violent wars, 36.1.10, 40.2.4
Joseph, son of Israhel, 36.2.6
Juda, 36.2.5
(M. Junianius) Justin, Pref. 4, 38.3.11
Juno, 20.4.11
Juppiter: of Elymais, 32.2.1f.; of
Dodona, 12.2.3, 17.3.4; evicts
Saturnus, 43.1.5; temple of
at Gordium, 11.7.4, 11.7.13,
11.7.15; priest of in Cyprus,
18.5.2; temple of (at Dion?) venerated by the Macedonians from
days of old, 24.2.8; temple of at
Antioch plundered by Alexander
Zabinaeus, 39.2.5f.; Clearchus
calls himself son of, 16.5.8
Jupiter Hammon. *See* Hammon

(Q.) Labienus, 42.4.7
Lacedaemon (Sparta), 2.15.4, 3.3.12;
Pythagoras spends time in,
20.4.4; attacked by the Thebans,
6.4.8, 6.7.1; fortified with walls,
14.5.6; captured by Antigonus
Doson, 28.4.14
Lacedaemonians (Spartans): legal
system of established by Lycurgus, 3.2.4ff., 3.3; wage three wars
against the Messenians, 3.4ff.;
found Tarentum, 3.4.11, 20.1.15;
at Marathon, 2.9.9; fight against
the Persians at Thermopylae,
2.11; advise the Athenians against
building walls, 2.15.1ff.; raid Persian territory under the leader-

Macedon(ia) (*continued*)
quered by Seleucus and Ptolemy,
17.2.5, 24.1.8; conquered by
the Gauls, 24.4.6, 25.1; taken
by Pyrrhus, 25.3.6; pillaged by
Alexander, king of Epirus, 26.2.9;
recovered by Demetrius, 26.2.11;
end of kingdom of, 33.2.6f.; number of kings of and years of their
rule, 33.2.6; receives a legal system from Paulus, 33.2.7
Macedonians: origins and history
of up to Alexander, 7-12; have
very ancient religion, 24.2.8;
emerge while the Greeks amuse
themselves, 6.9.6; exempted from
all obligations except military
service by Alexander, 11.1.10;
delighted at the loss of Alexander,
13.1.7; generals of following
Alexander, 13.1.10ff.; transfer
their allegiance to Olympias,
14.5.10; decree that Olympias
be executed, 14.6.6f.; where kings
of are buried and why, 7.2.2ff.
Maeotis, 2.1.19
Magabasus, 7.3.1, 7.3.7
Magas, king of Cyrene, 26.3.2
Magi: of the Babylonians, 12.13.3;
of the Persians, 1.9.9ff.; of the
Bactrians, 1.1.9
Mago, great general of the Carthaginians (sixth century), 18.7.19,
19.1.1
Mago, general of the Carthaginians:
supports the Romans against
Pyrrhus, 18.2.1ff.
Malchus, 18.7.2ff.
Mallius Malthinus (ambassador 89),
38.3.4, 38.3.8; in Cappadocia,
38.4.4
L. Manlius Vulso (consul 256),
41.4.3
Marathon, 2.15.18; plains of, 2.9.9;
battle fought at, 2.9.9, 2.11.2,
2.12.12, 2.15.18
Maratus, father of Pythagoras,

20.4.3
Mardi: subjugated by Alexander,
12.3.4; subjugated by Phrahates,
king of the Parthians, 41.5.9
Mardonius, 2.13f.
Margiani, 41.1.10
Mars: father of the Amazons,
2.4.13; father of Romulus and
Remus, 43.2.3, 43.2.7; grove sacred to, 43.2.3, 43.2.7
Marsian War, 38.4.13
Martesia, queen of the Amazons,
2.4.12f.
Masinissa, king of Numidia: ally of
the Romans, 33.1.2; has merit
among the Romans, 38.6.4f.;
grandson of, 38.6.6
Massilia: founded by the Phocaeans,
37.1.1, 43.3.4ff.; fights great wars
with the Gauls, 43.5.1; fights
great wars with the Ligurians,
43.3.13, 43.4.3ff., 43.5.1; acropolis of Minerva in, 43.5.6
Massilians: allied with the Spaniards
and the Romans, 43.5.3, 43.5.10;
fight the Carthaginians, 43.5.2;
wage war against Catuman-
dus, 43.5.5ff.; assist the Romans
with money, 43.5.9; make an
appeal on behalf of the Phocaeans, 37.1.1; send gifts for
Apollo, 43.5.8; honoured at
Rome, 43.5.10; an institution
of the, 43.4.11f.
Mauretanians, 19.2.4; their king,
21.4.7
Maxitani, 18.6.1
Medea, daughter of Aeëtes, the king
of the Colchians: wife of Jason,
42.2.12, 42.3.1; wife of Aegeus,
2.6.14; mother of Medus by
Aegeus, 2.6.14, 42.2.12
Medes: kingdom of established by
Medus, 42.3.6; subjugated by
the Assyrians, revolt and transfer
empire to themselves, 1.3; their
empire, 1.6.17, 1.7.2, 41.1.4,

Index to the Prologues

Again, this is an emended version of Seel's index of proper names in the prologues.

of, 35
Crisa, war of, 3
Croesus, king of Lydia, 1
Cyprus, 9, 15, 39, 40
Cyrene, 22, 26
Cyrus (Persian king), 1
Cyrus (brother of Artaxerxes), 5, 9

Dacians, 32
Dardani, 28, 29
Darius (son of Hystapes), 1, 2
Darius Nothus, 9
Darius (son of Arses), 10, 11.
Datis, 2
Decelian War, 5
Delphi, 24
Demetrius, son of Antigonus, 15, 16
Demetrius II (king of Macedon), 28
Demetrius (king of Cyrene), 26
Demetrius (son of Philip), 32
Demetrius, surnamed Soter, 34, 35
Demetrius (Nicator), 35, 36, 38, 39
Dercylides, 6
Dion, 21
Diodorus, 17
Diodotus I (king of Bactria), 41
Dionysius (tyrant of Heraclea), 16
Dionysius the elder of Sicily (Syracusan), 19, 20
Dionysius the younger, 21
Dorian people, 3
Dotames, satrap of Paphlagonia, 10
Dromichaetes, 16

Egypt, 1, 3, 10, 34, 38, 39; war with, 10
Epirus, 8, 16, 23, 28, 33; people of, 28; kings of, 17
Etruscans, 1
Eumenes (of Cardia), 13, 14
Eumenes (king of Asia), 32, 34
Eusebes (surname of Antiochus), 40
Evagoras, king of Cyprus, 9, 10

Titus Flamininus, 30, 31

Gabinius, 40

Gallograeci, 34
Gaul, 32
Gauls, 24, 25, 26; Gauls who live in Italy, 20; Gauls who took possession of Illyricum, 24, 32; (= Gallograeci), 25, 27, 32
Gaza, 15
Gela, 19
Greece, 2, 9, 12, 13, 15, 24, 31
Greeks, 3; Greeks who served under Cyrus, 5; who live in Italy, 20

Hannibal (the Carthaginian), 31, 32
Hellespont, 10, 14
Heraclea, 16
Heracleo, 39
Hercules, descendants of, 3
Himerus, 42
Himilco, 19
Hyrcanus, 36

Illyria, digression on, 32
Illyrian War, 25, 28; kings, 8
Illyrians, 7, 29
Illyricum, 15, 24, 32
India, king of, 15
Indian campaigns, 12; history, 41
Ionia, cities of, 1
Italy, 1, 12, 15, 17, 18, 20, 23, 25, 32
Italian campaigns, 20; beginnings, 12

Jason of Pherae, 6
Jews, 36, 39

Lacedaemon, 25
Lamian War, 13
Laodamia, 28
Latins (ancient), 43
Leuctra, 6
Liguria, 43
Lucanians, 12
Lydia, 1
Lydians, 1
Lysimachus, 15, 16, 17, 24

Macedon, kings of, 10, 30, 33

Textual Variants

	SEEL	YARDLEY-DEVELIN
Praef. 5	operam	operam omitted
2.4.29	et ante	sed ante
2.7.2	annua	annuis
2.10.13	easdemque	eademque
5.2.3	parta qui cum ... pensaret	partaque cum ... pensare
6.3.6	proelii	populi
13.4.5	regum	rerum
13.4.24	haec ... memoria	cum haec ... materia
13.6.10	Alexandro, Magni filio	Alexandri Magni filio
14.1.3	simul an ut	simul ut
15.2.8	odii	odiis
16.2.9	duxerat	dixerat
16.4.15	se, an sibi malint	se, si malint
18.7.7	Herculis	Herculi
28.3.5	Laudamia	Laodamia
31.2.3	urbanum	suburbanum
Prol. 40.7	Alexandriam	Alexandriae